P9-CNF-299

Modern Critical Interpretations

Modern Critical Interpretations

Charles Dicken's
Great Expectations

Edited and with an introduction by
Harold Bloom
Sterling Professor of the Humanities
Yale University

CHELSEA HOUSE PUBLISHERS
Philadelphia

© 2000 by Chelsea House Publishers, a division of
Main Line Book Co.

Introduction © 2000 by Harold Bloom

Printed and bound in the United States of America

10 9 8 7 6 5 4 3 2 1

∞ The paper used in this publication meets the minimum
requirements of the American National Standard for
Permanence of Paper for Printed Library Materials,
Z39.48-1984

Library of Congress Cataloging-in-Publication Data

Great expectations / edited and with an introduction by
Harold Bloom.
        p. cm. — (Modern critical interpretations)
    Includes bibliographical references and index.
    ISBN 0-7910-5661-9 (alk. paper)
    1. Dickens, Charles, 1812–1870. Great expectations.
  I. Bloom, Harold. II. Series.
PR4560 .G686   1999
823'.8—dc21   99-051594
                                          CIP

Contributing Editor: Jaynce Marson

Contents

Editor's Note

My Introduction explores some aspects of Pip's inwardness, and speculates upon Shakespeare's possible influence on Pip's capacity for change as he listens to his own narrative voice.

Murray Baumgarten centers upon Pip's learning to read and write, while Peter Brooks adroitly establishes the importance to the plot of Pip's interpretation of his own name.

The social limitations accepted by Dickens are noted by Carolyn Brown, after which William A. Cohen considers what he regards as latent erotic possibilities in *Great Expectations*.

Edwin M. Eigner shrewdly considers why the novel lacks a clown-figure, while David Gervais suggests how little time-bound *Great Expectations* now seems to be.

The late Elliot L. Gilbert relates Pip's inwardness to the Wordsworthian paradigm of *Tintern Abbey*, after which Gail Turley Houston finds in the book an ambivalent account of Victorian consumer society.

Jerome Meckier defends Dickens's revision of the novel's ending, while Christopher D. Morris affirms both endings.

James Phelan centers upon the problematic character of Wemmick, after which Jeremy Tambling invokes Foucault to affirm Dickens's modernity.

Dickens's reliance upon Shakespeare, emphasized rather differently in my Introduction, is seen by William A. Wilson as reflecting the particular influences of *Hamlet* and *A Midsummer Night's Dream*.

In a final essay, Anny Sadrin finds elements of both Odysseus and Oedipus in Pip's adventures.

Introduction

Pip is the most inward of all Dickens's major characters, and except for Esther Summerson in *Bleak House*, he also appears to be the Dickens-protagonist most overtly affected by his own pathos. In particular, he has a tendency to feel excessively guilty, almost in the Kafkan mode. An anguish of contamination seems to have reached out from Magwitch and Miss Havisham and invaded Pip's sensibility; this is profoundly irrational, and yet seems demonstrable. Himself not at all criminal, Pip carries an aura that we might associate with the hero-villain Hamlet. "Hero-villain" sounds odd for Hamlet, but pragmatically the Prince of Denmark is quite deadly. At play's end, Horatio and Fortinbras are the only survivors of any importance whatsoever. Pip, a far gentler person than Hamlet, is bad luck for his sister and for Magwitch, for Miss Havishan and Estella, even for the wretched Pumblechook and the malevolent Orlick. After all the disasters, Pip suffers his brainfever, and returns to an improved infancy with the Gargerys and their child, his godson, little Pip. Absorbing as all this is, it remains a puzzle why Pip should have tormented himself into a guilt-consciousness he simply did not deserve.

Dickens, unlike Jane Austen or Stendhal or Dostoevsky, is not a particularly Shakespearean novelist. He has more affinities with Ben Jonson than with Shakespeare, but if you go in search of inwardness then you must go to school with Shakespeare. *David Copperfield*, despite its autobiographical elements, would not refute Henry James's judgment that Dickens "has added nothing to our understanding of human character." *Great Expectations*, because it enters the abyss of Pip's inner self, *does* refute James. Something in Dickens, descending into Pip's psyche, called upon Shakespeare for aid, perhaps not altogether knowingly.

Pip's social identity is fathered by the secret patronage of Magwitch, who is also Estella's actual father. For Dickens, that hardly counts as extraordinary coincidence; in the world of the novels everyone is over-connected. But it does place a particular demand upon Dickens's genius; there is a profound link between Magwitch's love for Pip and Pip's suffering passion for Estella, though the connection necessarily is an uncanny one. Pip's inwardness has to apprehend the symbolic incest of his desire for the mocking Estella without comprehending it. So subtle and persuasive is Dickens's art of representation in *Great Expectations* that the reader experiences no surprise when the identity of Estella's father is revealed.

Magwitch, confronting Pip and Herbert together, plays the Ghost of Hamlet's father, but he is a Ghost who has come too late. Pip, gentlest of Hamlets, is no avenger: "Pip, revenge!" would be the silliest of outcries. Neither a dramatist nor a dramatizer, Pip joins Hamlet only as a sufferer, guilty and grieving. Hamlet mysteriously returns from the sea transformed, beyond melancholia and mourning. Pip goes under, is reborn very differently, and becomes a companion of his godson, little Pip. Dickens, theatrical to the core, values Hamlet as a self-dramatizer, but has little interest in Hamlet the intellectual. Pip does not feel disgust at unpacking his heart with words, and Estella is a counter-Ophelia. Perhaps Magwitch and Miss Havisham are counter-Ghosts, truly bearing the authentic guilt of the story.

I hold with those who believe that Dickens ruined the original ending, which held out no hope for Pip and Estella. The revised ending is equivocal, but perhaps not equivocal enough. You can end a *Hamlet* transcendentally, but not happily.

MURRAY BAUMGARTEN

Calligraphy and Code:
Writing in Great Expectations

Part of our pleasure in reading *Great Expectations* comes from watching Pip learn to write and read. No matter that right from the start he reads inappropriately, out of the intensity of his need. How else can we characterize an imagination that constructs a picture of his parents from the shape of the letters on their tombstones? In this book, he serves as the hero of mis-reading.

Participating with this heroic reader in the effort to become literate, we are yet separate from him. Though we identify with him, we as well repudiate him. His overdetermination—to pun on his tenacious desire and its psychological sources—leads to energetic confusion. We recognize that despite Pip's success in learning to read and write, "he falls continually into mistakes of interpretation," launching himself "too hastily into a world he has scanned but not yet understood." The tension of our participation with Pip in his alphabet adventures is resolved in the comic amusement with which we judge him a mistaken if eager student—by contrast with our own advantage of correctness.

Unlike the printed text of the novel that absorbs us, the material which the young Pip reads is handwritten. His imagination fastens eagerly upon the constitutive strokes of pen and chisel. Out of the letters of his father's and mother's names "in a time" as he says "long before the days of photographs,"

From *Dickens Studies Annual: Essays on Victorian Fiction* 11. © 1983 by AMS Press, Inc.

he derives an image of his parents' bodily form. "The shape of the letters on my father's" tombstone "gave me an odd idea that he was a square, stout, dark man, with curly black hair. From the character and turn of the inscription, 'Also Georgiana Wife of the Above,' I drew a childish conclusion that my mother was freckled and sickly."

Here writing has an ideographic quality; it is pictorial rather than or in addition to phonetic writing. In the child's eye, its calligraphic qualities release secrets which the printed world of books conceals. The letters of his parents' names serve as visual cues and clues. Having told us that he lived in the pre-history of photography, Pip then proceeds to give us snapshots of his experience, constructing them out of the lines and patterns of the alphabetic characters that form their names.

In its literal denotation, calligraphy means "beautiful writing." Nowadays, we think of it as fine penmanship. I use it to designate, following Dickens' own usage, writing that bridges hieroglyphic and phonetic systems. The *OED* lists Dickens' use of the word calligraphy as the first one after Milton's, and cites the following sentence from *Household Words*, "His calligraphy suggests . . . the skating of an intoxicated sweep over a sheet of ice." In effect, like Dickens in this sentence, Pip the conscious writer of his autobiography is telling us that he is using words to SEE through time to the subjects that acted in it—a theme close to the heart and work of Dickens' friend, Carlyle—rather than treating language as an enclosed symbol system with its own rules and values.

As Pip learns to read more conventionally, growing up and becoming acquainted with books, he begins to be enmeshed in the social "systems and processes of meaning." By contrast his writing will be an attempt to escape from the rigors of codes and structures into calligraphic possibilities, whereby the imagination can envision his experience in all its fullness. In the course of the novel we will confront, as Pip does, these two aspects of literacy: as writing it has calligraphic potential and can liberate the imagination; as reading it may be a code that directs and even imprisons the imagination in rules and laws.

The manifest theme of *Great Expectations*, reading is at the center of Pip's personal difficulties. We will come to recognize that the code of reading has the capacity to distort the world. It will warp Pip's character, and lead him to repudiate his childhood innocence; it will serve as the mark of his moral superiority, propelling him into a traumatic world of secrecy, intrigue, and duplicity. Whenever he reads something, whether it is the note telling him not to go home which Wemmick leaves for him, the letter he has written Joe on his slate, the novel he is pursuing just before Magwitch returns from Australia, or the deciphering of the features of the marsh with which the book opens, something drastic immediately follows. We are led to suspect that literary texts are potentially dangerous, for they have the power to affect and even skew reality.

In the course of the novel Pip reminds us that he is not only reading but writing the narrative of his life: the book is his confession and story. If we include the historical context of rising literacy as part of the explanation for this central phenomenon of the novel, we must also recognize the personal fact of Dickens' writing life as a contributing element. In making the text of his life for us and even himself to read, Pip is not only engaging the problematics of reading—the deciphering of words and codes—but the more active aspect of literacy: of writing as the encoding of language, and the heady liberation of the making of meaning. *Great Expectations* is not only about the consumption of words in reading but also their production in language as writing—the latent theme and dialectical subject of the novel.

Many of the crucial communications of this novel are relayed between characters through writing. Letters are delivered and notes passed from hand to hand; characters describe theirs lives as if they were taking place in a book. The implements of writing acquire symbolic force: Wemmick expresses astonishment by putting pen in mouth; Miss Havisham keeps a pencil around her neck; Mike is rebuked for crying by the comment that he is "spluttering like a bad pen."

The characters read each other as if they were alphabetic letters. Their most important meanings must be put into writing: Miss Havisham demands that Pip record his feelings in her copybook, for the written statement alone can serve as the testament of his forgiveness. In her last extremity, she repeats the same sentences over and over in the same rhythm as if they were the script of her deathbed scene.

Writing is not only a physical actuality in this novel but a metaphor used by the characters to describe and account for their own lives. At one point in relating his story, Magwitch "looked about him in a confused way, as if he had lost his place in the book of his remembrance." Somewhat earlier Pip "saw in everything the construction that my mind had come to, repeated and thrown back to me. My thoughts passed into the great room across the landing where the table was spread, and I saw it written, as it were, in the falls of the cobwebs from the centre-piece. . . ." Later on Pip describes Magwitch's behavior by recourse to an analogy with writing: "he had a barrack way with him of hanging about one spot, in one unsettled manner, and going through one round of observances with his pipe and his negrohead and his jack-knife and his pack of cards, and what not, as if it were all put down for him on a slate—." In this sentence life is imagined to have the routinized pace of words marching unalterably along the line.

We are Pip's accomplices in learning how to maneuver through this world of slate and chalk, paper, pen, and ink. In reading this written text we join him in the process of becoming educated adults, recapitulating our own schooling experiences as we participate in the plot—which is also a stratagem—that should lead an orphan to worldly wealth and a gentleman's status, thereby promising us an accounting for our own efforts.

For Pip as for us reading and writing are not just skills but semiotic codes constitutive of personality and social order. The ability to use them is the mark of his gentility. Magwitch defines a gentleman as someone who owns books "'mounting up on their shelves, by hundreds! And you read 'em; don't you? I see you'd been a reading of 'em when I come in. Ha, ha, ha! You shall read 'em to me, dear boy! And if they're in foreign languages wot I don't understand, I shall be just as proud as if I did.'"

When Pip leaves the illiterate world of Joe Gargery and the blacksmith's forge for London he encounters the ambiguous meaning of writing. Compeyson, the villain of the novel, is a "handwriting"-forger, who "writes fifty hands"—not like "sneaking" Pip whom Orlick accuses of writing "but one." Hard work at the village forge is an honest craft; but even if we believe Pip sincere, the suspicion remains that writing one's story is not by contrast conducive to truth-telling. After all is not *Great Expectations*, despite our absorption in it, just a novel that we are reading? something made up?

As we follow along in this fairy tale and wish fulfillment of upward social mobility across class lines, we share not only Pip's fears, the insults and injuries which he suffers, his shame and humiliation, but as well the guilty suspicion that the act of writing is a fiction in which we are implicated as potential forgers. We cannot forget the scene at the castle when Wemmick shows Pip among other curiosities "several manuscript confessions written under condemnation—upon which Mr Wemmick set particular value as being, to use his own words, 'every one of 'em Lies, sir.'" Furthermore, the punishment for lying and forgery, as we learn in Chapter 2, is that "People are put in the Hulks because they murder, and because they rob, and forge. . . ."

For Dickens, the writer, the written word like the world of books is suspect. By contrast with speech in which, face to face we can interrogate and examine the speaker, writing is abstract. Whatever our objections, the book cannot answer us, only insolently and without risk repeating the same thing. Reading and writing intrinsically partake of the arbitrary qualities of the alphabet on which literacy is based. In place of a person with whom we can physically interact, the written word plunges us into the interpretive hermeneutic, which as Nietzsche reminds us means "forcing, adjusting, abbreviating, omitting, padding, inventing, falsifying, and whatever else is of the essence of interpreting."

As Pip becomes a member of our genus, Alphabetic Person, growing up to be a reader, he leaves behind his childish pictorial imagination. By the end of the novel, Pip will say openly that he has "a taste for reading." *Great Expectations* will thereby remind us that even if literacy is the mark of the gentleman, reading has often made men and women mad. Not for nothing was *Don Quixote* one of Dickens' favorite books.

Pip accepts his ability to read as the signature of his moral superiority. For Pip reading becomes part of his idle expectant life. He believes his life is destined to have the happy ending of a fairy tale, for he reads the text that way. He is a consumer of words. By contrast, writing, the production of language, is meaningful work—the function it will have for Pip at the end of the novel, when he will earn his living as a clerk at Clarriker's. (Note the doubling of the meaning of clerk in the sound—and British pronunciation—of Clarriker's.)

In writing his autobiography, Pip in engaged in the making of a necessary fiction, himself. Pip's is not a unique activity. In the era of the production of cloth by machines, of the criss-crossing of a land by railroads, of the emergence of universal literacy as an ideal, his enterprise of ego development is representative. It is the democratic idea of having a self, being a character, and an individual, in which all will participate, including women.

Once the alphabet is invented, writing is no longer the sole "pursuit of scribes" or "preserved as 'a mystery' and 'secret treasure.'" It is the democratic vehicle making possible the production of the self. "By objectifying words, and by making them and their meaning available for much more prolonged and intensive scrutiny than is possible orally, writing encourages private thought; the diary or the confession enables the individual to objectify his own experience." And as we all know personally, literacy is the enabling condition for social mobility in the modern world.

The effort to master writing is ritualistic; it is a matter of repeating strokes on paper till the resulting character becomes automatic, and can be made without conscious thought. In order to reach this state, one must have talent and skill at doing something unnatural and artificial, something arbitrary. Literacy has a transformative impact on the social order. It also changes the writer. His psyche begins to be shaped by the process of reading and writing.

The literate ego knows how to differentiate itself from the flow of language of oral culture. It distinguishes between letters, and comprehends how they make words and words sentences, paragraphs, and pages. The process in which it engages in reading and writing is only one of the actions inherent in the modern notion of ego development. As it changes, this self will also come to discover that just as it is separated yet mysteriously and secretly linked to the words it reads and writes, so it is different from and yet secretly joined to the many roles it plays.

Becoming self-conscious about his writing, Pip believes he is now worthy of being read. He has become a text. His presumption is the mark of his self-importance and supposed moral superiority. By the end of the novel, Dickens has taken us through a course that weighs the costs and benefits of social mobility and does not yield an optimistic judgment. Pip leaves behind the innocence of his life with Joe for the travails of an education which will make him increasingly ashamed of his common boots and coarse hands. It will teach him to become a liar; he will discover that words are like costumes, and can be put on and off at will, so that the self can play many roles. Writing ushers him into the romantic world of Experience, as he leaves illiterate Eden. It is worth remembering that in Swift's fable, the rational Houyhnhnms who cannot lie, have no writing.

If Pip is the writer of his own story, then in the context of the novel, Magwitch is his author, as Miss Havisham creates Estella. Both Pip and Estella are new minted unnatural, artificial creatures—like the characters of the alphabet. Half brother and sister, they are the creatures of the writer, who authorizes their existence with the strokes of a pen.

Pip's education has a grotesque quality that hopefully separates it from ours. His is of a piece with Wopsle's Hamlet, in which all the characters are undecided as to their roles and play them seriously yet are laughed at for their pains. Pip's education partakes of his fairy-tale world. He thinks himself the knight of romance freeing the maiden, but he is in actuality closer to Mrs. Pocket's father who "had been knighted . . . for storming the English grammar at the point of the pen, in a desperate address engrossed on vellum." The assault on the alphabet partakes of the violence of Pip's wrenching from the bosom of his family upon the waving of the magic wand of expectation before him. As a result, he becomes transformed into the knight of the story, as his mind begins to work in the alphabetic logic of writing. Thus, his dreams take on the character of writing. "When at last I dozed, in sheer exhaustion of mind and body, it became a vast shadowy verb which I had to conjugate. Imperative mood, present tense: Do not thou go home, let him not go home, let us not go home. . . ."

Now Pip is fully a part of the alphabetic world. For him, as for us, the self is now made of words and sentences, those characters in which since the expulsion from Eden we have clothed ourselves. Pip's autobiography is an account of how the more he writes the story of himself, the less he can find it. As the Spanish philosopher Ortega y Gasset points out, the secret of writing is the making of the present self into an absence. Writing his own life, Pip defines its contours. By this process he makes its center, himself, into an absence, by which he loses his essential identity: it is written into his adventures as it is written out of himself. "The book is the absence of the author, and the written word the previous flight of the one who pronounces it. We have a speech without the speaker present."

In *Great Expectations*, Dickens explores the ambiguous meanings and values of literacy, in a style which seems not so much to be written as spoken. It has a calligraphic rather than a printed quality, preserving aspects of the oral speech of an era before widespread literacy. To read Dickens as we all know is not to decipher and decode the rules of grammar and the laws of syntax but to listen to someone speaking personally to us. His writing has the plentitude of face to face encounters, of speech itself.

Paradoxically, his writing has the power even of depicting in writing the abandonment of the personal relationships of oral culture, so richly and brilliantly imaged for us in the figures of Joe and Magwitch, as we join Pip in tracing the stumbling effort to participate in the fairy-tale world of literacy—a process that was to transform our ways of seeing and conceiving reality. Note how in Chapter 7, Pip manages to discover the alphabet in pictorial, tactile terms. I struggled "as if it had been a bramble-bush; getting considerably worried and scratched by every letter. After that, I fell among those thieves, the nine figures, who seemed every evening to do something new to disguise themselves and baffle recognition. But, at last, I began, in a purblind, groping way, to read, write, and cipher, on the very smallest scale."

This process echoes a similar educative effort in *Bleak House*, when Esther attempts to teach Charley how to make the letters of the alphabet. In this scene we gain a sense of how writing was learned then, not so different now despite Sesame Street, by the process of copying.

> "I had not been at home again many days, when one evening I went upstairs into my own room to take a peep over Charley's shoulder, and see how she was getting on with her copy-book. Writing was a trying business to Charley, who seemed to have no natural power over a pen, but in whose hand every pen appeared to become perversely animated, and to go wrong and crooked, and to stop, and splash, and sidle into corners, like a saddle-donkey. It was very odd, to see what old letters Charley's young hand had made; they, so wrinkled, and shrivelled, and tottering; it, so plump and round. Yet Charley was uncommonly expert at other things, and had as nimble little fingers as I ever watched.

'Well, Charley,' said I, looking over a copy of the letter O
in which it was represented as square, triangular, pear-shaped
and collapsed in all kinds of ways, 'we are improving. If we only
get to make it round, we shall be perfect, Charley.'

Then I made one, and Charley made one, and the pen
wouldn't join Charley's neatly, twisted it up into a knot.

'Never mind, Charley. We shall do it in time.'

Charley laid down her pen, the copy being finished;
opened and shut her cramped little hand; looked gravely at the
page, half in pride and half in doubt; and got up, and dropped
me a curtsy."

To Charley, Esther has authority in part because she is her writing teacher,
beginning to initiate her into the secret fellowship of writers. The intimacy
of this relationship is emphasized in *Great Expectations* when we discover that
part of the experience Biddy and Joe share and that leads them to marry is
the teaching and learning of reading and writing.

By contrast with their sharing, Pip increasingly uses his ability as a
reader and writer to reveal his supposed moral superiority to Biddy and
Joe. The child judges the adults who provide for him, perhaps as a way of
finding the possibility of equality in his deprived state. Pip concludes his
assessment of Joe's education with a phrase that links industrialization and
literacy while at the same time reversing the relations between adult and
child. "Joe's education, like steam, was yet in its infancy." For Pip, writing
and reading will become the beginning of his accomplishments. They are
the vehicles of his anticipated upward social mobility, and the expectation
not only of greater wealth but of moral superiority as well. He recapitulates
the historical experience by which oral culture is devalued and writing
replaces spoken communication as the transcendent value of western
culture. The subsequent plot reveals how Dickens is making an accounting
of the costs and benefits of modernization: writing, the production of
language, and the manipulation of words and capital have become the new
measure of human worth.

In the nineteenth century, Dickens is one of the great producers of
words. It was an era when Balzac was producing thousands of sentences on
the French *comédie humaine* and Dostoevsky was investigating the
psychology and urban malaise of his characters in volume after dramatic
volume. Other English writers of the Victorian era were also pouring out
words at an incredible clip, all before the invention of the typewriter, which
Tolstoy at the end of his career would use to substitute for the wife who
copied the manuscript of *War and Peace* seven times. Dickens' work, like

that of many of his contemporaries, is distinguished by plentitude. In sheer bulk and volume, it is a universe. Unlike their work, however, his is particularly notable for its self-conscious concern to map the social and psychological consequences of writing.

By the time he published *Great Expectations* in serial form in 1860–1861, Dickens had already written twelve novels, edited four magazines for which he had written at least a million words, and published two books of travel and social observation. He was forty-nine years old.

He began his career as a court reporter and transcriber of Parliamentary debates, which he reproduced for newspaper publication with phenomenal speed and accuracy. Like Pip, Dickens had taught himself to read and write; like David Copperfield he had taught himself to take shorthand before he was sixteen, very quickly becoming the best stenographer of his time. As Steven Marcus points out in a classic article, this talent of Dickens' helped make it possible for him to recast the conventional relation between speech and writing.

Once he had mastered the stenographic characters in a process that receives brilliant description in Chapter 38 of *David Copperfield*, they were no longer the constituents of an imprisoning code, Marcus points out, but the playful doodles of speech. The stenographic "characters, as he describes them in recollection, were themselves doodles—apparently random plays of the pen, out of which figures or partial figures would emerge and to which meaning could be ascribed." As a result, speech could "now be rendered not only in the abstract forms of cursive or printed letters and units; it could be represented *graphically* as well." Marcus emphasizes that this "experience of an alternative, quasi-graphic way of representing speech had among other things the effect upon Dickens of loosening up the rigid relations between speech and writing that prevail in our linguistic and cultural system." These flourishes of the pen, these squiggles and doodles, provide Dickens "with an experience of something that closely resembled a hieroglyphic means of preserving speech," making it possible for "the spoken language to enter into his writing with a parity it had never enjoyed before in English fictional prose. Speech here was not that traditional subordinate of its written representation; it could appear now in writing with a freedom and spontaneity that made it virtually, if momentarily, writing's equal." Dramatizing the acquisition of literacy in *Great Expectations*, and revealing the gulf between oral and written culture, Dickens occupies a particularly heady moment in western cultural history. He can look both ways, and bring into the future alphabetic code of the west the childhood experience of calligraphy, when the alphabetic character is both phoneme and picture.

In this novel as was the case throughout the nineteenth century, most reading was reading aloud; then writing must be the (sometimes) private act of making the characters that provide a public voice. Perhaps the act of decoding in which we are engaged parallel to that of the characters of *Great Expectations* will lead us as well to the greater magic of encoding—so that we like them may inscribe our selves in the world in which they too are circumscribed. Then our story would become more than a private possession, and be changed into public meaning. Like money that Wemmick refers to as portable property, our story would have added to the store of language and become something from which, like capital, we could all benefit.

Reading *Great Expectations* aloud, we become one of its community of readers. We are the witnesses to its experience. As Pip speaks to us we are not imprisoned in the code of reading, but rather liberated by calligraphic impulses; the characters of the novel, both alphabetic and fictive, are writ large as our meaning. We envision the scene, encounter the portrayed situation, and believe in this rendered world, for it is a true story. In referring to Marcus, I do not mean to make *Great Expectations* into an avatar of *Pickwick Papers*. Rather, it is to emphasize that our experience in reading this novel is not just Pip's deciphering of a code—not mere transcription—but the rhythm of participating in its production. Thereby, we share in a particular version of calligraphic experience. *Great Expectations* gives writing the qualities of speech, the flow of language unceasing and unending. We are sorry when it stops.

If we share in the education of the characters, the grotesque quality of their schooling distances us from it. When its serious meanings receive comic treatment, the validity of our own efforts as readers and writers is reinforced. The difficulties of their writing displace our own struggle in learning to read and write onto them; they serve to guide us across the threshold of literacy into the world of the capital accumulation and production of language. The novel asks if it is possible for us to be—unlike the child Pip—correct readers who are yet not imprisoned by the false expectations of books or class, nor deceived into devaluing those sentiments of innocence, sincerity, friendship, and help which the oral world of the blacksmith's forge stands for over and against the deceit and duplicity of town and city life. We do not seek to emulate Jaggers, for whom speech consists of cross-examination—that is, of treating oral communication as if it were a written contract. And if Jaggers, the lawyer, is one of the principal figures involved in writing in this novel, he is so as the embodiment of code: as writing that hides, represses, and deprives meaning of its pictorial and visual fullness.

By contrast, the comedy of Joe's letter writing reminds us how far we have come since childhood. If it helps us to forget the tribulations of our education, it also suggests the hope that the directness of oral speech may transfer to literacy, so that we may read and write the alphabet as calligraphy rather than code. We may hope that reading and writing will become easy enough so that it will not be for us, as it is for Joe, living in our Sunday clothes. The comedy of Joe's writing is emphasized in Pip's description, in which we also hear a touch of derision.

> At my own writing-table, pushed into a corner and cumbered with little bottles, Joe now sat down to his great work, first choosing a pen from the pen-tray as if it were a chest of large tools, and tucking up his sleeves as if he were going to wield a crowbar or sledgehammer. It was necessary for Joe to hold on heavily to the table with his left elbow, and to get his right leg well out behind him, before he could begin, and when he did begin, he made every down-stroke so slowly that it might have been six feet long, while at every up-stroke I could hear his pen spluttering extensively. He had a curious idea that the inkstand was on the side of him where it was not, and constantly dipped his pen into space, and seemed quite satisfied with the result. Occasionally, he was tripped up by some orthographical stumbling-block, but on the whole he got on very well indeed, and when he had signed his name, and had removed a finishing blot from the paper to the crown of his head with his two forefingers, he got up and hovered about the table, trying the effect of his performance from various points of view as it lay there, with unbounded satisfaction.

Pip's sarcastic description reveals the ways in which he has become alienated from the sources of his feelings by contrast with Joe. In so fully rendering Joe, the blacksmith coping with the difficulty of writing, Dickens reminds his reader not only of its importance but its increasing value in a world undergoing the revolution of industrialization and modernization that depends upon making unlettered folk into modern workers. What makes Joe special, however, is the way in which he never quite becomes fully literate and thus does not learn to forget the ways in which his person and identity are rooted in the oral culture of family, place, and time. He does not invest in his own ego, as Pip does, and Charley Hexam will in *Our Mutual Friend.*

By contrast, the pathos of Pip's situation as he learns to read and write is already apparent in his letter to Joe in Chapter 7.

One night I was sitting in the chimney-corner with my slate, expending great efforts on the production of a letter to Joe. I think it must have been a full year after our hunt upon the marshes, for it was a long time after, and it was winter, and a hard frost. With an alphabet on the hearth at my feet for reference, I contrived in an hour or two to print and smear this epistle:

'mI deEr JO I opE U r krWitE wEll i opE i shAl soN B haBelL 4 2 teeDge U JO aN theN wE shOrl b sO glOdd aN wEn i M preNgtD 2 u JO woT LarX an blEvE ME in FxN PiP.'

There was no indispensable necessity for my communicating with Joe by letter, inasmuch as he sat beside me and we were alone. But, I delivered this written communication (slate and all) with my own hand, and Joe received it as a miracle of erudition.

The next to last word of Pip's letter is a pun; he means, we think, in affection, but writes infection. The word reveals his conscious and unconscious meanings at the same time. More of him is inscribed in it than he knows. Writing is the dis-ease of his new condition—as well as ours.

PETER BROOKS

Repetition, Repression, and Return:
The Plotting of Great Expectations

W̲e have defined plot, for our purposes, as a structuring operation
deployed by narratives, or activated in the reading of narratives: as the logic
and syntax of those meanings that develop only through sequence and
succession. We noted that the range of meanings assigned to the word plot
in the dictionary includes a sense of the scheme or machination to the
accomplishment of some end—the sense apparently derived from the
"contamination" of the French *complot*—and we suggested that nineteenth-
century novels regularly conceive plot as *complot*: they are structured by a
plotting for and toward something, a machination of desire. Some narratives
clearly give us a sense of plotting and of "plottedness" more than others, and
in particular a sense that their central meanings come to us through plotting:
that there is no disjuncture between idea and symbol on the one hand, and
the requirements of narrative design on the other. Such a disjuncture will, I
think, be characteristic of the novel in its "modernist" and "postmodernist"
phases, where there is a pervasive suspicion that plot falsifies more subtle
kinds of interconnectedness. If the novels of Joyce and Woolf and Proust and
Gide, and then Faulkner and Robbe-Grillet, cannot ultimately do without
plotting insofar as they remain narrative structures that signify, they plot
with irony and bad conscience, intent (in their very different ways) to expose
the artifices of formal structure and human design. Whereas it was part of the

From *Reading for the Plot: Design and Intention in Narrative.* © 1984 by Peter Brooks.

triumph of the nineteenth-century novel in its golden age to plot with good conscience, in confidence that the elaboration of plot corresponded to, and illuminated, human complexities. The intimacy of Balzac, Dickens, Eugène Sue, Wilkie Collins (to name only the most popular) with a large audience inclusive of different social strata was both a result of and a license to the working out of their deepest intentions through plotted action, in a demonstrative mode.

I want in this chapter to discuss in the light of Freud's masterplot a novel that stands firmly within the golden age of plot, one that is centrally, unashamedly, and—at first glance—unsuspiciously concerned with issues of plot and plotting. It is indeed plotting, as an activity, as a dynamic machination, that may provide our best way into the reading of a fully achieved plot. And this activity of plotting may be most readily discernible in a retrospective first-person narrative. When we ask the questions, How do we find significant plots for our lives? How do we make life narratable? we find that the answers are most clearly dramatized in narratives of an autobiographical cast, since these cannot evade an explicit concern with problems of closure, authority, and narratability. As Sartre argued, autobiographical narration must necessarily be "obituary"—must in any event explicitly show margins outside the narratable, leftover spaces which allow the narrating *I* to objectify and look back at the narrated *I*, and to see the plotted middle as shaped by and as shaping its margins. Hence rather than such novels as *Bleak House* or *Our Mutual Friend*, highly elaborated lengthy arabesques of plot, I choose *Great Expectations*, a more compact example, but one that gives in the highest degree the impression that its central meanings depend on the workings-out of its plot. For in this fictional pseudo-autobiography, Dickens adopts the revealing strategy of taking a "life" and creating the demarcations of a "plot" within it. The novel will indeed be concerned with finding a plot and losing it, with the precipitation of the sense of plottedness around its hero, and his eventual "cure" from plot. The novel images in its structure the kind of structuring operation of reading that plot is.

I

Great Expectations is exemplary for a discourse on plot in many respects, not least of all for its beginning. For what the novel chooses to present at its outset is precisely the search for a beginning. As in so many nineteenth-century novels, the hero is an orphan, thus undetermined by any visible inheritance, apparently unauthored. This clears away Julien Sorel's problems with paternity. There may be sociological and sentimental reasons to account for the high incidence of orphans in the nineteenth-century novel, but clearly the parentless protagonist frees an author from struggle with pre-existing authorities, allowing him to create afresh all the determinants of plot within his text. He thus profits from what Gide called the "lawlessness" of the novel by starting with an undefined, rule-free character and then bringing the law to bear upon him—creating the rules—as the text proceeds. With Pip, Dickens begins as it were with a life that is for the moment precedent to plot, and indeed necessarily in search of plot. Pip when we first see him is himself in search of the "authority"—the word stands in the second paragraph of the novel—that would define and justify—authorize—the plot of his ensuing life.

The "authority" to which Pip refers here is that of the tombstone which bears the names of his dead parents, the names that have already been displaced, condensed, and superseded in the first paragraph, where Pip describes how his "infant tongue" (literally, a speechless tongue: a catachresis that points to a moment of emergence, of entry into language) could only make of the name, Philip Pirrip, left to him by the dead parents, the monosyllabic Pip. "So, I called myself Pip, and came to be called Pip." This originating moment of Pip's narration and his narrative is a self-naming that already subverts whatever authority could be found in the text of the tombstones. The process of reading that text is described by Pip the narrator as "unreasonable," in that it interprets the appearance of the lost father and mother from the shape of the letters of their names. The tracing of the name—which he has already distorted in its application to self—involves a misguided attempt to remotivate the graphic symbol, to make it directly mimetic, mimetic specifically of origin. Loss of origin, misreading, and the problematic of identity are bound up here in ways we will further explore later on. The question of reading and writing—of learning to compose and to decipher texts—is persistently thematized in the novel.

The decipherment of the tombstone text as confirmation of loss of origin—as unauthorization—is here at the start of the novel the prelude to Pip's *cogito*, the moment in which his consciousness seizes his existence as other, alien, forlorn:

> My first most vivid and broad impression of the identity of things seems to me to have been gained on a memorable raw afternoon towards evening. At such a time I found out for certain, that this bleak place overgrown with nettles was the churchyard; and that Philip Pirrip, late of this parish, and also Georgiana, wife of the above, were dead and buried; and that

Alexander, Bartholomew, Abraham, Tobias, and Roger, infant children of the aforesaid, were also dead and buried; and that the dark flat wilderness beyond the churchyard, intersected with dykes and mounds and gates, with scattered cattle feeding on it, was the marshes; and that the low leaden line beyond was the river; and that the distant savage lair from which the wind was rushing, was the sea; and that the small bundle of shivers growing afraid of it all and beginning to cry, was Pip.

"Hold your noise!" cried a terrible voice. . . .

The repeated verbs of existence—"was" and "were"—perform an elementary phenomenology of Pip's world, locating its irreducible objects and leading finally to the individual subject as other, as aware of his existence through the emotion of fear, fear that then appears as the origin of voice, or articulated sound, as Pip begins to cry: a cry that is immediately censored by the command of the convict Magwitch, the father-to-be, the fearful intrusive figure of future authorship who will demand of Pip: "Give us your name."

The scenario is richly suggestive of the problem of identity, self-consciousness, naming, and language that will accompany Pip throughout the novel, and points to the original decentering of the subject in regard to himself. For purposes of my study of plot, it is important to note how this beginning establishes Pip as an existence without a plot, at the very moment of occurrence of that event which will prove to be decisive for the plotting of his existence, as he will discover only two-thirds of the way through the novel. Alien, unauthorized, self-named, at the point of entry into the language code and the social systems it implies, Pip will in the first part of the novel be in search of a plot, and the novel will recount the gradual precipitation of a sense of plot around him, the creation of portents of direction and intention.

Schematically, we can identify four lines of plot that begin to crystallize around the young Pip, the Pip of Part 1, before the arrival of his "Expectations":

1. Communion with the convict/criminal deviance.
2. Naterally wicious/bringing up by hand.
3. The dream of Satis House/the fairy tale.
4. The nightmare of Satis House/the witch tale.

These plots, we will see in a moment, are paired as follows: 2/1=3/4. That is, there is in each case an "official" and censoring plot standing over a "repressed" plot. In terms of Pip's own choices, we could rewrite the formula:

3/4/2/1, to show (in accordance with one of Freud's favorite models) the archaeological layering of strata of repressed material. When the Expectations are announced by Jaggers at the end of part one, they will apparently coincide with Pip's choices ("My dream was out; my wild fancy was surpassed by sober reality"), and will thus appear to take care of the question of plot. But this will be so only on the level of official plots; the Expectations will in fact only mask further the problem of the repressed plots.

I choose the term "communion" for the first plot because its characteristic symbolic gesture is Pip's pity for the convict as he swallows the food Pip has brought him, a moment of sympathetic identification which focuses a series of suggestive sympathies and identifications with the outlaw: the bread and butter that Pip puts down his leg, which makes him walk like the chained convict; Mrs. Joe's belief that he is on his way to the Hulks; Pip's flight from the Christmas dinner table into the arms of a soldier holding out handcuffs, to give a few examples. Pip is concerned to assure "his" convict that he is not responsible for his recapture, a point he conveys in a mute exchange of glances which the convict understands and which leads him to make a public statement in exoneration of Pip, taking responsibility for stealing the food. This in turn provokes an overt statement of community with the outlaw, which comes from Joe: "We don't know what you have done, but we wouldn't have you starved to death for it, poor miserable fellow-creatur.—Would us, Pip?"

The fellowship with the convict here stated by Joe will remain with Pip, but in a state of repression, as what he will later call "that spell of my childhood"—an unavowable memory. It finds its official, adult, repressive version in the conviction—shared by all the adults in Pip's life, with the exception of the childlike Joe—that children are naturally depraved and need to be corrected, kept in line with the Tickler, brought up by hand lest their natural willfulness assert itself in plots that are deviant, transgressive. Pumblechook and the Hubbles, in their Christmas dinner dialogue, give the theme a choric statement:

> "Especially," said Mr. Pumblechook, "be grateful, boy, to them which brought you up by hand."
>
> Mrs. Hubble shook her head, and contemplating me with a mournful presentiment that I should come to no good, asked, "Why is it that the young are never grateful?" This moral mystery seemed too much for the company until Mr. Hubble tersely solved it by saying, "Naterally wicious." Everybody then murmured "True!" and looked at me in a particularly unpleasant and personal manner.

The "nateral wiciousness" of children legitimates communion with the outlaw, but legitimates it as that which must be repressed, forced into other plots—including, as we shall see, "binding" Pip as an apprentice.

The dream of Satis House is properly a daydream, in which "His Majesty, the Ego" pleasures himself with the phantasy of social ascension and gentility. Miss Havisham is made to play the role of Fairy Godmother, her crutch become a magic wand, explicitly evoked twice near the close of part 1. This plot has adult sanction; its first expression comes from Pumblechook and Mrs. Joe when they surmise that Miss Havisham intends to "do something" for Pip, and Pip comes to believe in it, so that when the "Expectations" arrive he accepts them as the logical fulfillment of the daydream, of his "longings." Yet to identify Satis House with the daydream is to perform a repression of all else that Satis House suggests and represents—all that clusters around the central emblem of the rotting bride cake and its crawling things. The craziness and morbidity of Satis House repose on desire fixated, become fetishistic and sadistic, on a deviated eroticism that has literally shut out the light, stopped the clocks, and made the forward movement of plot impossible. Satis House, as the circular journeys of the wheelchair to the rhythm of the blacksmith's song "Old Clem" may best suggest, constitutes repetition without variation, pure reproduction, a collapsed metonymy where cause and effect have become identical, the same-as-same. It is significant that when Pip returns from his first visit to Satis House, he responds to the interrogations of Pumblechook and Mrs. Joe with an elaborate lie—the story of the coach, the flags, the dogs fighting for "weal cutlets" from a silver basket—a phantasy that we can read as his response to what he calls a "smart without a name, that needed counteraction." All the attempts to read Satis House as a text speaking of gentility and social ascension may be subverted from the outset, in the passage that describes Pip's first impression of Miss Havisham:

> It was not in the first few moments that I saw all these things, though I saw more of them in the first moments than might be supposed. But, I saw that everything within my view which ought to be white, had been white long ago, and had lost its lustre, and was faded and yellow. I saw that the bride within the bridal dress had withered like the dress, and like the flowers, and had no brightness left but the brightness of her sunken eyes. I saw that the dress had been put upon the rounded figure of a young woman, and that the figure upon which it now hung loose, had shrunk to skin and bone. Once, I had been taken to see some ghastly waxwork at the Fair,

representing I know not what impossible personage lying in a
state. Once, I had been taken to one of our old marsh churches
to see a skeleton in the ashes of a rich dress, that had been dug
out of a vault under the church pavement. Now, waxwork and
skeleton seemed to have dark eyes that moved and looked at
me. I should have cried out, if I could.

The passage records the formation of a memory trace from a moment of
unmastered horror, itself formed in repetition of moments of past visual
impression, a trace the forces its way through the mind without being
grasped by consciousness and is refused outlet in a cry. Much later in the
novel, Pip—and also Miss Havisham herself—will have to deal with the return
of this repressed.

We have, then, a quadripartite scheme of plots, organized into two
pairs, each with an "official" plot, or interpretation of plot, standing over a
repressed plot. The scheme may lead us in the first instance to reflect on the
place of repression as one of the large "orders" of the novel. Repression plays
a dominant role in the theme of education which is so important to the novel,
from Mrs. Joe's bringing up by hand, through Mrs. Wopsle's aunt's
schoolroom, to Mr. Pocket's career as a "grinder" of dull blades (while his
own children meanwhile are "tumbling up"). Bringing up by hand in turn
suggests Jaggers's hands, representation of accusation and the law, which in
turn suggest all the instances of censorship in the name of high authorities
evoked from the first scene of the novel onward: censorship is repression in
the name of the Law. Jaggers's sinister hand-washings point to the
omnipresent taint of Newgate, which echoes the earlier presence of the
Hulks, to which Mrs. Joe verbally assigns Pip. Then there is the moment
when Pip is "bound" as apprentice blacksmith before the magistrates, in a
scene of such repressive appearance that a well-meaning philanthropist is
moved to hand Pip a pamphlet entitled *To Be Read in My Cell*. There is a
constant association of education, repression, the threat of prison,
criminality, the fear of deviance. We might note in passing Dickens's capacity
to literalize the metaphors of education—"bringing up by hand,"
"grinding"—in a manner that subverts the order that ought to assure their
figural validity. The particularly sinister version of the *Bildungsroman*
presented by *Great Expectations* derives in some measure from the
literalization of metaphors pertaining to education and upbringing. Societal
repression and censorship are, of course, reinforced by Pip's own, his
internalization of the law and the denial of what he calls the "old taint" of his
association with the criminal. The whole theme of gentility, as represented
by the Finches of the Grove, for instance, or the punishment of Trabb's boy,

consistently suggests an aggressivity based on denial. One could reflect here on the splendid name of Pip's superfluous valet: the Avenger.

The way in which the Expectations are instituted, in seeming realization of the Satis House dream, comprehends "bringing up by hand" (the other official plot) in that it includes the disciplines necessary to gentility: grinding with Mr. Pocket, lessons in manners from Herbert, learning to spend one's time and money in appropriate gentlemanly pursuits. There is in this manner a blurring of plot lines, useful to the processes of wish fulfillment in that education and indeed repression itself can be interpreted as agencies necessary to the pursuit of the dream. Realization of the dream permits acceptance of society's interpretations, and in fact requires the abandonment of any effort at personal interpretation: Pip is now enjoined from seeking to know more about the intentions of his donor, disallowed the role of detective which so much animates him in part three of the novel—when the Expectations have proved false—and is already incipiently present in part one.

Taking our terminology from the scene where Pip is bound as apprentice, we may consider that education and repression operate in the novel as one form of "binding": official ways of channeling and tying up the mobile energies of life. It is notable that after he has become apprenticed to Joe, Pip goes through a stage of purely iterative existence—presented in chapter 14—where the direction and movement of plot appear to be finished, where all life's "interest and romance" appear shut out as by a "thick curtain," time reduced to repetitive duration. Conversely, when the Expectations have arrived, Miss Havisham is apparently identified as the fairy-tale donor, and the Satis House plot appears securely bound, Pip need only wait for the next stage of the plot to become manifest. Yet it is clear that for the reader neither binding as an apprentice (the first accomplishment of an upbringing by hand) nor the tying up of Satis House as a fairy-tale plot constitutes valid and adequate means of dealing with and disposing of the communion with the convict and the nightmare of Satis House. The energy released in the text by its liminary "primal scene"—in the graveyard—and by the early visits to Satis House, creating that "smart without a name," simply is not and cannot be bound by the bindings of the official, repressive plots. As readers we know that there has been created in the text an intensive level of energy that cannot be discharged through these official plots.

In fact, the text has been working simultaneously to bind these disavowed energies in other ways, ways over which Pip's ego, and the societal superego, have no control, and of which they have no knowledge, through repetitions that, for the reader, prepare an inevitable return of the repressed. Most striking are the periodic fragmentary returns of the convict-communion material: the leg iron used to bludgeon Mrs. Joe, guns firing from the Hulks to signal further escapes, and especially the reappearance of Joe's file, the dramatic stage property used by Magwitch's emissary in a "proceeding in dumb show . . . pointedly addressed at me." His stirring and tasting his rum and water "pointedly at" Pip suggests the establishment of an aim (Pip calls his proceeding "a shot"), a direction, an intention in Pip's life: the first covert announcement of another plot which will come to govern Pip's life, but of course misinterpreted as to its true aim. With the nightmare energies of Satis House, binding may be at work in those repetitive journeys around the rotting bridal cake, suggestive of the reproduction or working through of the traumatic neurotic whose affects remain fixed on the past, on the traumatic moment that never can be mastered. For Miss Havisham herself, these energies can never be plotted to effective discharge; and we will have occasion to doubt whether they are ever fully bound for Pip as well. The compulsive reproductive repetition that characterizes every detail of Satis House lets us perceive how the returns of the convict-communion suggest a more significant working through of an unmastered past, a repetition that can alter the form of the repeated. In both instances—but ultimately with different results—the progressive, educative plots, the plots of repression and social advancement, are threatened by a repetitive process obscurely going on underneath and beyond them. We sense that forward progress will have to recover markings from the beginning through a dialectic of return.

II

In my references to the work of repetition as the binding of energies, I have been implicitly assuming that one can make a transfer from the model of psychic functioning proposed in *Beyond the Pleasure Principle* to the literary text, an assumption that no doubt can never be "proved" and must essentially find its justification in the illumination it can bring to texts. We saw in Chapter 2 that texts represent themselves as inhabited by energies, which are ultimately images of desire, and correspond to the arousals, expectations, doubts, suspense, reversals, revaluations, disappointments, embarrassments, fulfillments, and even the incoherences animated by reading. If we can accept the idea of a textual energetics, we can see that in any well-plotted novel the energies released and aroused in the text, especially in its early moments, will not be lost: the text is a kind of thermodynamic plenum, obeying the law of the conservation of energy (as well, no doubt, as the law of entropy). Repetition is clearly a major operative principle of the system, shaping energy, giving it perceptible form, form that the text and the reader can work with in the construction of thematic wholes and narrative orders. Repetition conceived as binding, the creation of cohesion—see the French translation of Freud's *Verbindung: liaison*, a word we would commonly use in the description of discourse and argument—may allow us to see how the text and the reader put energy into forms where it can be mastered, both by the logics set in motion by the plot, and by interpretive effort.

Repetition is, of course, a complex phenomenon, and one that has its history of commentary in philosophical as well as psychoanalytic thought. Is repetition sameness or difference? To repeat evidently implies resemblance, yet can we speak of resemblance unless there is difference? Without difference, repetition would be identity, which would not usually appear to be the case, if only because the chronological context of the repeated occurrence differs from that of the "original" occurrence (the "original" is thus a concept that repetition puts into question). In this sense, repetition always includes the idea of variation in time, and may ever be potentially a progressive act. As Kierkegaard writes near the beginning of *Repetition*, "Repetition and recollection are the same movement, only in opposite directions; for what is recollected has been, is repeated backwards, whereas repetition properly is repeated forwards." Freud, as we noted, considers repetition to be a form of recollection brought into play when conscious mental rememoration has been blocked by repression. Lacan argues that Freud distinguishes between repeating (*wiederholen*) and reproducing (*reproduzieren*): reproduction would be the full reliving, of the original traumatic scene, for instance, that Freud aimed at early in his career, when he still believed in "catharsis"; whereas repetition always takes place in the realm of the symbolic—in the transference, in language—where the affects and figures of the past are confronted in symbolic form. We can thus perhaps say that for Freud repetition is a symbolic enactment referring back to unconscious determinants, progressive in that it belongs to the forward thrust of desire and is known by way of desire's workings in the signifying chain, but regressive in its points of reference.

We cannot and should not attempt to reduce and resolve the ambiguities of repetition since they are indeed inherent to our experience of repetition, part of what creates its "uncanny" effect and allows us to think about the intractable problem of temporal form, in our lives and in our fictions. In *Great Expectations*, the repetitions associated with Satis House, particularly as played out by Miss Havisham herself, suggest the reproductive in that they aim to restore in all its detail the traumatic moment—recorded by the clocks stopped at twenty minutes to nine—when erotic wishes were abruptly foreclosed by Compeyson's rupture of faith. On the other hand, the repetitions of the convict material experienced by Pip all imply something to come—something to come that, as we shall see, will take him back, painfully, to the primal scene, yet take him back in the context of difference. Repetition in the text is a return, a calling back or a turning back. And as I suggested earlier, repetitions are thus both returns to and returns of: for instance, returns to origins and returns of the repressed, moving us forward in Pip's journey toward elucidation, disillusion, and maturity by taking us back, as if in obsessive reminder that we cannot really move ahead until we have understood that still enigmatic past, yet ever pushing us forward, since revelation, tied to the past, belongs to the future.

The novelistic middle, which is perhaps the most difficult of Aristotle's "parts" of a plot to talk about, is in this case notably characterized by the return. Quite literally: it is Pip's repeated returns from London to his home town that constitute the organizing device of the whole of the London period, the time of the Expectations and their aftermath. Pip's returns are always ostensibly undertaken to make reparation to the neglected Joe, an intention never realized; and always implicitly an attempt to discover the intentions of the putative donor in Satis House, to bring her plot to completion. Yet the returns also always bring his regression, in Satis House, to the status of the "coarse and common boy" whose social ascension is hallucinatorily denied, his return to the nightmare of unprogressive repetition; and, too, a revival of the repressed convict assumption, the return of the childhood spell. Each return suggests that Pip's official plots, which seem to speak of progress, ascent, and the satisfaction of desire, are in fact subject to a process of repetition of the yet unmastered past, the true determinant of his life's direction.

The pattern of the return is established in Pip's first journey back from London, in Chapter 28. His decision to visit Joe is quickly thrown into the shade by the presence on the stagecoach of two convicts, one of whom Pip recognizes as the man of the file and the rum and water, Magwitch's emissary. There is a renewed juxtaposition of official, genteel judgment on the convicts, voiced by Herbert Pocket—"What a vile and degraded spectacle"—and Pip's inward avowal that he feels sympathy for their alienation. On the roof of the coach, seated in front of the convicts, Pip dozes off while pondering whether he ought to restore the two one-pound notes that the convict of the file had passed him so many years before. Upon regaining consciousness, the first two words he hears, continuing his dream thoughts, are: "Two one-pound notes." There follows the convict's account of his embassy from "Pip's convict" to the boy who had saved him. Although Pip is certain that the convict cannot recognize him, so changed in age, circumstance, and even name (since Herbert Pocket calls him "Handel"), the dreamlike experience forces a kind of recognition of a forgotten self, refound in fear and pain:

> I could not have said what I was afraid of, for my fear was altogether underfined and vague, but there was great fear upon me. As I walked on to the hotel, I felt that a dread, much exceeding the mere apprehension of a painful or disagreeable recognition, made me tremble. I am confident that it took no distinctness of shape, and that it was the revival for a few minutes of the terror of childhood.

The return to origins has led to the return of the repressed, and vice versa. Repetition as return becomes a reproduction and re-enactment of infantile experience: not simply a recall of the primal moment, but a reliving of its pain and terror, suggesting the impossibility of escape from the originating scenarios of childhood, the condemnation forever to replay them.

This first example may stand for the other returns of the novel's middle, which all follow the same pattern, which all double return to with return of and show Pip's ostensible progress in the world to be subverted by the irradicable presence of the convict-communion and the Satis House nightmare. It is notable that toward the end of the middle—as the novel's dénouement approaches—there is an acceleration in the rhythm of these returns, as if to affirm that all the clues to Pip's future, the forward movement of his plot, in fact lie in the past. Repetition as return speaks as a textual version of the death instinct, plotting the text, beyond the seeming dominance of the pleasure principle, toward its proper end, imaging this end as necessarily a time before the beginning. In the moment of crisis before the climax of the novel's action, Pip is summoned back to the marshes associated with his infancy to face extinction at the hands of Orlick—who has throughout the novel acted the role of Pip's "bad double," a hateful and sadistic version of the hero—in a threatened short-circuit of the text, as Pip indicates when he thinks how he will be misunderstood by others if he dies prematurely, without explanation: "Misremembered after death . . . despised by unborn generations." Released from this threat, Pip attempts to escape from England, but even this voyage out to another land and another life leads him back: the climax of Magwitch's discovery and recapture are played out in the Thames estuary, where "it was like my own marsh country, flat and monotonous, and with a dim horizon." We are back in the horizontal perspectives and muddy tidal flats that are so much a part of our perception of the childhood Pip.

But before speaking further of resolutions, I must say a word about the novel's great "recognition scene," the moment at which the latent becomes manifest, the repressed convict plot is forcibly brought to consciousness, a scene that decisively re-enacts both a return of the repressed and a return to the primal moment of childhood. The recognition scene comes in chapter 39, and it is preceded by two curious paragraphs at the end of chapter 38 in which Pip as narrator suggests that the pages he has just written, concerning his frustrated courtship of Estella, constitute, on the plane of narration itself, a last binding of that plot in its overt version, as a plot of romance, and that now he must move on to a deeper level of plot—reaching further back—which subsumes as it subverts all the other plots of the novel: "All the work, near and afar, that tended to the end had been accomplished." That this long-range plot is presented as analogous to "the Eastern story" in which a heavy slab of stone is carved out and fitted into the roof in order that it may fall on "the bed of state in the flush of conquest" seems in coded fashion to suggest punishment for erotic transgression, which we may want to read as return of the nightmare plot of Satis House, forcing its way through the fairy tale, speaking of the perverse, sadistic eroticism that Pip has covered over with his erotic object choice—Estella, who in fact represents the wrong choice of plot and another danger of short-circuit. To anticipate later revelations, we should note that Estella will turn out to be approximately Pip's sister—natural daughter of Magwitch as he is Magwitch's adoptive son—which lends force to the idea that she, like so many Romantic maidens, is marked by the interdict, as well as the seduction, of incest, which, as the perfect androgynous coupling, is precisely the short-circuit of desire.

The scene of Magwitch's return operates for Pip as a painful forcing through of layers of repression, an analogue of analytic work, compelling Pip to recognize that what he calls "that chance encounter of long ago" is no chance, and cannot be assigned to the buried past but must be repeated, reenacted, worked through in the present. The scene replays numerous details of their earlier encounter, and the central moment of recognition comes as a reenactment and revival of the novel's primal scene, played in dumb show, a mute text which the more effectively stages recognition as a process of return to the inescapable past:

> Even yet I could not recall a single feature, but I knew him! If the wind and the rain had driven away the intervening years, had scattered all the intervening objects, had swept us to the churchyard where we first stood face to face on such different levels, I could not have known my convict more distinctly than I knew him now, as he sat in the chair before the fire. No need to take a file from his pocket and show it to me; no need to take a handkerchief from his neck and twist it round his head; no

need to hug himself with both his arms, and take a shivering turn across the room, looking back at me for recognition. I knew him before he gave me one of those aids, though, a moment before, I had not been conscious of remotely suspecting his identity.

The praeterition on which the passage is constructed—"no need . . . no need"—marks the gradual retrieval of the past as its involuntary repetition within the present. The repetition takes place—as Magwitch's effective use of the indicative signs may suggest—in the mode of the symbolic, offering a persuasive instance of Freud's conception of repetition as a form of recollection brought into action by repression and resistance to its removal. It becomes clear that the necessity for Pip to repeat and work through everything associated with his original communion with Magwitch is a factor of his "forgetting" this communion: a forgetting that is merely conscious. The reader has undergone a similar process through textual repetition and return, one that in his case has had the function of not permitting him to forget.

The scene of Magwitch's return is an important one for any study of plot since it demonstrates so well how such a novelist as Dickens can make plotting the central vehicle and armature of meaning in the narrative text. All the issues raised in the novel—social, ethical, interpretive—are here simultaneously brought to climax through the peripety of the plot. Exposure of the "true" plot of Pip's life brings with it instantaneous consequences for all the other "codes" of the novel, as he recognizes with the statement, "All the truth of my position came *flashing* on me; and its disappointments, dangers, disgraces, consequences of all kinds" (my italics). The return of the repressed—the repressed as knowledge of the self's other story, the true history of its misapprehended desire—forces a total revision of the subject's relation to the orders within which it constitutes meaning.

Magwitch poses unanswerable questions, about the origins of Pip's property and the means of his social ascent, which force home to Pip that he has covered over a radical lack of original authority. Like Oedipus—who cannot answer Tiresias's final challenge: who are your parents?—Pip does not know where he stands. The result has been the intrusion of an aberrant, contingent authorship—Magwitch's—in the story of the self. Education and training in gentility turn out to be merely an agency in the repression of the determinative convict plot. Likewise, the daydream/fairy tale of Satis House stands revealed as a repression, or perhaps a "secondary revision," of the nightmare. That it should be the criminally deviant, transgressive plot that is shown to have priority over all the others stands within the logic of the model derived from *Beyond the Pleasure Principle*, since it is precisely this plot that most markedly constitutes the detour from inorganic quiescence: the arabesque of the narratable. One could almost derive a narratological law here: the true plot will be the most deviant. We might be tempted to see this deviant arabesque as gratuitous, the figure of "pure narration." Yet we are obliged to remotivate it, for the return of the repressed shows that the story Pip would tell about himself has all along been undermined and rewritten by the more complex history of unconscious desire, unavailable to the conscious subject but at work in the text. Pip has in fact misread the plot of his life.

III

The misreading of plots and the question of authority brings us back to the question of reading with which the novel begins. Pip's initial attempt to decipher his parents' appearance and character from the letters traced on their tombstones has been characterized as "childish" and "unreasonable." Pip's decipherment in fact appears as an attempt to motivate the arbitrary sign, to interpret signs as if they were mimetic and thus naturally tied to the object for which they stand. Deriving from the shape of the letters on the tombstones that his father "was a square, stout, dark man, with curly hair," and that his mother was "freckled and sickly," for all its literal fidelity to the graphic trace, constitutes a dangerously figural reading, a metaphorical process unaware of itself, the making of a fiction unaware of its status as fiction making. Pip is here claiming natural authority for what is in fact conventional, arbitrary, dependent on interpretation.

The question of texts, reading, and interpretation is, as we earlier noted, consistently thematized in the novel: in Pip's learning to read (using that meager text, Mrs. Wosple's aunt's catalogue of prices), and his attempts to transmit the art of writing to Joe; the excessive dumb shows between Pip and Joe; messages written on slate, by Pip to Joe, and then (in minimum symbolic form) by the aphasic Mrs. Joe; the uncanny text of Estella's visage, always reminding Pip of a repetition of something else which he cannot identify; Molly's wrist, cross-hatched with scratches, a text for the judge, and eventually for Pip as detective, to decipher; Mr. Wopsle's declamations of *George Barnwell* and *Richard III*. The characters appear to be ever on the watch for ways in which to textualize the world, so that they can give their readings of it: a situation thematized early in the novel, at the Christmas dinner table, as Pumblechook and Wopsle criticize the sermon of the day and propose other "subjects":

Mr. Pumblechook added, after a short interval of reflection, "Look at Pork alone. There's a subject! If you want a subject, look at Pork!"

"True, sir. Many a moral for the young," returned Mr. Wopsle; and I knew he was going to lug me in, before he said it, "might be deduced from that text."

("You listen to this," said my sister to me, in a severe parenthesis.)

Joe gave me some more gravy.

"Swine," pursued Mr. Wopsle, in his deepest voice, and pointing his fork at my blushes, as if he were mentioning my christian name, "Swine were the companions of the prodigal. The gluttony of Swine is put before us, as an example to the young." (I thought this pretty well in him who had been praising up the pork for being so plump and juicy.) "What is detestable in a pig, is more detestable in a boy."

"Or girl," suggested Mr. Hubble.

"Of course, or girl, Mr. Hubble," assented Mr. Wopsle, rather irritably, "but there is no girl present."

"Besides," said Mr. Pumblechook, turning sharp on me, "think what you've got to be grateful for. If you'd been born a Squeaker—"

"He *was*, if ever a child was," said my sister, most emphatically.

Joe gave me some more gravy.

"Well, but I mean a four-footed Squeaker," said Mr. Pumblechook. "If you had been born such, would you have been here now? Not you—"

"Unless in that form," said Mr. Wopsle, nodding towards the dish.

The scene suggests a mad proliferation of textuality, where literal and figural switches places, where any referent can serve as an interpretant, become the sign of another message, in a wild process of semiosis which seems to be anchored only insofar as all texts eventually speak of Pip himself as an unjustified presence, a presence demanding interpretation.

The novel constantly warns us that texts may have no unambiguous referent and no transcendent signified. Of the many examples one might choose in illustration of the status of texts and their interpretation in the novel, perhaps the most telling is the case of Mr. Wopsle. Mr. Wopsle, the church clerk, is a frustrated preacher, ever intimating that if the church were to be "thrown open," he would really "give it out." This hypothetical case never coming to realization, Mr. Wopsle is obliged to content himself with the declamation of a number of secular texts, from Shakespeare to Collins's ode. The church indeed remains resolutely closed (we never in fact hear the word of the preacher in the novel, only Mr. Wopsle's critique of it), and Mr. Wopsle "has a fall": into play-acting. He undertakes the repetition of fictional texts which lack the authority of that divine word he would like to "give out." We next see him playing *Hamlet*, which is of course the text par excellence about usurpation, parricide, lost regal authority, and wrong relations of transmission from generation to generation. Something of the problematic status of textual authority is suggested in Mr. Wopsle's rendition of the classic soliloquy:

> Whenever that undecided Prince had to ask a question or state a doubt, the public helped him out with it. As for example: on the question of whether 'twas nobler in the mind to suffer, some roared yes, and some no, and some inclining to both opinions said "toss up for it"; and quite a Debating Society arose.

From this uncertainty, Mr. Wopsle has a further fall, into playing what was known as "nautical melodrama," an anonymously authored theater played to a vulgar public in the Surreyside houses. When Pip attends this performance, there occurs a curious mirroring and reversal of the spectacle, where Mr. Wopsle himself becomes the spectator, fascinated by the vision, in the audience, of what he calls a "ghost" from the past—the face of the novel's hidden arch-plotter, Compeyson. The vision leads to a reconstruction of the chase and capture of the convicts, from the early chapters of the novel, a kind of analytic dialogue in the excavation of the past, where Mr. Wopsle repeatedly questions: "You remember?" and Pip replies: "I remember it very well . . . I see it all before me." This reconstruction produces an intense visual, hallucinatory reliving of a charged past moment:

> "And you remember that we came up with the two in a ditch, and that there was a scuffle between them, and that one of them had been severely handled and much mauled about the face, by the other?"
>
> "I see it all before me."
>
> "And that the soldiers lighted torches, and put the two in the centre, and that we went on to see the last of them, over the black marshes, with the torchlight shining on their faces—I am

particular about that; with the torchlight shining on their faces,
when there was an outer ring of dark night all about us?"

By an apparently gratuitous free association, from Mr. Wopsle's play-acting, as from behind a screen memory, emerges a drama on that "other stage": the stage of dream, replaying a past moment that the characters have never exorcised, that moment of the buried yet living past which insists on repeating itself in the present.

Mr. Wopsle's career as a whole may exemplify a general movement in the novel toward recognition of the lack of authorship and authority in texts: textures of codes without ultimate referent or hierarchy, signs cut loose from their apparent motivation, capable of wandering toward multiple associations and of evoking messages that are entirely other, and that all speak eventually of determinative histories from the past. The original nostalgia for a founding divine word leads to a generalized scene of writing, as if the plotting self could never discover a decisive plot, but merely its own arbitrary role as plotmaker. Yet the arbitrary is itself subject to an unconscious determinant, the reproductive insistence of the past history.

Mr. Wopsle's career may stand as a figure for Pip's. Whereas the model of the *Bildungsroman* seems to imply progress, a leading forth, and developmental change, Pip's story—and this may be true of other nineteenth-century educative plots as well—becomes more and more as it nears its end the working through of past history, an attempted return to the origin as the motivation of all the rest, the clue to what must else appear, as Pip puts it to Miss Havisham, a "blind and thankless" life. The past needs to be incorporated *as past* within the present, mastered through the play of repetition in order for there to be an escape from repetition: in order for there to be difference, change, progress. In the failure ever to recover his own origin, Pip comes to concern himself with the question of Estella's origin, searching for her patronymics where knowledge of his own is ever foreclosed. Estella's story in fact eventually links all the plots of the novel: Satis House, the aspiration to gentility, the convict identity, "naterally wicious" (the status from which Jaggers rescued her), bringing up by hand, the law. Pip's investigation of her origins as substitute for knowledge of his own has a certain validity in that, we discover, he appeared originally to Magwitch as a substitute for the lost Estella, his great expectations a compensation for the impossibility of hers: a chiasmus of the true situation. Yet when Pip has proved himself to be the successful detective in this quest, when he has uncovered the convergence of lines of plot that previously appeared distinct and indeed proved himself more penetrating even than Jaggers, he discovers the knowledge he has gained to be radically unusable.

When he has imparted his knowledge to Jaggers and Wemmick, he reaches a kind of standoff between what he has called his "poor dreams" and the deep plot he has now exposed. As Jaggers puts it to him, there is no gain to be had from knowledge. We are in the heart of darkness, and the articulation of its meaning must simply be repressed. In this novel full of mysteries and hidden connections, detective work turns out to be both necessary and useless. It can offer no comfort and no true illumination to the detective himself. Like deciphering the letters on the tombstone, it produces no authority for the plot of life.

The novel in fact toward its end appears to record a generalized breakdown of plots: none of the schemes machinated by the characters manages to accomplish its aims. The proof *a contrario* may be the "oversuccessful" result of Miss Havisham's plot, which has turned Estella into so heartless a creature that she cannot even experience emotional recognition of her benefactress. Miss Havisham's plotting has been a mechanical success but an intentional failure, as her final words, during her delirium following the fire, may suggest:

> Towards midnight she began to wander in her speech, and after that it gradually set in that she said innumerable times in a low solemn voice, "What have I done?" And then, "When she first came, I meant to save her from misery like mine." And then, "Take the pencil and write under my name, 'I forgive her'!" She never changed the order of these three sentences, but she sometimes left out a word in one or other of them; never putting in another word, but always leaving a blank and going on to the next word.

The cycle of three statements suggests a metonymic movement in search of arrest, a plot that can never find satisfactory resolution, that unresolved must play over its insistent repetitions, until silenced by death. Miss Havisham's deathbed scene transmits a "wisdom" that is in the deconstructive mode, a warning against plot.

We confront the paradox that in this most highly plotted of novels, where Dickens performs all his thematic demonstrations through the manipulation of plot, we witness an evident subversion and futilization of the very concept of plot. If the chosen plots turn out to be erroneous, unauthorized, self-delusive, the deep plots when brought to light turn out to be criminally tainted, deviant, and thus unusable. Plot as direction and intention in existence appears ultimately to be as evanescent as Magwitch's money, the product of immense labor, deprivation, and planning, which is in the end forfeit to the Crown. Like money in its role as universal modern (capitalist) signifier as described by Roland Barthes in *S/Z*, tied to no referent (such as land), defined only by its exchange value, capable of unlimited metonymic circulation, the expectations of fortune, as both plot and its aim or intention, as vehicle and object of representation, circulate through inflation to devaluation.

The ultimate situation of plot in the novel may suggest an approach to the vexed question of Dickens's two endings to the novel: the one he originally wrote and the revision (substituted at Bulwer Lytton's suggestion) that was in fact printed. I think it is entirely legitimate to prefer the original ending, with its flat tone and refusal of romantic expectation, and find that the revision, with its tentative promise of reunion between Pip and Estella, "unbinds" energies that we thought had been thoroughly bound and indeed discharged from the text. We may also feel that choice between the two endings is somewhat arbitrary and unimportant in that the decisive moment has already occurred before either of these finales begins. The real ending may take place with Pip's recognition and acceptance of Magwitch after his recapture—this is certainly the ethical dénouement—and his acceptance of a continuing existence without plot, as celibate clerk for Clarrikers. The pages that follow may simply be *obiter dicta*.

If we acknowledge Pip's experience of and with Magwitch to be the central energy of the text, it is significant that the climax of this experience, the moment of crisis and reversal in the attempted escape from England, bears traces of a hallucinatory repetition of the childhood spell—indeed, of that first recapture of Magwitch already repeated in Mr. Wopsle's theatrical vision:

> In the same moment, I saw the steersman of the galley lay his hand on the prisoner's shoulder, and saw that both boats were swinging round with the force of the tide, and saw that all hands on board the steamer were running forward quite frantically. Still in the same moment, I saw the prisoner start up, lean across his captor, and pull the cloak from the neck of the shrinking sitter in the galley. Still in the same moment, I saw that the face disclosed was the face of the other convict of long ago. Still in the same moment, I saw the face tilt backward with a white terror on it that I shall never forget, and heard a great cry on board the steamer and a loud splash in the water, and felt the boat sink from under me.

If this scene marks the beginning of a resolution—which it does in that it brings the death of the arch-villain Compeyson and the death sentence for

Magwitch, hence the disappearance from the novel of its most energetic plotters—it is resolution in the register of repetition and working through, the final effort to master painful material from the insistent past. Pip emerges from this scene with an acceptance of the determinative past as both determinative and as past, which prepares us for the final escape *from* plot. It is interesting to note that where the "dream" plot of Estella is concerned, Pip's stated resolution has none of the compulsive energetic force of the passage just quoted, but is rather a conventional romantic fairy-tale ending, a conscious fiction designed, of course, to console the dying Magwitch, but possibly also a last effort at self-delusion: "You had a child once, whom you loved and lost. . . . She lived and found powerful friends. She is living now. She is a lady and very beautiful. And I love her!" If taken as anything other than a conscious fiction—if taken as part of the "truth" discovered by Pip's detections—this version of Pip's experience leads straight to what is most troubling in Dickens's revised version of the ending: the suggestion of an unbinding of what has already been bound up and disposed of, an unbinding that is indeed perceptible in the rather embarrassed prose with which the revision begins: "Nevertheless, I knew while I said these words, that I secretly intended to revisit the site of the old house that evening alone, for her sake. Yes, even so. For Estella's sake." Are we to understand that the experience of Satis House has never really been mastered? Is its nightmare energy still present in the text as well? The original end may have an advantage in denying to Pip's text the possibility of any reflux of energy, any new aspirations, the undoing of anything already done, the unbinding of energy that has been bound and led to discharge.

As at the start of the novel we had the impression of a life not yet subject to plot—a life in search of the sense of plot that would only gradually begin to precipitate around it—so at the end we have the impression of a life that has outlived plot, renounced plot, been cured of it: life that is left over. What follows the recognition of Magwitch is left over, and any renewal of expectation and plotting—such as a revived romance with Estella—would have to belong to another story. It is with the image of a life bereft of plot, of movement and desire, that the novel most appropriately leaves us. Indeed, we have at the end what could appropriately be called a "cure" from plot, in Pip's recognition of the general forfeiture of plotting, his renunciation of any attempt to direct his life. Plot comes to resemble a diseased, fevered state of the organism caught in the machinery of a desire which must eventually be renounced. Plot, we come to understand, was a state of abnormality or deviance, suggested thematically by its uneasy position between Newgate and Old Bailey, between criminality and the law. The nineteenth-century novel in general—and especially that highly symptomatic development, the detective story—regularly conceives plot as a condition of deviance and abnormality, the product of cities and social depths, of a world where *récit* is *complot*, where all stories are the result of plotting, and plotting is very much machination. Deviance is the very condition for life to be "narratable": the state of normality is devoid of interest, energy, and the possibility for narration. In between a beginning prior to plot and an end beyond plot, the middle—the plotted text—has been in a state of *error*: wandering and misinterpretation.

IV

That plot should prove to be deviance and error is fully consonant with Freud's model in *Beyond the Pleasure Principle*, where the narratable life of the organism is seen as detour, a deviance from the quiescence of the inorganic which has been maintained through the dynamic interaction of Eros and the death of instinct. What Pip at one point has called his "ill-regulated aspirations" is the figure of plot as desire: Eros as the force that binds integers together in ever-larger wholes, totalizing, metaphoric, the desire for possession of the world and for the integration of meaning—whereas, concomitantly, repetition and return have spoken of the death instinct, the drive to return to the quiescence of the inorganic, of the nontextual. Yet the repetitions, which have served to bind the various plots, both prolonging the detour and more effectively preparing the final discharge, have created that delay necessary to incorporate the past within the present and to let us understand end in relation to beginning. Through the erotics of the text, we have inexorably been led to its end, which is precisely quiescence: a time after which is an image of the time before. We have reached the non-narratable. Adducing the argument of "Remembering, Repeating, and Working Through" to that of *Beyond the Pleasure Principle*, we perceive that repetition is a kind of remembering, and thus a way of reorganizing a story whose connective links have been obscured and lost. If repetition speaks of the death instinct, the finding of the right end, then what is being played out in repetition is necessarily the proper vector of the drive toward the end. That is, once you have determined the right plot, plot is over. Plot itself is working-through.

   Great Expectations is exemplary in demonstrating both the need for plot and its status as deviance, both the need for narration and the necessity to be cured from it. The deviance and error of plot may necessarily result from the interplay of desire in its history with the narrative insistence on explanatory form: the desire to wrest beginnings and ends from the uninterrupted flow of middles, from temporality itself; the search for that significant closure that would illuminate the sense of an existence, the meaning of life. The desire for meaning is ultimately the reader's who must mime Pip's acts of reading but do them better. Both using and subverting the systems of meaning discovered or postulated by its hero, *Great Expectations* exposes for its reader the very reading process itself: the way the reader goes about finding meaning in the narrative text, and the limits of that meaning as the limits of narrative.

In terms of the problematic of reading which the novel thematizes from its opening page, we could say that Pip, continuously returning toward origins in order to know the plot whose authority would lead him to the right end but never recovering origins and never finding the authoritative plot, never succeeds in going behind his self-naming to a reading of the missing patronymic. He is ever returned to a rereading of the unauthorized text of his self-given name, Pip. "Pip" sounded like a beginning, a seed. But, of course, when you reach the end of the name "Pip," you can return backward, and it is just the same: a repetitive text without variation or point of fixity, a return that leads to an unarrested shuttling back and forth. The name is in fact a palindrome. In the rereading of the palindrome the novel may offer its final comment on its expectative plot.

What, finally, do we make of the fact that Dickens, master-plotter in the history of the novel, in this most tightly and consistently plotted of his novels seems to expose plot as a kind of necessary error? Dickens's most telling comment on the question may come at the moment of Magwitch's sentencing. The judge gives a legalistic and moralistic version of Magwitch's life story, his violence, his crimes, the passions that made him a "scourge to society" and led him to escape from deportation, thus calling upon his head the death sentence. The passage continues:

> The sun was striking in at the great windows of the court, through the glittering drops of rain upon the glass, and it made a broad shaft of light between the two-and-thirty [prisoners at the bar] and the Judge, linking both together, and perhaps reminding some among the audience, how both were passing on, with absolute equality, to the greater Judgment that knoweth all things and cannot err. Rising for a moment, a distinct speck of face in this way of light, the prisoner [Magwitch] said, "My Lord, I have received my sentence of Death from the Almighty, but I bow to yours," and sat down again. There was some hushing, and the Judge went on with what he had to say to the rest.

The passage is sentimental but also, I think, effective. It juxtaposes human plots—including those of the law—to eternal orders that render human attempts to plot, and to interpret plot, not only futile but ethically unacceptable. The greater Judgment makes human plots mere shadows. There is another end that recuperates passing human time, and its petty chronologies, to the timeless. Yet despite the narrator's affirmations, this other end is not visible, the other orders are not available. As Mr. Wopsle's case suggested, the divine word is barred in the world of the novel (it is suggestive that Christmas dinner is interrupted by the command to repair handcuffs). If there is a divine masterplot for human existence, it is radically unknowable.

In the absence or silence of divine masterplots, the organization and interpretation of human plots remains as necessary as it is problematic. Reading the signs of intention in life's actions is the central act of existence, which in turn legitimizes the enterprise of reading for the reader of *Great Expectations*—or perhaps, vice versa, since the reading of plot within the text and as the text are perfectly analogous, mirrors of one another. If there is by the end of the narrative an abandonment of the attempt to read plot, this simply mirrors the fact that the process of narration has come to a close—or, again, vice versa. But that there should be a cure from the reading of plot within the text—before its very end—and the creation of a leftover, suggests a critique of reading itself, which is possibly like the judge's sentence: human interpretation in ignorance of the true vectors of the true text. So it may indeed be: the *savoir* proposed by Balzac's antique dealer is not *in* the text. But if the mastertext is not available, we are condemned to the reading of erroneous plots, granted insight only insofar as we can gain disillusion from them. We are condemned to repetition, rereading, in the knowledge that what we discover will always be that there was nothing to be discovered. Yet the process remains necessary if we are not to be caught perpetually in the "blind and thankless" existence, in the illusory middle. Like Oedipus, like Pip, we are condemned to reinterpretation of our names. But it is rare that the name coincide so perfectly with a fullness and a negation of identity as in the case of Oedipus. In a post-tragic universe, our situation is more likely to be that of Pip, compelled to reinterpret the meaning of the name he assigned to himself with his infant tongue, the history of an infinitely repeatable palindrome.

CAROLYN BROWN

Great Expectations:
Masculinity and Modernity

Just as masculinity seems to dominate the world, so too does modernity seem the only mode of existing. As an atmosphere, a whole culture, it makes it difficult to become even dimly aware of the conceptual boundaries which construct and circumscribe our languages, our thoughts. Both, it seems, engage in the masquerade of universality, posing as the only mode of orientation to the world.

And yet what are these words? To what do they refer? How closely are they entwined? Are they, within our history, so intimately enmeshed as to constitute the same phenomenon? Can we indeed undo these universalities to reveal them as partial, as historical and discursive constructs, without setting up new universalities?

In this essay I will attempt to look at masculinity and modernity as motifs in Charles Dickens's *Great Expectations*. While my discussion will rely upon these as specific strands in the problem of 'identity,' I would like also to locate them as general phenomena. The perspective of 'post-modernism' offers a position, however fictional, which refuses the nostalgia usually present in critiques of 'modernity' and in refusing this nostalgia permits a critique of 'masculinity'.

Jürgen Habermas has brought to English readers' attention the work of Hans Robert Jauss on the term 'modern' which dates the word from its Latin form 'modernus' in the late fifth century. Thereafter,

From *Essays and Studies 1987*. © 1987 The English Association.

> . . . the term 'modern' appeared and reappeared exactly during
> those periods in Europe when the consciousness of a new
> epoch formed itself through a renewed relationship to the
> ancients—whenever, moreover, antiquity was considered to be
> a model to be recovered through some kind of imitation.

Habermas argues that a significant shift took place in the early nineteenth
century, which opposed an idealized Middle Ages to the antique ideals of the
classicists. During the course of the nineteenth century, this became an
aesthetic modernity 'that radicalized consciousness of modernity and freed it
from all specific historical ties'.

Craig Owens in an interesting essay has considered the construction of
discourse in dominance to the masculine, arguing that

> It is precisely at the legislative frontier between what can be
> represented and what cannot that the postmodernist operation
> is being staged—not in order to transcend representation, but
> in order to expose that system of power that authorizes certain
> representations while blocking, prohibiting or invalidating
> others. Among those prohibited from Western representation,
> whose representations are denied all legitimacy, are women.
> Excluded from representation by its very structure, they
> return within it as a figure for—a representation of—the
> unrepresentable (Nature, Truth, the Sublime, etc.). This
> prohibition bears primarily on women as the subject, and rarely
> as the object of representation, for there is certainly no
> shortage of images *of* women.

Together, these versions indicate a model of 'modernity' which is decentered,
yet constructed in dominance to, overdetermined by, the masculine.
'Modernity' and 'masculinity' are fragmented, historically structured and
historically dominant.

In this essay, I am interested in these aspects of our history as
constructing identities, and enabling those identities to be written, in
constructing a 'speaking subject'. *Great Expectations* is an account of
development of identity in a 'modern' world, but also (to me) an
extraordinarily masculine world. In this text, women are present only to be
incorporated into men, to be destroyed, or as narcissistic reflections. Insofar
as Pip's development of identity can proceed beyond an enclosed narcissism,
it operates primarily within a masculine homosocial world, within the
dynamics of power of that world, and within relations of love which occur

within those relations of power. This construction is geo-historically specific, and an essential component is the reviewing of traditional narratives at a time of change and transformation.

I will elaborate further on this complex formulation in the course of this essay, but I wish first to consider the specifics of English 'modernity' through two recent American texts. Marshall Berman's *All That Is Solid Melts into Air* takes its title from 'The Manifesto of the Communist Party', where Marx wrote of the 'constant revolutionizing of production, uninterrupted disturbance of all social conditions, everlasting uncertainty and agitation'. This is perceived by Berman as the essence of the modern, and his celebration of modernity through selected modernist texts excludes Dickens, and, excepting the Crystal Palace, Britain. Berman's perspective operates as it were negatively upon the subject of this essay. Martin J. Wiener opens his book *English Culture and the Decline of The Industrial Spirit* by observing that 'the leading problem of modern British history is the explanation of economic decline'. The Crystal Palace, which Berman celebrates as 'the most visionary and adventurous building of the whole nineteenth century . . . [a] lyrical expression of the potentialities of an industrial age' appears now as the beginning of the end of English modernity, of English modernism, of English hegemony. Wiener points out that 'planted within the Great Exhibition itself was a core of cultural opposition, represented by Augustus Pugin's Medieval Court'. English bourgeois culture turned to the construction of a faked and forged history.

Wiener argues that Dickens (whose writings have served as the basis of much of our theme-park history) apparently opposed the nostalgia for 'those infernally and damnably good old times', yet in later years moved 'towards an affirmation of a gentlemanly ideal . . . purged of its associations with class and social ambition'. Clearly, the 'gentleman ideal' is by no means dissociated from class and social ambition. Rather, in *Great Expectations* it points to a crucial moment of development of 'Englishness', as an identity based upon the 'gentlemanly ideal' formed within the intersection of historically located masculinities and modernities.

This identity was not 'imposed' in any simple way but was actively sought after as a mode of negotiating cultural transformations. Patrick Wright has recently drawn attention to Agnes Heller's formulation of the problem of identity in modernity. He cites from *A Theory of Feelings* Heller's observation that

> Bourgeois society is the first 'pure' society; natural or blood kinship no longer determines the path of the individual. At the same time it is a dynamic society, and increasingly so; the tasks

to be dealt with change continually from the point of view of every stratum and class, often even within the space of a generation. With the disintegration of community ties the individual becomes an 'accidental' individual [his class—or stratum]—is of accidental character but, at the same time he becomes a free individual as well, at least potentially.

Using *Great Expectations* as a 'memory which flashes up at a moment of danger', I would argue that the 'gentlemanly ideal', dislodged from a feudal location with the changes of English society, was not merely made available as a model for the rising bourgeoisie, but rather, disseminated through the proliferating products of the press, moved into the most unlikely places, operating within the reformation of English capitalism as it demanded competent clerical-managerial labour in its imperialist operations. Moreover, propagated through the English educational system it continues as an 'ideal', as a basis from which to write, to speak, to be heard.

The world of *Great Expectations* is in a process of rapid social and textual transformation. Edward Said has used the Hamlet scene in *Great Expectations* to demonstrate Derrida's points concerning the myth of presence in Western culture. I have not the space here to rehearse fully Said's excellent analysis of this scene, but what concerns us is the point that

> if we say that *Hamlet* as Shakespeare wrote it is at the centre or origin of the whole episode, then what Dickens gives us is a comically literal account of the centre not only unable to hold, but *being* unable to hold, producing instead a number of new, devastatingly eccentric multiples of the play.

Said demonstrates that the philosophic ideas of Jacques Derrida concerning 'voice, presence, and metaphysical "origins"' are assumed in a most unphilosophic way by Dickens; and if we consider the wonderful *bricolage* which is Shakespeare's *Hamlet* we have evidence that the posing of open, multi-referential texts against bourgeois notions of unified, realist, texts, or subjects, enables us to abandon a morality of the text, the subject, to consider its textuality, its historicity.

Apparently paradoxically, the world in which writing acquires such a reality, in which identity becomes so problematic, is a world of increasing organization, increasing regulation. From the beginning to the end of the novel, it is made clear what 'identity' means to Magwitch, who is a victim of the growing state apparatus of control and surveillance.

While the efforts of the State to locate and identify its individuals is but one aspect of the question of identity, of subjectivity, which is present in *Great Expectations* it is nonetheless vitally important. For it seems that in this Dickensian world, there is very little certainty of identity as an essential attribute, somehow tagged by a legal label. Rather identity is entangled within the operations of the legal system, within the operations of writing, from its outset. If we turn to Pip's relationship with Magwitch the matter will become clearer.

> 'I do not even know' said I, speaking low as he took his seat at the table, 'by what name to call you. I have given out that you are my uncle.'
>
> 'That's it, dear boy! Call me uncle.'
>
> 'You assumed some name, I suppose, on board ship?'
>
> 'Yes, dear boy. I took the name of Provis.'
>
> 'Do you mean to keep that name?'
>
> 'Why, yes, dear boy, it's as good as another—unless you'd like another.'
>
> 'What is your real name?' I asked him in a whisper.
>
> 'Magwitch,' he answered in the same tone: 'chrisen'd Abel.'
>
> 'What were you brought up to be?'
>
> 'A warmint, dear boy.'
>
> He answered quite seriously, and used the words as if it denoted some profession.

For Magwitch, recognition in London, identification as the same (*idem*), convicted, person, can only bring death on the gibbet. His refuge is in a *provis*-ional name, by which he can function in society (and to which he is indifferent) without incurring the penalty of the Law, Death, which will stop the fluctutation of identity. Yet, in fixing the identity finally, Death also brings annihilation.

The organization and regulation of society depends upon making people accountable for their actions, by insisting upon a continuation of identity, a retention of a name, a label, in order to locate potentially mobile and fluid existences. During the eighteenth century, and increasingly in the nineteenth century, an immense apparatus is constructed to fix, locate, and stabilize the young and mobile population brought forth by the social and economic changes. Births, deaths, and marriages must be registered. It becomes essential to belong to a certain geo-political unit, a nation-state.

Existences become regulated, according to a system which becomes increasingly homogenized, in order to control an increasingly heteogeneous social body.

The world of *Great Expectations* is a transitional world. Pip moves between the small local scale of organization in the village in Kent, and the vast global system which radiates from London. Yet perhaps to put it like this is to overstate the opposition. For the world of *Great Expectations*, in the village almost as much as the city, is not only extraordinarily violent, but abounds in orphans, in non-existent or inadequate parenting. Pip has been raised by his sister, Mrs Joe, whose husband is no candidate for the role of surrogate patriarch. Yet Pip's environment is stable compared to the account which Jaggers (the intermediary between the regulatory apparatus and those it desires to regulate) gives of the state of children in the early nineteenth century. It is an account of anarchy. "'. . . all he saw of children, was, their being generated in great numbers for certain destruction . . . being imprisoned, whipped, transported, neglected, cast out, . . . and growing up to be hanged.'"

Great Expectations is told by the adult. It is a *bildungsroman* which seems to lead nowhere, but to enable this narrative to be recounted, this identity to be fixed and located. For, as the developing nineteenth-century state organizes identity, 'identity' comes to be problematic to the individual subject. The mobility of existences places considerable stress upon subjectivity: in a dis-continuous existence, continuities become necessary. Narcissism (for what form can be more narcissistic than the autobiography?) becomes a necessary device for survival. It becomes essential to write a 'self', to construct an order from the chaos, to locate oneself in some way within the ordering of power.

Great Expectations opens with the presentation of Pip in the graveyard, viewing his family. He names himself first. He is 'Pip'; he has acquired this name through his inability to speak his father's name which he has been given. He shares his father's name, even as he differentiates himself from it. This self-naming, this differentiation, has been accepted by those who surround him. Pip's father's name is presented in relation to Pip, not as quoted from the tombstone, unlike his mother's name. 'Also Georgiana, his wife' is more central within that first paragraph as a name, than the father's, perhaps as a part of Pip's infancy. 'Also Georgiana' is nonetheless defined in relation to her husband, as a supplement to the (assumed but absent) centrality of the father's name at the head of the tombstone.

The moment at which Pip's identity is established, his consciousness assumed, is the moment preceding Magwitch's appearance. This trauma is that which constructs identity, making possible the reviewing of the acquisition of consciousness. The events before the trauma acquire their significance in the light, or the shadow, of the trauma. Pip's account constructs the events thus:

> My first most vivid and broad impression of the identity of things, seems to me to have been gained on a memorable raw afternoon towards evening. At such a time I found out for certain, that this bleak place overgrown with nettles was the churchyard; and that Phillip Pirrip, late of this parish, and also Georgiana wife of the above, were dead and buried; . . . and that the low leaden line beyond, was the river; and that the distant savage lair from which the wind was rushing, was the sea; and that the small bundle of shivers growing afraid of it all and beginning to cry, was Pip.

The nature of the 'father' who ushers Pip into the Lacanian Symbolic, is that of a *carnivalesque* Patriarch. Using threats of penetration, mutilation, and absorption ('. . . I'll cut your throat!' 'What fat cheeks you ha' got.' 'Darn me if I couldn't eat them. '. . . I'll have your heart and liver out') Magwitch directs Pip against his home, confounding that order. Like the wolf in *Little Red Riding Hood*, like the witches greeting Macbeth, *Mag-witch* is the harbinger of disruption. Threatening the body of the barely established consciousness of the 'small bundle of shivers', he upturns Pip not only physically, but conceptually. Transgressing the small world by bursting in from outside, Magwitch, as anarchy, brings consciousness to Pip, not only as self, but of all things as a source of fear.

This account of the assumption of consciousness, bears all the marks of the 'agonising transition', but the archetype of the Oedipal family, with a maternal Imaginary, is present in *Great Expectations*, as an 'original' known only by a parodic echoing. 'Also Georgiana' occupies the role of mother, but is known only through the writing on her tombstone, which thus confirms her absence. Pip's acquisition of consciousness is a messy, untidy, process, in which writing, divorced from any authentic source, plays an essential part. It is between the 'real' world and the 'textual' world of writing and reading that Pip is formed. It is between reading the inscriptions on the tombstones and the assault by Magwitch that Pip comes to consider his 'self'.

At the end of the first chapter, Pip constructs the world around him in terms of horizontal lines, with two vertical lines, intersecting. One is a guide for voyagers, the other a sign of the law:

> The marshes were just a long black horizontal line then, as I stopped to look after him; and the river was just another

horizontal line, not nearly so broad nor yet so black, and the
sky was just a row of long angry red lines and dense black lines
intermixed. On the edge of the river I could faintly make out
the only two black things in all the prospect that seemed to be
standing upright; one of these was the beacon by which the
sailors steered—like an unhooped cask upon a pole—an ugly
thing when you were near it; the other a gibbet, with some
chain hanging to it which had once held a pirate.

This typographical world in which Pip exists, exhibits signs of other worlds,
other existences, but also of danger, of death. These signal the inhospitable,
hostile world in which an 'identity', some stable ensemble must be inscribed.

Following the narration of his encounter with Magwitch and the Law,
Pip relates his experiences in the acquisition of literacy at the evening school
kept by Mr Wopsle's great-aunt, assisted by her granddaughter, Biddy. Just
as the landscape has appeared as a threatening series of lines, so do letters and
numbers appear as physical entities.

Much by my unassisted self, and more by the help of Biddy
than of Mr Wopsle's great-aunt, I struggled through the
alphabet as if it had been a bramble-bush; getting considerably
worried and scratched by every letter. After that, I fell among
those thieves, the nine figures, who seemed every evening to do
something new to disguise themselves and baffle recognition.
But, at last I began, in a purblind groping way to read, write
and cipher, on the very smallest scale.

The devices of representation have a physical presence and importance, and
their promiscuous intermingling 'organizes' Pip's perception of himself and
the world. It is an organization of scraps of inaccurate fragments. Of his
reading of the family tombstones Pip recalls that 'my construction even of
their simple meaning was not very correct' and that his understanding of the
Catechism as a declaration to '"walk in the same all the days of my life," laid
me under an obligation always to go through the village from our house in
one particular direction.' This is not a simple account of a childish
incomprehension, for it is made clear that similar states of ignorance exist in
the entire village, all of whom, it seems, share the 'Educational scheme' of
Mr Wopsle's great-aunt. Narrative, as a coherent linear form, does not
organize this world: rather there is a jumble of garbled odds and ends, an
ensemble of the flotsam and jetsam of discourse. It is not only that the realm
of writing manifests itself in fragments, it is also that the reading, the

meaning that these acquire, are various and unpredictable. Nevertheless they are ordered in some way, and desires are ushered into existence, and take effect on the real world. Pip writes his first letter to Joe, a year after his encounter with Magwitch. It is a wonderfully graphic piece of writing setting out his desires to teach Joe, to be apprenticed to him, to be close to him. Through the distance provided by writing, Pip 'speaks' his desires, although 'there was no indispensable necessity for my communicating with Joe by letter, inasmuch as he sat beside me and we were alone'.

Writing connects Pip to his parents, separates him from his sister, and permits the declaration of love for Joe. It acquires a reality in the child's life, and directs him to a desire of being the Prince to the Sleeping Beauty hidden behind those thickets of discourse. Thus, in this reading, Pip's first and indeed crucial action is the acquisition of literacy, which pre-dates his encounter with Magwitch, with Satis House, yet is fixed and reinforced by those encounters.

I have noted the absence of a maternal figure for Pip. The discovery of the masculine world is an essential aspect of the narrative. It is Magwitch, not Miss Havisham who is the fairy godmother to this Cinderella; and, as with the Miss Havisham–Estella relationship, it is quite clear what this relationship is based upon. Pip's filial position is purchased by the convict's money, and Pip is living out the convict's carefully nurtured fantasies of revenge:

> 'And then, dear boy, it was a recompense to me, look'ee here, to know in secret that I was making a gentleman. The blood horses of them colonists might fling up the dust over me as I was walking; what do I say? I says to myself, "I'm making a better gentleman nor *you*'ll ever be!" When one of . . . I says to myself, "If I ain't a gentleman, nor yet ain't got no learning, I'm the owner of such . . . a bought-up London gentleman?"'

Perhaps it is a mark of how endemic are the expectations that one can buy vicarious satisfaction through another, that Pip's abhorrence, dread, and repugnance of the source of his great expectations have been termed 'snobbish'. For not only is it made clear that it is a network of criminality and capitalism in which he exists (rather than Miss Havisham's tastefully unstated *rentier* income), but that he is the product of these forces, that his desires for gentility have been shared by Magwitch. He is the product of Magwitch's desires, and is possessed by him.

Magwitch's displaced desires for gentility make it clear that Pip's wishes are not an isolated and eccentric desire, but a widespread social phenomenon: Magwitch's reasons are made clear, and his demonstration that it is money which buys the 'character' of a gentleman is borne out. Ironically, Pip's 'gentlemanly' refusal of Magwitch's money is backed up by the State which sequesters Magwitch's money as it kills him.

Pip's collapse following Magwitch's death results in a breakdown of identity:

> That I had a fever and was avoided, that I suffered greatly, that I often lost my reason, that the time seemed interminable, that I confounded impossible existences with my own identity; that I was a brick in the house wall, and yet entreating to be released from the giddy place where the builders had set me; that I was a steel beam of a vast engine, clashing and whirling over a gulf, and yet that I implored in my own person to have the engine stopped, and my part in it hammered off; that I passed through these phases of disease, I know of my own remembrance, and did in some sort know it at the time. That I sometimes struggled with real people, in the belief that they were murderers, and that I would all at once comprehend that they meant to do me good, and would then sink exhausted into their arms, and suffer them to lay me down, I also knew at the time. But, above all, I knew that there was a constant tendency in all these people—who when I was very ill, would present all kinds of extraordinary transformations of the human face, and would be much dilated in size—above all, I say, I knew that there was an extraordinary tendency in all these people to settle down in the likeness of Joe.

Pip is rescued from the nightmare of anonymity and confusion by Joe, who rescues him from absorbtion in a terrifying industrial psychic world, where 'real people' are assumed to be murderers. Joe becomes, in the words of Dickens's draft, a ministering angel; the vision of Joe is a loving reconciliation to the world, a rebirth with Magwitch eliminated. It is a touching relationship. Joe functions in the novel as the embodiment of 'home', 'sanctifying' what is otherwise a bleak, inhospitable, unpleasant and violent community. Joe provides the point at which the loss of the ties of childhood, of community, is rendered mythical. Joe sanctifies masculinity.

I have noted that Pip's casting of himself in the role of Miss Havisham's Cinderella turned Prince to Estella's Sleeping Beauty is a mistaken narrative, one which attributes a power of transformation to women when they in the 'real' story have none. Moreover, Miss Havisham bears an uncanny resemblance to Also Georgiana:

> Once I had been taken to see some ghastly waxwork at the Fair, . . . Once, I had been taken to one of our old marsh churches to see a skeleton in the ashes of a rich dress, . . . Now, waxwork and skeleton seemed to have dark eyes that looked out for me.

> . . . I began to understand that everything in the room had stopped . . . a long time ago . . . Without this arrest of everything, this standing still of pale decayed objects, not even the withered bridal dress on the collapsed form could have looked so like grave-clothes, or the long veil so like a shroud. So she sat, corpse-like, as we played at cards.

This corpse-like maternal phantom lingers throughout the novel, even after a partial and *pre-mortem* cremation. Miss Havisham is not the only woman in the novel to suffer death-in-life. The vigorous Mrs Joe is struck down by Orlick with Magwitch's leg-iron; Estella's once murderous mother, whom Pip first sees after going to *Macbeth*, is kept well under control by Jaggers. Through the apparently naive and gentlemanly Pip, *Great Expectations* creates a world in which only the biddable Biddy, and the sweet betrotheds of Wemmick and Herbert can survive.

The sexual politics of Estella's upbringing are explained to Pip by Herbert. She is "'hard and haughty and capricious to the last degree, and has been brought up by Miss Havisham to wreak revenge on all the male sex.'" Estella's role as guerrilla in the gender war meets with failure; she is made to marry the brutal Bentley Drummle, 'who . . . used her with great cruelty'. Estella resembles those narcissistic women described by Freud as being particularly attractive to men. The normal male, according to Freud (*On Narcissism*) displays 'complete object-love of the attachment type', which 'displays the marked sexual overvaluation which . . . corresponds to a transference of (the original) narcissism to the sexual object.' The object choice is the narcissistic woman who takes herself as object. Freud elaborates:

> The importance of this type of woman for the erotic life of mankind is to be rated very high . . . The great charm of narcissistic women has, however, its reverse side; a large part of the lover's dissatisfaction, of his doubts of the woman's love, of his complaints of her enigmatic nature, has its root in this incongruity between the types of object choice.

This description traces the terrain of Pip's experiences, of his desires. Constructed as a reflection of 'normal' masculine narcissism, Estella is denied any autonomy. Pip's extraordinary declarations, disperse and incorporate her at the same time.

> ' . . . You are part of my existence, part of myself. You have been in every line I have ever read, since I first came here, the rough common boy whose poor heart you wounded even then. You have been in every prospect I have ever seen—on the river, on the sails of the ships, on the marshes, in the clouds, in the sea, in the streets. You have been the embodiment of every graceful fancy that my mind has ever been acquainted with . . . Estella, to the last hour of my life, you cannot choose but remain part of my character, part of the little good in me, part of the evil.'

Arguably, Pip's search for Estella's true identity, as daughter of the Magwitches, as well as the adopted daughter of the phantom bride, can be seen as a displaced search for his own identity. That Magwitch is Pip's 'second father' conjures up that wisp of incest so beloved by the Gothic, and also incorporates Estella with Pip. It would seem that the desires for gentility, apparently unleashed by Satis House, are nothing more than a reflection back from the enigma of woman, which can yet be blamed upon the reflecting surface.

Great Expectations, then, presents the formation of an identity of a 'gentleman', or rather of a clerk, a businessman, who will go aboard to work 'for profits', although, we are reassured that the firm was 'not in a grand way of business, but we had a good name', This identity is located at the period of British ascendency over the globe. It is constructed in a network of the movements of the growing legal system, the movements of expanding capitalism, the movements of a proliferating writing of fragmentary narratives, dislocated from their existence in traditional and stable settings. In the interstices of these systems, it seems that 'identity' is an uncertain matter: yet it takes, for Pip and for Magwitch, the form of desiring to acquire the characteristics of the dominant class, which then come into play in quite different formations.

I have made use in this essay of *Great Expectations* in order to attempt to draw out some points which, while hardly novel, are worth repeating. *Great Expectations'* status, not only as literary 'classic' but also as a children's book, its presence in our culture, rendered this attempt, for me at any rate, particularly interesting. It is a disconcerting tale. While Pip may grow to reconcile his gentlemanly ideal to his employment in the world of commerce—and in this sense it is an expression of that rising sector of finance capital, which will become of increasing importance in the British economy—we should observe the exclusions, and prohibitions within this development. (During the nineteenth century, and continuing now, a regime of education is developed which is far more carefully controlled than Pip's, but also building upon this 'ideal' masculine world.) Wiener notes that the English public school had 'become by the end of Victoria's reign the shared formative experience of most members of the English elite'. The gentlemanly ideal was also applied to girls' schools, and it is not insignificant that Radclyffe Hall in constructing the paragon lesbian-novelist for *The Well of Loneliness* made 'Stephen' into the gentlemanly ideal, complete with fencing skills and silk shirts. Perhaps neither class nor gender was any substantial impediment in accepting the mould, which operates as an entry point into an active subjectivity: so long as either discrepancy could be repudiated in the embracing of the image of the dominant class, in order to claim a share in its privileges, which included, not least, the right to speak.

WILLIAM A. COHEN

Manual Conduct in Great Expectations

If one were writing the masturbator's guide to the English novel, certain correspondences would soon become evident. Like the novel, the discourse that constitutes masturbation (as a medical condition, a moral sin, a personal identity, a psychological stage) first arose early in the eighteenth century; like the novel, too, it achieved full cultural currency by the Victorian period and began its decline early in the present century. By the middle of the nineteenth century, both masturbatory practice and novel-reading were firmly installed in popular imagination and culture. With the cultural designation of these practices as significant, anxieties about an unregulated, excessively productive imagination arose, impelling both anti-onanist doctrine and anti-novel invective. Through famously repressive techniques, medical authorities sought to control the onanistic vice that, as we now suppose, they thereby invented; the novel, meanwhile, so perilously implicated in encouraging kindred forms of imaginative self-abuse, had to find ways of managing the erotic reveries it was accused of arousing in its readers.

Having been stigmatized for its association with fantasy, the novel eventually internalized and accommodated that charge. By the mid-nineteenth century, fictional narratives were seeking to exonerate themselves from incrimination in readers' imaginations. Even as the novel strove to redirect its

---

From *ELH* 60, no. 1 (Spring 1993). © 1993 The Johns Hopkins University Press.

readers *away* from masturbatory vice, however, this now-dominant form of imaginative literature could hardly cease its sexual provocations. The novel increasingly learned how to perform this simultaneously regulatory and arousing function while having (perhaps until Hardy) ever *less* to say about sex overtly. Through specifiable narrative techniques, the Victorian novel at once encrypted representations of sexuality and demonstrated a frantic need for managing and redeeming sexual practices.

In the masturbator's guide to the English novel, at least under the heading "men's bodies," Charles Dickens would doubtless merit a good deal of attention. Charley Bates, a character in *Oliver Twist* (1837–39), first alerts us to the valence of the term in Dickens's corpus. When, as sometimes happens, he is called "Master Bates," we are assured of not being able to lose sight of the pun; yet when, more usually, he is referred to as "Master Charles Bates," we are guaranteed to continue imagining it—like the onanist, always fantasizing about what isn't at hand in order to keep aroused what is. The volatility of Charley's name might in itself make us suspicious, for in the mouth of the narrator it constantly shifts toward and away from the little joke. When he first appears, for instance, he is described as "a very sprightly young friend . . . who was now formally introduced to [Oliver] as Charley Bates." Further down on the page, he is referred to as "Mr. Charles Bates." Finally, he delivers the gear for cleaning up whatever mess his name might imply: "'Wipes,' replied Master Bates; at the same time producing four pocket-handkerchiefs."

The peculiar attention to the young scoundrel's name is dramatically amplified by the following exchange:

> [The Dodger] looked down on Oliver, with a thoughtful countenance, for a brief space; and then, raising his head, and heaving a gentle sigh, said, half in abstraction, and half to *Master Bates*:
>
> "What a pity it is he isn't a prig!"
>
> "Ah," said *Master Charles Bates*; "he don't know what's good for him."
>
> The Dodger sighed again, and resumed his pipe: as did *Charley Bates*. They both smoked, for some seconds, in silence.
>
> "I suppose you don't even know what a prig is?" said the Dodger mournfully.
>
> "I think I know that," replied Oliver, looking up. "It's a th–; you're one, are you not?" inquired Oliver, checking himself.
>
> "I am," replied the Dodger. "I'd scorn to be anything else." Mr. Dawkins gave his hat a ferocious cock, after

delivering this sentiment, and looked at *Master Bates*, as if to
denote that he would feel obliged by his saying anything to the
contrary. (emphasis added)

Through this, one of the many scenes depicting Oliver's initiation into the
secret community of male adolescence, the term "prig" floats with as much
instability as that of "Master Bates." The gloss on "prig" that Oliver is
incapable of uttering is presumably "thief," yet the persistence with which
the term goes undenoted throws us deliberately back upon the signifier—
where, with the alacrity of any English schoolboy, we might take the usual
phonemic detour from a bilabial to a fricative and detect a "frig" (Victorian
slang for manual stimulation of the genitals). If the revelation that Master
Bates himself is a "prig" merely establishes a relation of synonymity, the
Dodger nonetheless asserts superiority over the smaller boys with his
"ferocious cock."

Dickens's linguistic attention to the male body and male eroticism
compels all his *Bildungsromane* to trace not only their heroes' social,
emotional, and intellectual development, but their sexual maturation as well.
While *Oliver Twist* confines its fantasies about boys' budding bodies to
closeted puns, *Great Expectations* (1860–61) refers those same sexual feelings
back onto the bodies of its characters. In so doing, however, the later novel
relegates sexual sensations to part of the body different from those in which
they are usually imagined to originate; *Great Expectations*, on this reading,
manages to anatomize whole species of erotic dispositions without ever
mentioning sex.

Let us look, for example, at a scene in *Great Expectations* thematically
paralleling the one I have discussed in *Oliver Twist*, in which Dickens raises
the issue of masturbation by referencing it in such a way as to announce the
impossibility of articulating it as such. The scene that probably constitutes
Dickens's most vivid account of the pleasures and anxieties of autoeroticism
occurs just when one would expect it in the maturation of the novel's
prepubescent hero. Soon after the primal scene of his encounter with
Magwitch in the graveyard, still stunned by the fear of it, and a long way
from knowing what it means, Pip lifts a slice of bread-and-butter from his
sister's table and hides it for later delivery to the convict. Pip, the Dodger
might say, thus becomes a prig. And like Oliver's truncated definition of
"prig," which in refusing the signified turns us back upon the phoneme (thus
stimulating, as Roland Barthes would suggest, the desire to eroticize—if not
to frig—the sign), Pip's language also abjures denotation: "Conscience is a
dreadful thing," he states, "when it accuses man or boy; but when, in the case
of a boy, that secret burden co-operates with another secret burden down the

leg of his trousers, it is (as I can testify) a great punishment." Pip carefully avoids a definition of that "secret burden"; his ambiguity, now semantic instead of phonemic, allows the bread-and-butter to function as an alibi for the arousal that he is—as anyone familiar with the perturbations of male adolescence can attest—at such pains to conceal.

Having secreted the morsel down his pants leg, Pip continues to be harassed by his "wicked secret" through the novel's early scenes. When he undertakes the chore of stirring the Christmas pudding, he finds himself altogether discomfited : "I tried it with the load upon my leg (and that made me think afresh of the man with the load on *his* leg), and found the tendency of exercise to bring the bread-and-butter out at my ankle, quite unmanageable. Happily, I slipped away, and deposited that part of my conscience in my garret bedroom." Stealing the meager repast does not merely coincide ("co-operate") with the primary arousal ("another secret burden down the leg of his trousers"): it literalizes the economic metaphor, by which masturbation is classically imagined, of counterproductive labor. Likewise, while the load of which Pip relieves himself surreptitiously in his bedroom signals the irresistible culmination of such titillation, it also completes the analogy between masturbation and theft through a common charge of wastefulness. The trail of butter down his leg points further toward that scene in which, on his first night in London, a now-idle gentleman-Pip claims to detect in his bed "much of [a boiled fowl's] parsley and butter in a state of congelation when I retired for the night." Whether through the profligacy of moneyed leisure or the degeneracy of desperate theft, autoeroticism is figured as wasteful sexual energy.

If the discovery of these suspiciously buttery emissions in Pip's bedroom suggests an excessively lubricious reading strategy, disavowal of this discovery would itself partake of the very paranoia that structures Pip's response. For in the scene we have been examining, Pip is quick to identify himself with the criminal. First, through corporeal metonymy (that oedipal limp) he links himself to the shackled Magwitch. Further, in abetting the convict, Pip fears he may *become* a convict, by virtue of the paranoiac imagination that affiliates his crime (and his body) with an illegality whose discipline is materialized almost immediately in the soldiers on the doorstep. Victorian proscriptions of self-abuse and the concomitant vigilance in preventing their infringement notoriously inspired the kind of guilt this passage bespeaks among habituated onanists. Not least in an effort to resist the continuing allure of the prohibitions against a practice otherwise thoroughly banalized today, this reading will insist that *Great Expectations* is imbued with lessons about the erotic dispositions of bodies. Rather than recapitulate the protagonist's phobic recoiling against sexual possibilities, I will, in what follows, propose to locate at the very heart of the Victorian literary canon a deeply saturated perversity. One of the nineteenth-century novel's principal accomplishments is to formulate a literary language that expresses eroticism even as it designates sexuality the supremely unmentionable subject. While the regulatory, often punitive dimension of these articulations cannot be overestimated, there is a comparable danger in recognizing nothing other than their prohibitive aspect, thereby merely relocating the critical institutions that have traditionally prevented readers from identifying erotic pleasures—call them perversions—within so respectable a text as *Great Expectations*. The novel both arouses and coerces its readers' desires; tracing the productive interplay of pleasure and power allows not only a reconception of this classic work but a charting of Victorian sexual ideology's formidable operations.

Thanks to the Victorian novel's renowned loquaciousness, the subjects it cannot utter generate particularly nagging silences. How can we make these silences speak? Precisely through attention to the rhetoric of unspeakability: such tropes as periphrasis, euphemism, and indirection give rise to signifying practices that fill in these enforced absences. Even as sexuality is unspeakable, it—or what was, historically, coming to be designated "it"—is everywhere being spoken. The novel, we will see, encrypts sexuality not in its plot or in its announced intentions, but in its margins, at the seemingly incidental moments of its figurative language, where, paradoxically, it is so starkly obvious as to be invisible. The novel directs out attention to its visibly invisible surface with its manifest interest in the materiality of the sign; it offers a model for such reading in, for instance, young Pip's assumption that "the shape of the letters" on the tombstones conveys the physical appearance of his parents, or in the silenced Mrs. Joe's ideogram for Orlick—the hammer—which everyone misreads *as* a letter. If the very letters that constitute its matter bear meanings beyond the literal, then by analogy we can detect other sorts of hidden information in aspects of the novel's surface usually considered so conspicuous as to be undeserving of comment. The arena of the unnoticeable (or what it comes down to, the unnoteworthy) shelters what can hardly be thought, much less articulated, in the novel; here instantiated in a specifically literary register is the institutionalization of the unspeakablity of sex, which has, as Foucault demonstrates, been generative, not repressive, of discourses on sexuality.

The placement of hands on genitals remains a secret in the Victorian novel, but like all secrets it wants to be told. The scene with which we have been concerned, of masturbation's near exposure, is only the most explicit instance of a pattern that runs throughout *Great Expectations*, a pattern which figures the sexual caress not in the genitals that are handled but in the hands that do the touching. From this early point, at which the boy's bulge virtually speaks its own name, the narrative quickly relegates such unutterable instances of provocation and arousal to the commonplace, benign, and unblushing representation of characters' hands. In a genre that forbids direct observation of genitals in action, this manual code gives voice to what otherwise cannot be spoken. The sexual secrets of the Victorian novel, that is to say, have not been silenced, but are audible instead in a different key.

Why hands? An account of their place in Victorian culture would consider the wealth of tracts on chirology, palmistry, and graphology from the period, as well as such anatomo-spiritual works as Sir Charles Bell's popular treatise *The Hand; Its Mechanism and Vital Endowments, as Evincing Design.* The fact is not simply that the hand was paid a great deal of attention, but that—given the extent of Victorian self-regulation both literal and sartorial—it was one of the few anatomical parts regularly available *for* attention: the usual costume of middle-class English adults in the nineteenth century covered all of the body but the head and the hands. Much has been made of the former body part, the head, both in literary representation and in those famous Victorian pseudo-sciences, phrenology, and physiognomy. But critics have had little to say about the other part of the body that could be examined—the hand. Nineteenth-century observers felt the hand to be fully saturated with information about its possessor's character; a book entitled *The Hand Phrenologically Considered: Being a Glimpse at the Relation of the Mind with the Organisation of the Body* (1848) exemplifies the Victorian investment in readings of the hand, the technicist discourse of the work enabling it to sidestep the dubiety of palmistry:

> The hand not only affords us characters by which the age and sex may be determined, it is likewise an index of the general habit of body, of the kind of temperament, and of the mental tendency and disposition. . . . A soft, thick hand, loaded with fat, denotes little energy of character, and a soft yielding, inactive disposition; while on the contrary, a thin, bony, or muscular hand indicates a rough, active, energetic nature.

Whether through its physiology, the lines that mark it, or the writing with which it is synonymous, the hand is so freighted with significance as to reveal all the vital information about the body and mind behind it.

For the Victorian reader, the hand would immediately be available both as a site of sexual signification and as a dangerous sexual implement. Hands are particularly important to any rendering of masturbation, as the putative etymology of the word suggests: *manus* (hand) + *stuprare* (to defile).

Preferring a Greek derivation, urologist William Acton suggests "chiromania" as a synonym for onanism, which he states, in *The Functions and Disorders of the Reproductive Organs* (1857), "can be properly applied, in the case of males, only to emission or ejaculation induced by titillation and friction of the virile member with the hand." In his account of the usual symptomatology of the onanist, Joseph W. Howe argues in *Excessive Venery, Masturbation and Continence* (1887) that hands deserve the special attention of "the experienced eye": "The superficial veins of the integument covering the hands and feet on the dorsal aspect, are very much enlarged or dilated. . . . The hands are often moist and clammy. While the patient is sitting, his shoulders stoop, and both hands are generally place on the inside of the thighs." Despite anti-onanists' attempts to constrain hands, their resistance to being covered (one can manage, as Miss Skiffins demonstrates, only so far with gloves on) marks their importance: the hand is the only exposed site of sexual communication below the neck.

I cite Victorian manual and medical authorities not to establish any specific resonance with *Great Expectations* but instead to demonstrate the kinds of attention that the hand received in the period. We need not show that, say, Dickens was familiar with *Onania* in order to prove Pip a masturbator; we hardly want to, in fact, for the novel nowhere delivers the reified identity of "the onanist." The history of masturbation is both institutional *and* private (however oblique our access to the latter), and its story is one of both proscription and excitation. Given the novel's implication in both efforts—warning against and encouraging solitary vice— my interest here is in tracing the enfolding of that erotic/somatic practice in particular literary structures, specifically in linguistic formations of codification, connotation, and euphemism. These rhetorical strategies, it must be emphasized, are not intentional reactions to sexual prohibitions (the result of repression or censorship) but generative possibilities for sexual meanings that cannot yet recognize themselves: within a constellation of broader, including non-literary, discursive systems, such strategies contribute to the *production* of sexuality as the very category of the unspeakable. Rather than take the novel as a document in the institutional history of masturbation, then, my concern is to consider masturbation as a figure in the history of the novel.

When hands take on a specifically sexual meaning, I have suggested, they speak of masturbation; but their sexual qualities are also *generalizable*. The metonymic association of hands with autoeroticism functions as a conduit between representation and sexuality, but it does not restrict manual signification to a solitary sexual act. *Great Expectations* constructs its sexual taxonomy through its representation of hands, and while its master trope is therefore masturbation, the novel oversees a remarkably wide range of what will come—not least through the genre's own efforts at discriminating types—to be known as sexualities. I will consider the links between the overt representation of the manual, on the one hand, and the mystification of sexuality, on the other, first through the novel's thematics of male masturbation; I will then proceed to broaden the manual/erotic affiliation and examine the hand's capacity to signify non-solitary sexuality, specifically through its potential for both inciting and regulating male homoeroticism; finally, I will assess the novel's efforts at representing and managing women's sexuality through increasingly phantasmatic conjurations of the female hand. As exemplar, the novel trains the bodies of its characters—as instructor, those of its reader—in exceedingly particular lessons; it becomes, in this peculiar sense, a novel of manners.

Like many avid masturbators, Pip is deeply ashamed, and just short of growing hair on his palms, he transfers his generalized sense of guilt onto the hands themselves. Pip is sorely touched by Estella's disdainful remark upon their first meeting: "'And what coarse hands he has!'" He responds, "I had never thought of being ashamed of my hands before; but I began to consider them a very indifferent pair. Her contempt for me was so strong, that it became infectious, and I caught it." Pip's hands focus and localize the virulent shame that, articulated here in the register of social class, bears with it all the marks of a sexual embarrassment. What he learns from Estella, that is to say, is that embodied signs of labor are distasteful; the way in which he learns it, though, is through the shaming of a physical exposure, having his vulgar, vulnerable members seen by a girl. The disgrace that attaches to the hand would, to Dickens and his audience, as surely be coded for that other subject routinely repressed—work—as it would be for sex. Humiliation over the laboring (productive) hand converges on shame over the autoerotic (wasteful) one.

Pip's rough appendages perennially trouble him, and the novel meticulously traces the coalescence between the laboring hand and the masturbatory one under the sign of embarrassment. When he tells his family tall tales of his first visit to Satis House—his initial step out of the working class—he strikes the pose of the guilt-ridden onanist: "They both stared at me, and I, with an obtrusive show of artlessness on my countenance, stared at them, and plaited the right leg of my trousers with my right hand." Once he comes into his expectations, Pip's newfound riches—or is it his newly bulging body?—plague him with another kind of awkwardness: "I went circuitously to Miss Havisham's by all the back ways, and rang at the bell constrainedly, on account of the stiff long fingers of my gloves." This manual erection coincides with Pip's rising expectations, as overt anxiety about class again takes the narrative form of a sexualized humiliation. The process of Pip's *Bildung* is an aggressive repudiation of the labor inscribed on his body: it tells the story of his refusal to *be* a hand. Consequently, he takes the rowing master's compliment that he has "the arm of a blacksmith" as the worst kind of insult.

In the logic of the plot, Pip can finally overcome the blackening of the forge—the shame of the laboring hand—with burns of another sort: after rescuing Miss Havisham, he notes, "When I got up, on the surgeon's coming to her with other aid, I was astonished to see that both my hands were burnt; for, I had no knowledge of it through the sense of feeling." These burns finally serve as a badge of honor, not shame, for Pip, a mark of adult arrival that overwrites his adolescent humiliation. This trial by fire obliterates at once his infantilized relation to Satis House and the calloused hands of his youth: he is required to pass through it in order to locate the appropriate alloerotic, heterosexual object. In this developmental narrative, which the novel overtly endorses, Pip's desires are ultimately as self-regulating as the free market that Adam Smith had envisioned as being—or being ruled by—an invisible hand.

When masturbation and labor are supplemented with a third sense of the hand—writing itself—the manual shame embedded in the narrative discloses its profound effects. Unlike most first-person novels, *Great Expectations* lacks an explicit scene of writing—that scene before the beginning and after the end in which readers are offered an account of the text's genesis. Like the worker, the writer is ashamed of his hand; he insists upon effacing (though perhaps succeeds only in displacing) the signs of his own manual labor at bringing the novel into being. Though we never witness the inscription of the novel itself, the narrative obsessively renders the exertions of the writing hand: from Pip's early problems learning to cipher ("getting considerably worried and scratched by every letter") down to his final scrivening labor for the Firm whose name merely embellishes that of his occupation—"I was clerk to Clarriker and Co."—the hero writes throughout the story. We would expect the writer's hand, like the productive one of the laborer, to exhibit the telltale marks of its toil (callouses, ink stains, cramps)—to bear witness to the work of what Melville dubs "a poor be-inked galley-slave, toiling with the heavy oar of a quill, to gain something wherewithal to stave off the cravings of nature"—but the narrator never displays his laboring hand. Only when he lives as a gentleman does Pip have the leisure to read, and he then does little else; writing is thus as much a mark of the protagonist's class descent (the economic necessity of writing) as of his rise (the intellectual ability to do so). We are prohibited from seeing Pip write this fiction for reasons both economic and sexual: on one side, the writing of this life is itself the signal of a fall in class terms, which must be occluded; on the other, any exposure of himself in the act of imagining his life would violate the autoerotic scene with which the solitary reverie, accompanied by manual manipulation, has already been aligned. Writing, like masturbation, cannot be narrated outright—yet it also *needn't* be, for it has already left its mark (spilled its ink) everywhere; it too is made shameful, so chastened by that interiorized conduct manual, the conscience, that it is evident only in its traces. Whether it covers work, writing, or sex, the coy hand thus seems to signal displacement itself.

The young Pip conforms most nearly to the identity of the onanist not because, as in some historical narrative, he envinces characteristics typical of the contemporary pathology, but because in his case hands take over the expression of emotions such as shame, self-assurance, arousal, or dejection more usually affiliated with sexuality. If Pip's hands encode certain features of autoeroticism, we might inquire how they became so accomplished. The narrative offers an initial, ontogenetic explanation: from the first, Pip avers that his sister "had established a great reputation with herself and the neighbours because she had brought me up 'by hand,'" and that he knows "her to have a hard and heavy hand, and to be much in the habit of laying it upon her husband as well as upon me." Here is one source, then, for so total a cathexis of the hand: it is both the punished and the punisher, the organ that sins and the one that disciplines. And while Pip's hands designate him a masturbator, Mrs. Joe's serve rather unambiguously to phallicize her (particularly through their tool, Tickler)—at least until her penchant for dealing blows is dealt a stronger one and she is silenced "by some unknown hand," which unsurprisingly turns out to be Orlick's "murderous hand."

To the muscular femininity of his surrogate mother's "bad cop," Pip's father-figure correspondingly exhibits the sentimental masculinity of a "good" one:

> Joe laid his hand upon my shoulder with the touch of a woman.
> . . . O dear good Joe, whom I was so ready to leave and so
> unthankful to, I see you again, with your muscular blacksmith's
> arm before your eyes, and your broad chest heaving, and your
> voice dying away. O dear good faithful tender Joe, I feel the
> loving tremble of your hand upon my arm, as solemnly this day
> as if it had been the rustle of an angel's wing!

The portrayal of Joe is in keeping with the usual representation of male sentimentality; the class signification of bodily attributes provides that the very "muscular blacksmith's arm" which could so humiliate Pip on the

Thames crew team functions, in the forge from which it derives, as the sign of an unimpeachably wholesome and regenerate masculinity. The antithesis of his wife's hand, the "woman's touch" that characterizes Joe's paradoxically serves to fortify, not to destabilize, the edifice of his virility, even as it threatens Pip, the precarious arriviste, whose feminized masculinity has an entirely different class valence. Where Mrs. Joe's hand trains Pip's through violence and terror, Joe's works more subtly, as a nostalgic—but for all that, no less thoroughly repudiated—negative exemplar. The child is always in danger of being slapped by "mother" for touching himself; the gentleman is always in danger of becoming as manly as "father"—and thus losing his class standing—or seeming as womanly as him—and thus losing his manhood.

Though Pip's body is schooled in a gender curriculum whose first instructors are, by virtue of their class status, comically reversed, the simplicity of this role reversal ensure that the inculcation will do its work all the same. It might be imagined that in such a scheme, Pip's early assimilation to a masturbatory erotics functions in keeping with a developmental narrative, so that his discovery of an interest in Estella can sweep over the adolescent vice and mature heterosexuality install itself. In fact, the presence in the novel of several other immature male characters with a predilection for self-abuse suggests the very normality of Pip's habit, if not of its persistence in his story. Instances of what teenage boys still term pocket-pool abound: young Pip "religiously entertained" the belief that his deceased "five little brothers . . . had all been born on their backs with their hands in their trousers-pockets, and had never taken them out in this state of existence"; Orlick typically "would come slouching from his hermitage, with his hands in his pockets"; and Bentley Drummle "sat laughing in our faces, with his hands in his pockets." The model of normative development we will wish to call seriously into question, but for now we shall consider the challenge offered by the fact that the behavior of at least one adult character in the novel is equally, though different ways, coded for autoeroticism.

The characteristics we associate most with the body of Pip's guardian, Jaggers, are those of touching himself—his trademark "biting the side of his great forefinger"—and otherwise drawing attention to his unaccountably large hands (Pip notes the solicitor has "an exceedingly large head and a corresponding large hand"). His classic pose: "The strange gentleman . . . with a manner expressive of knowing something secret about every one of us . . . remained standing: his left hand in his pocket, and he biting the forefinger of his right." Even if we overlooked the finger he keeps in his mouth, we could hardly avoid noticing the one stashed in his pocket—for Pip's isn't the only pants leg found bulging with secret burdens. "[Jaggers] pushed Miss Havisham in her chair before him, with one if his large hands, and put the other in his trouser-pocket as if the pocket were full of secrets." Jaggers's case is somewhat more profound than that of the boys who pocket their hands, both because he is the only adult to do so and because the secrets in his pockets connote the other reason for keeping one's hands there: to lay hold of money. Both Pip and Drummle keep their wealth so concealed, and, as Pip executes the pun on the family name, he relies on our knowledge that while the money is kept in pockets, it is not in the Pockets: "Both Mr. and Mrs. Pocket had such a noticeable air of being in somebody else's hands, that I wondered who really was in possession of the house and let them live there, until I found this unknown power to be the servants." Jaggers is famous for ensuring that, as he says, "the secret was still a secret," and it is his skill at keeping secrets in his pocket that makes him so adept at getting money (even if not spending) there as well. Through Jaggers, the novel lends vivid materiality to the familiar Victorian analogy—condensed in the theory of "spermatic economy"—between male sexuality and a money economy.

If Jaggers's version of autoeroticism functions in one sense as that which is sublimated by his acquisitiveness and in another as, say, the bodily inscription of his propensity for taking charge of others' secrets, in a third sense it registers the consistent pattern of his solipsistic withdrawal from scenes of potential erotic engagement. Again taking hands as our clue, we first recognize his distaste for human contact in his Pilate-like hygiene mania:

> I embrace this opportunity of remarking that he washed his clients off, as if he were a surgeon or a dentist. He had a closet in his room, fitted up for the purpose, which smelt of the scented soap like a perfumer's shop. It had an unusually large jack-towel on a roller inside the door, and he would wash his hands, and wipe them and dry them all over this towel, whenever he came in from a police-court or dismissed a client from his room.

Jaggers's approach is often signaled by the advance guard of this scented soap—a redolence perhaps attributed to the massive surface area of the organs in question. Jaggers's attention to others' hands amounts to no less a form of self-involvement that his fastidiousness about his own. In one instance, he takes a peculiar interest in Bentley Drummle: before the dinner party he throws for Pip and his "intimate associates," Jaggers remarks, upon first laying eyes on Drummle's form, "'I like the look of that fellow'"; "'I like the fellow, Pip; he is one of the true sort,'" he repeats after dinner. In an effort to get a better look at the body of "the Spider," Jaggers stages a competition among the boys by provoking Pip's future rival to demonstrate the strength of his arm:

> [Drummle] informed our host . . . that as to skill he was more than our master, and that as to strength he could scatter us like chaff. By some invisible agency, my guardian wound him up to a pitch little short of ferocity about this trifle; and he fell to baring and spanning his arm to show how muscular it was, and we all fell to baring and spanning our arms in a ridiculous manner.

Like the comparison of equipment usual in any high-school boys' locker room, this scene belies the pretense of romantic rivalry (it predates Bentley's interest in Estella) with its own gleeful erotics. Yet for all the zeal of his "invisible agency," Jaggers's taste for Drummle—and in particular, for his arm—is "quite inexplicable." The plot never sufficiently rationalizes it, except through some vague notions of the solicitor's perverse contrariety. Likewise, the occasion that this arm-wrestling provides for showing off Molly's superior strength—"'Very few men have the power of wrist that this woman has'"—remains largely unexplained, as does the sadomasochistic dramatization of this master/servant relationship. Wemmick's later explanation—"'She went into his service immediately after her acquittal, tamed as she is now'"—merely asserts its own insufficiency; surely if all Jaggers wanted was a domestic servant he needn't have taken in "a wild beast tamed." Though they work according to the novel's usual manual semiotics, these sites of Jaggers's prospective erotic interest rapidly lose their motivation; the plot abandons them as false leads, and Jaggers seems finally more interested in keeping his hands to himself than in pursuing others'.

If the lawyer appears to suffer from an unaccountable withholding, he can at least be said to have made professional use of this attribute, as Pip testifies in describing one of his most effective litigious techniques:

> He always carried (I have not yet mentioned it, I think) a pocket-handkerchief of rich silk and of imposing proportions, which was of great value to him in his profession. I have seen him so terrify a client or a witness by ceremoniously unfolding this pocket-handkerchief as if he were immediately going to blow his nose, and then pausing, as if he knew he should not have time to do it before such client or witness committed himself, that the self-committal has followed directly, quite as a matter of course.

Jaggers's large-handed handkerchief trick gives bodily, objective form to the particular erotic disposition we have identified with him: autoeroticism as a mode of refusing alloeroticism. Not unlike the flirtation between "prig" and "Master Bates" in *Oliver Twist*, this spectacle—in the context of Jaggers's finger-biting and pocketed secrets—texually codes the sexualization of refusal that it cannot name. And while Pip's frigs result in sticky messes (butter down the pants leg, butter in the bed), Jaggers turns refusal—here, to allow the phlegm to come—into *ars erotica*. Through the representation of an adult character coded for onanistic behavior, Dickens gives literary form not so much to a Victorian pathology or sexual identity as to a particular "perverse" sexual practice. Though Pip and Jaggers both bespeak autoeroticism, they personify two very different modalities of it, neither in an especially proximate relation to the classic onanist of Tissot or Acton: Pip's practice is guilty, excessive, uncontrolled, a sexualized strategy for repudiating the manual labor he abhors; Jaggers's is manipulative, parsimonious, recoiling, a performance and extension of his economic motivations. To insist upon the conformity of literary characters to the genuinely repressive models of medical authorities may itself be to fall victim to a coercively normative, normalizing sexuality; instead, without obliging ourselves to abandon the postulate that all sexuality is shot through with ideology, can we imagine that the novel engages sexualities unaccounted for by official pathologies?

The solitary hands we have observed thus far in *Great Expectations* are marked, via a metonymic connection, for male masturbation: when hand and genital organ touch, the former (speakable) can connote the latter (unspeakable). The novel's erotic investment in hands is so general, however, as to allow for metaphoric links as well, so that sexual practices less directly managed by the hand may nonetheless be imagined as manual. We now shift our attention from singular hands to redoubled ones in order to read sexuality: the moments at which two men's hands are engaged arise first, in the most highly socialized form of male hand-holding—the handshake—and then, in the other shape they principally assume in the novel, pugilism. Returning to Jaggers, we again find his mode of refusal striking. While he is frequently "throwing his finger at [one] sideways," and is quick to lay a hand on Pip's shoulder or arm, he rarely takes the young man in hand. Indeed, Jaggers is all but unwilling to extend his hand—and the largeness of his endowment makes the fact of his withholding all the more disappointing:

> It was November, and my guardian was standing before his fire
> leaning his back against the chimney-piece, with his hands

under his coat-tails.

"Well, Pip," said he, "I must call you Mr. Pip to-day. Congratulations, Mr. Pip."

We shook hands—he was always a remarkably short shaker—and I thanked him.

A man who has so noticeably large a hand and yet is such a "remarkably short shaker" will always fail to satisfy. As Pip comes to learn, however, handshaking in the world of this novel has a curiously negative valence in any case.

The handshake is the one social ritual by which men—most especially those who are strangers—routinely touch each other. It functions to draw people together by holding them apart: it interposes hands between other body parts as a safe form of contact. Why, then, this shortness on the part of Jaggers's shaker? Why, even more pertinently, the castigation of this ritual in the form of Pumblechook's unctuous insistence on it? One recalls how the seedsman, after learning that Pip has come into his expectations, clings to the boy with an obsequiousness as oppressive as the proverbial cheap suit that Pip has just come from being fitted for by Tabb.

> "But do I," said Mr. Pumblechook, getting up again the moment after he had sat down, "see afore me, him as I ever sported with in his times of happy infancy? And may I—*may*—I ?"
>
> This May I, meant might he shake hands? I consented, and he was fervent, and then sat down again.
>
> "Here is wine," said Mr. Pumblechook. "Let us drink, Thanks to Fortune, and may she ever pick out her favourites with equal judgment! And yet I cannot," said Mr. Pumblechook, getting up again, "see afore me One—and likewise drink to One—without again expressing—May I—*may* I—?"

Pumblechook's sycophancy is insatiable, at least so long as Pip stays in the money; once Pip is "brought low," however, the hand is extended "with a magnificently forgiving air," and Pip notes "the wonderful difference between the servile manner in which he had offered his hand in my new prosperity, saying, 'May I?' and the ostentacious clemency with which he had just now exhibited the same fat five fingers." Here is the novel's signal instance of a hand freighted with meaning, yet what it bespeaks is not the efficacy of gestural communication. Instead, at the moment it raises the possibility that in the most familiar code of manual conduct—the handshake—something might supervene upon the literal, the narrative can be nothing but derisive (as if to confirm that hands are evocative only where they are not, in the novel's conscious terms, meant to be so). At the point where connotations of the manual—including but not limited to the erotic—seem most likely to proliferate, the mode of parodic excess preempts all meanings but the most repugnant hypocrisy.

Though Pip's hand may remain insufficiently chafed by Pumblechook's grip, in the progressive tale of his body's schooling it receives a final chastening lesson. Jaggers's second, Wemmick, is noted for parodically representing the schizophrenic divide between the office persona of the bureaucratic modern man and his home life ("'the office is one thing, and private life is another'"). While on the job, Wemmick faithfully emulates the withholding posture of his employer: "Something of the state of Mr. Jaggers hung about him too, forbidding approach beyond certain limits." And like Jaggers, Wemmick finds distasteful Pip's provincial penchant for handshaking:

> "As I keep the cash," Mr. Wemmick observed, "we shall most likely meet pretty often. Good day."
> "Good day."
> I put out my hand, and Mr. Wemmick at first looked at it as if he thought I wanted something. Then he looked at me, and said, correcting himself,
> "To be sure! Yes. You're in the habit of shaking hands?"
> I was rather confused, thinking it must be out of the London fashion, but said yes.
> "I have got so out of it!" said Mr. Wemmick—"except at last. Very glad, I'm sure, to make your acquaintance. Good day!"

The perplexity that Wemmick evinces at Pip's quaint amiability here is only elucidated later. For the man of business, handshaking is shown to have practical purposes: besides the exhibition of the "portable property" he has acquired from condemned prisoners ("he wore at least four mourning rings"), he reserves demonstrative use of his hands for its utility *as* a sign. As he leads Pip on a tour of Newgate prison, the narrator notes: "He tuned to me and said, 'Notice the man I shall shake hands with.' I should have done so, without the preparation, as he had shaken hands with no one yet." After the brief conversation between Wemmick and the designated man, "They shook hands again, and as we walked away Wemmick said to me, 'A Coiner, a very good workman. The Recorder's report is made to-day, and he is sure to be executed on Monday.'" Wemmick hopes to land a bit of portable property from the condemned man, and reserves his embrace to satisfy this materialistic impulse. His handshake, like Pumblechook's, foregrounds its own function as coded behavior; divested of any erotic significance, Wemmick's secret handshake holds no secret (except so far as the unwitting Coiner is concerned) because its code is transparent. No wonder he is so reluctant to take up Pip's hand when they first meet: to do so would, in Wemmick's bodily lexicon, be transparent to marking him for the gallows.

While the handshake routinizes and sublates manual contact among characters, the other context in which hands regularly meet—fisticuffs—tends in a rather different direction. Unlike the ostentatious signification with which the text loads handshaking (a system of meaning, I have argued, so manifest that it paradoxically empties itself out), the novel's most fully embodied moments of physical violence are either so curiously undermotivated or so thoroughly overdetermined as to proliferate the meanings available to a manual semiotics. Although in the logic of the novel's plot, fights interpose at junctures of fierce romantic rivalry, the *narration* of the battles consistently provides the occasion for the playing out of erotic contact, both homo- and heterosexual, between combatants. Insofar as this precipitate collapse of the pugilistic into the erotic becomes a problem for Victorian masculinity, we might take John Sholto Douglas, Marquess of Queensberry, as the figure effectively to drive a wedge between them. By dint of historical "accident," the very man who, in 1867, codified the rules of "fair play" in boxing—thereby regulating and legitimating the procedures for homosocial sparring—was destined to initiate the century's most notorious legal proceeding for homoerotic touching—thereby taking the lead in the fin-de-siècle anathematization of homosexuals.

At Pip's first encounter with Herbert Pocket, for instance, the relationship is one of immediate and unmediated physical aggression: "'Come and fight,' said the pale young gentleman." As Herbert's provocation appears wholly unmotivated, he soon supplies the incitement it is felt to require: "'I ought to give you a reason for fighting, too. There it is!' In a most irritating manner he instantly slapped his hands against one another, daintily flung one of his legs up behind him, pulled my hair, slapped his hands again, dipped his head, and butted it into my stomach." To such ungentlemanly conduct the gentleman's reaction—that is, the bellicosity Herbert desires— itself must be reconfigured, albeit in hindsight, as a form of chivalrous combat for feminine affections. Thus, Pip's payoff for sparring with Herbert is the opportunity to kiss Estella, the scene's unseen observer. Yet even if this putative erotic aim were capable of sustaining a state of arousal, it would nonetheless function only retrospectively and defensively as the alibi for the more provoking touches elaborated in the battle with Herbert. In fact, Pip feels as a result that he has prostituted himself, "that the kiss was given to the coarse common boy as a piece of money might have been, and that it was worth nothing." In compensation for the tussle's lack of motivation, then, the text supplies a series of rationales—ranging from insult to romance to monetary recompense—whose insufficiency is demonstrated by the very rapidity of their deployment.

However persuasive the pretext for pugnacity in the novel may be (in this case, hardly at all), it thus functions primarily as the occasion for physical contact between adversaries—contact whose cathexes evince a logic quite different from the plot's. And while the sensory modality of the novel's eroticism is primarily tactile, there is a peculiarly embodied form of the visual—an assaultive kind of looking—which also partakes of these haptic significations. In the present scene, the bout between Herbert and Pip is preceded by both narrator-Pip's account of Herbert's awkward frame (he later discreetly terms it "a little ungainly") and Herbert's somewhat more suspect examination of Pip's physique. In a remarkable description of his adversary's seminudity, Pip recounts:

> [Herbert] fell to pulling off, not only his jacket and waistcoat, but his shirt too, in a manner at once light-hearted, businesslike, and bloodthirsty.
>
> Although he did not look very healthy—having pimples on his face, and a breaking out at his mouth—these dreadful preparations quite appalled me. . . . He was a young gentleman in a grey suit (when not denuded for battle), with his elbows, knees, wrists, and heels, considerably in advance of the rest of him as to development.
>
> My heart failed me when I saw him squaring at me with every demonstration of mechanical nicety, and eyeing my anatomy as if he were minutely choosing his bone.

The investment of Pip's narration in looking at and rendering the repulsive particulars of his antagonist's body is strangely at odds with the character's professed distaste for the figure that Herbert cuts. And at the moment that Pip, almost despite himself, catalogues the corners of the pale young gentleman's frame, Herbert returns the gaze. The fight then proceeds from this curiously cruising scrutiny; from sizing up to feeling up, we will see, the novel's pattern is here established.

The striptease that Pip witness at his introduction to Herbert enacts a form of male-male persual not uncommon in Dickens's work. Such an androphilic once-over is most fully elaborated in the following passage in *The Old Curiosity Shop* (1840–41):

> Mr. Swiveller looked with a supercilious smile at Mr. Cheggs's toes, then raised his eyes from them to his ankle, from that to his shin, from that to his knee, and so on very gradually, keeping up his right leg, until he reached his waistcoat, when he raised his eyes from button to button until he reached his chin, and travelling straight up the middle of his nose came at last to his eyes, when he said abruptly, "No, sir, I didn't."

The point at which one man can no longer anatomize another's body—"and so on very gradually"—is always telling. But as if to rectify Herbert's enticing literalization of that familiar gaze ("he undressed me with his eyes"), the revelation moves in the opposite direction when the two meet again, now grown up. As Pip first espies the mature Herbert mounting the stairs, he reverses the striptease both by clothing his friend and by moving this time from the head downward: "Gradually there arose before me the hat, head, neckcloth, waistcoat, trousers, boots, of a member of society of about my own standing." Here the progressive dressing (of a nude ascending a staircase) ensures their rivalry is at an end; proleptically asserting a Freudian developmental mythology, it insists that a more happily socialized and sublimated relation will ensue.

The relationship most thoroughly structured around hand-to-hand combat, of course, is not finally Pip's friendship with Herbert but his enmity with Orlick. This conflict too originates in an aggressive looking: "I had leisure to entertain the retort in my mind, while [Orlick] slowly lifted his heavy glance from the pavement, up my legs and arms, to my face." Even in the midst of Orlick's climatic attack on Pip, he pauses for a leisurely gander at his victim—a glance that can afford to be less furtive than earlier: "'Now,' said he, when we had surveyed one another for some time, 'I've got you.' . . . 'Now, wolf,' said he, 'afore I kill you like any other beast—which is wot I mean to do and wot I have tied you up for—I'll have a good look at you and a good goad at you. Oh, you enemy!' . . . Then, he took up the candle, and shading it with his murderous hand so as to throw its light on me, stood before me, looking at me and enjoying the sight."

Violence is visualized before it is actualized; but Orlick's is of a specially ferocious variety, requiting not only specular conjuration but verbal confirmation as well. For however violating this staring-down may be, its narration is always coy in the elision of certain body parts. The linguistic analogue to the so-far-and-no-farther gaze is a device (comparable to the "prig" from *Oliver Twist*, the "secret burden" from Pip's childhood) by which the novel evokes, while still refusing to denote, terms for male sexuality around Orlick. "He pretended that his christian name was Dolge—a clear impossibility—but he was a fellow of that obstinate disposition that I believe him to have been the prey of no delusion in this particular, but wilfully to have imposed that name upon the village as an affront to its understanding." With no other objection than this—that in its inscrutability the name simply *feels* obscene—Pip implies that a lack of definition itself signifies a transgression against propriety. Pip's assertion of this name's "impossibility" aims to bolster the straightness and clarity of his own narrative, a species purportedly remote from the obscenity of Orlick's indirection; yet the proximate impossibility of his own name belies this effort, as the novel's opening words attest: "My father's family name being Pirrip, and my christian name Philip, my infant tongue could make of both names nothing longer or more explicit than Pip. So, I called myself Pip, and came to be called Pip." The case for the perversity of connotation becomes unequivocal in the next instance:

> "Well the," said [Orlick], "I'm jiggered if I don't see you home!"
>
> This penalty of being jiggered was a favourite supposititious case of his. He attached no definite meaning to the word that I am aware of, but used it, like his own pretended christian name, to affront mankind, and convey an idea of something savagely damaging. When I was younger, I had had a general belief that if he had jiggered me personally, he would have done it with a sharp and twisted hook.

Here the insistent non-meaning of the word rebounds upon the victimized body with a sexual signification that cannot otherwise be uttered. The denotative refusal entailed in the "supposititious case" functions as a place-holder for sexual meanings, not simply by obliterating some other, straightforward language (as in this example, by eliding the term "buggered"), but by producing those meanings *as* inarticulable.

Orlick's visual and verbal pugnacity toward Pip issues in the inevitable corporal confrontation between them, at the sluice-house by the limekiln at novel's end. In returning to characters' bodies, the scene naturally refers us, through its usual synecdochal route, to their hands. Throughout the final chapters Pip is sorely disabled by the burns his arms received at Satis House; Orlick's attack is so effective in part because it exacerbates Pip's condition. As the lights go down Pip finds himself pinned to the wall:

> Not only were my arms pulled close to my sides, but the pressure on my bad arm caused me exquisite pain. Sometimes,

a strong man's hand, sometimes a strong man's breast, was set against my mouth to deaden my cries, and with a hot breath always close to me, I struggled ineffectually in the dark, while I was fastened tight to the wall. "And now," said the suppressed voice with another oath, "call out again, and I'll make short work of you!"

Faint and sick with the pain of my injured arm, bewildered by the surprise, and yet conscious how easily this threat could be put in execution, I desisted, and tried to ease my arm were it ever so little. But it was bound too tight for that. I felt as if, having been burnt before, it were now being boiled.

If the hand of Pip's that touches his own body is regularly subject to rebuke, the one that feels (and is felt by) other men is even more thoroughly penalized. Yet here the brutal ferocity of "a strong man's hand" and its arousing caress are absolutely coterminous. Fearsomely violent as this assault is, its erotic sensations are manifest: "strong man's breast" set against Pip's mouth, and, in return, the attacker's own "hot breath" against him, serve to literalize the lickerish "kiss" inhering in Orlick's surname. As if to draw on Pip's youthful training matches with Herbert and Bentley—as if to dramatize the tantalizing prospect of being "jiggered"—this serious adult business with Orlick enacts all the erotic potential of murderous male combat. The particular correspondence that the novel has established between the manual and the genital only barely prepares us for the scene's concatenation of terror and tenderness, of the one hand that savors to inflict pain and the other that anguishes to endure it.

At this point we can identify—though, as I will suggest, only prematurely—what might be termed the novel's homophobia. On the one hand, it denies the handshake any of the erotic valence we might well expect to attend this ritual: either because of the refusal of others (Jaggers or Wemmick) or because Pip's own repulsion (at Pumblechook), this manual contact is insufficient to bring men together. On the othet hand, Pip's pugilistics with Herbert, Drummle, and Orlick (as well as Magwitch's with Compeyson) represent a form of contact too close for comfort: however ecstatically and erotically charged one may suspect these passages of being, the form they take—of increasingly savage violence—must sit uneasily with any gleefully homotropic reading. If, that is to say, the cost of men touching men is that one of them be pummeled, we must recognize a certain ideological resistance in the text to such an erotics. To this apparent dead end, however, the novel proposes several alternate routes. Thanks largely to the fluidity with which *Great Expectations* structures the thematic of hands, we are left not with an antitheses between homophobic and homophilic, but rather with an apparatus that ultimately brings these two terms—not to mention their hetero counterparts—into a relatively stable and consolatory relation of mutually reinforcing regulation.

For one instance, let us, in pursuing our investigation of pugilism, witness the novel's strenuous effort to redeem it for normative heterosexuality. Earlier I ascribed Wemmick's refusal to shake Pip's hand as much to the single-mindedness of his economic motives in the workaday world as to any phobic pathology. When turning to his erotic interests at home, however, we find Wemmick himself must overcome another's refusal, in the resistance of his fiancée, Miss Skiffins, to yield to his hands. Upon meeting her, Pip "might have pronounced her gown a little too decidedly orange, and her gloves a little too intensely green"; he notes further that "Miss Skiffins . . . retained her green gloves during the evening as an outward and visible sign that there was company." Like her suitor, Miss Skiffins knows full well the hand's capability to signify: these gloves ensure her genteel incapacity for domestic labor as much as they conceal her dishpan hands (she "washed up the tea-things, in a trifling lady-like amateur manner that compromised none of us. Then, she put on her gloves again"). But while the gloves afford Miss Skiffins an "outward and visible sign" of *class* propriety, their verdancy promises a *sexual* steaminess as surely as her unwillingness to remove them withholds it.

The elaborate charade by which Wemmick makes a pass at his inamorata confirms this dynamic; it is his hands now that her gloves must peel off:

> As Wemmick and Miss Skiffins sat side by side, and as I sat in a shadowy corner, I observed a slow and gradual elongation of Mr. Wemmick's mouth, powerfully suggestive of his slowly and gradually stealing his arm round Miss Skiffins's waist. In course of time I saw his hand appear on the other side of Miss Skiffins; but at that moment Miss Skiffins neatly stopped him with the green glove, unwound his arm again as if it were an article of dress, and with the greatest deliberation laid it on the table before her. Miss Skiffins's composure while she did this was one of the most remarkable sights I have ever seen, and if I could have thought the act consistent with abstraction of mind, I should have deemed that Miss Skiffins performed it mechanically.
>
> By-and-by, I noticed Wemmick's arm beginning to disappear again, and gradually fading out of view. Shortly

afterwards, his mouth began to widen again. After an interval of suspense on my part that was quite enthralling and almost painful, I saw his hand appear on the other side of Miss Skiffins. Instantly, Miss Skiffins stopped it with the neatness of a placid boxer, took off that girdle or cestus as before, and laid it on the table.

By contrast with the performances of sexual excitation we've previously observed, this one can afford to be frankly erotic. Yet even as this pantomime of heterosexual courtship struggles to establish a relation to the normative, it repeatedly collapses into the realm of proscribed sexuality. Even—perhaps especially—when the flavor of eroticism is most vanilla (heterosexual, monogamous, genital), its pungency does not diminish against the palate; through the very nearness of its *exposure* in the narration, the representation of sexuality here continues to sting the readerly tongue. The "slow and gradual elongation of Mr. Wemmick's mouth" and the collateral distention of his arm, for example, only barely keep under wraps the other turgidity to which they give rise. The "mechanical" procedure of Miss Skiffins's resistance itself is metaphorized as *déshabillement* (she "unwound his arm again as if it were an article of dress, and . . . took off that girdle"), as though to confirm that so hot a refusal functions as an enticement to arousal. Furthermore, however superficially normative this passage's sexual thematics may be, the *mise en scène* returns us to a spectacle of sexual impropriety: unusual in the novel, Pip is here positioned as observer of others' erotic play, and his "interval of suspense . . . that was quite enthralling and almost painful" bespeaks a more-than-passive relation to the scene. Indeed, the pas de deux between Wemmick's arm and Miss Skiffins's gloves titillates Pip into a state of voyeuristic autoeroticism no different from that which novels themselves had been accused of arousing.

Finally, the contest between "his hand" and her "green glove" drifts irresistibly toward an allegory of fisticuffs. The narrative alighment of the modest maiden to "a placid boxer" installs the scene among those of intermasculine, androphilic pugilism; at its most explicit moment of heterosexual pursuit, then, the novel's erotic language modulates into the definitionally male and homosocial. For all that Miss Skiffins boxes with kid gloves on, it seems to say, she throws her punches with determination. Yet if in one sense the current of fistic homoeroticism unsettles the characters most preoccupied with bourgeois propriety, the Wemmick-Skiffins match, as we'll see, also works in the other direction (not unlike the Marquess of Queensberry) toward the reform and sanitization of boxing itself.

Indeed, the novel works arduously to redirect the erotic divagations set loose here. Lest the state of premarital arousal prove unsustainable, Miss Skiffins eventually removes her green gloves (still fully cognizant of their utility as signifiers) as a means of marking a new order of conjugally sanctioned eroticism. Arriving at church with Wemmick, Pip observes: "That discreet damsel was attired as usual, except that she was now engaged in substituting for her green kid gloves, a pair of white." Refusal having been abandoned as an erotic mode, domesticity triumphs in the Castle at Walworth: "It was pleasant to observe that Mrs. Wemmick no longer unwound Wemmick's arm when it adapted itself to her figure, but sat in a high-backed chair against the wall, like a violoncello in its case, and submitted to be embraced as that melodious instrument might have done." The spur to desire is now so fully normalized by the institution of marriage that it loses its edge: although Wemmick evinces no sign of disappointment, one need only set an ungirdled boxer beside an encased 'cello to determine which woman— Miss Skiffins or Mrs. Wemmick—is the more enticing. In the miniature, mechanical, businesslike form that the Wemmicks lend it, the marriage plot's usual propensity for damage is made starkly evident: characters' bodies are disciplined into conformity, domesticity cancels eros, married life instantly obliterates memories of the prior excitation requisite for having brought it about. Here proven in its punishing aspect is a cardinal rule of the novel genre: that nuptials represent the end, not the beginning of things.

The fights we have examined illustrate different modes of repression, in varying degrees of punitiveness, for managing and disciplining the play of hands. In each instance, the sexual possibilities generated by hands are expunged from the plot—from the register of articulated representation—by means of violence, only to resurface in the contours of the narrative voice, where they can pass by virtue of going unheard inside the novel. Male homosocial desire is expressed as brutality, while premarital sex is narratable only insofar as it fuels the hegemony of matrimony. But in addition to these transformations of errant manual desire accomplished through battle, the novel manages other, less violently chastening ones. Against the compulsions of the handshake and the fistfight, we will want now to consider the *consensual* modality of male manual regulation in the novel.

Through the shift from denuding to redressing, I have suggested, Herbert's youthful belligerence is rehabilitated as properly sublimated, adult male homosociality. Following his adolescent ineptitude in the boxing ring, moreover, Herbert's mastery of the hand correspondingly matures as well. Although we learn surprisingly little about his grown-up appendages, this lack is more than compensated by the peculiar knack he develops for tending to Pip's hands—a taste initiated, perhaps, in those first moments of "eyeing"

[Pip's] anatomy as if he were minutely choosing his bone." Indeed, Herbert's proclivity is confirmed both by his impulse, almost immediately upon becoming reacquainted with Pip, to christen him "Handel" and by his own surname, Pocket, the usual receptacle for hands in the novel. At their first dinner in town, Herbert interlards his conversation with a course in table manners for the newly arrived Pip, instructing him in the proper handling of utensils and other matters of the body's polite disposition at table ("'the spoon is not generally used over-hand, but under,'" etc.). Herbert interjaculates this manual conduct lesson (as if to literalize a parody of the silver-fork novel) through his recounting of Miss Havisham's history. In the second installment of this tale—when Pip realizes that Magwitch is Estella's father—Herbert is again preoccupied with the condition of his friend's hands, this time changing the bandages that cover Pip's burns ("'Lay your arm out upon the back of the sofa, my dear boy, and I'll sit down here, and get the bandage off so gradually that you shall not know when it comes'"). Through both stories, then, the narrative interpolates information about Pip's hands, as though, at these crucial moments of the protagonist's overt erotic interest, the novel's encrypted sign of that desire need literally be close at hand.

Th story that Herbert tells in the midst of his bodywork on Pip is not merely incidental: significantly, this narrative concerns the conspiracy of Miss Havisham's half-brother, Arthur, with her fiancé, Compeyson, to defraud her:

> "I has been supposed that the man to whom she gave her misplaced confidence, acted throughout in concert with her half-brother; that it was a conspiracy between them; and they shared the profits."
>
> "I wonder he didn't marry her and get all the property," said I.
>
> "He may have been married already, and her cruel mortification may have been a part of her half-brother's scheme," said Herbert. "Mind! I don't know that."
>
> "What became of the two men?" I asked, after again considering the subject.
>
> "They fell into deeper shame and degradation—if there can be deeper—and ruin."

The implication of a debased, presumably homosexual criminality in this last line derives its force from the contrast with the scene of its narration. Compeyson's story functions as a cautionary tale about the dangers of excessive intimacy between two young men; conversely, Pip's and Herbert's is the comfortably homosocialized relation, where eros is sublimated as pugilism, camaraderie, bachelor-marriage, and eventually marriage brokering. While in the boys' earlier encounter (the adolescent sparring match) eroticism was registered only as a "supposititious case," their newfound intimacy (the now far gentler touching) can be more frankly denoted. In forming the frame of an interpolated tale (which itself has an antithetical disciplinary moral) the hand-holding dispersed throughout the present scenes is rendered explicitly—it *is* the scene of narration—by virtue of being more highly socialized.

For Magwitch, the other figure given to excessive handling of Pip, socialization again requires a transposition of eros from narrative discourse to plot, though in his case the change is accomplished through more radical means. From the first, Magwitch embodies a certain pedophilia: the novel's opening, showing his combined aggression and affection for Pip, suggests a species of man-boy love, and it is primarily through his man-handling of Pip that we come to register such pederastic impulses. At their initial encounter, "The man, after looking at me for a moment, turned me upside down, and emptied my pockets"; and, "After darkly looking at his leg and me several times, he came closer . . . took me by both arms, and tilted me back as far as he could hold me." The recognition scene between patron and protégé stages the climax of the touching here initiated, in the form of an erotic ballet performed by the hands:

> I saw, with a stupid kind of amazement, that he was holding out both his hands to me . . . He came back to where I stood, and again held out both his hands. Not knowing what to do—for, in my astonishment I had lost my self-possession—I reluctantly gave him my hands. He grasped them heartily, raised them to his lips, kissed them, and still held them. . . . At a change in his manner as if he were even going to embrace me, I laid a hand upon his breast and put him away. . . . I stood, with a hand on the chair-back and a hand on my breast, where I seemed to be suffocating—I stood so, looking wildly at him, until I grasped at the chair, when the room began to surge and turn. He caught me, drew me to the sofa, put me up against the cushions, and bent on one knee before me; bringing the face that I now well remembered, and that I shuddered at, very near to mine. . . . The abhorrence in which I held the man, the dread I had of him, the repugnance with which I shrank from him, could not have been exceeded if he had been some terrible beast. . . . I recoiled from his touch as if he had been a snake. . . . Again he

> took both my hands and put them to his lips, while my blood
> ran cold within me. . . . He laid his hand on my shoulder. I
> shuddered at the thought that for anything I knew, his hand
> might be stained with blood.

This narration has a perilously overt sexual charge: one need hardly cite the
bended knee, the kissing of hands, the prostration on the couch, the insistent
caresses, to locate the courtship conventions of which it partakes. Pip's gag
reflex serves to bolster, not to diminish the eroticism of the episode, for it
demonstrates his revulsion to be as highly cathected as the convict's
attraction. The narrative attention to Magwitch's manipulation, in its root
sense, empowers his cataclysmic revelation even as it threatens to run out of
control through a homoeroticism we are made to feel and, through Pip, to
feel repulsed by. But like his former partner, Molly, this "terrible beast" must
be tamed as well.

How does the novel recuperate Magwitch's erotic palpation and Pip's
corresponding palpitation? For Pip, the immediate antidote to the fearsome
caress of the grizzled convict's "large brown veinous hands" arrives in the
form of his companion's reassuring embrace: "Herbert received me with
open arms . . . got up, and linked his arm in mine." Through the
developments of the plot, moreover, Pip is capable of turning Magwitch's
lecherous pawing back upon him, lending it a normalized, moralized
signification. On his deathbed, Magwitch again feels Pip's hands, now
silently communicating through a sentimentalized hand-holding. "He had
spoken his last words. He smiled, and I understood his touch to mean that
he wished to lift my hand, and lay it on his breast. I laid it there, and he
smiled again, and put both his hands upon it." Then, as if to repay Magwitch
for the earlier episode, Pip makes his own revelation:

> "You had a child once, whom you loved and lost. . . . She
> is living now. She is a lady and very beautiful. And I love her!"
> With a last faint effort, which would have been powerless
> but for my yielding to it and assisting it, he raised my hand to
> his lips. Then, he gently let it sink upon his breast again, with
> his own hands lying on it.

Pip is at last able to translate his benefactor's uncomfortable stroking into
heterosexual terms, now giving that touch a proper meaning *in* the plot: he
transposes it onto the heterosexual economy by lending it the valence of the
"consent of a beloved's father to a suitor's entreaty." Much as he has had to
endure Magwitch's caress, that is to say, the hand he now can own to wanting

is Estella's, in marriage. Those earlier, less fully accountable hand-squeezings are now available to him reworked retrospectively as the beneficence of a future father-in-law. Pip can afford to be "yielding" and "assisting" to the old man's supplications by virtue of his knowledge that whatever homoerotic force they might once have had has been defused and rewritten—written into the story proper—as straight desire.

Both Magwitch and Herbert partake of a homoerotic handling of Pip and both must be retrofitted in order to discipline those desires. Whether through visceral repugnance or progressive socialization, the novel attempts to school the men's bodies in normative heterosexual touching. It is not only through other men that Pip learns these lessons, however, for the women in his story must also undergo dramatic transformations in order to rectify the manual problems they present. The two modes of regulating sexuality that we have identified for the men—the violently coercive and the consensual— also structure female eroticism. While Biddy submits to her training for respectable femininity, Molly resists domestication to the utmost; Estella, meanwhile, never has the option of choosing because she never properly has any desires that require management. The novel, moreover, makes a distinction between male and female sexuality broadly conceived, through its phantasmatic construction of the latter, which functions largely in the service of a solitary male dream of its own sexual capacity. In situating erotic subject and object in the same body, autoeroticism, as we have seen, alienates the onanist from himself, thereby paradoxically constituting him *as* a subject. Rarely more than fantasy objects, the female characters buttress the narrative's masturbatory mode, for the novel's sexual architectonics bars them from sustaining a position as desiring subjects.

Biddy and Pip start out as perfect counterparts, their as-yet ungendered identities equally oriented around the manual. "She was an orphan like myself," says Pip; "like me, too, had been brought up by hand." Also like Pip, Biddy exhibits a hand replete with the dirtying signs of both manual labor and onanistic indulgence: "Her hands always wanted washing," Pip notes early on; and at one point, to reassure him, "she put her hand, which was a comfortable hand though roughened by work, upon my hands, one after another." For all their youthful likeness, however, the specter that Biddy presents of female masturbation and of an affirmative female desire is more than Pip can abide. The novel manages the anxiety Biddy inspires by ascribing to her all the dreariness of provincial working-class life, the ignominy of which is routed specifically through the femininity of her touch. The uncleanliness of her hands distresses Pip rather vividly at the point he repudiates her: while they converse, Biddy is shown "plucking a black-currant leaf," "looking closely at the leaf in her hand," and "having rubbed the leaf to pieces between her hands—and the smell of a black-currant bush has ever since recalled to me that evening in the little garden by the side of the lane." Like Jaggers's, Biddy's hands generate a characteristic aroma; but where "scented soap" indicates a fastidious mysophobia, the provocative image of Biddy's "black-currant bush" bespeaks an *odor di femina* that sends Pip running. If we didn't already suspect this hedge of signaling a demonstrative and menacing female sexuality, two other references would ensure that we do so. One: the alibi that Jaggers provides for Molly's wrist ("much disfigured—deeply scarred and scarred across and across"), the sign of a more fearsome—and therefore more severely chastised—feminine sexuality: "She had struggled through a great lot of brambles which were not as high as her face; but which she could not have got through and kept her hands out of; and bits of those brambles were actually found in her skin and . . . the brambles in question were found on examination to have been broken through, and to have little shreds of her dress and little spots of blood upon them here and there." Two: the image Pip conjures up for his youthful acquiescence to Biddy's guidance through the thicket of language: "By the help of Biddy . . . I struggled through the alphabet as if it had been a bramble-bush; getting considerably worried and scratched by every letter." The women who navigate these pungent, puncturing bushes offer more of an affront to male sexuality and authority than the novel cares to sustain.

If in Pip's imagination Biddy represents a distressing (all too available, all too appropriate) sexual possibility, whatever desires she herself can be said to express finally appear thoroughly managed and manageable. Her feminine pliancy is evident from the first in her concern for others' hands: when they are children, Biddy tutors Pip, remedying his early orthographic troubles; when, with no apparent discomposure, she eventually transfers her affections from nephew to uncle, she also trains Joe's maladroit hand. Through a disturbing but not unfamiliar bit of Dickensian sleight of hand, the minimal degree of erotic errancy that Biddy has displayed is fully recuperated in the redirection of her interest toward Joe. He, for one, can identify with having dirt under the nails ("'No, don't wipe it off—for God's sake, give me your blackened hand!'" Pip cries to him), though upon moving into the Gargery household, Biddy concomitantly improves her personal hygiene: "I became conscious of a change in Biddy . . . her hands were always clean." Ultimately the new Mrs. Joe exhibits a hand fully accommodated to matrimonial-maternal orthodoxy: "Biddy looked down at her child, and put its little hand to her lips, and then put the good matronly hand with which she had touched it, into mine. There was something in the action and in the light pressure of

Biddy's wedding-ring, that had a very pretty eloquence in it." Light though it may be, the wedding ring exerts sufficient pressure to remind Pip of the female trajectory parallel to, but divergent from, his own.

Unlike Miss Skiffins, who requires combat—however figurative—to bring about the bliss of connubial sterility, Biddy accedes willingly to marital hegemony. Molly, by contrast with both, perpetrates the story's only interfemale bout, and she is consequently subject to an even more violent form of correction. Intervening in the boys' dilettantish display of arm-wrestling aptitude, Jaggers reveals Molly to be the real heavyweight among the novel's prize-fighters: "'There's power here,' said Mr. Jaggers, coolly tracing out the sinews with his forefinger. 'Very few men have the power of wrist that this woman has. It's remarkable what mere force of grip there is in these hands. I have had occasion to notice many hands; but never saw stronger in that respect, man's or woman's, than these.'" While the boys' sparring connotes a certain homoeroticism, the sexual provocation of Molly's violence is identifiable only through the extraordinary means requisite to its suppression. Even the titillating gaze we've come to associate with such manual displays is here rendered paralyzing, as the Medusa one cannot but look upon: "We all stopped in our foolish contention. . . . When she held her hands out, she took her eyes from Mr. Jaggers, and turned them watchfully on every one of the rest of us in succession." Seduction here amounts to a rage kept in check by its ritual humiliation. No mere "placid boxer" in drag (unlike Miss Skiffins's, these hands are always available for viewing), Molly exhibits a savagery that the narrative's libidinal economy can barely contain.

Wemmick later comes to narrate Molly's story, explaining the source of those mysterious scars and that "force of grip":

> "[Molly] was tried at the Old Bailey for murder, and was acquitted. . . . The murdered woman—more a match for the man, certainly in point of years—was found dead in a barn near Hounslow Heath. There had been a violent struggle, perhaps a fight. She was bruised and scratched and torn, and had been held by the throat at last and choked. Now, there was no reasonable evidence to implicate any person but this woman, and, on the improbabilities of her having been able to do it, Mr. Jaggers principally rested his case. You may be sure," said Wemmick, touching me on the sleeve, "that he never dwelt upon the strength of her hands then, though he sometimes does now. . . . [Molly] was so very artfully dressed from the time of her apprehension, that she looked much

slighter than she really was; in particular, her sleeves are always remembered to have been so skilfully contrived that her arms had quite a delicate look. She had only a bruise or two about her—nothing for a tramp—but the backs of her hands were lacerated, and the question was, was it with finger-nails?"

In form, Molly's battle with her rival differs little from the other bouts of jealousy in the novel; the fact, however, of the players' gender-reversal (here two women fight for the love of a man), as well as the fight's more serious consequences (the death of one combatant, the other's loss of her child), makes a difference. Pugilism, as we've seen, even when heterosexual, relies on intermasculine codes of conduct to generate its eroticism; when two women fight, crossing the border to sexuality is a more perilous prospect. To fight *as a woman*, this narrative suggests, is a deadly undertaking, because it threatens normative femininity so radically: the possibility of an *avant la lettre* lesbian eroticism here is rapidly chastened and expunged, for female sexuality undergoes the most rigorous surveillance.

Instead of demonstrating pure animus, then, Molly represents so high-voltage a current of sexual violence that its erotic charge must be defused through the most repressive means conceivable. The punishment she suffers for her manual conduct is a life-sentence of "taming" at Jaggers's hands, but more is at stake in her representation than a wholesale denial of female eroticism: she exemplifies the way in which repression functions as a vigilant and perpetual *management* of eros. Jaggers, as we've noted, exhibits a sadistic pleasure in displaying and exercising the "wild beast tamed" to the cohort of young men he gathers for dinner:

> "If you talk of strength," said Mr. Jaggers, "*I'll* show you a wrist. Molly, let them see your wrist."
>
> Her entrapped hand was on the table, but she had already put her other hand behind her waist. "Master," she said, in a low voice, with her eyes attentively and entreatingly fixed upon him. "Don't."
>
> "*I'll* show you a wrist," repeated Mr. Jaggers, with an immovable determination to show it. "Molly, let them see your wrist."
>
> "Master," she again murmured. "Please!"
>
> "Molly," said Mr. Jaggers, not looking at her, but obstinately looking at the opposite side of the room, "let them see *both* your wrists. Show them. Come!"

> He took his hand from hers, and turned that wrist up on
> the table. She brought her other hand from behind her, and
> held the two out side by side.

This sadomasochistic tableau *is* the taming technique to which Wemmick has alluded—a performance Jaggers clearly must stage with some regularity in order to keep his handmaid in line. The sheer power of Molly's hands requires the sheer coercion of Jaggers's discipline; his delight at showing her off derives not from admiration of her strength but from pride in having controlled it.

In the magnetic field of the novel's eroticism, Molly occupies the negative pole; what, then, ought we to make of the connection between her and Estella, so clearly designated the protagonist's sexual cathode? Pip first suspects their relationship when, shortly after Jaggers's exhibition of Molly, he has an uncanny feeling upon meeting the grownup Estella:

> What *was* it that was borne in upon my mind when she stood
> still and looked attentively at me? . . . As my eyes followed
> her white hand, again the same dim suggestion that I could
> not possibly grasp, crossed me. My involuntary start
> occasioned her to lay her hand upon my arm. Instantly the
> ghost passed once more, and was gone.
>   What *was* it?

Pip regards Estella's pointing finger, and following the novel's usual exchange, his inability literally to "grasp" his feeling is transferred onto, and compensated by, Estella's laying *her* hand on him. At their next meeting, Estella's hand again disturbs him: as he sees "her face at the coach window and her hand waving," he is once more startled by an ineffable likeness: "What *was* the nameless shadow which again in that one instant had passed?" In being designated "nameless," this relation—unlike those other terms ("secret burden," "jiggered") whose namelessness remains implicit—ceases to be so: the novel of course finally can name it, denominating this uncanniness *maternity*. And as soon as namelessness is articulable, it has consequences in the plot.

Pip at last lights upon the "one link of association" that confirms the affiliation he suspects: having witnessed "the action of Estella's fingers as they worked" at knitting, he then finds "a certain action of [Molly's] fingers as she spoke arrested my attention. . . . The action of her fingers was like the action of knitting. . . . Surely, I had seen exactly such eyes and such hands, on a memorable occasion very lately! . . . I had passed by a chance swift from Estella's name to the fingers with their knitting action, and the attentive eyes. And I felt absolutely certain that this woman was Estella's mother." More surprising than the revelation of Molly as Estella's mother is the suggestion that Pip could establish that relationship based on the appearance of their hands—for other that this "action of knitting," they have nothing common. The very attempt to align these two sets of hands by force of uncanny conjunction only points up the antithesis between them: Molly's are marked while Estella's are blank; Molly's signify (even if what they designate is sexuality held in check) while Estella's do not. For Estella is so insistently the object of erotic denotation that her depiction virtually evacuates the connotative register in which we have located sexuality elsewhere in the novel.

The link to Molly persists in interfering with Estella's appropriateness as Pip's amorous desideratum, but the novel sufficiently manages this taint to keep it from tarnishing the daughter even as it continually condemns the mother. In a rare moment of offering advice, Jaggers discourages Pip from revealing Estella's pedigree, arguing, "'Add the case that you had loved her, Pip, and had made her the subject of those "poor dreams" . . . then I tell you that you had better—and would much sooner when you had thought well of it—chop off that bandaged left hand of yours with your bandaged right hand, and then pass the chopper on to Wemmick there, to cut *that* off too.'" For Pip "to establish her parentage" would be "to drag her back to disgrace," and consequently to annihilate his own "dreams"; in Jaggers's image, it would amount to amputation—or, by the logic of hands in the novel, castration. This exposure would associate Estella with Molly, whose brutally inscribed flesh has always engendered castration anxiety; the Estella whom Jaggers counsels Pip not to reveal is thus in a true sense Molly's daughter—one with fantastically disabling sexual powers.

Pip of course resists the impulse to disclose Estella's origins, and in so doing he both protects her from "disgrace" and saves himself from the threat of dismemberment. In fact, Estella has never seemed particularly dangerous, for while her mother is perpetually and actively tamed, Estella is so almost by definition. Her irascible demeanor, and the sexual frigidity that accompanies it, have less to do with serving her own desires than with her fashioning as a suitably impossible object for the male characters captivated by her looks. To the extent that Estella appears as a desiring subject, she does so as the "mere puppet" of her guardian, Miss Havisham; and as if to ensure that the willfulness evident in her aggressive passivity will be utterly disarmed, she receives a decisive pummeling at the hands of her husband, Drummle. Unlike those of the other female characters we have considered, Estella's hands are virtually maintenance-free; there is little of interest to say about them, except that little is said of them. Since she signals the overt representation of the subject's desire, Estella's appearances in the narrative obviate the necessity for sex appeal to reside wholly in the linguistic timbre. As if to amplify the silence of her own desire, Estella is shown simply to have a "white hand"; and although Pip can fondle it, hers is possibly the least erogenous hand in the book:

> "I am beholden to you as the cause of [Miss Havisham's relatives] being so busy and so mean in vain, and there is my hand upon it."
>
> As she gave it me playfully—for her darker mood had been but momentary—I held it and put it to my lips. "You ridiculous boy," said Estella, "will you never take warning? Or do you kiss my hand in the same spirit in which I once let you kiss my cheek?"
>
> "What spirit was that?" said I.
>
> " . . . A spirit of contempt for the fawners and plotters."
>
> "If I say yes, may I kiss the cheek again?"
>
> "You should have asked before you touched the hand. But, yes, if you like."
>
> I leaned down, and her calm face was like a statue's.

Estella succeeds as Pip's proper erotic object by the very thoroughness of her deeroticization in the narrative; she does not simply represent the refusal ordinarily requisite to provoke desire but is *constitutively phantasmatic*. Though we are meant to register Pip's arousal at the alluring sight of her, the narrative voice—otherwise so rich in provocative periphrasis—becomes laryngitic around her "beauty," relying on such tropes as "indescribable majesty and . . . indescribable charm." While the novel elsewhere registers eroticism in a combination of denotative refusal and connotative titillation, at the points of Pip's greatest official erotic interest, these strategies are reversed: in asserting *fortissimo* Pip's desire for Estella, the narrative need no longer marshal its battery of *sotto voce* techniques. At the moment desire's tale can be told, the narrative modulates into abstract diction, abandoning all of its prior engagement with corporeality: "She was so much changed, was so much more beautiful, so much more womanly, in all things winning admiration had made such wonderful advance, that I seemed to have made none."

For those who take the singular voicing *in* the plot of Pip's feelings for Estella to indicate the text's only genuine eroticism, the novel reads as a conventional romance. Such readers, however, are obliged to account for the fact that, even in its famously revised ending, *Great Expectations* resists bringing about the usual novelistic resolution in matrimony. As though to clear the space necessary for sanctioned, sanctified heterosexual romance, male homoeroticism is finally repudiated and female subjectivity thoroughly thwarted; yet we are left wondering why, despite these preparations, the romance plot is not more emphatically accomplished. One might, of course, point to the final version of the novel's ending, where Pip records the sensation of "what [he] had never felt before . . . the friendly touch of the once insensible hand." If the novel does, as Bulwer Lytton wished, conclude in happy domesticity, then its last sentence—"I took her hand in mine, and we went out of the ruined place . . . "—would provide a coherent resolution for its manual thematics. Yet the suspended animation entailed not only by the preservation of the original ending but by the ambiguity of the final version itself ("I saw no shadow of another parting from her") makes so smug a termination precarious. Despite critical attestations of its plot's "perfection," the fact that the story is waylaid *before* the threshold has left readers notoriously unsettled about its ultimate outcome.

Why should a novel with such copious erotic investments finally fail to resolve the most basic romance plot? One answer is that its strategies for regulating the vagaries of sexual desire simply prove *too* effective: they discipline all sexuality, even the most orthodox, quite out of existence. Not only are female domination, male homosexuality, onanism, and sadomasochism eliminated, but genitally oriented, maritally legitimated heterosexual monogamy itself comes to seem impossible. Though the novel entertains a range of sexual designations, exchanges, developments, and diffusions, the sexual hegemony in which it issues becomes so powerful as finally to suspend not only that order's own ideal—institutionalized heterosexual monogamy—but anything that exceeds the fantasy of the solitary subject.

Yet despite the apparent elimination of all erotic possibilities, this sole remainder—the solitary imagination—suggests that bodily self-regulation may generate its own rewards. For even as the novel inculcates lessons about sexual continence in its audience, it agitates and incorporates the erotogenic pleasures of solitary reading. Indeed, the very irresolution of the ending offers an alternative to erotic abjuration, one that animates the oscillation between the hegemony of the marriage plot and the violence of its refusal. Rather than resolving all the previous travails of hands through the story, the novel's ultimate ambivalence may instead reinscribe the mode of sexual deferral by which it has operated from the first: in the manner of an imaginary object held perpetually at bay by autoerotic reverie, its eroticism can persist precisely by being suspended as undecidable. Just as Estella can never be more to Pip than a "poor dream"—the object of solitary sexual fantasy—so the residum of the novel's ending finally demonstrates the sustainability, rather than the complete evacuation, of the masturbatory thematic that has mobilized its eroticism throughout. The ambiguity of the ending thus accomplishes a shift in the location of the novel's erotics that I have already suggested: in its finality it extinguishes the evocative narration through which sexuality has been connoted; but in the irresolution of its plot—its denotative practice—it now preserves those concerns as strictly undecidable. Even as it draws to an end, the novel resituates masturbation—sustains it, that is to say, by refusing closure. The originary sexuality that enables the novel's flood of erotic potentials, masturbation also serves as the remainder left behind when all other possibilities have been forsworn.

EDWIN M. EIGNER

The Absent Clown in Great Expectations

"The two endings of *Great Expectations*," as Edgar Rosenberg notes in a recent issue of *Dickens Studies Annual*, "have generated enough talk in the last thirty years to call for some sort of moratorium." It is a vain hope. The questions raised are so compelling and of such significance to Dickens studies that even those of us whom Rosenberg pleasantly refers to as "the 100-odd commentators (hyphen optional) who have specifically addressed themselves to the double ending" can hardly be expected to be satisfied with only one go at it. In my own previous contribution, I suggested that Bulwer-Lytton would have recommended the change from the originally planned and already drafted unhappy ending because he believed such a conclusion would be psychologically damaging to its readers, who had been encouraged to identify closely with the hero through more than eight months of weekly serial publication. I would also maintain that Dickens was prepared to take such advice so readily because it expressed an aesthetic of his own. Dickens had himself been struggling through from pessimistic premises to triumphantly optimistic conclusions from the very beginning of his career. The recognition of this fact is what make it difficult for me at least to stay silent on the business of the endings, for it was the first time in a quarter-century of writing inspiriting fiction that Dickens had even thought to deny his romantic male hero the conventionally happy ending of undisillusioned comedy.

From *Dickens Studies Annual: Essays on Victorian Fiction* 11. © 1983 AMS Press Inc.

It is true that Dickens had guillotined a hero to death just two years earlier, but Sydney Carton of *A Tale of Two Cities* is anyway, as we shall see later on, not of the class of Dickens heroes who ever gets the girl. It is also true the Dickens had permitted the death of Little Nell and that he had condemned the heroine of *Hard Times* to live childlessly and without a suitable second marriage. But female characters in Dickens, since they are frequently more symbolic than real, seldom invite the kind of reader identification the Pip and his many predecessors do.

Faced with the anomaly of an unhappy ending for the hero of *Great Expectations*, critics have been asking the question: "What went wrong?" And the most frequent answer has been that Dickens' vision gradually darkened and his sense of personal guilt deepened in his later novels until in this one he was no longer capable, at least on a first try, of pulling the tired old rabbit out of the hat. I think, however, that from as early as *Oliver Twist* his vision had been a dark one, and that his heroes had always had a sufficient load of guilt to deal with. Pip's guilt, for instance, is not significantly greater than that of say, David Copperfield, who introduced the seducing serpent into the closest thing he had ever known to Eden, and who wished his first wife to death because she did not suit him. Yet Dickens had always before been able to come up with the magic when he needed it. I should like, therefore, to turn the usual question around. Instead of asking "What goes wrong in *Great Expectations*" or "How has the problem become more serious?" I should like to ask "What doesn't go right this time?" or "What ingredient is missing here from the solution?"

But before we can get to either of these questions, we shall have to take leave of *Great Expectations* for some time so that we can try to discover the nature of the magic which produced the happy endings in the previous works and where it came from. And since *Great Expectations* is generally regarded a *Bildungsroman*, we shall begin with Dickens' first effort in that genre, *Nicholas Nickleby*, a novel written when the author was supposedly as full of self-confidence as in 1861 he was reputedly full of doubts. In the past two years, his first five books, including two novels, had been or were being published, and he had been named editor of an important new monthly magazine. He had married and was supporting an extended family, including his ne'er-do-well parents. It was a moment, perhaps, for a twenty-five-year-old success to write a book about "making it."

The year in which *Nicholas Nickleby* was begun, 1838, was also the right time in the history of English fiction for the writing of a *Bildungsroman*. Steven Marcus has argued from internal evidence, that Dickens had read Carlyle's *Sartor Resartus* before he began writing *Oliver Twist*. If not, then he is likely to have encountered it when it came out in book form for the first time in England during the summer of 1838, for now Carlyle had published *The French Revolution* and was already something of a celebrity. Eighteen-thirty-eight was also the year of *Alice*, the second part of Edward Bulwer's early *Bildungsroman*. The first part, *Ernest Maltravers*, had been published the year before and speedily acquired by Dickens from his friend, John Forster. Bulwer was at this time the most consistently popular serious novelist in England, and Dickens was already paying the elder writer the compliment of writing *Oliver Twist* in the genre of the Newgate Novel, established by Bulwer at the beginning of the decade.

Both *Sartor* and *Maltravers-Alice* were obviously *Bildungsromane* in the German tradition, rather than traditional English novels of personal development, and both authors made it plain that they had been influenced by *Wilhelm Meister*. Bulwer wrote in a Preface to *Ernest Maltravers* that he "left it easy to be seen that I am indebted to Goethe's *Wilhelm Meister*," and Carlyle had, of course, translated the work into English in the previous decade.

The importance of the influence on Dickens of these Goethean *Bildungsromane* by Carlyle and Bulwer is that they would have encouraged him to apply mystical solutions to experiential or realistic problems. The subtitle of Bulwer's *Alice* is *The Mysteries*; Carlyle's hero is saved by a vision; just as Wilhelm Meister himself ultimately achieves his harmonious development through a mystical initiation. I cannot demonstrate that Dickens read *Wilhelm Meister* at this time, but I suspect he did, not only because Goethe was being so highly recommended to him, but because a couple of months after the 1838 book publication of *Sartor Resartus*, Dickens' Nicholas Nickleby, as Marcus also points out, in fairly obvious imitation of Goethe's hero, became a member of a provincial theatrical company.

The episode in *Wilhelm Meister* is interesting for its famous digression on *Hamlet* and full of significance for the rest of the story; in *Nicholas Nickleby* it is hilarious and, as I shall be arguing, it forms the foundation of the structure not only for the remainder of this novel but for the rest of Dickens, as well. Nicholas leaves Vincent Crummle's theatrical company in order to rescue his sister from a situation taken directly from the popular Victorian stage: Kate's honor is being compromised by their wicked and greedy uncle, who is using her as sexual bait to entrap dissolute noblemen into his money-lending schemes. And, once this melodrama has been solved through Nicholas's theatrical heroics, the novel almost immediately reestablishes itself as a Regency Christmas or Easter pantomime.

Since it is the pantomime which, as I believe, provides the magical solutions in *Nicholas Nickleby* and the subsequent novels of Dickens, and since I intend ultimately to explain the unhappy ending of *Great Expectations* by showing how and explaining why that work is defective as a pantomime,

I must pause here to establish Dickens' interest in this theatrical genre and to give some idea of what a pantomime was in Dickens' imagination.

Dickens' interest in the legitimate theatre, especially at this time in his career, hardly needs to be documented again. Suffice it to say that he nearly became an actor and that part of the accomplishment of the amazing two years just passed had been the production of three of his plays. Pantomime, however, was sub-theatrical. Allardyce Nicoll gives the nineteenth-century version of it only a paragraph in his exhaustive *A History of English Drama, 1660–1900*, and it was not held in much better repute during Dickens' time. In 1841 the critic of the *Theatrical Inquisitor* wrote this of the genre:

> It can hardly be expected that we should enter into a detail of the disgraceful mummeries which custom has sanctioned. The dignity of criticism would be degraded, and we shall rather content ourselves with entering into a decided though unavailing protest against what we consider as an insult to the common understanding of mankind. Pantomimes are a farrago of nonsense suited only to the vulgar and illiterate.

And, indeed, Dickens, himself, seems to have regarded the pantomime as a sort of theatrical ash heap, for a number of his not very hopeful characters end up in it, beginning with the pathetic dying clown in the first number of *Pickwick Papers* and ending with Wopsle of *Great Expectations*.

Nevertheless, the pantomime seems always to have exercised a powerful fascination on Dickens. References to it occur in a number of his novels; he wrote articles on the subject in the years before both *Nicholas Nickleby* and *Great Expectations*; and in 1855 he staged a family production of a James Robinson Planché Christmas pantomime in his own home. Most important, in 1837 he edited, actually he rewrote, the *Memoirs of Joseph Grimaldi*, the great clown who was to the pantomime and, according to some commentators, to the Regency Theatre in general, what Charlie Chaplin was to silent film and twentieth-century drama.

The two articles just mentioned give some understanding of what Dickens saw in the pantomime. In 1837 he wrote:

> Before we plunge headlong into this paper, let us at once confess to a fondness for pantomimes—to a gentle sympathy with clowns and pantaloons—to an unqualified admiration of harlequins and columbines. . . . We revel in pantomimes . . . because . . . a pantomime is to us, a mirror of life; nay more, we maintain that it is so to audiences generally, although they are

not aware of it, and that this very circumstance is the secret cause of their amusement and delight.

Twenty-three years later, in the second article, he went on to say that the pantomime is therefore more effective than a sermon as a moral teacher. Attending a pantomime at a cheap theatre, he is

> pleased to observe Virtue quite as triumphant as she usually is out of doors, and indeed I thought rather more so. We all agreed (for the time) that honesty was the best policy, and we were as hard as iron upon Vice, and we wouldn't hear of Villainy getting on in the world—no, not upon any consideration whatever.

The dramatic form which Dickens revelled in and admired so bore practically no resemblance to the pantomimes which are performed in English theatres these days around Christmastime. Indeed the pantomime of his childhood imagination, the Regency pantomime of Joseph Grimaldi, was already beginning to change beyond recognition in the 1830s. The pantomimes Dickens remembered were in two parts. The "opening" combines a mythological narrative or fairy tale with a simple love story in which, usually, an avaricious old man tried to force his daughter to marry an unacceptable but wealthy suitor instead of the young man she obviously preferred. This was the business of a few very brief and slackly written scenes. When things looked hopeless for the lovers, there appeared a benevolent spirit—Mother Goose, Friar Bacon, the Spirit of Adventure, the Fairy Fantassina, etc.—who converted them into Harlequin and Columbine. The father was also transformed into an aged Pantaloon and the unacceptable suitor into one of two characters, Clown or Lover. If into the latter, then Clown was created from one of the other characters around the father, most frequently from his incompetent and clumsy servant. Now the main business of the evening began, the Harlequinade, which consisted of an hour or more of comic songs, farce ballet, and slapstick mime, in which Harlequin pursued Columbine and the others pursued Harlequin. The problems were the same as in the "opening," but now the old power structure has been wonderfully turned on its head because Pantaloon, hampered by the clumsiness or the contrivance of Clown, was constantly eluded by the youthfully agile Harlequin, who was aided, moreover, by a psychologically suggestive magic bat, capable of immobilizing his pursuers or altering any circumstances in which he found himself trapped. When, at length, Harlequin won Columbine, he carelessly lost the magic bat to

Pantaloon or Clown and needed to be rescued one more time by the Benevolent Spirit, who, of course, never failed to appear.

Dickens was attracted to this form of drama for a combination of reasons: for one thing, pantomime, like his own novels, intertwined fairy tales with more realistic though still romantic love plots; for another thing, it changed genres abruptly; and, most significantly, it resolved seemingly irresolvable situations by means of magic. Thus, as soon as the melodramatic interlude is over in *Nicholas Nickleby*, a pantomime "opening" establishes itself: the hero sees and falls hopelessly in love with a young girl whose weak and selfish father has promised her to a septuagenarian lecher, the miserly partner of Nicholas's wicked uncle. There is also a clownish servant, Newman Noggs, and *twin* Benevolent Spirits, the Cherryble brothers.

The Benevolent Spirits of *Nicholas Nickleby* were strongly criticized as "unrealistic," and so Dickens dropped or disguised this element in most future works, or he presented them without apology as supernatural figures, as in the Christmas Books; but the heroines of the subsequent novels are almost always accompanied by the other four: a weak or somehow defective parent or guardian, a wicked and/or lustful suitor, Harlequin, whom Dickens described as just an ordinary man "to be found in no particular walk or degree, on whom a certain station, or particular conjunction of circumstances, confers the magic wand," and finally, almost extraneously, the clownish servant. Newman Noggs of *Nicholas Nickleby* is described as

> A tall man of middle-age with two goggle eyes whereof one was a fixture, a rubicund nose, a cadaverous face, and a suit of clothes (if the term be allowable when they suited him not at all) much worse for wear, very much too small, and placed upon such a short allowance of buttons that it was quite marvellous how he contrived to keep them on . . . [He] rubbed his hands slowly over each other, cracking the joints of his fingers, and squeezing them into all possible distortions. The incessant performance of this routine on every occasion, and the communication of a fixed and rigid look to his unaffected eye, so as to make it uniform with the other, and to render it impossible for anybody to determine where or at what he was looking were two among the numerous peculiarities of Mr. Noggs.

This unprepossessing character, the clownish servant, is, I have become convinced, the most powerful force for redemption in Dickens' imagination. In the Dickens pantomime he is Columbine's magic rescuer. After *Nicholas*

Nickleby, moreover, he is often her uncritical admirer or hopelessly unrequited lover: Tom Pinch of *Martin Chuzzlewit*, Mr. Toots of *Dombey and Son*, Micawber of *David Copperfield*, Guppy of *Bleak House*, John Chivery of *Little Dorrit*, Sydney Carton of *A Tale of Two Cities*. He is a drunk or a profligate or an imbecile; at best he is only simple or foolish. Yet without him, it seems there is no happy ending. When Dick Swiveller becomes distracted with the Marchioness, Little Nell dies, and when the clownish or dissipated servant happened to be female, as in *Hard Times*, or the Little Em'ly plot of *David Copperfield*, or the Edith plot of *Dombey and Son*, the heroine is condemned to remain childless and unmarried. It is a character, obviously, of extreme power. Why is he so important to Dickens, and where did he derive his amazing magic?

To answer these questions, we must, I believe, return to Christmas and Easter pantomimes from which the clownish, secret lover or worshipper was taken. Clown was the only English pantomime figure who did not come directly from the Italian *commedia dell'arte*, but since he was, like the others, an improvised character, he shared their tendency to change and develop according to the qualities of the important actors who impersonated him. In the eighteenth century, Clown was the English rustic Clodpoll, and he did not become an important figure in the pantomime until Signor Giuseppi Grimaldi, the father of Joseph Grimaldi, combined him with the sad clown, Pierrot, who is vainly and blunderingly in love with Columbine. The elder, or rather, the eldest Grimaldi, for there were ultimately to be three generations of them, was known as "the rough and tumble Pierrot," and he made Clown into the most prominent character in the pantomime.

His son, Joseph Grimaldi, completed the transformation of the role and revolutionized both the pantomime and British slapstick comedy. As Richard Findlater writes,

> [Joseph Grimaldi] changed Pantaloon's servant—who had sometimes been Pierrot, but was more often a rustic booby or (synonymously) a clown—into the prime mover of the pantomime. . . . In a formalized white mask of bismouth make-up with bright rouged triangles on his cheeks, wearing a comic wig (bald-pate or blue-crested, or oddly tufted) and a caricature livery of vividly ornamental shirt, tunic and baggy breeches, Clown persecuted Pantaloon, lusted after Columbine, guzzled on a grand scale, stole and was robbed, cheated and was gulled, beat people up, pushed them over, tripped them up, and was himself mercilessly thrashed, kicked and cudgelled.

David Mayer, the best historian of the Regency pantomime, writes that Grimaldi's Clown

> has a buoyancy, a barely suppressed impudence and irreverence that encouraged pantomime audiences to share vicariously, and willingly condone his seeming impatience with manners, his mocking of class distinctions, his disregard for propriety, and his absolute disrespect for authority. If Clown had fixed traits, they were all ones that mocked conventions and exposed social habits pretending to morality or self-conscious graciousness. He rebelled against stuffiness and tradition and did what others wished to do but never dared. If Clown encountered another's property he would break it if fragile, wear it if portable, paint it or deface it if immovable. If there was a woman, old or young, he would make advances; if there was food he would eat it gluttonously; if the food were someone else's he would first steal it. The law held terror for him only when he was in danger of being caught. He was a happy criminal who knew neither shame nor guilt nor repentance. He was a mimic, a coward, a lazy rascal, an energetic imposter. He humiliated the mighty, the cruel, the pretentious, and the over-bearing, and his own encounters with pain and embarrassment were noisy, ludicrous, and brief.

Findlater calls him "a Cockney incarnation of the Saturnalian spirit; a beloved criminal, free from guilt, shame, compunction, or reverence for age, class or property."

As might be expected, such a character could not long remain Pantaloon's tool, however clumsy, in the battle against the young people. In fact, he is the natural enemy of Pantaloon, who represents the establishment, and while Clown may be forced to live as Pantaloon's servant, he can be expected to undermine his master in every imaginable way. A. E. Wilson writes of pantomimes in which Clown takes a bribe from Harlequin to aid in Columbine's escape and then frustrates Pantaloon's pursuit; pretending to help the old man, he "constantly plays cruel tricks on him and puts him on the wrong scent."

The magnificent collections of published and unpublished pantomimes at the Huntington Library clearly demonstrate Clown's progressive liberation from Pantaloon during the course of Joseph Grimaldi's career. ΔΙΟΝΥΣΙΑ ΤΡΙΕΤΗΡΙΚΑ, or *Harlequin Bacchus* (1805) shows Clown as "a blundering zany." In *Harlequin in His Element*, a Grimaldi vehicle of 1807,

Clown does not need to be bribed. He picks his master Pantaloon's pockets in one scene, and in another he "sweeps his stick around, breaks Guardian's [Pantaloon's] shins, and knocks him down—Clown discovers his mistake, pretends to cry, but laughs aside." In *Harlequin and Fortunio* (1815), the ancestor of the Planché pantomime Dickens staged in his home forty years later, Grimaldi as Clown performed his most heroic acts of eating and drinking and was thus able to defeat the antagonist and become "Champion of the Fair in Distress." The Clown in *Harlequin and Friar Bacon* (1820) was no longer even in Pantaloon's employ; Grimaldi here was the servant of the Benevolent Spirit and is thus the old man's enemy from the outset. And in another pantomime of the same year, *Harlequin and Cinderella*, Grimaldi played the servant Pedro, hopelessly in love with the heroine and desperately opposed to her persecutors.

There is another, more personal or psychological reason which, I believe, made the Clown figure vital to Dickens' imagination. *Nicholas Nickleby* has long been understood as the book in which the author made defensive sport of his own scatterbrained mother. And there is also, of course, a more serious side to the portrait. When Ralph Nickleby is trying to make a prostitute of his niece, Mrs. Nickleby, the girl's mother, steadfastly and selfishly refuses to see the threatening danger and degradation. In much the same way Dickens understood that his own mother had closed her eyes to his deep humiliation as a laboring hind at Warren's Blacking. As Dickens wrote in his posthumously published memoir, "I never afterwards forgot, I shall never forget, I never can forget, that my mother was warm for my being sent back." The portrait of Mrs. Nickleby is Dickens' supremely comic indictment of his mother's unforgiven selfishness. Micawber of *David Copperfield* is understood to be Dickens' similar tribute to his ne'er-do-well and pretentious father, and to his part in the same episode from the author's youth, but my assertion that Micawber, Swiveller, Newman Noggs and the others are all versions of a single character, suggests that John Dickens got into his son's novels much earlier; that he got into them, indeed, at the same time as his wife did, in *Nicholas Nickleby*.

John Forster notes a circumstance which argues a connection in Dickens' imagination between the pantomime Clown figure of the novels and the author's father. Reporting on Dickens' work with the manuscript of *Memoirs of Joseph Grimaldi*, Forster mentions that "Except for the Preface he did not write a line of this biography, such modifications or additions as he made having been dictated by him to his father; whom I often found in exalted enjoyment of the office of amanuensis." If so, imagine the satisfaction self-righteous young Charles got by dictating the following sentences to his neglectful father:

> [Grimaldi] devoted the whole of his leisure time to the society and improvement of his son. As he could not bear to part with him, and was wholly unable to make up his mind to send him to any great boarding school, he was partly educated at the same school at which his father had been a pupil and partly by masters who attended him at home. The father appears to have bestowed great and praiseworthy care upon his education.

Or picture a self-satisfied Dickens dictating these words to the irresponsible parent whose debts he was constantly being required to pay:

> [Grimaldi's success} shows that industry and perseverance of Grimaldi, and the ease with which, by the exercise of these qualities, a very young person may overcome all the disadvantages and temptations incidental to the most precarious walk of a most precarious pursuit and become a useful and respectable member of society.

As a book about the theater, *Memoirs of Joseph Grimaldi* is a constant disappointment. Dickens must have had practically nothing to begin with, not even Grimaldi's original manuscript, but a much shortened rewrite by the hack, Egerton Wilks, who obviously did his best to convert Grimaldi's life into a sort of Tom and Jerry *Life in London*. So little of the actor Grimaldi seems left that one critic "wonders whether Dickens is reporting Grimaldi or creating him." But what is clearly remarkable in Dickens' version of the *Memoirs* and what is most Dickensian, as well, are the relations between parents and children. Joseph's father is described as a neurotic and brutal monster, constantly brooding on his death, beating his children, and conjuring up elaborate tests of their love for him. Joseph Jr., on whom, as we have seen, the actor lavished such care and love, and about whom he entertained great hopes, threw away the successful career in the theater his loving father had fashioned for him and died a very young man. Kathleen Tillotson speculates that the death ·of the drunken clown, told in "The Stroller's Tale" in *Pickwick Papers*, "may be modeled after J. S. Grimaldi, who died of delirium tremens." If so, then it is perhaps significant that Dickens gave *his* first dissipated clown the first name of his own father.

Dickens saw Joseph Grimaldi himself, the man and not the character he portrayed, as "remarkably temperate," although not really capable of keeping the money he earned. "He was a man of the most childlike simplicity. . . . He was innocent of all caution in worldly matters." Among Clown-rescuers in Dickens, he most resembles, I believe, Tom Pinch of *Martin Chuzzlewit*, who innocently persists in his admiration for Pecksniff, the Pantaloon of the story, until Mary, the Columbine, tells him of the hypocrite's attempted seduction of her. Tom is, like Grimaldi, a much more industrious worker than John Dickens was, but his is also one who did not know very well how to take care of himself. Like all the other Clowns, however, he is capable of turning the entire plot around.

The proper work to test out some of the foregoing ideas is *David Copperfield*, not only because of the long-acknowledged connection between Micawber and Dickens' father, or because *Copperfield* is the first of Dickens' fictionally autobiographical *Bildungsromane*, or even because it is, I believe, the first novel of Dickens in which the hero actually attends a pantomime (Chapter 19), but also because it contains four heroines, three of whom have full pantomime constellations of attendant male characters. Dora, the fourth heroine, has no father after the first few chapters in which she appears, no wicked or lustful seducer, and no Clown-rescuer. As a result, perhaps, she is very short-lived. The other heroines fare better.

Little Em'ly has a strong figure in Daniel Peggotty and a powerful seducer in James Steerforth. The romantic lover, Ham, perhaps because he is only a stand-in for David, would obviously have been wrong for her even without Sterrforth's interference. Em'ly accepted him, and thus began her desperation, only to please Mr. Peggotty, who, like many of the parent figures, is thus the source of the trouble, albeit the innocent source. Em'ly is saved by the most dissipated and seemingly least consequential character in the novel, the prostitute Martha, and the result of such a rescue by a female, as noted before, is a not unhappy but a nevertheless childless spinsterhood.

Annie Strong's parental liability is her mother, who selfishly engineered Annie's marriage to the aged Dr. Strong. When Strong turns out ironically to be Annie's romantic lover, Mrs. Markleham promotes marital discord and even encourages a seduction by Annie's worthless cousin, Jack Maldon. There results a serious misunderstanding between husband and wife, which is averted only through the interference of Mr. Dick, the clownish, mild lunatic.

Of course, the principal heroine of *David Copperfield* is Agnes, who has a perfect romantic lover in David, although he does not know it for some time, and a most imperfect, though loving father in Mr. Wickfield. It is the situation in *Nicholas Nickleby* all over again, as the weakness and self-indulgence of the father threaten to deliver the dutiful daughter into the skinny and lascivious arms of Pantaloon, this time Uriah Heep. David cannot do anything about it; he is only a Harlequin. But once again Pantaloon's abject servant, whom Uriah calls "a dissipated fellow, as all the world knows" (Chapter 52) has a strong feeling of admiration for the heroine:

> "Miss Wickfield," said Mr. Micawber now turning red, "is, as she always is, a pattern, and a bright example. My dear Copperfield, she is the only starry spot in a miserable existence. My respect for that young lady, my admiration for her character, my devotion to her for her love and truth, and goodness!"

And a few episodes later, on one of the most dramatic magic shows in all of Dickens, he explodes Heep to save his mistress.

So it always happens in Dickens. Harlequin's lady-love, made vulnerable by her parent, has to be rescued from the wicked seducer by the saturnalian energy of her inept or dissipated, clownish admirer. And we come back, therefore, to the question we started with. Why does this not happen in *Great Expectations*? And the question is not only "How come Pip does not get Estella in the original ending, but why does Dickens allow Estella to fall into the spidery arms of Bentley Drummle even for a moment?"

Well, for one thing, John Dickens died five months after the conclusion of *David Copperfield*, and in the most uncomical manner imaginable, following unsuccessful emergency surgery, performed without chloroform, for a bladder disease. Dickens called it "the most terrible operation known in surgery," and he described the room in which he saw his father immediately afterwards as "a slaughter house of blood." As Robert Newsom explains, the operation not only mutilated Dickens' father, it literally unsexed him by making a vagina-like "incision between the anus and the scrotum." John Dickens remained in his son's creative imagination thereafter, but his characteristics seemed no longer suitable for the sexually irrepressible and energetic clown figure. He has been recognized instead as John Jarndyce of *Bleak House* and William Dorrit of *Little Dorrit*.

In the novels after *David Copperfield*, the Clown figure does not disappear, but there is a marked difference in him. Guppy in *Bleak House* (1852–53) plays the Clown's part, discovering the resemblance between Esther and Lady Dedlock and thus facilitating the mother's significant acknowledgement of her daughter, but he does not act disinterestedly as the others do; rather he is trying, with his detective work, to win her. In *Hard Times* (1854), the real Clown runs away in the opening chapters, and his part must be played by his daughter, Sissy Jupe, with all the usual consequences to the heroine for having been rescued by a female. In *Little Dorrit* (1855–57) Young John Chivery, the son of the turnkey at the Marchalsea Prison, is a suitably ridiculous figure, but the strength of his unrequited love for Amy undercuts the comedy of his contemplated suicides and the sentimental epitaphs he composes for himself. There is, moreover, a large measure of self-sacrifice involved when he acts to bring Arthur and Amy together at the conclusion. And with Sydney Carton of *A Tale of Two Cities*, although it is easy enough to recognize in him the same wasteful drunkenness and the same enslavement to the character who represents the novel's evil, which were immediately apparent in such previous Dickensian Clowns as Nogg, Swiveller, and Micawber, there is no comedy at all either in his dissipation or in his self-sacrificing rescue of the heroine. And for the first time readers of Dickens wondered if the heroine had not chosen the wrong lover.

I suspect it is the death of Sydney Carton, even more than the death of John Dickens, which finished off the Clown and made him unavailable for use in *Great Expectations* (1860–61). That death had been building throughout the decade and is so powerful an act of the imagination that it could not be easily undone. Moreover, in *A Tale of Two Cities*, the Clown is for the first time the double Harlequin, with whom Dickens was accustomed to identify, so that Carton's death must have felt something like a suicide for the author.

Reading the first number on December 1, 1860, experienced Dickens watchers might have spotted Joe Gargery as the Clown. Even the name is suggestive, for it had by this time become customary to call English clowns Joey, after Grimaldi. And in the thirty-fifth number, as he is nursing Pip through his delirium, Joe's face, like that of a pantomime character, undergoes "all kinds of extraordinary transformations" beneficial to Pip's redemption. But Joe has too much dignity to get involved with the Satis House world, and cannot therefore be expected to rescue Estella, as well.

In the second weekly number, Wopsle appears, speaking just the right sort of pretentious diction. And, indeed, before the novel is over, he becomes not only a Clown but even a Benevolent Spirit in a real pantomime which Pip attends. Moreover, the kind of information he gives Pip after this performance—that Compeyson is abroad—is just the sort of revelation we expect to get from the Clown in Dickens. Unfortunately, though, it also has no relation to Estella.

The most promising Clown in *Great Expectations* is Wemmick. He is properly eccentric, and he is, after all, Jaggers' servant; and while Jaggers is not himself the wicked or lustful lover of the novel, he does feel a strong interest in and an immediate affinity for the character who fills that role, Bentley Drummle, his fellow spider. Wemmick is, moreover, in a professional position to learn the sort of information which might prevent Estella's capitulation to Drummle. His first name is John, and he seems well enough disposed towards Pip to want to serve him.

On the other hand, Wemmick is hardly what we might call "a cockney embodiment of the Saturnalian spirit." He has a warm human nature, but he keeps it locked safely behind the moat in Walworth. In Little Britain, his place of business, he is man without sentiment. No one calls him John there. The compromise he has made, which is that of modern, urban man, preserves his own sanity; but it hardly makes him an enemy to hypocritical Pantaloon and the establishment he stands for. Applecarts are portable property, after all, only when you do not upset them, and as Wemmick says in the scene at Jaggers' office when his employer discovers he has an old father and pleasant and playful ways, "If I don't bring 'em here, what does it matter?" What, indeed?

But although there is no real help to be looked for from Wemmick, Dickens cannot help teasing us with him. Or perhaps he is teasing himself. At the end of the chapter in which Estella breaks the news to Pip that she intends to marry Drummle, and after Pip, having burst into tears, makes his way to his lodgings, the night porter hands him a note from Wemmick— "DON'T GO HOME." But the communication, it turns out, has nothing to do with Estella. In the succeeding chapters, Pip gives up reading the papers, so that he will not accidentally learn of the marriage. The news is ultimately broken to him by Jaggers, but in an ambiguous manner: "So, Pip! Our friend the spider . . . has played his cards. He has won the pool." And a few speeches later, after he *and* Wemmick speculate, to Pip's extreme pain, that Drummle may come to beat Estella, Jaggers drinks to "Mrs. Bentley Drummle." Still, neither we nor Pip know if Jaggers is announcing a marriage or only an engagement. There may still be time. Pip and Wemmick leave Jaggers' house and head towards the castle in Walworth. As usual, Wemmick's humanity begins to return, somewhat slowly this time, and he tells Pip the story of Molly, the murderess, and her child, who is of course Estella. Pip asks:

> "Do you remember the sex of the child?"
> "Said to have been a girl."
> "You have nothing more to say to me to-night?" [Pip asks]

> "Nothing," [Wemmick replies] "I got your letter and destroyed it. Nothing."
> We exchanged a cordial Good Night, and I went home, with new matter for my thoughts, though with no relief for the old."

And so there is to be no rescue.

In the last pages of the novel, Dickens desperately tried every mystical trick he could think of to absolve the hero's guilt and come out with a happy ending. Pip is put through a series of rigorous penitences: he is humiliated by poverty and, along with Magwitch, before the bar of justice. He even undergoes a number of ritual deaths: by sickness, by Orlick's violent hands, by water, and by fire. But it seems that nothing works in Dickens when the Clown's magic fails.

In December, 1860, when the writing of *Great Expectations* was still in its early stages, Dickens went to the theatre to see a pantomime. Bringing the dead back to life was a special feature of the pantomime, as Dickens had noted in an 1853 article in *Household Words*, but if Dickens was hoping to reanimate his Clown at this performance, he was disappointed. By this stage of its development or degeneration, the harlequinade element of the pantomime had been swallowed by the "opening," which sometimes lasted now for three hours or more. Moreover, neither Grimaldi or any of his great pupils, Tom Matthews or Jefferini, were still on the stage to play the Clown, whose magic had anyway disappeared along with the significance of the harlequinade, which was either kept on these days as a sort of afterpiece with no plot connection to what came before, or else dispensed with entirely. This was, indeed, a sorry age for an old magician. Dickens wrote that the pantomime he saw was "dull." An old pantomimist he met in the street after the performance told him, "There's no right feeling in it" anymore.

Sydney Carton's death in *A Tale of Two Cities* is presented as a Crucifixion. It should therefore have been followed by a resurrection. Here, perhaps for the first time, the inimitable Dickens showed himself weaker in imagination than his own Creator. Instead of three days, it took Dickens five years to reanimate his Clown-redeemer. When he did come up with Sloppy of *Our Mutual Friend*, who returns Silas Wegg to the ashes, it was only with the help of his supreme and most daring invention of a Benevolent Spirit, Mr. Boffin, the most powerful magician in all the novels, the most powerful magical figure, I believe, since Prospero. In the meantime, however, during those five years when the Clown was dead, his saturnalian energy and mystical power were missing, and Dickens could not, on his own, imagine a happy ending for *Great Expectations* and any real redemption or *Bildung* for that novel's guilty hero.

DAVID GERVAIS

The Prose and Poetry of Great Expectations

> By the wilderness of casks that I had walked on long ago, and
> on which the rain of years had fallen since. . . . I made my way to the
> ruined garden.
>
> Great Expectations, Chapter 49

It is not that the wine becomes thinner in Dickens' later comedy, nor that
its richness turns to a sediment, but laughter is put to different purposes. Its
bracing wildness is disciplined by art. If art is what we hope for from later
Dickens—from *Great Expectations* especially—we will see this as a good thing.

Twenty-two chapters into *Nicholas Nickleby*, Mr. Vincent Crummles
and his troupe of traveling players hijack the novel. The comedy they furnish
spills across the book as the main plot marks melodramatic time. The
theatrical humors expand like a concertina for a hundred pages or so. This
comedy is not without *point* though far less of it might have made Dickens'
point for him if that had been all his inspiration asked. But the diffuse
exuberance of his delight in the Crummles company is in itself a sufficient
theme for expression. When, in *Great Expectations*, Mr. Wopsle (or
Waldengarver) plays Hamlet, this comic buoyancy is still there but in a
carefully framed and muted fashion. Dickens is concerned not to let the fun
upset the mood of Pip's story. Wopsle's antics are not the glorious throwback
to the earlier comic largesse that Victorian readers pined for; what was mirth

From *Dickens Studies Annual: Essays on Victorian Fiction* 13. © 1984 AMS Press Inc.

in *Nickleby* now pinpoints a painfully uneasy consciousness of human self-deception, too near the bone for laughter to last long. Wopsle is very funny but the comedy feels more constrictive than exhilarating: our laughter is quenched by Pip's rueful, embarrassed smile. The end of laughter is significance; it is organized to that effect. Perhaps a better example of this—for Mr. Wopsle does have his slapstick side—would be Trabb's dreadful boy taunting Pip in his brand-new suit: "Don't know yah!" Such comedy concentrates our attention on what is essential to a general sense of Pip's "expectations." Trabb's boy's character only flowers to help Dickens make us understand Pip better. He is not an individual on the same liberal terms as, say, Miss Petowker from Drury Lane is.

This distinction between early and later Dickens will matter more or less depending upon what we choose to look for from the riches of Dickens' works. The present article is looking for their poetry. Its purpose is to ask how far they, or any great novels, can deserve the description "poetic," despite their prose medium. T. S. Eliot long ago remarked that a Dickens comic character—his example was Young Bailey—strikes us with the same poetic immediacy, a character in a phrase, that we find in Dante or Shakespeare. This idea has not been much developed, perhaps because it might make us think that the essentially poetic Dickens is not the weaver of the prison "symbol" in *Little Dorrit* but the creator of all those early comic figures who so freely express their own being without having it reined in by the ulterior motives of the author/artist. Artistic consciousness (not the same thing as art) plays only a small part in the creation of a Pecksniff. This is why thinking about what is poetic in a later novel like *Great Expectations* needs to begin with the early novels. There is no point in seeing *Great Expectations* in isolation as an entire and perfect chrysolite: it raises questions about all the other novels, and its very difference from many of them is precisely what obliges a critic to keep them always in mind when thinking about it. It may seem more obviously like a poem than they do, but to say so need not be to say that it represents the deepest poetic voice at Dickens' command. It may simply come closer, in the tristful harmony of its tone, to what the nineteenth century habitually thought of as making for the poetic.

I

Even readers who normally look askance at Dickens have been haunted by *Great Expectations*. They see it as his one assured "artistic success"—the other books being sprawling or shapeless by comparison. But why not approach the novel by the opposite route? Examine not what it has that the other novels lack; rather, explore those qualities which they possess in abundance but which, in its economy, *Great Expectations* measures out much more sparingly. It has never seemed wholly convincing that the majority of readers up to Chesterton were simply wrong to prefer the earlier Dickens. They had at least a case to put and they still do. By now, however, the pall of incense that we have inhaled from the critics of *Great Expectations* is so thick that it may even prevent us from breathing the scent of the rose itself. A symptom of this is that the novel is often praised by comparing it to other novelists, like George Eliot, with whom Dickens is normally felt to have little in common. Its unique beauty is put down to its "art" and the way is then open for the symbol-prospecting and the intellectual sleuthing after shipshape "themes" that bedevil modern Dickens criticism. With students, for example, it has become, in my experience, something of a sacred cow and a little less alive in consequence. This is why I propose to argue that its extraordinary subtlety and richness have their source in something deeper than either its "art" or its "themes" (through both of which we may too easily feel that we *know* what the novel does and says) and that, at times, these more conscious elements in it can impede and distract us from its true poetry.

To read *Great Expectations* is, first of all, to listen to it. It is the gravely lyrical tone that Dickens sustains in the pondering rhythms of Pip's voice that makes us so intensely susceptible to his experience. In no other nineteenth-century novel I can think of , except for *L'Education Sentimentale*, is narrative so musical. Yet if its cadences are essential to its power, they may also be inseparable from its limitations. Its incantatory rhythms, dying falls and beautifully turned sentences lodge in the mind. For example:

> I saw that the bride within the bridal dress had withered like
> the dress, and like the flowers, and had no brightness left but
> the brightness of her sunken eyes.

Such stately magic is not what we recall either from the early books or of the galvanic prose of *Bleak House* or *Our Mutual Friend*. None of them seeks to sustain for so long [or would if they could] the note of trancelike and meditative lassitude that informs what Graham Greene finely calls "Dickens' secret prose." In them, energy would have made off with half the controlled beauty of a recollection like the following, which, for all its mounting drama, seems to spring from some central tranquillity in Pip:

> Ours was the marsh country, down by the river, within, as the
> river wound, twenty miles of the sea. My first most vivid and
> broad impression of the identity of things, seems to me to have

been gained on a memorable raw afternoon towards evening. At such a time I found out for certain, that this bleak place overgrown with nettles was the churchyard; and that Philip Pirrip, late of this parish, and also Georgiana wife of the above, were dead and buried; and that Alexander, Bartholomew, Abraham, Tobias, and Roger, infant children of the aforesaid, were also dead and buried; and that the dark flat wilderness beyond the churchyard, intersected with dykes and mounds and gates, with scattered cattle feeding on it, was the marshes; and that the low leaden line beyond was the river; and that the distant savage lair from which the wind was rushing, was the sea; and that the small bundle of shivers growing afraid of it all and beginning to cry, was Pip.

Pip is then surprised by Magwitch ("Hold your noise!"); but even in the next paragraph, he is never jolted out of these delicately weighed rhythms which savor their own note of subdued drama ("and that . . . and that") and rich suggestiveness ("the low leaden line beyond," "the distant savage lair"). Within the drama of childhood grief that the narrator recalls, there is a less dramatic note, a solemn lingering pathos, almost a mournfulness, that, for its greater actuality, would remind us of elegiac poems like "Tears, Idle Tears" and "Dover Beach." This plangency is as much part of the spell the passage casts as is the mounting emotion of its repetitions. If it makes the prose seem deliberately less elastic than other late Dickensian prose, a new firmness and authority accrues from its slowness. The movingly delayed image of Pip as a "small bundle of shivers," for instance, is the touch of a writer who knows how to bide his time. Each detail in the passage is left to fill the mind at its own appropriate pace. Neither is this special sense we have of the mental depth of Pip's story to be put down to its being told by an introspective melancholic. If we think back to poor Arthur Clennam, watching the rose petals on the "river of time," we can see how surely Dickens avoids sentimental self-indulgence here. There is none of that listlessness (the obverse of Dickens' satiric violence and declamation) in the voice he finds for Pip. This voice, though, is not to be summed up; it strikes us as being like a part in a play that an actor has to discover how to interpret. For *Great Expectations* is one of the few novels whose prose can be read and reread as poems are, aloud. Every reading can disclose new suggestions in its music.

If this (or something like it) is the impression we get from a page of *Great Expectations*, what impression do we take from the earlier books? It is even harder to put one's finger on the sources of their comic strength, even if we can identify the fierce, raw-blooded tradition of Jonson, Hogarth, Fielding, and Smollett that nurtured it. Yet even Fielding stretches his comic canvas too tight on a frame of moral abstractions—Pride, Vanity, Affectation—to match Dickens' exuberant delight in the ridiculous and the bizarre. The dignity of eighteenth-century satire (Pope takes himself so much more seriously than do Rabelais and Molière) was incompatible with the Dickensian desire to make fun of life itself. Dickens could be unsubtle and browbeating as a satirist, but he was always blessedly free of the posture of noble spleen. To the lord of misrule who wrote *Pickwick*, nothing was immune from laughter, least of all fine sentiments. His humor is like a fountain, not a deadly jet; it is too overflowing to be trained in any one set moral purpose. Gloriously injudicious, fueled by equally huge stores of love and hate, its human relish for mischief saves it from seeming compulsive or devouring. Dickens breathed so naturally in this air of delighted disrespect for life that his comedy seems to liberate us from our habitual reserves and inhibitions, from that constant temptation to take ourselves seriously which so often stops us from being serious. His laughter has a power which vaults over any formal plan to instruct by pleasing and finds its moral wisdom in a blithe transcending of all moralizing. Dickens may make us think in terms of black and white, like Hogarth with his good and bad apprentices, but his blackness can comprehend Pecksniff's drunken advances to Mrs. Todgers, his whiteness, Mr. Pickwick getting hot under the collar. The comedy is more concerned to enact and embody moral qualities than to pass judgment on them. This is especially so with the early books, though their overt morality can be cruder; even with so brilliant a later comic character as Harold Skimpole we always feel more keenly that we are being asked to discriminate and judge.

In its irresistible flow of emotion, Dickens' early comedy shows an indirect affinity with something in tragedy. The copious hilarity hints that the young Dickens held a tragic expressiveness of emotion within his immense potential. The very bounciness of his "happy" endings suggests as much, for a strong imagination of possible happiness is as vital to tragedy as is the sense of pathos. Both modes find their resolution in a catharsis. An early reader of *Martin Chuzzlewit* could reasonably have speculated that anything tragic that Dickens might write later would be more likely to derive from the same sources as his comedy than from his simply seeing through the glib optimism on its surface. It follows, I believe, that any diminution in the flow of spirits in the later books does not mean that their tragic possibilities are necessarily enhanced in consequence. Only our own century could have swallowed the notion that the movement from Pickwickian cheer to the dark melancholy of *Edwin Drood* was, *per se*, an index of growing profundity. It is possible to argue that the later novels are not so much deeper as more depressing and that depression can work, as sometimes in Hardy, as a kind of protective insurance against the onrush of tragedy. For instance, the steady note of resignation in the voice of Pip the narrator perhaps makes renunciation—of Estella, of Biddy, of England—less intolerable to him than it would have been to the more aspiring David Copperfield. Pip turns out more an Horatio than a Hamlet, a stoic who contains his sorrows. Certainly his inner life strikes us as deeper and richer, but it is not wider in its emotional range. That David is in the end only called upon to resign himself to his own good fortune does not mean that, when he does suffer (as at Steerforth's death), his suffering is less intense than Pip's. Pain and grief may nearly be ironed out of the final number of *Copperfield*, but our last terrible glimpse of Rosa Dartle and Mrs. Steerforth, for example, perhaps gives us a more acute sense of the irreversible waste of a life than anything that Pip has to tell us.

Much could, of course, be said against the distinction made here; but for the present I want to leave it unexamined in the reader's mind while I develop its main implication: that there is a greater emotional energy in the early comic Dickens than he can always find in later books. For although there is enormous energy behind a *Bleak House*, it is a more organizing kind of energy; it cannot be assumed to share the spontaneity of the best things in earlier novels. In even the lightest early comic scenes, we sense a creative energy that springs from deep below Dickens' will to shape his material. He voices his high spirits freely and firmly; there is no call for the romantic notion of the artist as half-enslaved to his own demonic creativity. What Henry James liked to call "good humour" balances the writing. Yet in some of the more boisterous comedy, there can be a sense of the *manic* too, of an aboundingly anarchic spirit walking a risky tightrope off which hilarity may topple into hysteria. The laughter keeps us on the edge of our seats as it mounts, especially if it also promises the cathartic unmasking of one of the villains. In both the discomfiture of Heep and the death of Bill Sikes, Dickens quite openly offers us release in a sort of mob emotion, letting us hate and love more wildly than we normally can allow ourselves to do. Such comic delirium is not found in classic writers of comedy like Molière or Chaucer, but, whether this suggests that Dickens' energy is unresolved or too easily resolved, part of the plesaure of the early books lies in the way they refuse to put the brake on it. The pressure of laughter is free to rise and rise over long passages and even chapters. A brief example, much simpler than such instances as the writhings of Uriah Heep or the deranged *non sequiturs* of Mrs. Nickleby, must suffice. It describes the election scene at Eatanswill, a Hogarthian subject that, in Dickens, radiates a rough but innocent spirit of anarchic joy. The crowd had just caught Mr. Pickwick in the act of kissing his hand to Mrs. Pott:

> "Oh, you wicked old rascal," cried one voice, "looking arter the girls, are you?"
>
> "Oh, you wenerable sinner," cried another.
>
> "Putting on his spectacles to look at a married 'ooman!" said a third.
>
> "I see him a vinkin at her, with his vicked old eye," shouted a fourth.
>
> "Look arter your wife, Pott," bellowed the fifth;—and then there was a roar of laughter.
>
> As these taunts were accompanied with invidious comparisons between Mr. Pickwick and an aged ram, and several witticisms of the like nature; and as they moreover rather tended to convey reflections upon the honour of an innocent lady, Mr. Pickwick's indignation was excessive; but as silence was proclaimed at the moment, he contented himself by scorching the mob with a look of pity for their misguided minds, at which they laughed more boisterously than ever.
>
> "Silence," roared the mayor's attendants.
>
> "Whiffin, proclaim silence," said the mayor, with an air of pomp befitting his lofty station. In obedience to this command the crier performed another concerto on the bell, whereupon a gentleman in the crowd called out "muffins"; which occasioned another laugh.
>
> "Gentlemen," said the mayor, at as loud a pitch as he could possibly force his voice to, "Gentlemen. Brother Electors of the Borough of Eatanswill. We are met here today, for the purpose of choosing a representative in the room of our late——"
>
> Here the mayor was interrupted by a voice in the crowd.
>
> "Suc-cess to the mayor!" cried the voice, "and may he never desert the nail and sarspan business, as he got his money by."
>
> (Chapter 13)

The gusto comes across even in the cold half-light of quotation. So too does the warmth within Dickens' irreverence. The fun is not simply at the expense of the unlucky mayor; it includes within itself a broad ring of fellow-feeling that enlists the reader in a nonsatirical way. Yet the passage is not merely jovial, as some of the cruder touches of the prose might suggest. The rowdy crowd displays a hint of savageness that, though kept in abeyance, is not neutralized. It contributes a reckless crescendo to the scene, giving an edge as well as a glow to the comedy. This wide-awake and jostling conviviality remains within call even in far more distraught scenes like the flight of Jonas Chuzzlewit or Fagin's last night in Newgate; though they unleash less biddable emotions, they still retain the comic gift of making us respond, not as solitary readers, but as members of a united audience. The word "manic" can be applied to the cumulative effect of both sorts of writing. We feel it in long narratives as an emotional rhythm which mounts and mounts toward some climax of mirth or fear that, as we read, seems never to come. A sense of being propelled through the novel in the emotional grip of the author is with us in both Eatanswill and Newgate. Dickens' energy is sustained, but it does not expend itself. Only so could the idea of a Mr. Pickwick have swelled to three volumes.

What might be called the Butt and Tillotson view of middle Dickens describes how the maturing writer of novels like *Dombey and Son* learned to contain and discipline his genius within a conscious thematic structure. I have always thought that this view, so tempting to the academic mind, unwittingly suggested that Dickens was in fact constructing a more wily superego for the mastery of an inventiveness which, after his heady *début*, must have proved extremely taxing to live with. His will to order *Dombey* must surely have come from something less simply rational in him than his increasing craft as a serial writer. The mastery of his material must have involved self-mastery too. So, at least, I infer from the fact that Dickens' growing impulse to structure his novels coincided with a new kind of comic character, one consumed with pent-up anger, stifling and fulminating in some little pocket of the novel, his wildness on a leash, a casualty of the Victorian world's repressive decorum who gasps for air. The fuming Major Joey Bagstock, playing with his name while his identity disintegrates, can stand as an epitome of many such characters whose need to order the self actually disorders it. He is a profound creation in the way his anger is so close to his high spirits that both go bad together. Anger and conviviality are near akin in Pickwick too, but Bagstock's rage merely exacerbates his feelings, whereas Pickwick's endearing bouts of indignation provide a release. Bagstock can never let off all the steam he needs to let off. His fantasies, finding no echo outside of self, flourish like rampant weeds and stifle any real feelings he has. Much the same is true of characters as ostensibly different as Mrs. Skewton, Mr. Gridley, Mr. Pancks and even Mr. Bounderby. It is not far-fetched to detect something of their thwarted feelings in many of Dickens' chief characters. A touch of frustration makes even Steerforth and Heep a little akin, though one broods and the other squirms. The languor of the one and the servility of the other disguise an equal longing to boil over. Each is made vivid for us by what he holds back from expressing. That, for all his outbursts, is Bagstock's problem too.

It is the way of manic emotion to intensify in proportion to its falling short of any lasting catharsis. (We see it in art too, in the work of writers like Balzac and Dostoevsky.) Dickens understood this Sisyphean character of some kinds of emotional energy very well and pondered it often. There is a brilliant double study of it in *Little Dorrit*, in the scenes where the driven Mr. Pancks tries to pacify Mr. F's terrible Aunt. Mr. Pancks, who grinds out his life of rent-collecting with a pounding and purposeless energy, catches a glimpse of his own madness fully grown in the old lady's arbitrary hostility. She projects her bitterness quite irrelevantly, on harmless victims like Clennam, while he dreams of the day when he will shear the flowing locks of his benign but bogus employer, Mr. Casby. He knows that his only real outlet is business and that it has no more real meaning for him than her zany aggression offers to her. Dickens as always looks for comedy in the disturbing mechanisms which imprison a person within the self, but whereas the madness of, say, Mrs. Nickleby's elderly admirer who threw vegetables to her seemed a refreshing and salutary display of a person luxuriating in his own idiosyncrasy, Mr. F's Aunt disorientates us as much as she does Clennam. What strange principle makes her tick? She is as much of a mystery as Blake's tiger. The same Dickensian obsession with how it feels to be a self appears in Steerforth's brooding fear of his own nature. As Ursula Brangwen says when her sister admires Gerald Crich for having so much "go," "Yes, but where does his go go to?" Steerforth was partly Dickens' way of wondering what outlet his world could offer for his own "go." The nagging questions that trouble what Shaw called his "dismal Jemmies"—Clennam, Wrayburn, Pip—are the same ones that haunt more explosive depressives like the Man from Shropshire. All of them live off the disquiet and the sense of persecution that undermine them, just as Gridley needs Chancery in order to express the energy inside him:

> . . . if I took my wrongs in any other way, I should be driven mad! It is only by resenting them, and by revenging them in my mind, and by angrily demanding the justice I never get, that I am able to keep my wits together. . . . There's nothing between doing it, and sinking into the smiling state of the poor little mad woman that haunts the court. If I was once to sit down under it, I should become imbecile.

This problem of the channeling of energy played, I believe, no small part in Dickens' own justly admired organizing of fictions like *Dombey* and *Bleak*

House. Great Expectations differs from them not least because its hero has more in common with the crushed Richard Carstone than with the inflammable Gridley.

Dickens' interest in a great range of emotion did not result simply in the invention of a gallery of characters. The emotions he embodied so liberally in them also shaped the ebb and flow of his narratives. Santayana celebrated the strength of love in his work and, by implication, its complementary strength of hatred. Between them they inspire the powerful oscillating rhythms of his most characteristic books. The beauty of *Copperfield*, for instance, resides in its rhythmic alternations of mood between the comic and the tragic, the buoyant and the anxious. Mr. Micawber may be said to sum up the whole book. The dramatic set pieces such as the shipwreck or the exposure of Heep are only part of the story. We are carried to the crest of their waves by the general swell of the narrative. Felicity of rhythm also distinguishes the telling of *Great Expectations*, a novel written with Copperfield very much in mind. Yet the rhythm of the later book is far more muted and modulated, far less springy. The range of emotional contrast seems less, as if it had been composed and subsumed into the harmonious narrative tone. The kind of intimate eavesdropping on Pip that it invites is rarely possible with the livelier David. Why is this? Does it mean that *Great Expectations* is somehow less Dickensian or more than Dickensian? What is meant when Dickens is said to have "matured" between the two novels? I raise these questions, not to make value judgments, but to try to see more clearly what it is that has for so many readers made the later novel distinct and unique in Dickens' work. Those things that I have pointed to as more characteristic of earlier books provide a frame and reference in this task. It can be assumed that though they may have taken a different and less obtrusive shape in *Great Expectations*, they cannot have been entirely excluded from it. The kind of mental energy, with its terrible self-repeating patterns, which Dickens expressed in a Bagstock and a Gridley never simply goes away.

II

One fancies that Hamlet meant every bit as much to the Dickens of *Great Expectations* as he did to Mr. Wopsle. The voice with which Pip recounts his "first most vivid and broad impression of the identity of things" has the music of soliloquy, quite shorn of rhetoric. Graham Greene speaks of "that sense of a mind speaking to itself with no one there to listen." Pip's tone invites barely conscious thoughts into his mind, thoughts that remain unsaid in his workaday world. Though his grave, meditative rhythm is strongly measured, it never suggests someone who is trying to rationalize his experience: its antitheses and pauses are not logical but a patient waiting for the truth to emerge.

It is the prose, then, which first tells us that *Great Expectations* has more to offer than the edifying acuities of the *bildungsroman*. The almost magically natural way Dickens sustains it throughout the novel is enough to tell us to expect more than just the moral progress of a "character," some subtler version of Wopsle's much admired *Tragedy of George Barnwell*. Pip's voice-music embodies something too deep to be seen simply in ethical terms. We are listeners first and judges only later and only then because the mature Pip succumbs more and more to his need to judge himself. But to the end, we always feel in him a mystery which no amount of self-rebuke and resignation can ever wholly illumine. Without such resonance, Dickens' fable would not have been so elusive and rich as readers always find it. A proposition to begin from is, then, that the novel's central and explicit moral concerns are sustained and animated by a more imaginative soil than ethics alone could provide. Often, of course, the moral and the imaginative work organically together (in Magwitch's first appearances, for example) while, at other times, they conflict. What is very hard to determine, but quite crucial, is whether it is only Pip the narrator who is trying to impose a moral pattern on his life or whether the novelist himself connives at moralizing his own poetry. Could it be that, in some beautiful and subtle way, Dickens' final complexities actually pass us off with a simpler, more novel-like novel than the poetry and comedy of the early chapters had led us to expect?

To compare the voice of chapter 1 with the words Pip later finds to express his remorse towards Joe ("I only saw in him [Magwitch] a much better man than I had been to Joe") is to wonder whether Pip is always as successful in evoking the unvoiced regions of his mind as the evenness of his tone suggests. His reconciliation with Joe is moving as are, in their way, the solemn white lies and the New Testament allusion that herald Magwitch's death, but such scenes seem bare of that rich aura of fantasy that clings to the marshes. To point to such contrasts with the earlier novels in mind is to notice that, with all its marvelous literary tact, *Great Expectations* nowhere seems to brim over and overflow as they do. It seems to resolve its energies into form without effort, without seeming contained in that volcanic way that makes Major Bagstock so alarming and *Dombey and Son* itself so near to bursting through its tight network of moral significances, dotted about it like so many parking meters. To discuss the novel's form is, in consequence, also to inquire into the fate of the energy we see in Pip as a child, since that form functions as an expression of the sadder and wiser Pip, who narrates the whole story. Does this Pip leave anything out of the picture he gives of himself? If so, does Dickens find a way to tell us what he omits? These questions are literary as well as psychological. Any answer to them has to decide how far Pip's poetry is shaped naturally and how far it is squeezed into the final classic form the novel takes.

Perhaps it was wrong to refer so soon to the overexplicit sublimations of a scene like the death of Magwitch. Pip's self-examinings do not always contain a ready moral, even in those later moments when he seems to whittle down his inner life to a grim pendulum movement between egoism and guilt. We need not pounce first on his self-recriminations when he tells us what to think of himself, as Q. D. Leavis did in her lust for clear meaning. For most readers his story unfolds more like some symbolic dream whose meanings peep out at us, as if from behind dark trees, and then are hidden. To insist on this is not to imply that Dickens was unaware of the meaning of his own fable. Something like Satis House is clearly not such a profound reflector of Pip's psyche just by chance and intuition. It is not my point to read *Great Expectations* as a piece of unconscious self-revelation, the way Roger Garis does, against its own grain. It is too perfectly orchestrated on the imaginative level for that to be convincing. It is possible to wish that Dickens had treated Pip's development rather differently, that he had not brought him out quite where he did at the end, but not that he was really saying something else behind his own back. When he made Pip resigned, damping down the fires of his selfhood, he kept faith with the emotion he had to express. Garis's *Great Expectations* might possibly be more Dickensian after the denotative manner of *Bleak House*: it would not have the beauty of the novel that we read.

Nowhere do the beauty and mystery of the book come together more vividly than in the first spectral apparition of Miss Havisham, all "waxwork and skeleton." The early chapters have been brought to a point in this one strange image of a life that has been wasted away by its own passion. The liturgical movement of the prose seems to set her at a remove from real living:

> It was not in the first few moments that I saw all these things, though I saw more of them in the first moments than might be supposed. But, I saw that everything within my view which ought to be white, had been white long ago, and had lost its lustre, and was faded and yellow. I saw that the bride within the bridal dress was withered like the dress, and like the flowers, and had no brightness left but the brightness of her sunken eyes. I saw that the dress had been put upon the rounded figure of a young woman, and that the figure upon which it now hung loose, had shrunk to skin and bone.

The incantatory chiming of the repetitions in this makes us dwell on Miss Havisham as if we saw her in slow motion. Despite the highly melodramatic subject, there is none of Dickens' usual kinesis. The hush in Pip's voice is too considered for excitement. A phrase like "It was not in the first moments that I saw all these things" has rather the still, visionary mood of some Romantic poetry, where the simplest words are given an unusual poise and weight, the mood of things like:

> . . . it had past
> The lily and the snow; and beyond these
> I must not think now, though I saw that face—
> But for her eyes I should have fled away.

For Miss Havisham is as much part of a spiritual vision as is Moneta. Only the later Dickens could have made her so haunting in so unflashy a way. Yet if the rhythm of his prose here is endlessly suggestive, it is also an index of his powerful conscious control over his material. The quietly inexorable momentum allows no let-up and no quickening of its steady pace: "I saw that the bride within the bridal dress had withered like the dress, and like the flowers, and had no brightness left but the brightness of her sunken eyes. I saw that the dress. . . . " The effect, as in Keats's poem, contrives to seem both very written and as if the words had been taken down in dictation. Yet Dickens' prose is too subtle to seem to push Miss Havisham into the shape he wants her to take. There is no tension even though he chooses to orchestrate his outlandish and manic creation with a strongly Apollonian music. She moves to his tune, keeping time perfectly. Here, at least, the form of the novel gives a sense of rightness, of rightness that, curiously, enhances our sense of her strangeness. The scene never appears patterned, even though Miss Havisham seldom looks like bursting through the scams of the form of the novel in the way many a Dickens character does.

Another way in which Dickens wraps *Great Expectations* in a pervasive air of psychological mystery is by his alertness to Pip's instinctive habit of reading himself into his world and of taking his world into his own inner thoughts, until there seems to be a dreamlike—but very real—continuity between them. In Dickens' great comic characters, the inner life is all tuned outward, toward us; they trump us, in a dazzling *fait accompli*, with an otherness that brooks no questioning of its source. An observer may well see our own mental life in this sharply outlined way, as a cluster of vivid signs without decipherable causes. But we are never characters to ourselves in this clear-cut way. This is why Pip, who is so short on the quirkiness that makes Micawber burst off the page crying, "I am me," can still afford a spacious lodging for our sense of how it feels to live in the self. Pip's life constitutes a mystery of himself; he broods constantly on just those thoughts from which Micawber seems so exhilaratingly exempt; he is obsessed by the Hamlet-like riddle, "What am I?" This mystery lies at the heart of Dickens' cryptically romantic fable of spider-like fairy godmothers, aloof princesses, and escaped convicts. Without it we might hear the metronome beat of Pip's self-irony, but we would not listen to his voice as if we were listening to our own.

Pip only makes any headway into his own "poor labyrinth" by recognizing that of the other people who shape and give meaning to his life. Mrs. Joe, Magwitch, Miss Havisham, Estella, Mr. Jaggers—they are all deeply bound into his consciousness, both its inner and its outer objects. They haunt him like parts of himself, of his guiltiness and desires and fears, just as the desolate marsh landscape of his childhood does. What he says about Estella belonging to "the innermost life of my life" applies, in varying ways, to all of them. Their goodness, like their badness, is incorporated into his imagination and, working there, becomes a constituent of his own moral nature. No clear line demarcates him from his world, no seam or joint to facilitate the definitions of the moralist. The distinctness of a Micawber or a Murdstone invites and sharpens moral judgment. Probably Micawber would not exist unless we kept a sort of balance sheet on him, to weigh his feckless gaiety against his selfishness, at the back of our minds. Pip, without this high relief of personality, has been shaped by others into whom his own grief and desire have been projected; the real world laid out before him is the repository of emotions which he himself has imputed to its symbolic landmarks of beacon and gibbet. Thus, the fears implanted in him by being brought up "by hand" and that make him a "self-tormentor" are always liable to reappear outside him, in the startling actuality of the "two fat sweltering one-pound notes" or the great, accusing forefinger of Mr. Jaggers. Such things help us understand and place his proneness to self-recrimination, just as they make us see how his misuse of his "expectations" arises out of the "spell" of his strange childhood. This being so, mere clarity of moral judgment on Pip's conduct neither could nor should be the upshot of our dealings with the mystery into which *Great Expectations* plunges us. In the first place, by being taken so far into Pip's confidence, into his own view of his life, we have no firm vantage for judging him other than the one he himself offers. We are not obliged always to accept Pip's own version of himself. Would one expect impartiality of self-judgment from anyone with *that* kind of formation? Even if we sometimes feel that Pip the narrator has contrived to distill his remarkable experiences into clear-cut ethical terms, we still go on attending to the mystery of his story, to the poetry as well as the moral prose. For, though his imagination may cause him to misread that story and make it more romantic than it is, we are surely not meant to feel that Estella and Satis House and his own hopes in them simply collapse like a house of cards to leave us with only a bitter sense of "*illusions perdues*." I do not, however, use the word "mystery" as a means of exculpating Pip from his sins or to play down Dickens' concern with his responsibility for what he becomes. The book does not ask for a wishy-washy kind of sympathy for its hero. The very mysteriousness of the story makes an overcomfortable sense of fellow-feeling with Pip impossible.

In speaking of the sense of "psychological mystery" in *Great Expectations*, I mean that its moral content, at its deepest, lies at a different level from that of Pip's own overt self-judgments. For instance, there is one telling difference between the child Pip and the Pip of Volume III, the Pip who will tell the story. As a child, he judges himself every bit as harshly as he does when he takes Magwitch down the river at the end; but in the early chapters, we know just how limited those judgments are, what crude instruments they make for understanding what is happening to him. We even laugh a little at his disproportionate anguish over something as comic as the pork pie. But by Volume III, it is less clear how far we are being asked to see round Pip's self-judgments. Sometimes it seems as if his sad, penitent self-rebukes are meant to represent a true self-knowledge. We hear him at the confessional and commend him for seeing the error of his ways: ". . . I lay there, penitently whispering, 'O God bless him [Joe]! O God bless this gentle Christian man!'" Pip sounds just like a little bit like Tiny Tim here. It is, in short, the directly moral moments which import a little softening sentiment into this grave and unremitting novel. More profound, in the scene just quoted from, is the sense that Pip, beneath his gentlemanly carapace, is still the same child of the marshes that he was at the beginning. The perception may be in danger of being sentimentalized by the presence of "gentle Joe," but it belongs to a deeper moral level in the book: Pip is so real because, more than with almost any character in fiction, we feel in him the continued presence of the undeciphered child on which his adult self has been built. His behavior to Joe and to Magwitch accounts for only a part, and that the easiest part, of what there is to judge and understand in him. When Pip sees in Magwitch a "much better man than I had been to Joe," it may well seem a moot point whether this is the final truth which resolves the book's psychological mystery or whether, instead, Dickens may not be conniving with the narrator to corroborate his hero's own indelible feelings of guilt.

Great Expectations owes some of its renown in our century to the fact that we have subscribed heavily to the notion that what we learn about life we learn—if at all—from experience, that self-doubt is the necessary prelude to self-knowledge. It is worth asking whether such an idea could provide Dickens with enough room for that celebration of natural energy which is usually such a spontaneous part of his characterization. To do this one needs to look at Pip's moments of self-chastisement. They include some of the rare occasions when his wise and even tone of voice falters. An early one, in chapter 6, has him reflecting on his failure to confess to Joe that he has stolen food from the pantry:

> In a word, I was too cowardly to do what I knew to be right, as I had been too cowardly to avoid doing what I knew to be wrong. I had had no intercourse with the world at that time, and I imitated none of its many inhabitants who act in this manner. Quite an untaught genius, I made the discovery of the line of action for myself.

The word "cowardly" is simply insensitive, as is Pip the narrator's ponderous sarcasm. Why call himself "untaught," given the strange and fierce duress under which he had acted? Instead of witnessing the mysterious birth of compassion out of terror, we get facetious copybook sermonizing. Pip's real anguish of mind is substituted by a picture of the moral man tut-tutting at the thoughtlessness of his youth. It is surely the child Pip who has the finest moral sense, who plays Maisie to his older self's Mrs. Wix. The narrator only seems to want to disguise and dilute the traumas of his younger self. He is less interested than he should be in remembering the emotional intensity which prompted him to act as he did. So we wonder whether he really can still remember what it was that made him invent the dogs with the veal cutlets and also made him love Estella.

Pip's *ex post facto* earnestness, then, is not quite convincing as the main legacy from the "spell" of his childhood. It seems too orthodox an outcome to the very special events that shape his life. This is not to deny that a certain ordinariness is integral to the kind of maturity Dickens suggests: a normal, unidiosyncratic narrator, able to drop into the background, to eavesdrop and whisper asides, suits the novel's general meanings better than some more Copperfieldian master of ceremonies would. But we need not feel as bound as Pip is to the moral truths that gnaw at his conscious mind. They are always symptoms of the particular individual he is too. And at another level of the prose, we can hear a voice less prone to praise or blame, a voice that is more merciful to others than it is to itself, and more honest about them. Here, for instance, from his description of his sister's funeral:

> It was the first time that a grave had opened in my road of life, and the gap it made in the smooth ground was wonderful. The

figure of my sister in her chair by the kitchen fire, haunted me night and day. That the place could possibly be, without her, was something my mind seemed unable to compass. . . .

Whatever my fortunes might have been, I could scarcely have recalled my sister with much tenderness. But I suppose there is a shock of regret which may exist without much tenderness.

This voice is larger and subtler than the self-expiatory one, though recognizably akin to it. The interplay of the two is not, however, any simple index of discrepancy and contradiction in the telling of the story. Both represent parts of the whole Pip. A problem only arises when the narrator unwittingly denigrates the inner life of his younger self, wishing to make his history exemplary, and one voice begins to drown out the other. This is more likely to happen toward the end of the novel, but the potential for it is there from the start. What is at stake is the fate of energy in the somber, twilit *Great Expectations* world. We already have a hint of this in the fate of Mrs. Joe. On the rampage with "tickler" and tar-water, she is a rebarbative but exciting figure, full of a coarse and spiteful life; but, after she has been attacked by Orlick and pacified, her image becomes more easy to assimilate into the tone of melancholy reminiscence. In this her fate resembles that of Magwitch, who, by the end, is well on the way to gentle Joedom. Pip's own energy is most pointedly downgraded in his relations with Herbert Pocket. He first meets Herbert when a "prowling boy" in the ruined garden of Satis House where Herbert challenges him to a boxing bout. Pip draws blood. The "pale young gentleman" is weak, fool-hardy and plucky; the forge child has real blood in his veins. For a long time this impression does not change much. Herbert is still innocent and ineffectual as Pip's roommate in London, needing Pip just as much as Pip needs him. He admires in Pip a complexity that is happily absent from his own open nature. Yet, by the end of the novel, Pip has come to look up to Herbert's as the finer character and one that reminds him of his own faults:

We owed so much to Herbert's ever cheerful industry and readiness, that I often wondered how I had conceived that old idea of his inaptitude, until I was one day enlightened by the reflection, that perhaps the inaptitude had never been in him at all, but had been in me.

The betraying note of facetiousness reminds us that we know better than to believe him. Pip surely needs some finer reason for rapping himself so often over the knuckles than a desire to become a "pale young gentleman." He is a sort of Hamlet who aspires to play Horatio. In the process, he tends to look down on his past self with something of the condescension to which he once treated Joe. It is as if he wanted to look back on a world that has been defused, a world in which Magwitch has become Provis, as if the very telling of his story is an attempt to make safe some unexploded bomb that lies in his memory. This is not, of course, the whole story—Pip's music would seep out of his voice if it were—but there is nonetheless something diluted in the novel's measured prose, some energy that has been too perfectly harnessed. Pip's moral maturity entails some thinning down of his blood. It is perhaps not unrelated to this that most of the novel's richest comedy comes in the opening chapters, before Pip learns to emulate the gentlemanly self-control of the Pockets.

                                        III

If the meanings of *Great Expectations* were all lodged within the confines of Pip's moral sense, its last volume would boil down to no more than a mood of chastened despondency, calculated to numb the egoist in us. But Pip's depressed wisdom is only a part of the book's final music. Its poetry, bred from the strangeness and terror, can still flare up and cast its light into the corners which morality has left obscure. In a scene that has been thought melodramatic but which to me is one of the great moments in the novel, the scene where Miss Havisham sets herself on fire, the same heightened emotion that made the first apparition of Magwitch so electrifying comes to the fore again. In the long interim the "rain of years" has changed Pip: he feels not fear, but a kind of exulation as her rescues Miss Havisham. The fire is purgatorial in its effect, though to describe it in such moral terms is not to place it on the same psychological level as Pip's admiration for Herbert. What actually characterizes the scene is an absence of introspection. Pip's emotions are conveyed without comment through his sense impressions, shown rather than told. An essential aspect of his experience is that while it lasts, to adopt Wordsworth's phrase, "thought was not." From the ruminative and dejected figure who patrols the ruined garden, the fire stirs Pip into acting and understanding as in a flash of vision. The scene is wonderfully sustained, but only a sample quotation is possible:

> . . . I saw her running at me, shrieking, with a whirl of fire blazing all about her, and soaring at least as many feet above her head as she was high.
>   I had a double-caped great-coat on, and over my arm another thick coat. That I got them off, closed with her, threw

her down, and got them over her; that it dragged the great cloth from the table for the same purpose, and with that I dragged down the heap of rottenness in the midst, and all the ugly things that sheltered there; that we were on the ground struggling like desperate enemies, and that the closer I covered her, the more wildly she shrieked and tried to free herself; that this occurred I knew through the result, but not through anything I felt, or thought, or knew I did. I knew nothing until I knew that we were on the floor by the great table, and that patches of tinder yet alight were floating in the smoky air, which, a moment ago, had been her faded bridal dress.

Then, I looked round and saw the disturbed beetles and spiders running away over the floor, and the servants coming in with breathless cries at the door. I still held her forcibly down with all my strength, like a prisoner who might escape; and I doubt if I knew who she was, or why we had struggled, or that she had been in flames, or that the flames were out, until I saw the patches of tinder that had been her garments, no longer alight but falling in a black shower around us.

The feeling of this passage is as much one of elation as of horror and there is a loveliness which is not grim in the "black shower" of tinder from the bridal dress. There is no one linear meaning to what happens. Pip's very manner of saving Miss Havisham is a sort of aggression; he may be exorcising something in her, liberating her true self or trying to suppress her will to die. The burnt garments may be the cue for Pip's later action of readmitting the sunshine to the darkened rooms or they may prefigure Miss Havisham's imminent death. What is unmistakable in the automatic, trancelike nature of his response to the fire is that it represents some release from his usual self-consciousness. The fact that his energy is linked to the final pacification of Miss Havisham, that the passion goes out of her to be replaced by a submissive need for his forgiveness, is profoundly characteristic of the novel as a whole. She had been, after all, one of the mainsprings of his childhood fantasy. To speak, however, of this great scene as merely a sublimation for Pip would be trite, because it is also an ordeal; and he is far from being its hero or the lucky beneficiary he hoped to be when he first met her. Psychological insight is too completely translated into action for the reader to moralize. Besides, not all of Pip's youthful dream has been dissolved. He still loves Estella, however helplessly, and it is in that love that Dickens concentrates his study of the passionate side of Pip's nature. She brings all his intense passivity into play.

In Miss Havisham, the libido that survives in the shape of a self-destructive will has an intensity that Estella's cool beauty and Pip's yearning for her both lack. A great deal of the fire in Pip's experience comes to him from other people—Mrs. Joe, Magwitch, Miss Havisham herself—but if Estella is desirable, she feels no desire herself. Her starlike coldness inspires in him a love that is warm enough to act to claim its object. It is the fact that she is out of reach that makes her so desirable:

> When I first went into it [the ruined brewery], and, rather oppressed by its gloom, stood near the door looking about me, I saw her pass among the extinguished fires, and ascend some light iron stairs, and go out by a gallery high overhead, as if she were going out into the sky.

Pip's abiding sense of Estella is given early: a lighted candle receding down the darkened passages of Satis House, beckoning as it recedes. The afterimage of her that lingers with him is cold and beautiful like diamonds. Whether she scorns or beguiles him, her spell arrests him in a dumb and unresolved longing. Not that the novel puts her on a pedestal, like Agnes: Pip cannot help seeing her as a very real, as well as very elegant, young lady too. There is a hint of the theatrical about her, but she is not ethereal. It is, indeed, precisely the discrepancy between what he wishes her to be morally and what he fears she really is that entices Pip. He loves her for what is unlovable in her, for her very indifference. It is inside this treacherous rift between desire and its object that Eros has delicately insinuated himself.

Pip's love enables him to go on inhabiting the same old territory of guilt and self-dispraise of his childhood. For all her beauty, Estella could never have made him want to call the Jacks Knaves but for what Mrs. Joe had done to him. It is as though some hidden complicity between his persecuting sister and Miss Havisham has fitted him to love Estella. She is shaped to despise him as he is shaped to feel despised. This lack of freedom in his desire makes his love seem romantically star-crossed so that, for all her spitefulness, Estella can still symbolize for him everything beyond the forge that his imagination craves for. She holds sway in his memory, the chief link between his life with and his life without expectations, a link with his pre-London world which, unlike Joe, he can still acknowledge to the Finches of the Grove. Estella occupies such an expanse of time in his mind, from before puberty to manhood, that she comes to seem like a symbol of sexuality itself, not just *one* beautiful woman. No other woman plays any real part in his life. Dickens is nowhere more sensitive than in his treatment of this fixation to the way every individual life creates a distinct sexuality of its own. That Pip's love is unrequited is not due simply to Estella herself (Bentley Drummle is rumored to have beaten her) but to his own delighted pain in contemplating her in a beautiful beyond outside him. His love, like Miss Havisham's, sets her aside from life. Because of it, he sets aside a part of himself as well. She never again kisses him so spontaneously as on the day when she watched him knock down Herbert Pocket.

The means which give us Pip's feeling for Estella are essentially poetic. She is not presented as a case for the psychologist or the moralist, any more than she is that to Pip. In this he is simply truthful, not deceived. A New Testament ethic, coupled with an acute consciousness of class, may provide the spur for a better understanding of Joe or Magwitch, but they would be too prosaic to fathom his love for Estella. She makes all his usual moral categories dizzy. This is not because she is simply an accomplished tease; it is Pip who teases himself. Part of her charm for him is an exquisite frigidity that allures and then rebuffs him. She is only superficially narcissistic and takes the praise she receives from men only on another's behalf. Personally, she is rather bored by her beauty. This listlessness makes her a more malleable image for Pip's fantasy and, if she manipulates him, he also manipulates her in his mind. Their relations make a haunting image of Eros in one of his most poignant guises—the tremulous deadlock of adolescent yearning—but it is a bloodless Eros that they show us. In Estella, as the novel renders her, the flesh seems distilled without being quite spiritualized; she is poised gracefully between being a body and a dream. It is in Pip's nature to cling to such an image and consonant with much else in his history that he should be smitten by a woman the very thought of whom seems to quell his blood. Possibly, Dickens wished to hint that his devotion was a way of coping with his fear of Estella's real sexuality. Certainly, her marriage to the bearish and insensitive Drummle can be taken as a sort of riposte to Pip's own lack of aggression. But it would be wrong to proffer any too definite interpretation of a love whose description is so much more atmospheric than analytic. This is the part of the novel where Dickens leaves most to our imagination and most avoids glossing the mystery he evokes.

The treatment of death in *Great Expectations* has something in common with its faintly wistful treatment of love. In the presence of death, Pip best understands both himself and others. Deaths like his sister's, Magwitch's and Miss Havisham's are the stepping stones over which he treads through life. His tone of voice constantly modulates from reminiscence to the mood of an epitaph (in a sense the whole book *is* an epitaph). The deaths in *Great Expectations* feel more elegiac than those in earlier books: we are too attuned to them in advance for them to surprise us. Sensation would be discordant; we hear instead the beat of muffled drums. If there is sentimentality in

Magwitch's death, it is of a hushed sort, remote from the voracious emotionalism that brings the curtain down on Little Nell. Pip never saws the air; he thinks of death as a diminuendo, a peaceful seeping away of such energy as the dying person still has.

Within this muted atmosphere, Dickens maintains his old fascination with the last moments of consciousness. He is drawn to death by its disclosure of a vital spark in people, beneath the level of moral differences, that seems to hover most vividly on the brink of extinction. This spark is brightest in the starving Magwitch on the marshes, in the paralyzed Mrs. Joe beckoning to Biddy to bring the slate and in the terrified Pip about to be murdered by Orlick. It is there too in the returned Magwitch for a while, as we see from the wild weather that brings him back, yet little vestige of it remains in the touching prison scene when he looks for the last time at the white ceiling of his cell and all is swathed in a consoling sublimity. It is telling that at this moment Pip lies to him about Estella, while the truth-seeking narrator makes not the faintest demur. There is an interesting contrast to this scene in *Our Mutual Friend*, in the great chapter where Rogue Riderhood, having been run down in his wherry by a steamer, is taken to the Jolly Fellowship Porters to be revived. Here, death claims an utter truthfulness from all present:

> See! A token of life! An indubitable token of life! The spark may smoulder and go out, or it may glow and expand, but see! The four rough fellows seeing, shed tears. Neither Riderhood in this world, nor Riderhood in the other, could draw tears from them; but a striving human soul between the two can do it easily.
>
> He is struggling to come back. Now he is almost here, now he is far away again. Now he is struggling harder to get back. And yet—like us all, when we swoon—like us all, every day of our lives when we wake—he is instinctively unwilling to be restored to the consciousness of this existence, and would be left dormant, if he could.
>
> (Book III, chapter 3)

Riderhood's "little turn-up with death" leaves him unchanged, whereas the "warmint" in Magwitch disappears and he seems word-perfect to make a good end. The differences between then apart, I think this is why Magwitch's death never grips us with the common feeling of mortality felt by the motley waterfront group around Riderhood. When Pip prays, "O Lord, be merciful to him, a sinner!" we have half-forgotten what Magwitch needs to be forgiven for. To think back from this hallowed moment to the escaped felon shivering on a gravestone is, however moved we may be, to feel regret that the poetic fable of volume I has become, by volume III, such a perfectly controlled moral fable. The fact that Magwitch's last scene is so perfectly written only makes one wonder whether the perfection of *Great Expectations* itself may not also be its greatest drawback.

IV

The cadenced quietness of the novel's prose, muted to naturalize the fantastic story, is peculiarly fitted to express a placed and governed emotion. Much tension seems to have been resolved before Pip's feelings find utterance. His surprising story is told in tones of dreamlike unsurprise. It is this, and not some masterful authorial organization, which makes us feel that the book is all cut from the one seamless cloth, perfectly sustaining its own inner decorum. In other words, it offers a pleasure that is more frequently found in verse than in prose fiction. If at times it tries to shake off its symbolism, it still remains symbolic in a way that *Little Dorrit* is not. Its symbols can never be severed from the story in which they live and be put on exhibition: there is nothing in it like the much rehearsed "prison symbol." To reduce the novel's poetry to a deposit of prose meaning would be to present Pip's sufferings as more easily negotiable, more morally explicable, than they really are. He is one who will always carry the baffling fable of his past about inside him. For him, as for us, the story fends off interpretation. What gives gravity to his voice is not so much moral knowledge as an undersense of wondering and cherished disquiet. This makes his tone too constant to generate anything like the intense emotional crescendos of the earlier Dickens novels, the impassioned build-ups to things like Nicholas's thrashing of Squeers or the shipwreck in *David Copperfield*. This is perhaps why *Copperfield*, with all its pulled punches, can voice a wild cry of regret that is beyond the melancholy Pip, to whom sadness is a kind of native element. In *Great Expectations* Dickens' great emotional range is harmonized to aesthetic ends and this makes the novel less hard to take than one at first expected. One looks vainly at the placid death of Magwitch for that fierce beauty of tragic terror which, albeit warmed by romance, is there in the sight of the drowned Steerforth. For it is easier to come to terms with dejection than with tragedy, with a life that is half-fulfilled than with a life that has been shattered to its foundations. In a sense, Pip lacks the emotional energy to suffer as much as David does; *Great Expectations* speaks of energies that prove more tame and tractable than those which fuel the earlier novels. This goes for both of its endings; neither is satisfactory, though the second works aesthetically. Each of them seems too resigned to the idea that passion can never flare up again; each of them takes a secret pleasure in its own sadness:

> The silvery mist was touched with the first rays of the moonlight, and the same rays touched the tears that dropped from her eyes.

The dying fall is right. Once more emotion has been exquisitely shaped. We forget that what really counts is not whether Pip finally wins or loses Estella but whether anything remains in either of them to make love between them still imaginable.

This is not to argue that Pip simply moves from feeling disconsolate toward a quiet consolation. There is also resolve and buoyancy in his voice. During the escape down the river we are told that Magwitch was neither "disposed to be passive or resigned" nor at all "anxious" and his state of elastic equanimity supplies Pip with an ideal for himself. We see it in the way he stands by Magwitch at the trial. But too much weight should not be put on what is affirmed in such scenes. Rarely, in *Great Expectations*, is the birth of goodness accompanied by any access of strength: in the paralyzed Mrs. Joe and the dying Magwitch, as in the reformed Pip (tended by Joe), goodness and debility go hand in hand. Miss Havisham has to be destroyed to be redeemed and Satis House pulled down for it to have that chiming beauty of a stage set which makes it a fit setting for Pip's and Estella's last meeting. The haunt of Pip's wild fancy concludes, half-symbol, half-backdrop, as the canvas for what Dickens, in exorcising it, called a "pretty piece of writing." The magic wand of his art has been waved one last time. If the subdued beauty it creates is pleasurable in its pathos this is partly because it is a beauty which does not much consort with exuberance or delight.

It seems, then, that moral awareness not only liberates Pip by the end but that, with the connivance of Dickens' art, it also diminishes things in him which stood in need of liberation. Much has to remain absent from his voice for its music to be so unbroken. Perhaps as a result of his pressing wish to be a good man, he reneges on some of his bodily energy. As Trabb's Boy remarks after the limekiln ordeal, "Ain't he pale, though?" At times, indeed, he almost resembles the "pale young gentleman," quelled into making the best of life, with honesty if without enthusiasm:

> I must not leave it to be supposed that we were ever a great House, or that we made mints of money. We were not in a grand way of business, but we had a good name, and worked

for our profits, and did very well.

This decent, undistinguished Pip, full of prosaic wisdom, so moving in his honesty, has somehow dwindled from the Everyman figure one looked to find in him in volume I. What is missing in him is not just the higher culture, as Bernard Shaw predictably felt, but something which, faced with the attenuated vitality of his lonely self, we can find in abundance in Dickens' less "artistic" books. To say so is not to wish that *Great Expectations* had ended more romantically than with the picture of an upright Victorian merchant; it is rather to surmise that when Dickens wrote it he was consciously and unerringly holding a part of his genius in check. Perhaps he could only describe sadness like Pip's by keeping it aesthetically in check.

This essay has spoken often of the "poetry" of *Great Expectations* because readers have always sensed in it a rhythm below the words which carries the words along, as the rhythm of verse does. There is nothing new in this deliberate confusing of prose and verse. Clough, for instance, did it when contrasting the poetry of his day with *Bleak House*:

> The true and lawful haunts of the poetic powers [are] no more upon Pindus or Parnassus [but] in the blank and desolate streets, and upon the solitary bridges of the midnight city, where Guilt is, and wild Temptation, and the dire compulsion of what has once been done. . . . there walks the discrowned Apollo, with unstrung lyre.

If Clough is right in thinking Dickens more like the great poets than were his verse-writing contemporaries then it seems to me to follow that a full sense of the greatness of his work is only possible if we think of it alongside the poets'. It is after all arguable that Shakespeare had a greater influence on his novels than did any previous novelist.

As well as conscripting the word "poetry," however, this essay has also made frequent recourse to the word "art." I do not mean the same thing by these two words, though what they refer to inevitably overlaps and interweaves as we read *Great Expectations*. By "art" I mean that which controls and shapes emotion into form; by "poetry," that which art has shaped, the bedrock of firsthand emotional experience that form animates and preserves. They trespass on each other, of course, being "blossoms upon one tree," but there is an important difference between them. If art articulates poetry, it may also exert control over it, rather as the Apollonian controls the Dionysian in Nietzsche's account of Greek tragedy. This control may be beneficent or repressive, making a work truer or falser to its original sources. We may see Dickens' control of the tone of Pip's self-knowledge as marking a triumph of the superego or, conversely, find in its framed and rounded art the perfect medium for a muted hymn to an adulthood tinged with regret for the fantasy region of childhood. The purpose of this essay is not to adjudicate this question but simply to ask whether the form and the poetry of the novel match each other as perfectly as is often said. Does Pip's faultless telling of his tale make over to us all of the potential meaning and emotion in the book? This question in no way belittles a great novel. If *Great Expectations* is a classic, it is one because of more than just the aesthetic pleasure we take in its telling. To praise it just as an "artistic" success is to pitch one's praise far too low.

We are still too near to the Victorians—nearer than we used to be—to say whether *Great Expectations* is enough of a classic to come free of the particular culture from which it grew. There is surely something in it which, recalling the sentiment of other writers of the time, will prompt the description "Victorian." But though Pip's voice often puts us in mind of the melodious gravity of a poet like Tennyson, it feels less bound to its age than Tennyson's and has a clearer ring. Tennyson had often to ginger up his authentic sadness with a sort of silver-plated rhetoric. He never forgets that he is wearing his laurel crown. For example:

> So be it: there no shade can last
>   In that deep dawn behind the tomb,
>   But clear from marge to marge shall bloom
> The eternal landscape of the past. . . .
>
> (*In Memoriam*, xlvi.)

Pip is never so self-consciously grandiose as this splendid quatrain is. His poetry is more instrumental and less ornamental. It sounds most clearly in plain statements, for example in "I have forgotten nothing in my life that ever had a foremost place there, and little that ever had any place there." Great as a poem like *In Memoriam* is, it is more tied to its times; when it tries to rise above them (as in "Strong Son of God, immortal Love") it feels, however eloquent, too dateably nineteenth-century. There is something in *Great Expectations* that, by facing Victorian England so squarely, transcends it, something subtler than its art and deeper than its morals, for which poetry is as good a name as any. Other Dickens novels are in some respects greater or more "Dickensian," but this is one whose magic most eludes every attempt to define and pin it down. It is a Scarlet Pimpernel among novels, unparaphraseable as good poems are, a mystery that grows more mysterious as it is explained.

ELLIOT L. GILBERT

"In Primal Sympathy":
Great Expectations *and the Secret Life*

> . . . what we have loved, others
> will love, and we will teach them how.
> —Wordsworth, *The Prelude*

In his Preface to the first edition of *Martin Chuzzlewit*, a novel which in a number of significant ways resembles the later, more mature *Great Expectations*, Charles Dickens declares that he set out to write the earlier book "with the design of exhibiting, in various aspects, the commonest of all vices." Always a purveyor of mysteries, a lover of secrets, Dickens declines to be more explicit about the exact nature of the vice he means his story to illustrate, but his biographer, John Forster, leaves no doubt in the matter. *Martin Chuzzlewit* is designed, Forster writes, "to show, more or less by every person introduced, the number and variety of humours and vices that have their root in selfishness."

Selfishness is indeed a common vice, perhaps too common, too ubiquitous to be the main theme of any popular work of fiction. One might even argue that novels cannot be written on any other subject. And it is true that if by selfishness Dickens means nothing more than a general preoccupation with private ambition and personal appetite, then such a theme hardly seems special enough to require mention in a preface. What is clear from *Martin Chuzzlewit*, however, and even clearer from *Great Expectations*, is that for

From *Dickens Studies Annual: Essays on Victorian Fiction* 11. © 1983 by AMS Press, Inc.

Dickens the term "selfishness" had a much broader significance, was in an important way associated with the nineteenth-century's well-known effort to redefine, in every area of human experience, the concept of self; was in fact a name for what the novelist plainly saw as the master social, political, economic, and metaphysical problem of the age.

In his perception of those years as a time of nearly pathological individualism and self-consciousness, Dickens was certainly correct, for toward the end of the eighteenth century, people had begun—more widely and more intensely than they had ever done before—to lead secret lives. I do not mean by this term that a whole civilization suddenly embarked on a clandestine and licentious career of the sort celebrated in the anonymous autobiography, *My Secret Life*. (Though such a career would come to be seen by many Victorians as an inevitable result of the radical turn-of-the-century redefinition of self.) Instead, I mean to identify by the phrase "secret life" that dramatic turning inward, that interiorization of reality, with its consequent emphasis on the private experience of the individual, so characteristic of late eighteenth- and early nineteenth-century Romanticism.

Nor do I mean to suggest that such turning inward, such a determination to live a secret life, is a uniquely nineteenth-century phenomenon. Intense individualism, with its assertion of the primacy of the inner life, has appeared in one form or another in all ages. Christianity is the form this impulse most memorably took two thousand years ago; "the heresy of the free spirit" is the way one scholar designates the same concept in its medieval manifestation; and Cartesian philosophy, concerned as it is above all with "a subject receiving experience," is a powerful seventeenth-century version of this idea.

Nevertheless, the late eighteenth- and early nineteenth-century celebration of self was unique in at least one way. Where previous upsurges of individualism had always had to move against the grain of prevailing, solidly authoritarian political and social structures, Romantic emphasis on the sovereignty of the inner life could draw support from a growing perception of that sovereignty in many areas of human experience. Thus, where a literary critic is able to explain nineteenth-century poetic theory by stating that "to receive true glimpses of the real nature of things, the human mind must, at least temporarily, withdraw its attention from practical mundane affairs and concentrate it upon the inner life," Alexis de Tocqueville can use virtually the same language to define the new American democracy, saying of it that "every man finds his belief within himself . . . [and] all his feelings are turned in on himself." The century of Dickens is, then, more universally, more all-pervasively a century of self than any age had ever been before, and it is for this reason that the novelist devoted not just one book but, in some way or other, every book he ever wrote to examining the consequences, both good and bad, of living what I have called a secret life.

Perhaps the most troublesome consequence of the Romantic theory of self stems, ironically, from one of that theory's greatest strengths: its emphasis on what Coleridge called "the shaping spirit of imagination." "To the Romantic poets," Masao Miyoshi writes in *The Divided Self,*

> the imagination is a mode of transcending raw reality, a means of overcoming the world as given. . . . The imagination is here [an] active agent, shaping the world as it finds it, creating it anew with each vision. The world as given is continually being transformed into a Higher Reality of the poet's own making.

Not concealed by the generally approving tone of this passage is the metaphysical perilousness of the procedure Miyoshi describes. For it is clear that one inevitable result of the interiorization of reality sanctioned by Romanticism must be an undermining of the autonomous, independent reality left behind, must involve a questioning of the very existence of such an autonomous reality.

This problem had early been foreseen in the pre-Romantic philosophy of Bishop Berkeley and in the even more influential writings of David Hume, for whom, as one commentator has remarked, "the existence of an external world with fixed properties [was] really an unwarranted assumption." And these ideas had, again, a currency far beyond the interests of philosophers and poets. Wordsworth, we know, famously described a period in his childhood when

> I was unable to think of external things as having external existence, and I communed with all that I saw as something not apart from but inherent in my own immaterial nature. Many times while going to school have I grasped at a wall or tree to recall myself from this abyss of idealism to the reality.

But only a few years later, Tocqueville was discussing this same withdrawal from reality as a practical political problem, declaring as a prime weakness of democracy that it

> makes men forget their ancestors, clouds their view of their descendants, and isolates them from their contemporaries. Each man is forever thrown back on himself alone, and there is a danger that he may be shut up in the solitude of his own heart.

Nothing more clearly testifies to the nineteenth-century's preoccupation with "the abyss of idealism" than the number and the range of the images it created to illustrate its fear of a solipsistic isolation from the world. Premature burial, for example, was the fate Edgar Allan Poe obsessively reserved for characters "shut up in the solitude of their own hearts." Prisons were another major symbol of the pathological internalization of experience, Walter Pater, for one, finding all of life reduced to the "impressions of the individual in his isolation, each mind keeping as a solitary prisoner its own dream of a world." Just as powerfully, the silence and ultimately the disappearance of God were signs for Victorians of a serious loss of connection with any authoritative reality independent of the self. "I am on fire within," cries the self-absorbed, guild-ridden protagonist of Tennyson's "The Palace of Art," "There comes no murmur of reply"; words echoed by the narrator of Robert Browning's "Porphyria's Lover" as he clings hour after hour to the body of the mistress he has murdered:

> And thus we sit together now,
>   And all night long we have not stirred,
>   And yet God has not said a word!

Perhaps most curious and idiosyncratic is Thomas Carlyle's employment of eating as a metaphor for the solipsistic interiorization of reality, the conversion of an autonomous universe into one more element of self, the imposition of one person on another. "The least blessed fact one knows of," writes Caryle in *The French Revolution*, "on which necessitous mortals have ever based themselves, seems to be the primitive one of Cannibalism: That *I* can devour *Thee*."

The proliferation of such images in nineteenth-century literature—burial alive, imprisonment, silence, cannibalistic consumption—suggests how deeply the age was obsessed with selfishness in the broadest sense of that word, how much it feared the darker and more uncontrollable consequences of what I have called the secret life. Victorian writers began, Miyoshi declares, "with the knowledge of the Romantic failure in self-discovery," and a major strain of Victorian culture may thus be characterized as an intensive effort to reverse, or at least to slow, the inward journey Romanticism had so hopefully begun.

One comparatively naive attempt at such a reversal is already hinted at in Wordsworth's grasping at a wall or tree to recall himself from his solipsistic self-absorption, an act reminiscent of Dr. Johnson refuting Berkeley by kicking a stone. There is a certain innocent appeal in these gestures, gestures which, in the face of profound epistemological scepticism, simply assert as self-evident the reality of the external universe. Another well-known instance of such bluff British empiricism can be found in John Ruskin's essay on the Pathetic Fallacy. There, in response to the statement of a philosopher that "everything in the world depends upon his seeing or thinking of it, and that nothing, therefore, exists but what he sees or thinks of," Ruskin considers it entirely sufficient to declare that there is "something the matter" with the man and to denounce him for his "egotism, selfishness, shallowness, and impertinence." More sophisticated, though not—finally— more responsive to the challenge of Romantic inwardness, is the philosophy of Positivism, a dominant intellectual force in England from the middle of the nineteenth century. For the Positivist, to quote one commentator, the "final point of reference is the reality of the natural world, the objective world as in itself it really is, apart from the mediating human consciousness." Carlyle, with a very different philosophical outlook, also counsels escape from self into an objective universe of action. In *Sartor Resartus*, he urges those who would seek their inner natures to turn outward, work in the world, and discover themselves in their own products.

These and may other responses to Romantic subjectivity make up the familiar picture of Victorian thought and culture. The responses were of two basic kinds. First, there were those which attempted, at every level, to deny if not the existence then the priority of the secret life. Victorian culture was in many ways a surface phenomenon, with artifacts elaborately decorated to conceal their function, clothing ingeniously cut to conceal the female form, a complex code of conduct designed to suppress sexuality, and a hierarchy of social virtues at the summit of which stood respectability.

The second kind of Victorian response to Romanticism consisted of frenetic activity in the world, an unprecedented busyness whose deepest metaphysical intention was to permit escape from the self into some independent reality, into a much-desired otherness. The intention may have been reasonable, but the method was fatally flawed; for unavoidably, in building in the world the Victorians built in their own image. Inevitably, English Industrialism imposed English values on other races. It was precisely in this that the pathos of the nineteenth-century dilemma lay. For in seeking to avoid the Romantic trap of subjectivity and self, the Victorians chose to subordinate their inner lives to a seemingly objective materialism in which, in the end, they were able to find only their own selves again.

II

Charles Dickens, born when the influence of Romanticism was at its peak, and later to be the great popular novelist of the high Victorian period, lived and worked at the junctions of these two powerfully opposed cultural ideas, and achieved the success he did in part because he knew how to give these ideas vivid and dramatic expression and, just as importantly, because he was able, especially in his later work, to provide a plausible resolution of such seemingly irreconcilable philosophical positions. Much of the drama in the novels takes the form of the opposition of two very different kinds of characters. In the first group are men and women so locked into themselves, so trapped in secret lives of their own devising, that they have largely lost connection with an independent reality, with what Positivism called the "true order" of the world around them. They represent for Dickens, in Miyoshi's phrase, "the Romantic failure in self-discovery."

Many such characters are essentially comic, benign examples of our universal human tendency to live in the world as we would like it to be rather than as it is: Mr. Pickwick, for whom everything must be assigned its Pickwickian meaning, and Mr. Micawber, for whom sooner or later everything will "turn up"; Mrs. Gamp, whose world is peopled with her own inventions, and Mrs. Gamp's opposite number, Mrs. Billikin in *Edwin Drood*, who causes people to disappear simply by refusing to notice them; Mrs. Jellyby, for whom the present place and the present moment fade before a vision of distant and future benevolence; Mr. Podsnap, for whom anything un-English does not exist; and perhaps the most consummate solipsist in all the novels, Mr. Sapsea, whose "frantic and inconceivable epitaph for Mrs. Sapsea" to use Chesterton's phrase, is the very apotheosis of self-absorption.

Sometimes such characters, without entirely losing their comic appeal, acquire more sinister dimensions. There is, for example, Montague Tigg, who creates himself anew and imposes himself on others by the simple expedient of changing his name to Tigg Montague; Harold Skimpole, whose infantile egoism distorts not just his own private world but the world of all those around him; and the Barnacle Clan, whose Circumlocution Office, for all its appearance of connection with the running of the state, is entirely self-referential, irrelevant to everything but its own existence. Then there are the true criminals, who, in Dickens' novels, are almost invariably trapped in nightmare worlds of their own creation, who live the ultimate secret lives. One thinks of Fagin in his last hours, dying over and over again in imagination; of Jonas Chuzzlewit, haunted by the apparition of his murder victim; of John Jasper and his drug-induced visions which impose his own fantastic passions on the everyday world, driving him to cry out, at one point, "The echoes of my own voice among the arches seem to mock me . . . Must I take to carving demons out of my heart?" And over all these novels broods the grand Dickensian metaphor of the prison—from the Fleet to the Marshalsea to the Bastille to Newgate—in part because of the writer's own personal associations with the image, but more importantly because there could be no more fitting symbol in the nineteenth century of the "failure of self-discovery," of incarceration in the "abyss of idealism." Not even Mr. Pickwick is spared, for to seek to retreat into a world everywhere marked with one's own name is already to be a kind of prisoner.

All of these elements appear with a peculiar intensity in *Great Expectations*, as though in this novel Dickens set out to make his closest examination of the social and metaphysical problems presented by the Romantic celebration of self. Self-reflexive characters and their imprisonment, actual or symbolic, crowd the story, from a minor but emblematic figure like Old Bill Barley, who never leaves his room and whose primitive self-assertion takes the form of repeated announcements of his own name, to Magwitch in the hulks, to the insufferable Mr. Pumblechook, trapped in a lie he has told so often that it has wholly replaced reality, to the quintessential solipsist, Miss Havisham, who, by sheer force of a perverse will, brings even time to a stop to commemorate her private grief.

We realize that the road Pip must travel in his life will be a difficult one when we note that there is a prison at each end. At home there is the gothic Satis House, in which Miss Havisham has self-indulgently locked herself away, and in London there is Newgate, representative of all the greed and egotism and violence that comprise Little, rather than Great, Britain. Indeed, we might perhaps see in this road, as in Pip's whole career, Dickens' deliberate symbol of the journey of mid-century England away from the Romantic prison of the secret life and toward the Victorian prison of materialism.

Pip's own journey along this road begins when, turned upside down by Magwitch, he finds that the whole world has turned upside down with him. His natural conclusion that the universe must therefore be coextensive with his own mind is precisely the Berkeleian idealism from which it takes him the rest of the novel to recover, an idealism Dickens slyly associates with the boy's regular imbibing of tar water, the popular nostrum originally concocted by (and still in the mid-nineteenth century credited to) Bishop Berkeley. In the end, what Pip learns from his journey is that it is a capital mistake to have expectations—to suppose that the world will agree to shape itself to anyone's preconceptions and desires—a mistake which leaves him painfully unprepared for life's surprising and dangerous autonomy.

Of course, we must not be misled by the fact that Pip is himself the victim of other people's solipsism—of Miss Havisham's and Magwitch's and even Pumblechook's private fantasies—into missing this point about his own manipulation of reality. In the abyss of idealism, everyone is necessarily the figment of someone else's imagination, even while supposing himself to be the center of his own universe. H. M. Daleski suggests that the expectations of many of the characters in the novel "have their source in a desire for change, for the transformation of an existing situation; and the expectations are sustained in each case by the belief that such a transformation may be effected *through the agency of another*" [italics mine]. But such expectations of change at the hands of another do not reflect genuine belief in a reality independent of self. Instead, because they are only further examples of wishful thinking—Miss Havisham's hope of achieving revenge through Estella, Magwitch's plan to escape the stigma of his past through Pip, and Pip's desire to change his own status with the aid of a patron—such expectations merely serve to confirm the unavoidability of solipsism, the ubiquitousness of self.

A second, contrasting category of characters in Dickens' novels consists of men and women who reject the secret life, with its treacherous subjectivity, in favor of a Positivistic "objective world as in itself it really is," who seek to avoid the "abyss of idealism," the prison of self, by rigorously directing their energies outward, by heeding Carlyle's well-known exhortation to "Produce! Produce!" The most famous of these characters is undoubtedly Ebenezer Scrooge, ferociously dismissing every appeal to emotion as humbug and putting his faith instead in such palpable social institutions as stock exchanges, prisons, and workhouses. But Scrooge-like figures are everywhere in the novels: Mr. Merdle, "immensely rich," Dickens tell us, "a man of prodigious enterprise [whose] desire was to the utmost to satisfy Society, whatever that was"; Mr. Dombey, a wealthy merchant who ruthlessly suppresses all tender feelings and who, significantly, lives in a London whose interior is being torn out to make room for a railroad; Thomas Gradgrind, proprietor of a Positivist educational theory whose chief objective is the stamping out of fancy; Edward Murdstone, of whom Dickens writes "He had that kind of shallow black eyes—I want a better word to express an eye that has no depth in it to be looked into."

Characters like these clearly have in common a worldly success gained at the expense of their own interiority, share the Victorian commitment to surfaces which requires the severing of connections with an inner life in order to permit the establishment of corresponding connections with an outer one. At first glance, the logic of such a procedure seems unimpeachable. In "The Palace of Art," for example, Tennyson's protagonist must renounce her at first complacent and later nightmarish secret life if she wishes to enter into useful relationships with others, and there is an easy moral symmetry in such an arrangement that must have appealed to early Victorian readers. But Dickens certainly means us to recognize, from our experience with his novels, the inadequacy of such a theory, means us to notice that such a procedure inevitably leads his characters not out of the prison of self but more and more irretrievably into it.

Why this should be so becomes clearer when we look at a few of the philanthropic figures in the stories. Especially in the earlier books, philanthropists are represented by such stock characters as Mr. Brownlow in *Oiver Twist* and the Cheeryble Brothers in *Nicholas Nickleby*, Dickens apparently unconcerned with motivation, with the psychology of metaphysics of charitable actions, and taking generosity at its face value. Elsewhere, however, the novelist is more analytic, more cynical, perhaps, and so we find such creations as Mrs. Pardiggle, a Visiting Lady of "rapacious benevolence" who bullies her reluctant children into participating in her charitable activities, and who likes nothing so much as lecturing to destitute slum-dwellers who have expressly asked her to stop. We have, as well, the Reverend Luke Honeythunder, a violent lover of humanity who demands strict compliance with his own moral vision and whose philanthropy is, Dickens informs us, "of that gunpowderous sort that the difference between it and animosity is hard to determine."

This treatment of philanthropy in Dickens' novels must be considered in the context of the prevailing Victorian attitude toward charity, an attitude which Alexander Welsh has described as

> chiefly distinguished by its emphasis on the character of the recipient . . . an emphasis that inverts the long tradition of Christian charity as a practice contributing to the salvation of the charitable. The elevating influence of the gift on the giver is never denied, but the giver is asked to subordinate this (almost selfish) consideration to a concern for the effect of his gift on the recipient's character—an effect that is regarded as dubious at best.

Such a statement makes it clear why philanthropy must necessarily fail in its effort to achieve an escape from self into a genuine relationship with others. For if, on the one hand, philanthropists take pleasure in their own generosity, if beneficent characters like Mr. Brownlow and the Cheerybles have, as Humphry House puts it, "their full return in watching the happiness they distribute and in the enjoyment of gratitude and power," then they are guilty of a kind of selfishness; at the very least their openhandedness is tainted with vanity. Alex Zwerdling sums up this particular Victorian anxiety very well when, in discussing Esther Summerson in *Bleak House*, he explains that her reluctance to break with John Jarndyce and accept Allan Woodcourt results from her terror "not of hurting Jarndyce but of pleasing herself." If, on the other hand, philanthropists should in fact succeed in suppressing all personal satisfaction, their act of charity must nevertheless compromise the autonomy, the otherness of the recipients, manipulate and impose on them even as Merdle and Dombey and Gradgrind, without any charitable intentions, manipulate and impose on the people with whom they live and the worlds in which they act. The stain of self in Dickens' fiction thus goes deep, indeed seems ineradicable, and the spectre of Carlyle's cannibalism is never far away; only not now saying "I can devour thee," but more chillingly, "Try as I will, I cannot *keep* from devouring thee."

Such cannibalism, such devouring is a key metaphor in *Great Expectations*, a story which, from the Christmas dinner at the forge to the grim, elegant suppers at Jaggers's house, is—as Angus Wilson reminds us—full of unpleasant feasting. The book opens, of course, with Pip being forced to act under the literal threat of being eaten. The young man who is to roast and consume Pip's heart and liver, perhaps initially a Mrs. Harris-like figment of Magwitch's imagination, must inevitably be equated with the corrosive and manipulative Compeyson. His name meaning, literally, "co-countryman," Compeyson is everyone's secret companion, dark double, diabolical inner voice: like Magwitch, a prisoner; like Miss Havisham, a marriage partner; like Orlick, a criminal; like Pip, a gentleman. Ubiquitous and morbidly energetic, Compeyson is the representative inhabitant of a universe of isolation, despair, and death in which each person sees, endlessly duplicated, only his own likeness.

Miss Havisham too is an eater of hearts, first of her own and then of Estella's, consuming the girl and reconstituting her as the instrument of an alien vengeance, obliging her to be an eater of hearts as well. Even Magwitch's philanthropy, though it derives from genuine gratitude, is devouring, falling unavoidably into the two corruptions of charity identified by sceptical Victorians. First it is manipulative; Magwitch tries to shape Pip to his own perverse image of a gentleman, controlling even his choice of a name. Then it is self-serving; Magwitch returns to England so that he may himself enjoy the fruits of his philanthropy, that he may get a "full return in watching the happiness he has distributed and in the enjoyment of gratitude and power." Thus interpreted, generosity in the story is only another name for selfishness, charity another name for vanity, a vanity particularly subtle in its danger because it comes in the guise of self-abnegation: "the vanity of penitence," as Pip says to Miss Havisham, "the vanity of remorse, the vanity of unworthiness, and other monstrous vanities that have been curses in this world."

III

What escape, then, is possible from the conflict between Romantic solipsism and an equally self-serving Victorian materialism? If, on the one hand, Romantic celebration of the inner life leads inexorably to isolation, to imprisonment in the self, to a Byronic stalking apart in joyless reverie, and if, on the other hand, Victorian renunciation of self in favor of work in the world not only fails to demolish that prison but makes it even sturdier and more secure, how can it ever be possible to cast off the oppressive burden of ego and enter into genuine relationship with others?

It is fair to say that this is always a key question in Dickens' novels. His characters, as has often been noted, are the great monologists of English fiction, speaking much more often to assert themselves and their idiosyncratic views than to enter into real communication with the rest of humanity. Frequently orphans, they are, in Tocqueville's words, "ignorant of ancestors, uncertain of descendants, isolated from their contemporaries." They move at random through a concealing fog that represents the alienating influence of nineteenth-century materialism, and nothing seems more unlikely than that they should ever connect with others like themselves. Indeed, we might well ask whether, in the light of this analysis, it makes sense even to talk about such connection.

To this question at least, Dickens would certainly answer "yes," for what is clear from the novels is the strength of his belief in a universal ordering principle, what one critic has called the "tight web of cause and effect beneath the apparent chaos of daily affairs." Another commentator identifies this order more precisely, observing that in Dickens' work as a whole, "the apparent randomness of existence conceals an underlying providence," a providence frequently taking the form of elaborate coincidence as a device for commenting on the complex connections which, in this view, always exist among people, even when they suppose themselves to be most imprisoned, most isolated from one another. In *Great Expectations*, Dickens develops a network of connections, at a deep level of his plot, meant to be perceived only retrospectively by both readers and characters, meant to show, in Dickens' own words, "by a backward light, what everything has been working to—but only to *suggest*, until the fulfillment comes." This is the real secret life of the novel, a force for wholeness and order awaiting its moment, one of which occurs at the death of Magwitch. At the bedside we find a settled calm, the bitterness and ignorance that have at one time or another separated Pip, Magwitch and Estella are all suspended. Pip talks to the dying man about the mutual relationships—"You had a child whom you loved and lost. She lived and found powerful friends. She is living now. She is a lady and very beautiful. And I love her!"—and for a moment we glimpse the secret life of the novel moving like a healing current, asserting connections that had always existed but had never till now been recognized. "It is in this way," writes Dorothy Van Ghent, "that the manifold organic relationships among men are revealed, and that the Dickens world—founded on fragmentariness and disintegration—is made whole."

That it is only at this depth that the dilemma of self and other can be resolved, Dickens makes clear in the chapter immediately following, the scene of Pip's illness and recovery. A scene similar to this one occurs in *Martin Chuzzlewit* where young Martin, a prototypical Pip, riddled with the spiritual disease he calls, "Self, self, self," falls physically ill and is nursed back to health by his ever-cheerful friend Mark Tapley. In the earlier book, however, this incident is related entirely from the outside and we are left to guess at the actual process of the protagonist's regeneration. In *Great Expectations*, that process is what chiefly interests the author, the process of spiritual recovery from the disease of self.

What we learn is that the first step toward such a recovery is *not* to reject the inner life and turn outward to the world, however logical such a process may seem. We have seen what that decision can lead to. Instead, we discover, paradoxically, but in the great mystical tradition, that recovery requires plunging deeper into that interiority, an act at first so unimaginable that for Pip it needs physical illness to initiate it. As his disease takes effect, Pip begins by falling deliriously into the painful isolation of personality which has always been his spiritual affliction, into the secret life that alienates and imprisons and from which he longs to escape. "I implored in my own person," he recounts one of his nightmares during this period, "to have the engine stopped and my part in it hammered off."

In such dream work, itself a form of autobiographical story-telling like the book Pip will one day make of his life, elements that seem meaningless and absurd have in reality been constructed by a highly complicated activity of the mind which renders everything significant and which, moreover, obligates us to seek, by Dickens' "backward light," the providential and/or psychological order underlying apparently random experiences and coincidental events. For Pip, as identity begins to disintegrate under the influence of fever—is "broken by illness" as he puts it and for which he is afterwards grateful—he sinks deeper and deeper, past personality, in a silence beyond monologues, finding at last, at this depth, a second secret life, the true secret life that frees, connects, and heals, "our own only true, deep-buried self," as Matthew Arnold puts it in *Empedocles on Etna*, "being one with which we are one with the whole world." Significantly, it is at this depth that Pip is restored to Joe, with whom—and the phrase takes on special meaning in this *extremis*—he was "ever the best of friends." For it is permanence and continuity that is celebrated by the secret life at this level, greetings across gulfs, Joe and the young Pip raising their half-eaten bits of bread to one another in silent communion.

That word is suggestive of the elements of the Christian story that provide another deep pattern for the novel. The book opens at Christmas, Pip is present at the weird resurrection of Magwitch from behind the elder Pirrip's tombstone, on the horizon of the marshes are two gibbets and a beacon light, Jaggers washes his hands after each trial, Pip is rudely baptized in the Thames, when he is ready to leave England, he informs us, in Christ's words to the rich man, "I sold all I had," and so on. Not that Dickens intended a rigorous retelling of the Christian story in nineteenth-century terms, but as the premier Western myth of the fall into self and the recovery from it, the New Testament narrative inevitably offered useful points of reference.

Most striking, perhaps, of those points is the fact that in the Christian story, metaphors which, for the nineteenth century, were representative of alienation and despair, convey instead the ideas of connection and hope: Christ's imprisonment *gives* him to the world rather than sequestering him from it, his "premature burial" leads not to death but to life, the silence of God at the crucifixion is an invitation to, not an expulsion from, Paradise. Even more remarkable is the reversal of the metaphor of eating. Where, in Carlyle, that "I can devour *Thee*" is "the least blessed fact one knows of," a futile transaction in which the victim is diminished while the devourer gains only more self, during a communion ceremony, both eater and eaten are augmented. In *Great Expectations*, it is Joe's life that most clearly embodies these reversals of metaphor. Unlettered, silenced by his inadequate formal education, Joe is nevertheless spiritually eloquent. At the forge, a prison to Pip, Joe is entirely at home, and when he is nursing Pip, giving freely of his time, money, and substance in a way that ought rationally to deplete him, he in fact enlarges remarkably, becomes omnipresent, offers, to his hallucinating patient, "all kinds of extraordinary transformations of the human face" which sooner or later settle down into the likeness of Joe.

One of the elements of Christianity most attractive to Dickens, one critic comments, was the creed of "the fatherhood of God [which] allowed for a kind of ancestor worship." Certainly, the many orphans or abandoned children in Dickens' fiction questing for reunion, either actual or symbolic, with lost parents, suggest how essential Dickens believed such reunion to be for the achievement of spiritual health. "Father is so much kinder that he used to be," Scrooge's sister happily reports, "that home's like heaven." To discover the lost father is to discover one's own place in the beneficent order of the generations, to escape from the prison of self into the amplitude of a universal community, to establish connections with ancestors, contemporaries, and descendants, connections whose disappearance from nineteenth-century society Tocqueville found so ominous. Certainly, from the moment Pip, in the depths of his illness, recognizes in Joe his spiritual father, a father he has been seeking since the first page of the novel, all traces of snobbish alienation from his own past vanish. Simultaneously, he becomes capable of a more generous judgment of his friend, Herbert Pocket, and later there is even a little Pip to carry on his name.

The darker fate of Estella only emphasizes the importance Dickens assigned to reunion with the father as a means of escape from the prison of self. Like Pip, Estella is brought up as an orphan, but unlike Pip, she has no Joe to represent the benign fatherhood of God. Magwitch, her natural father, she never knows, and the morally ambiguous Jaggers, who in fact "gives" her life, is himself a pathologically isolated figure, victim of a cold and alienating intellect gruesomely symbolized by the severed heads in his office. Cut off from connection with the world on this side, she is further isolated by the vengeful, witch-like Miss Havisham. For in the Victorian scheme, in which marriage is a woman's best hope of entering into the broad community of the father, the single woman is the ultimate metaphor for spiritual isolation, and to be left at the altar is to be condemned to a life sentence of solitary confinement, a sentence Miss Havisham ruthlessly executes upon herself in the name of a despised patriarchy and which she attempts, all too successfully, to impose on her ward.

The theme of the fatherhood of God is comically exploited in the Wemmick episodes. A character who, with his absurdly elaborate contrivances for isolating himself from the world, ought to symbolize solipsistic despair, Wemmick is, instead, shown to be spiritually healthy because he is the selfless preserver of a paternal community. Every one of Wemmick's actions is taken, very literally, in the name of the father, and indeed, the Aged Parent can be seen as Dickens' wry satire on gloomy Victorian pronouncements about the superannuation and silence of God. Like that Hardyesque God, the Aged P. cannot hear and is incapable of replying coherently to questions addressed to him. But there the comparison ends, for his is not the censorious silence of rejection and abandonment but rather the loving silence of a mutual understanding that requires nothing to be said.

Such a silent communion is for Dickens, as it was for Carlyle, a clear sigh of spiritual health, the health of people secure in their own natures and participating so unself-consciously in the universal order that they have no need for words to influence or manipulate one another. Both writers seem to be echoing here Keats' famous contrast between the elector of Hanover, who governs his petty state, and knows how many straws are swept daily from the causeways in all his dominions, and has a continual itching that all the housewives should have their coppers well scoured, and the ancient emperors of vast provinces, who had only heard of the remote ones and scarcely cared to visit them.

Such negative capability as the ancient emperors displayed, such un-cannibalistic acquiescence in the uniqueness and sovereignty of others, has, we know, always been characteristic of Joe. From the start, exposed to the energetic cannibalism of Mrs. Joe, he seeks to protect Pip while unconditionally loving both. Later, he readily destroys Pip's apprenticeship papers, umcomplainingly relinquishing control over the boy while rejecting the worldly Jaggers's offer of compensation. His act is an authentically philanthropic one, asking nothing for itself and freeing rather than manipulating the recipient.

That by the end of the story Pip has become the true son of this spiritual father is perhaps clearest from the silence which he maintains about the money he had given to Herbert Pocket. Where Miss Havisham seeks credit for philanthropy she has not performed, and Magwitch taints his genuine philanthropy with a desire for gratitude, Pip finds his greatest happiness in self-abnegation, in a withholding of himself which, paradoxically, leads to the deepening of his relationship with his friend. Looking back, from this vantage point of the novel's end, on Pip's pilgrimage, we can see that Dickens has indeed been offering it as a paradigmatic nineteenth-century journey. Beginning where Romaticism itself began, in the ultimate isolation of the graveyard, among graveyard poets and the tombstones of his prematurely buried siblings, and moving out into an encounter with frenetic Victorian materialism which only increases that isolation, Pip is shown undergoing a symbolic death of the self through which he is able to discover a place beyond personality where true community is possible.

IV

It is natural for the reader of *Great Expectations* to wonder, however, whether such a resolution is a universal or an influential or even a convincing response to the nineteenth-century crisis of self, or for that matter to the situation presented in the novel. Certainly, it was not the only response available to Dickens' contemporaries. Just three years after the novelist's death, for example, Walter Pater was proposing, in his "Conclusion" to *Studies in the History of the Renaissance*, from which I have already quoted, that the effort to escape from the prison of self be abandoned in favor of an ecstatic cultivation of that imprisonment. And there can be no doubt that it was Pater's recommendation rather than Dickens' that more deeply influenced the last third of the nineteenth century. Indeed, an unsentimental reader may wonder if Dickens himself could seriously have believed that the tepid mysticism of a conventional—even an exhausted—Christianity was at all adequate to resolve the long-standing post-Romantic problems of epistemological scepticism and the secret life.

Ironically, Pater's advice, which in the context of these problems as presented by Dickens is in fact a counsel of despair, seems to lead to more intense and more joyous experience than does the resigned, autumnal resolution of *Great Expectations*, a resolution which, for many readers, appears to reflect its author's own spiritual exhaustion at this stage of his career. "What is lacking in Dickens' magical solution," asks Edwin Eigner about the novel, "that it fails this time to bring off the conventional happy ending?" The question clearly alludes to the absence of a celebratory marriage of hero and heroine at the end of the book, in either of the two final passages, but it also comments on the protagonist's long exile from his homeland, on the unexciting commercial career to which all his hopes for a dramatic life have led him, and in general on the low energy of the story's last pages.

It is particularly the absence of an intense, life-affirming energy, an energy we have come to expect from our reading of Dickens' earlier works, that we note in the resolution of *Great Expectations*: the absence of any equivalent, for example, of Scrooge's inspired declaration that, in his newly recovered innocence, he has become a baby again, or of the transfiguring fancy of Sairey Gamp, whose creativity, one commentator remarks, fills "the void in her life . . . casting the glow of imagination over the sordidness and solitude [of her world]". The sober *dénouement* of *Great Expectations* is hardly the place for Scrooge's magical return to a pre-lapsarian state of grace. The warning message Pip had earlier received—"Don't go home!"—has become, by the end of the story, a more poignant "Can't go home," the young man's exile from England representing, as well, an irrevocable exile from the Eden of childhood. Nor will any Mrs. Gamp-like inventiveness serve this time to "cast a glow" over a sordid world. Pip's wildly fanciful story of his first visit to Satis House is by the end of the novel repudiated in favor of the subdued, serious-minded autobiographical account which we call *Great Expectations*. No wonder readers find unconvincing any suggestion that the book is about—in the words of one critic—"the Christian love and 'true fatherhood' by which [Pip], and not he alone, may be redeemed." It is precisely such redemptive energy that appears to be missing from the story's resolution, and the "lack" of which, as Edwin Eigner puts it, constitutes the work's "failure to bring off the conventional happy ending."

To speak of a "conventional" happy ending, however, is to speak of one's *expectations* for a story, and here we may begin to better understand the significance of the muted conclusion Dickens supplied for his novel. For in a book about the dangers of indulging in unreasonable expectations, there could hardly be a wittier or more dramatic achievement for the author than to demonstrate to his readers that they are susceptible to the same solipsistic preconceptions as his protagonist, hardly a more effective device than to cause the audience to make the same mistake as the hero, the better to reveal the seductive nature of that mistake. Where, after all, have our disappointed expectations for the resolution of the novel come from if not, as Edwin Eigner suggests, from Dickens' own earlier fictions, from his many irresistible invitations to us to believe wholeheartedly in the ability of Scrooge to be a baby again and of Mrs. Gamp to "fill the void of her life" with tales of her own making; if not, in short, from his consistently and famously encouraging us in the Romantic faith that a world created by the imagination is better and more appealing and ultimately truer than any Positivistic universe "as in itself it really is?" And such an idea is exactly analogous to Pip's own Romantic reliance on a magical rescue from "sordidness and solitude."

But in *Great Expectations*, the familiar Dickensian formula no longer applies. The passionate energy and creativity of Pip's fiction about Satis House, for example, a fiction appealing even to Joe, who, like the reader, knows it is a lie but wishes it were true, is presented here not as part of the resolution of the hero's difficulties but as itself the problem, an early instance of Pip imposing his own vision on the world. And to the extent that readers are delighted by the imaginative vitality of this fiction and feel disappointment at Pip's subsequent metamorphosis into sober autobiographer, they too are falling into what Dickens would have us understand is Pip's own self-indulgent error, into the familiar error of all readers everywhere who desire a favorite author to go on fulfilling their conventional expectations of him. "In the wilderness," lamented a reviewer of *Little Dorrit* in *Blackwood's Magazine*, "we sit down and weep when we remember thee, O *Pickwick*!" But in *Great Expectations*, Dickens would have us recognize, the somber conclusion of the story constitutes not a loss of power and authority but a gain; the muted, autumnal tomes of the book's last pages, he wants us to see, depict not the feebleness of disappointed desire but the tranquility of recollected emotion.

The Pip whose voice we hear narrating the story of *Great Expectations* is, we must not forget, a memoirist, a man quietly revisiting his own hectic past, and it is surely appropriate that Dickens, whose narratives tend often to circle back to their beginnings, should have found a Wordsworthian resolution for a story whose origins lie so deep in the Wordsworthian "abyss of idealism." Dickens' debt to Wordsworth, particularly to the latter's exploration of childhood innocence through the process of recollection, is great, his books owing much, Angus Wilson comments, "to the ethics of the *Lyrical Ballads.*" Other critics have noted this same indebtedness. Barry Westburg, for example, speaks of the importance of memory in Dickens' psychological scheme, commenting that "he dealt with it more fully than any other writer of his time (except possibly Wordsworth, whose *Prelude* was published the same year as *Copperfield*).

The theme of childhood revisited is a familiar one in early nineteenth-century literature, "often represented," M. H. Abrams points out,

> as a circuitous journey back home. So represented, the protagonist is the collective mind or consciousness of men, and the story is that of its painful pilgrimage through difficulties, sufferings, and recurrent disasters in quest of a goal which, unwittingly, is the place it had left behind when it first set out and which, when reachieved, turns out to be better than it had been at the beginning,

The journey described by Abrams is a mystical one, most schematically depicted in the works of Dickens by Scrooge's astonishing recovery of his own youthfulness. But there is a danger inherent in such a mystical resolution, one apparent to even the most sympathetic readers of *A Christmas Carol.* For the fact that Scrooge's innocence is reachieved *in his own person* inevitably compromises its integrity, raising the possibility that the old man's revival may be just one more convolution of ego, a further solipsistic manipulation of reality rather than the genuine recovery from the disease of self it is supposed to represent.

Perhaps this is why a maturer Dickens found the Wordsworthian model of a return to the past *through another* so much more appropriate for a story like *Great Expectations.* The paradigm of this Wordsworthian strategy is, of course, "Tintern Abbey," an elegiac poem in which, after "a long absence" from an intensely experienced scene, the narrator is able to recover some of the power of that old emotion by emphatically participating in his sister's experience of the same scene. Such recovery is necessarily at one remove from, and less passionate than, the original solitary moment, but it achieves a sweetness of its own through being shared, through its confirmation of the fact that beyond Pateresque self-reflexiveness there exists genuine otherness as an alternative to solipsistic isolation. "What we have loved," Wordsworth declares at the end of the *Prelude*, "others will love, and we will teach them how," such teaching or reporting further emphasizing the human obligation to, and connection with, others. The "Intimations Ode" makes the same point even more directly. Beginning with its famous concession that the ecstatic personal moment can never be recovered, it philosophically accepts as substitute the consolation of community inherent "in the primal sympathy / which having been must ever be."

Great Expectations, I am suggesting, derives in part from this Wordsworthian model. The well-known lines from "Tintern Abbey," for example:

> These beauteous forms,
> Through a long absence, have not been to me
> As is a landscape to a blind man's eye;
> But oft in lonely rooms, and 'mid the din
> Of towns and cities, I have owed to them,
> In hours of weariness, sensations sweet . . .

have their somewhat soberer counterpart in the opening passage of Chapter 59 of the novel:

> For eleven years I had not seen Joe nor Biddy with my bodily eyes—though they had both been often before my fancy in the East—when, upon an evening in December, an hour or two after dark, I laid my hand softly on the latch of the old kitchen door.

After the nearly fatal illness which purges him of ego, and after "many wanderings, many years / Of absence," Pip revisits the scene of his early life. There he finds his old place filled by a young child bearing his own name and recognizes the obligation which such an experience places on him to record his history so that "what we have loved, / Others will love." The tone of such a history must necessarily be subdued and elegiac, not as a sign of its author's spiritual exhaustion but as an indication of his newly acquired "philosophic mind." The community beyond personality that Pip has discovered is also beyond the manic, self-advertising fables that provided a specious vitality earlier in the book. Christian acquiescence in "the primal sympathy / Which having been must ever be"—here validated by its Wordsworthian analog—always expresses itself most authoritatively, Dickens suggests, through silence.

V

To talk of the silence of an autobiographer may at first seem paradoxical. Technically speaking, the only voice we ever hear in *Great Expectations* is Pip's, but what the young memoirist's story appears to tell us is that representation in general, and language in particular—both spoken and written—are all too frequently distorters of reality, concealing rather than revealing truth. "Have you seen anything of London, yet?" Joe is asked, and in some bewilderment he replies:

> Why, yes Sir . . . me and Wopsle went off straight to look at the Blacking Ware'us. But we didn't find that it come up to its likeness in the red bills at the shop doors.

Throughout the novel, words are shown to be deceptive and imprisoning: susceptible to misunderstanding, as Pip misunderstands "wife of the above," or to misspelling and misconstruction, as Pip's "BlEve ME in FxN" may be misconstrued; capable of imposing one person on another, as indenture papers do, or of lying outright, as in Pip's story about Satis House, or Pumblechook's self-congratulations, or Jaggers's collection of convict memoirs.

All these instances suggest that language is unavoidably an instrument for manipulating reality, for imposing one's own vision on others, for promoting self-consciousness and irony and isolation. To speak or to write, however scrupulously, is of necessity to deceive, to create a private, alternate universe and thus to destroy all possibility of that self-abnegation and community which it is Pip's intention to urge in his cautionary story. Certainly, the depiction of Joe in *Great Expectations* supports this view. Unlettered and therefore "silent," Joe is the least manipulative character in the novel, the one who engages life most directly and authentically, who grasps most unironically the self-evident proposition that "lies is lies." Yet it would be a great mistake to suppose that the story means to resolve this dilemma of language by equating virtue with illiteracy or by celebrating Joe's naiveté over Pip's dearly bought sophistication as the more desirable human state.

One critic seeks to deal with the paradox of Pip's "silent" narration by distinguishing between "lies and fictions in general," through which Pip originally enters the fallen world of self, and "confession, that frees him from [that world]." The distinction is a reasonable one, emphasizing the difference between language intended to impose solipsistically on others and language meant to facilitate surrender of self to a larger order. Pip's careful reportage, for example, never calling attention to itself as reportage, never inviting us to impugn its motives, clearly seems to belong in this latter category. In the end, however, we have no choice but to question the good faith of *any* linguistic reconstruction of reality, however well-intentioned. For as Frank Kermode argues in *The Sense of an Ending*, the chief objective of the novelist, autobiographical or otherwise, is to impose some personal structure on what appears to be the chaos of experience.

Kermode derives this view principally from his observation of fiction's need—a need nor shared by life—to come to a satisfactory or at least to a significant conclusion. But when we examine the ending of *Great Expectations* we find its writer remarkably—if unintentionally—withholding the final assertion of authority, of self, as if understanding, at least intuitively, how essential his own silence is to the credibility of the novel's resolution. Everyone knows how Dickens, having written the so-called "unhappy" ending of his story, the ending in which Pip and Estella meet briefly and then part, was then convinced by his fellow novelist Edward Bulwer-Lytton to write a second, "happy" ending in which the two meet and remain together. Consideration of this matter has tended to focus on two questions: which of the endings is better (critics take both sides), and what was Dickens' motive for making the change (did he do it simply to improve sales or for some other reason)?

We can pretty well dismiss the notion that Dickens acted out of crass commercialism. Bulwer-Lytton is on record elsewhere as stating that whether a book ends happily or not rarely affects sales, and as Edwin Eigner puts it,

> from several letters to other writers we can reconstruct at least the nature of Bulwer's advice [to Dickens], and I believe we can conclude that it was based on esthetic principles which, however faulty they may be judged, should not be dismissed as either commercial or merely conventional.

Whatever we think of the quality of the emendation, however, and whatever we may conclude about Dickens' motives for making the change, there is one striking fact about which there can be no dispute. People who purchase modern editions of *Great Expectations* find themselves reading a novel with two endings. That Dickens never intended the endings to be printed together is beside the point. As far as our actual experience is concerned, *Great Expectations* presents its readers (and perhaps even its characters) with a choice of how the story should conclude.

At least one consequence of the alternative endings is to create the effect of an extraordinarily autonomous fictional world, one free even of authorial control and intention. Dickens' willingness to surrender some of his authority to Bulwer is itself an unusual instance of self-abnegation in a normally independent writer. Is it possible that, for the moment, Dickens was under the spell of his own story and its thesis, that he really perceived the prime value to be the withholding of self, an acquiescence in forces different from, and perhaps greater than his own? How, after all, could the ending of a story as rich and complex as this ever be limited to a single possibility? An author may all along have his secret intentions for the ending of his novel, but what of the novel's own, perhaps deeper intentions? If, as Murray Baumgarten suggests in another essay in this collection, writing has the capacity to "imprison the imagination . . . warp the world," what we may be seeing in the double conclusion of *Great Expectations*—and two endings imply, of course, an infinite number—is a chastened Dickens, struggling against the selfishness of language to allow for possibilities in the world that even this most imaginative of English novelists knew he could not imagine.

This striking authorial "silence" represented by Dickens' submission to Bulwer and his consequent creation of the two endings of *Great Expectations*, like the equally notable substitution in the book of a tone of settled melancholy for the usual Dickensian ebullience, are the key elements in this major Victorian response to the ubiquitous nineteenth-century dilemma of the secret life. I have already identified that dilemma as a conflict between healthy self-expression and solipsism, a conflict whose resolution appears to have presented more and more difficulties as the century advanced. Wordsworth, for example, aware as he was of the dangers of idealism, nevertheless found it unqualifiedly blissful to be young and self-absorbed, and his development of an emphatic philosophy to take the place of potentially imprisoning youthful passions seems to have been accomplished cheerfully enough. By mid-century, however, such comparatively naive delight and maturation were hardly possible, and especially in Dickens' later novels an ineradicable self-consciousness and even self-parody intrude, often introducing a hectic note into their liveliest comic passages and darkening their moments of self-abnegation.

Readers today can trace, in this movement from the magisterial resignation of Wordsworth to the melancholy submission of Dickens, a line of development in nineteenth-century culture leading inexorably toward *fin-de-siècle* nihilism; toward, for instance, a naturalistic fiction in which human lives are not so much secret as—to use Hardy's term—obscure, in which men and women are abandoned by an unfatherly universe to an isolation from which there is not even the possibility of escape into a community beyond self. In this line of development, Dickens clearly occupies a middle position as the typical Victorian wanderer between two worlds, worlds represented by the two endings—one falteringly romantic, the other incipiently nihilistic—that he wrote for *Great Expectations*. Such a middle position has obvious advantages for the artist, discouraging simplistic formulations of problems, guarding against easy answers. Certainly, it is the delicate balance maintained among conflicting claims in *Great Expectations*, the aesthetically and philosophically rich texture of the story that has earned it its current status as the most respected of its author's novels. The balance can perhaps best be seen in the oxymoronic "silent" speech through which the story is told by its reticent narrator, in the willing relinquishment of will which is the essence of its ambivalent resolution. In the persistent nineteenth-century conflict between self-expression and solipsism, there could be no more complex or resonant figure than Pip, the passionate dreamer turned acquiescent realist who, choosing to renounce self, chooses to tell the story of that choice.

GAIL TURLEY HOUSTON

"Pip" and "Property":
The (Re)Productions of the Self in Great Expectations

One of the important perceptions of Dickens' fiction is of Victorian society as one in which the weak support the strong, the starving underwrite the satiated, the poor prop up the rich, the children sustain the parents—and the female upholds the male. Indeed, the typical Dickensian heroine is a nourishing mother figure who herself is usually motherless. Central to most of Dickens' novels, this heroine in her self-denial creates for the hero a safe and sacred haven from the rapaciousness of the market. Nevertheless, these same heroines also underwrite the economic ambition they are intended to mediate. As Mary Poovey suggests, in Victorian England the alienation of male labor was made tolerable by representing female work within the domestic sphere as selfless and self-regulating, and therefore not alienated. Hence, it was assumed that the "non-competitive, non-aggressive, and self-sacrificing" private sphere of women domesticated without curbing the "competitive, aggressive, and acquisitive" public sphere of the male dedicated to success and money.

This pattern is borne out in Dickens' fiction in a number of ways. For example, in *The Old Curiosity Shop*, Nell's ascetic control of her body and her maternal care for her grandfather mute but also magnify his grotesque obsession with gambling and wealth. Likewise, Mary Graham's "self-possession and control over her emotions" tame the senior Martin

From *Studies in the Novel* 24, no 1 (Spring 1992). © 1992 by University of North Texas.

155

Chuzzlewit's selfish materialism, and thus validate his wealth, as she makes him rich in feeling. Herself starved for affection, Florence Dombey becomes a nurturing angel to her financially and emotionally bankrupt father at the same time that she underwrites Walter Gay's "Dick Whittington" aspirations to marry the daughter and heir and become financially successful.

This pattern culminates in Dickens' autobiographical novel *David Copperfield*, in which David depends on Agnes to domesticate his "undisciplined heart." Thus, married to the self-denying Agnes, Copperfield's self-indulgent actions and thoughts are redeemed. Moreover, in depicting Agnes as a maternal, self-sacrificing heroine who is the inspiration for himself as aspiring author, David casts a positive aura on his own ambitions that might otherwise be construed as, in his words, "sordid things." Hence, emphasizing Agnes' role as amanuensis, literary helpmeet, and muse, David focuses on his motives as secular prophet and downplays his own profit motive. Indeed, the underside of David's excessive humility about his own profession is Heep's aggressive profession of his "humble" aspirations.

Great Expectations, Dickens' second attempt at a fictional autobiography, is an about-face, for the key women in the protagonist's life are anything but maternal. In fact, in this late novel, the long suppressed Dickensian female defies her maternal role. Clearly Pip seems doubly bereft of maternal nurture through the death of his mother and the accession to that role by Mrs. Joe. In fact, named after Pip's mother—and with everything that implies about the senior Georgiana Pirrip's nurturing abilities—Pip's sister regrets having to have been his second "mother." Bitter that circumstances have forced her into being the self-denying mother figure, Mrs. Joe physically and emotionally starves her brother, become son. Likewise, she forces him to pay a high price—and that is to be taken literally—for her maternal service(s). With her arsenal of needles and pins sticking to the bodice of her apron, this "all-powerful sister" is literally the bad breast. Miss Havisham, whom I will discuss in more detail later, is another surrogate mother to Pip. Not the "fairy godmother" Pip thinks she is, Miss Havisham manipulates Pip in order to enslave him emotionally in the same way that she forms her adopted daughter, Estella, in order to cannibalize her.

Certainly Dickens sets Biddy up as a potential wife and mother figure for Pip, but here again a contrast with *David Copperfield* is enlightening. In *David Copperfield* Dickens describes David's romantic love for Agnes as the culmination of a ragged young boy finding his way home to his mother. Similarly, Pip romantically sees himself as "one who was toiling home barefoot from distant travel, and whose wanderings had lasted many years," and he hopes that Biddy can receive him "like a forgiven child (and indeed I am as sorry, Biddy, and have as much need of a hushing voice and a soothing hand)." But in a surprising scene, Dickens denies his hero the self-denying heroine. Indeed, Biddy will not be the mother figure—the good breast—for Pip, for she rather abruptly "baffles" Pip's plans by marrying Joe. Nevertheless, she remains a touchstone for the hero's romantic intentions. For instance, pointedly questioning why he would love someone who calls him coarse and common, Biddy asks Pip if he wants to be a gentleman, "to spite her [Estella] or to gain her over?" Pip responds that he doesn't know, to which Biddy replies: "if it is to spite her . . . I should think . . . that might be better and more independently done by caring nothing for her words. And if it is to gain her over, I should think . . . she was not worth gaining over."

Thus, true to her name, Biddy is something of a hen pecker, but her catechisms of Pip are incisive and just. One wonders, then, why neither Pip nor Dickens is capable of taking her sensible advice. But, in fact, with Estella Dickens seems ready to delineate a very different kind of woman, for, considering her predecessors, the ingenue Estella is an astonishing Dickensian heroine. Like Nell, Mary Graham, Florence, Agnes, Esther, and Little Dorrit, she is without a nourishing mother figure, but in this novel the lack of a loving mother results in the creation of a "Tartar," Herbert Pocket's epithet for Estella. Furthermore, as Estella tells Miss Havisham,

> Mother by adoption, I have said that I owe everything to you. All I possess is freely yours. All that you have given me, is at your command to have again. Beyond that, I have nothing. And if you ask me to give you what you never gave me, my gratitude and duty cannot do impossibilities.

Obviously, Miss Havisham uses this child for her own warped purposes, but in producing Estella to take revenge on the men who took public and economic advantage of her private sexual desires, Miss Havisham only succeeds in duplicating the experience for her own adoptive daughter, making her a thing to be bartered in the marriage market.

Moreover, trained in the accomplishments of the ideal Victorian woman, Estella as Dickensian heroine has finally necessarily become what Victorian and Dickensian expectations must naturally—or, rather, unnaturally—result in: she is the nightmare version of the Victorian female bred to have no desires, no appetites, trained to be desired and to be the object of appetite. Clearly Estella views herself as Miss Havisham's ornamental object, to be dangled before men to tantalize them and break their hearts. Thus, groomed to be the absent center of the Victorian male's affections, Estella incites obsessive emotional responses in men while she herself is without feelings. Dickens, of course, reviles the kind of system that would create such a creature, yet it is undeniable that his own earlier powerful portrayals of ascetic heroines helped to create this distorted version of the ideal female. Pip's remark to Estella that "you speak of yourself as if you were some one else," reveals Dickens' implicit and incisive awareness of the results of Pip's—and for that matter, his own—sexual and economic obsessions. Indeed, Estella's self-forgetfulness resonates on the self-forgetfulness of Dickens' previous heroines, for Estella's alienation from the self is the underside of the earlier Dickensian heroine's self-denial.

Struggling with his own self-aggrandizing personality, Dickens' alterego, then, comes face to face with a ravishing, sensual, but heartless woman. Pip cannot help but empathize with her, but he also cannot rise above his own rationalization of his desire. If in Dickens' autobiographical *David Copperfield* Agnes' self-denying female economy underwrites David's self-indulgent, aggressive male economy, we must question what happens in Dickens' later semi-autobiographical novel when Estella's warped female economy underlies Pip's, for like David, Pip places the responsibility for his own character on the woman he loves:

> Truly it was impossible to dissociate her [Estella'a] presence from all those wretched hankerings after money and gentility that had disturbed my boyhood—from all those ill-regulated aspirations that had first made me ashamed of home and Joe—
> . . . In a word, it was impossible for me to separate her, in the past or in the present, from the innermost life of my life.

The ominous suggestion that Estella made Pip avaricious becomes almost a threat when Pip states to her, "Estella, to the last hour of my life, you cannot choose but remain part of my character, part of the little good in me, part of the evil." In contrast to *David Copperfield*, in which Dickens portrays male ambition as refined by an ascetic female, the reasoning of *Great Expectations* is that, not the devil, but Estella made me do it.

In his study of the Naturalist novel, Mark Seltzer tracks the ways that writers like Frank Norris counter two generative forces, production and reproduction, as signified in the masculine steam machine and the mother. Brilliantly arguing that Naturalist fiction assumes that genetically males live according to a principle of loss and females according to a principle of profit, Seltzer points out that such a discourse posits the contradictory spheres of the public and the private, work and home, the world and family, and the economic and the sexual. Though Seltzer's focus is on American Naturalist fiction, his contrast of male production and female reproduction is useful in analyzing the meaning of *Great Expectations*, for in this later autobiographical novel Dickens is far more conscious of how economics infiltrate the construction of the self. Indeed, in *Great Expectations* the making of the self rests in the space between the meanings of reproduction and production, the maternal and the material, the home and the market. Thus, perhaps more so than in any other of his novels, in *Great Expectations* Dickens realistically examines the possibility of inhabiting the sphere of reproduction, which in his previous works was that place or person—usually female and maternal— through which the individual is validated as a human being with feelings. To put it more precisely, in Dickens the sphere of reproduction is in essence a kind of actual or metaphorical return to the bosom of the family.

The problem, as Seltzer is so aware in his analysis of the Naturalist novel, is that though the productive and reproductive spheres are separate, they also interpenetrate, for the one sphere produces the goods while the other produces the consumers of those goods. Thus the sphere of production infiltrates that of reproduction, creating the self caught in the cycle of consumption, as the individual becomes a thing, reared to consume and to be consumed. Therefore, in contrast to Dickens' earlier works, in which he represents the heroine as a haven from aggressive economies, in *Great Expectations* both hero and heroine are constructed, that is, made economically. In fact, Dickens comes to realize that the possibility of escaping the market and effecting a return to the mother is practically nil. Indeed, Pip's—and, for that matter, Estella's—maternal guardians, who are supposed to be their nurturers, end up being their business managers.

That production infiltrates reproduction is apparent in the fact that the Victorians referred to private, sexual matters in rather public, economic terms. For example, the Victorian slang phrase for male orgasm was "to spend." Therefore, when Victorian men were trained to "save" themselves for marriage it was in both economic and sexual terms: they were required to put off marriage until they had saved enough in the bank to be financially stable; but it was also necessary to put off "spending" in sexual terms. Hence, Samuel Smiles' blithe assertion that the capitalist is a man "who does not spend all that is earned by work," but rather is a man prepared to deny "present enjoyment for future good," results in the ludicrous situation that Fraser Harrison describes: "Celibate and capitalist alike resolutely fought off the desire to spend." Herbert Pocket's emotional and economic reasoning regarding his engagement to Clara is a fictional example of this Victorian attitude: "the moment he [Herbert] began to realize Capital, it was his intention to marry this young lady. He added as a self-evident proposition, engendering low spirits, 'But you *can't* marry, you know, while you're looking about you.'"

In the opening chapter of *Great Expectations* Dickens immediately confronts the reader with this question of who "made" Pip. Indeed, in contrast to the young Copperfield's first sense of the "identity of things" as residing exclusively in the maternal reproductive sphere, Pip's budding sense of the "identity of things" is a combination of familial and economic bonds: in the graveyard scene Pip first registers his beginnings in the deceased father and mother and his kinship to five brothers, but then his "second father" Magwitch appears, who, of course, is the benefactor who will produce Pip and his great expectations. What with the absent family unit, particularly the mother, very little in the way of maternal nurture protect Pip from falling from the sphere of reproduction into that of production, for in this state of affairs he is destined to become associated with property one way or another. As Biddy teaches Joe and Joe keeps repeating, when the hero first learns of his great expectations, there are really only two words to describe the change: "Pip" and "Property," and the sense is as much Pip becoming property as inheriting it.

In fact, before he received his great expectations, Pip, who was "raised by hand," was in the same situation as Herbert Pocket, who is always "looking about me" for his opportunity to become a self-made "capitalist." Juxtaposed, the suggestion that Pip was "raised by hand," and Pocket's continual assertion that he is always "looking about" for something seems to contrast the modes of reproduction and production; nevertheless, in actuality the two refrains tend to merge those meanings. For example, Herbert's "looking about" for a "capitalist" position refers to his economic need, but that stress is also partially the result of having to look out for himself as a child in a family that "tumbles" children up, clearly portrayed as more the fault of Pocket's mother than father. As Herbert explains to Pip, the offspring of a family in which children are unfathomably produced rather than reproduced, are quick to look about them both for opportunities to marry and enter the market.

Of course "raised by hand," meaning literally the laborious and usually unsuccessful Victorian practice of feeding orphans or abandoned infants by hand rather than by bringing in a wetnurse, signifies Pip's physical lack of the breast in the primal infantine stage, but it also implies his lack of maternal love. Thus, given her brother's fragile beginnings, it is ironic that the woman who raised him by hand, Mrs. Joe, believed Pip should not be "Pompeyed," that is, pampered. And, in fact, the phrase "raised by hand" comes to mean Mrs. Joe's physical abuse of her brother. Furthermore, Mrs. Joe also expects remuneration for having raised Pip by hand, for obviously she hopes to advance her own fortunes by placing him at Miss Havisham's. Her ally, Pumblechook, coopts the phrase, and, by acknowledging that his niece raised Pip by hand, gives added weight to his own claim that he is Pip's mentor in economic terms (and thus deserving of Pip's newly inherited "Capital") when he ludicrously suggests that he "made" Pip. Pip thinks and hopes that "Miss Havisham was going to make my fortune on a grand scale," but he is repulsed that he is the gentleman Magwitch has "made" and "owns."

Fallen into the world of production and consumption, Pip is not born; he is made, and that makes him particularly vulnerable in the cannibalistic world of Victorian England. James E. Marlow suggests that for the reader of *Great Expectations* "the dread of being eaten structures the novel." Asserting that after 1859 "the themes of orality, predation, and the translation of human flesh into economic gain—all metaphoric cannibalism—dominate [Dickens'] fiction," Marlow argues that by this point Dickens believed that cannibalism was not just an "aberration" in ogres like Quilp, but rather "a custom sanctioned by the ideologues of capitalism" such as Merdle and Casby. Indeed, in *Great Expectations* production displaces reproduction whenever the individual is abandoned or betrayed by family, more particularly, by the mother.

With no nourishing mother figure, Pip becomes the object of market relations, learning only to consume or be consumed. Certainly, the masterplot of Pip's rise to and fall from fortune indicates Pip's sense of self as devoured or devouring. Gluttony and starvation oscillate in Pip as his often violent assertion of hunger conflicts with his sense of being devoured. In his "first most vivid and broad impression of the identity of things," Pip is confronted by a convict who threatens to eat Pip if he does not bring him food and a file. As Magwitch later explains to Pip, he turned to crime because he was starving and no one ever "measured my stomach," for "I must put something into my stomach, mustn't I?" Furthermore, when asked what his occupation is, the convict replies, "Eat and drink . . . if you'll find the materials." However, eating and drinking in a society that tolerates starvation—physical or emotional—may be defined as robbery, and Dickens does seem to suggest that any kind of market relations between human beings is a kind of robbery, or, worse, cannibalism. Thus, Pip becomes like "my convict": the starving child of his sister's "bad breast," he broods "I was going to rob Mrs. Joe," and metaphorically assaults the surrogate mother's bad—unreproductive—breast by invading his sister's pantry.

But, as Marlow suggests, the scene that follows indicates that "Pip's dread of being eaten was founded long before the arrival of Magwitch." Young Pip seems in constant danger of being eaten by adult swine. In the Christmas Day feasting scene tales of the eating of children act as appetizers for the adults. Wopsle begins the linguistic cannibalism:

"Swine," pursued Mr. Wopsle, in his deepest voice, and pointing his fork at my blushes, as if he were mentioning my christian name; "Swine were the companions of the prodigal. The gluttony of Swine is put before us, as an example to the young." (I thought this pretty well in him who had been praising up the pork for being so plump and juicy.) "What is detestable in a pig, is more detestable in a boy."

Pumblechook takes up the sermon, focussing on the "boy" Pip. He opines, "If you'd been born a Squeaker," which Mrs. Joe heartily affirms he was, "You would have been disposed of for so many shillings according to the market price of the article, and Dunstable the butcher . . . would have shed your blood and had your life." The suggestion, of course, is, and Marlow alludes to it as well, that Pip's relations with his sister and her uncle are "market" relations, their chief interest in him being both what fortune they can accrue through him, and making him repay them for how much effort and energy they have spent on raising him. To extend the metaphor, in a later scene, Joe clumsily remarks of Pip's London apartments, "I wouldn't keep a pig in it myself—not in the case that I wished him to fatten wholesome and to eat with a meller flavour on him." This remarkable statement by the "angel" of the novel suggests just how much Pip is consumable "property," subject to the market and its consuming practices.

Nevertheless, the epithet "swine" indicts the hero as a devouring as well as devoured self, for, in addition to describing Pip as victim, it is also used, of course, to refer to a person with an inordinate appetite. Pumblechook notes that when Pip leaves for London to fulfill his expectations he is "plump as a Peach," whereas in his diminished state he returns as "little more than skin and bone." It might be taken literally, then, when Joe visits Pip in town and exudes that he has "growed" and "swelled" as he becomes "gentle-folked." In fact, like most of Dickens' young heroes and heroines, Pip is "uncommonly small," yet like young Oliver and David, who are accused of wanting "more," and being a "boa constrictor," respectively, Pip is accused of "bolting." Like his predecessors, Pip is both innocent and guilty when it comes to being accused of gluttony. On the one hand, this ostensible ingestion is an empty consumption, for the hungry boy foregoes eating the bread in order to feed it to the escaped convict, yet his guardians accuse him of "bolting."

But, on the other hand, Dickens never leaves these accusations of his hero's inordinate appetite alone. Quite commonly he complicates the hero's motives, suggesting that there is a kind of oscillation between guilty desires and innocent victimization. Thus, when Pip feeds Magwitch with the hoarded slab of bread and butter, the convict actually does bolt the wadded up supper, as Pip watches with the fascination of revulsion: "He swallowed, or rather snapped up, every mouthful, too soon and too fast . . . In all of which particulars he was very like the dog." But, of course, Pip both directly and implicitly compares himself to "bolting" canines, an animal image like the swine imagery the implies both voracious gluttony and victimization and starvation. Estella offers Pip "bread and meat" as if he were "a dog in disgrace," and it is also telling that Pip's fanciful description of his first visit to Miss Havisham's includes four "immense" ravenous dogs that "fought for veal-cutlets out of a silver basket." In the same interlude, after young Pip pummels Herbert Pocket, he regards himself "as a species of savage young wolf or other wild beast," an image reiterated at the end of the novel when a murderous Orlick refers to Pip as "wolf."

Pip's first impression of Miss Havisham, that she is "immensely rich" and lives in a "large and dismal house barricaded against robbers," also suggests his unconscious motives. In other words, already having "robbed" his sister, Pip now desires to rob Miss Havisham of her material and maternal wealth. However, her domicile is a fallen and unfruitful paradise. Indeed, the home of Satis, which reproduced Miss Havisham, is infiltrated by the market because it is also the house of Satis, a brewery where her father produced the family's wealth. Likewise, market relations penetrate marital relations, for Satis House is where Miss Havisham has been the victim of her own brother's and lover's economic designs. Consequently, in the next generation, the cycle of production infiltrates reproduction again as the motherless Miss Havisham becomes the unnatural mother to Estella. Thus, though "Satis" is the root of satiation and satisfaction, Satis House is unsatisfying, unnourishing, and barren. Indeed, Satis House may represent a fundamental contradiction of the Victorian economy in the startlling and simple revelation that abundant wealth is founded on deprivation. In other words, there must be poor Magwitchs for there to be wealthy Miss Havishams.

Nevertheless, in *Great Expectations* Dickens reveals that both rich and poor fill the roles of consumer and consumed, as consuming and being consumed almost become interchangeable states. Hence, caught in the cycle of production and consumption, Miss Havisham, like Pip, devours others and is herself devoured. Indeed, to a certain extent, Miss Havisham equates herself with her own digestive processes, about which she is morbidly self-conscious. In fact, the reader does not see Miss Havisham eat or drink: "She has never allowed herself to be seen doing either . . . She wanders about in the night, and then lays hands on such food as she takes." Such self-imposed physical and emotional deprivation on the part of this wealthy woman reveals a number of things. Most important, I suggest, is the contrast of Miss

Havisham's asceticism with Little Nell, Florence, Agnes, and Little Dorrit and their insistent indifference to eating. In fact, I believe that in *Great Expectations* Dickens faces the fact that in a consumer society the lack of appetite in a character like Miss Havisham is a grotesque display of the miraculous anorexia that the younger Dickens had expected to mediate aggressive market demands.

Indeed, as Miss Havisham ascetically nibbles in her decaying house, she watches the natural world—or rather, supernatural—mimic the intrusion of the economic and public into her very private sphere as spiders invade and devour her decomposing wedding cake. Dickens' representation of such public and private consumption is unforgettable, for Miss Havisham's bridal "feast" remains like "a black fungus" on the table where "speckled-legged spiders with blotchy bodies [run] home to it, and [run] out from it, as if some circumstance of the greatest public importance had just transpired in the spider community." At the same time, this "feast" also represents Miss Havisham's moral decay and her acquiescence to the demands of the market, revealed in the fact that she can only express her emotional responses in images of devouring. Indeed, in *Great Expectations* the cliché of being eaten up by revenge almost becomes actuality when Miss Havisham remarks, "The mice have gnawed at it [the wedding cake], and sharper teeth than teeth of mice have gnawed at me." A displaced representation of anthropophagy, the arachnid feast is not only a gothic image of the market dynamics. This construct of consuming also displays the incursion of the financial into the familial, for Miss Havisham's cousins wait to "feast" on her at her death, on the same table where the spiders feed on her rotting bridal cake.

Perhaps, then, it is not too far-fetched to suggest that the spider community may represent all England itself actively engaged in the perpetuation of its own consumption. In fact, *Great Expectations* suggests that consumer society is the ultimate gothic horror. Indeed, this novel almost endlessly produces gothic or comic oral images of ingestion for the reader's consumption, from Miss Havisham, who "feasts" on Estella, "as though she were devouring the beautiful creature she had reared"; to Wemmick "putting fish into" his "post-office" mouth, and bullying customers as a kind of "refreshment" or "lunch"; to the "heavy grubber" Magwitch who threatens Pip that "your heart and your liver shall be tore out, roasted and ate"; to the fish-mouthed Pumblechook who stuffs himself with food at Mrs. Joe's funeral.

It is only natural, then, that Pip represents Orlick's attempt to kill him as an expression of violent appetite: Orlick "slowly unclenched his hand and drew it across his mouth as if his mouth watered for me." Obviously, such oral imagery may be Pip's projection of his own ravine, for as Pip explains,

Orlick hates him because he fears Pip will "displace him," but in fact Pip displaces onto Orlick his own violent anger towards his sister and her bad breast. As Orlick ominously reveals of the bludgeoning of Mrs. Joe: "I tell you it was your doing—I tell you it was done through you." I need not retrace Julian Moynihan's excellent essay on this projection; suffice it to say, that like an Oedipus figure seeking the perpetrator of his sins, Pip "revengefully" vows to pursue Orlick, or "anyone else, to the last extremity," when it is his own tail he chases and swallows, and his own tale he must ingest.

Once again, Pip is both innocent and guilty as Dickens dramatically underscores Pip's rationalized and displaced appetite for revenge at the same time asserting that Mrs. Joe, Miss Havisham, Estella, Pumblechook, and Magwitch are to blame for the hero's fall into the sphere of production. In any case, Dickens calls each to a violent accounting: Orlick brutally attacks Mrs. Joe and robs and beats Pumblechook, while Compeyson assaults Magwitch; in two instances Pip fantasizes Miss Havisham as hanging, and he is there when she rather spontaneously combusts. And to punish the heartless heroine, heavy-built Drummle, nicknamed the "spider"—surely an evocation not only of the spider feast, but also of Miss Havisham feasting on her adopted daughter—beats Estella. His physical abuse, of course, leads to the abasement that purportedly makes the heroine worthy of Pip's love.

The novel, then, persistently manufactures images of Pip's innocence and guilt. But it must stop somewhere, and Dickens must redeem his alter-ego from the cycle of production and consumption. Thus, in the end, after all those who claimed to have "made" Pip receive their just desserts, in Dickens' displaced system of tit for tat, Pip, as a kind of outcast in India, spends his energy for eleven years paying his financial and emotional debts. Obviously Dickens cannot fully disentangle his hero from market relations, because, in fact, Pip's calculated debt-paying really provides no redemption, nor does the protagonist's hinted marriage to Estella, for these only seem to perpetuate the dynamics of production. After all, in a capitalist society, the notion of paying for one's sins is hardly to the purpose.

Dickens allows Pip only a brief return to the ideal reproductive sphere through the characters who seem most immune to the desire for money: Joe and Biddy. Joe, for instance, shies away from a premium Miss Havisham offers him for putting Pip into his indentures. Likewise, he castigates the intimidating, money-conscious Jaggers for his "bull-baiting and badgering" insistence that "Money can make compensation to me for the loss of the little child—what come to the forge—and ever the best of friends!" In fact, Pip's deepest regret is that he never acknowledges properly that it is Joe who has made him, or rather, reproduced him. Joe, who has "the touch of a woman," spiritually and physically nurses Pip, acting in the end as his true mother:

when Pip is ill, Joe wraps him up and carries him "as if I were still the small helpless creature to whom he had so abundantly given of the wealth of his great nature." This illness offers Pip his only chance in actual and figurative terms of having all his debts canceled. In fact, even the ideas of debt and the market dynamics of production and consumption are repealed when Joe freely pays Pip's creditors. Thus, for an Edenic while Pip is no longer equated with "property." That reproduction of Pip—"I again"—is wonderfully recreated in Joe and Biddy's young son, named after Pip, who under the "good matronly hand" of Biddy and the woman's touch of Joe, returns the protagonist, at least for awhile, to the condition of the child's bonding with the maternal.

Nevertheless, the ending of *Great Expectations* is troubling, and we know, of course, that Dickens had difficulty concluding his story. The main problem with the ending(s) is not that Dickens cannot bring about his protagonist's permanent regeneration. I suggest, instead, that the conclusion is problematic because Dickens ends up affirming and advocating what he also reviles in a consumer society: the necessity for the powerless to underwrite the powerful. In Dickens' earlier fiction that quite typically means that the heroine, though herself motherless, must be a self-sustaining source of nurture and nourishment to the emotionally starved hero. In the later *Great Expectations*, though Dickens rigorously explores the effects of a market economy on his protagonist, Pip's momentary but transcendent rebirth is at the expense of the female, for Dickens fails to redeem Estella from the sphere of production. Indeed, he forces her back into the mold of his earlier ascetic heroines. Thus, this physically abused, motherless heroine is still an ornament, for neither Pip nor the reader has any conception of what Estella's desires or hungers might be, only that she has been "bent and broken" into "better shape" in order to fulfill Pip's desires.

JEROME MECKIER

Charles Dickens's Great Expectations: *A Defense of the Second Ending*

The notion persists that George Bernard Shaw persuasively championed the original ending for *Great Expectations*. Enlarging upon his often unreliable pronouncements, defenders of the first ending have been legion. Technically, however, Shaw was not allied to either side. He was of two minds: the second ending seemed "psychologically wrong" but "artistically much more congruous than the original," for "the scene, the hour, the atmosphere are beautifully touching and exactly right." Convinced that Dickens had "made a mess of both endings," Shaw supplied the "perfect ending" himself. Instead of the possibility of belated happiness with Estella, Pip is paid off with a gallon of peaceful resignation: "Since that parting," Shaw's Pip concludes, "I have been able to think of her without the old unhappiness; but I have never tried to see her again, and I know I never shall."

This Shavian solution could simply be appended to the first ending. But since it mentions "parting," a crucial word used twice in the second ending, Shaw presumably wanted his compound sentence to oust Dickens's last paragraph; Pip's new statement would then follow Estella's resolve to continue "friends apart." Shaw desired unmistakable finality yet failed to avoid a degree of uncertainty: does Pip mean that he will never see Estella again or simply never *try* to? If the latter, he remains vulnerable to

From *Studies in the Novel* 25, no. 1 (Spring 1993). © 1993 by the University of Texas.

unpremeditated encounters. Shaw's double "never" may prove no more definitive than Dickens's single "no" in "no shadow of another parting."

Choosing between alternative endings is one thing, tampering with them another. Shaw was inept at both. The elimination of Dickens's final one-sentence paragraph nullifies Pip's comparison of the "evening mists" to the "morning mists" that he observed at the conclusion of the First Stage; it also dulls the implicit analogy of Pip and Estella leaving the "desolate garden" to Adam and Eve emerging from Eden. Shaw would have canceled two of the congruencies that create the appropriate hour and the perfect atmosphere.

When Shaw restored the so-called unhappy ending to the text proper for the Limited Editions Club edition, he printed the allegedly happier second ending in an "Editor's Postscript" to his "Preface." This cost Pip and Estella two years of life. In the revised ending, Dickens reunited them the day after Pip's return, instead of allowing "two years" to pass as happens in the original ending. Dickens realized that he had made the lovers younger: no longer 33 or 34 after ten years of separation, they were now a less mellow 31 or 32. To compensate, Dickens added three years to Pip's sojourn abroad, altering "eight years" in the first sentence of chapter 59 to "eleven" for the revised ending. Ignoring Dickens's revamped time scheme, Shaw pasted the earlier ending onto the text—that is, he substituted "It was two years more" for "Nevertheless, I knew" right after the sentence that ends "Biddy, all gone by." Because the "eleven years" of the revised ending remained in the opening sentence, Shaw separated Pip from Estella for 13 years, aging both of them to at least 36, considerably older than Dickens intended.

Were commentators to emulate Shaw, devising the ideal ending for *Great Expectations* might become as consuming a pastime as inventing denouements for *The Mystery of Edwin Drood*. Here, for example, is Douglas Brooks-Davies's proposal: "the evening sunlight of the moment when I left Satis [House] holding Estella's hand was so bright," Pip recalls, "that it banished all shadows—even the metaphorical shadow of the parting that we were soon (and permanently) to endure." Having studied the controversy, Brooks-Davies's Pip attempts to blend the psychological aptness of the first ending with the atmospheric rightness of the second. This compromise only exaggerates Shaw's mistake, for it is self-contradictory and therefore false to *both* endings to force the allegedly superior context of the revision to restate the supposedly truer message of the original.

Scene, hour, and atmosphere not only seem "right" in the revised ending, but are also inherently promising—romantic rather than terminal. Handholding cannot be twisted into a prelude to permanent separation. In contrast, Estella's willingness "to shake hands," to let byegones be byegones, can be seen as more of a masculine gesture that keeps the Piccadilly Pip at a distance, as does her sitting in a carriage while he remains on foot. Dickens's Pip and Estella have experienced a critical re-encounter, arguably more critical in the revision than in the original, yet Brooks-Davies reduced the magic moment his couple share to an optical illusion, a trick of light and shade. His Pip and Estella are dazzled by a sunshine so powerful it can temporarily sweep away all obstacles, even a shadow that is strictly "metaphorical."

For Dickens's Pip, however, resplendent sunlight late on a December eve is out of the question. By the time he walks the four miles from Joe's forge to Satis House, "the day had quite declined." Granted, "the evening was not dark"; still, Pip notes that "the stars were shining beyond the mist, and the moon was coming." The real Pip and Estella rendezvous at twilight, the hour for lovers and the part of day metaphorically suited to their reduced expectations. There can be no sundrenched reunion scene, the exuberance of noon-day having long since faded for them both.

Shaw's insistence that Dickens faltered twice has prompted some opponents of the second ending to jettison both endings. But sidestepping dissatisfaction with the second ending by lopping off the original and the revised is just as irresponsible as inventing a third conclusion or grafting the first onto the second. Merely because the Piccadilly meeting is absent from Dickens's working notes, Robert A. Greenberg decided that Dickens originally intended to stop with chapter 58: "Pip was to remain in the East, and the action was to end on an ironical, though not totally unaffirmative note." Does it matter if Dickens failed to include a reunion for Pip and Estella in the two pages of "General Mems." he jotted down about the time he began chapter 48? Designed to assist him through the final twelve chapters, these notes need not have contained everything of import, not do they deserve absolute authority, as if they automatically overruled second thoughts during composition. Dickens's working plans turned out to be far from infallible: Pip was supposed to save Magwitch from drowning; Herbert was to go abroad *after* Magwitch's trial. If reunion must not occur because it was never mentioned, one should also strike Wemmick's wedding and Pumblechook's comeuppance, two other developments that Dickens did not foresee (or feel obliged to predict).

Perhaps Dickens envisioned the Piccadilly reunion with sufficient clarity not to list it beforehand; maybe he invented it on the spur of the moment. Whichever the case, once Pip told the dying Magwitch that his long-lost daughter lives and that he, Pip, loves her (ch. 56), Dickens surely recognized that the final scene had to be some form of re-encounter.

Curiosity about Estella's fate, not just lingering questions about the extent of Pip's maturation, demanded a reckoning. The real issue is which ending better provides one.

Just as Brooks-Davies compounded Shaw's error, Milton Millhouser magnified Greenberg's: he tried to halt *Great Expectations* twice prior to the reunion at Satis House. If the novel actually comes to a stop on either of these occasions, the ending Dickens supplied and then revised can be discounted as a superfluous third resolution. Echoing Greenberg, Millhouser was willing to desist with Pip's return to the forge and his apology to Biddy and Joe; his preference, however, was Pip's post-Egypt visit—the first eleven paragraphs of chapter 59.

Stopping with chapter 58 truncates the novel's mounting emphasis on return as a vehicle for reconciliation. In chapter 49, responding to Miss Havisham's note, Pip revisits Satis House for the first time in five chapters. Miss Havisham gives him £900 for Herbert's partnership, informs him of Estella's marriage, and then begs and obtains his forgiveness for having tortured him with Estella. In chapter 56, as the returned convict expires in the prison infirmary, Pip implores God's forgiveness for him; and in chapter 58, a convalescent Pip, having come back to the forge, entreats Joe and Biddy, whom he has neglected for the past six years: "pray tell me, both, that you forgive me!" Surely it was also imperative that Pip and Estella make their peace; indeed, Dickens chose to improve on the first ending in this regard, for he replaced the formal handshake in the original with Estella's earnest plea that Pip again say to her, "'God bless you, God forgive you!'"

A decade of self-imposed exile in the Egypt of the 1830s was doubtless penitential—closer in extent to Magwitch's involuntary sixteen years in Australia, which may explain why Dickens prolonged Pip's absence from eight years to eleven. But once the novelist allowed Pip to return, he was obliged to bring him into contact with *all* of the people from whom he may be said to have fled in chapter 58. Paradoxically, Millhouser's inclusion of chapter 59's first eleven paragraphs truncates the novel just as sharply as Greenberg's choice of chapter 58 as the terminus; in fact, it makes Estella's exclusion seem more conspicuous. First Pip returns to the forge, this post-Egypt visit, in Millhouser's opinion, offering proof that he has found his "métier," completed his "moral education." Then he takes little Pip to visit the graves of Philip and Georgiana Pirrip, an outing that, in repeating the novel's opening scene, constitutes another instance of return as reconciliation: Pip has finally come to terms with his earliest childhood fears and disappointments. To have ended with Pip assuring Biddy of having "quite forgotten" Estella would tax credulity; it would violate the chapter's pattern of settling unfinished business.

Not only anticlimactic, Pip's disinterestedness would also be false to the note of expectancy that Dickens sounded simply in returning Pip to England. In a novel about the intricacies and ironies of expectation, Philip Pirrip cannot end his lifestory by safely ruling out any more of them—that is, by proclaiming his "poor dream," in effect, his life, entirely over, even if that is as much as some readers believe he deserves. Pip's sense of finality—"all gone by, Biddy, all gone by"—goes contrary to life as the novel has presented it; like the double "never" in Shaw's so-called "perfect ending," it crumbles beneath the weight of its twofold insistence.

Dickens's actual conclusions struck Millhouser as no more than alternative appendices to an already completed novel: whichever one chooses, he maintained, "the impression" persists "that the book is hurried to a conclusion, through scenes about which the author does not greatly care." Passing judgment against Dickens for haste and indifference is most unfair in view of his enduring difficulties with chapter 59: he first completed it on 11 June 1861, discussed it with Bulwer-Lytton at Knebworth from 15–18 June, toiled on the revision until 23 June, revised in proof the final sentence of the revised ending, and then revised that sentence again for the Library Edition of 1862. So he devoted, in all, several months of rethinking and superintendance to a chapter that fills less than half a dozen pages in print.

The point to reemphasize is that *Great Expectations* is Estella's story, too, not just Pip's, yet neither of Millhouser's alternatives divulges her fate. Incredibly, she would not even be mentioned by name if only the first eleven paragraphs of chapter 59 were retained, although, like Pip, we do not need to be told the missing antecedent in Biddy's question: "Have you quite forgotten her?" Were the novel to end with Pip's departure for Egypt (Greenberg's suggestion), the protagonist's last mention of Estella would be to the dying Magwitch in chapter 56, and his declaration of love at that juncture ("And I love her!") would remain totally futile. In Millhouser's version, Pip's last interview with Estella would occur fifteen chapters prior to the conclusion—i.e., in chapter 44, where she announces her plans to take what Pip calls the "fatal step" of marrying Drummle. If the novel terminated without either the original or the revised ending, Drummle's fate, the outcome of his marriage to Estella, would be another loose end.

That Dickens was right to return to Estella in the original ending and then to increase her role in the revision is easier to credit when one realizes how may assessments of the novel find her change of heart abrupt and unconvincing despite the expansion. "The shaping of a lifetime," Edgar Johnson objected, is "miraculously undone." As a consequence, H. M. Daleski added, Pip will "live on unearned income in his emotional life" much as he did in his career as Magwitch's gentleman. But the past eleven years, many of them spent in miserable bondage to Bentley Drummle, have been as penitential for Estella as they were for Pip, whose self-exile we have already compared to Magwitch's term of transportation. Pip and Estella undergo parallel periods of self-imposed suffering and regret. Unfortunately, the novel does not dramatize either period. Consequently, Estella's conversion through pain and sorrow comes as a surprise to some readers, unlike Pip's turnabout which enjoys greater visibility because it begins when he softens toward Magwitch.

In order to give Estella her due, Dickens inserted four brief paragraphs in chapter 59 just before he sent the final installment to *Harper's*, publisher of the serial version in America. Starting with her statement that she has "often thought of" Pip, Estella tells how hard she tried at first not to remember the love she had foolishly "thrown away." One may still feel that her change of heart, no matter how long and arduous Dickens makes her claim it was, conflicts with her upbringing, but Dickens used the second ending to address this problem more directly than he had in the original ending. Her "suffering," Estella explicitly states, "has been stronger than all other teaching." In the first ending, it was merely "stronger than Miss Havisham's teaching," an assertion directly to the point yet, in Dickens's reconsideration, less forceful than the subsequent generalization, which adds Drummle's unkind schooling to her adopted mother's.

What Shaw, Brooks-Davies, Greenberg, and Millhouser really wanted from Dickens's second ending was not a lesser degree of happiness but a greater sense of finality. Shaw and Brooks-Davies obtained it by putting additional words into Pip's mouth; Greenberg and Millhouser tried to take words out. Both parties disliked the element of ambiguity in the second conclusion. Shaw and Brooks-Davies pushed the novel forward to achieve greater resolution; Greenberg and Millhouser pulled back, searching for the latest point in the text at which matters seemed entirely unambiguous. Shaw and Brooks-Davies damaged the setting and atmosphere they professed to admire; Greenberg and Millhouser left Estella's situation unresolved, thereby imperiling the conclusiveness they coveted. Efforts to replace, supplement, or eliminate Dickens's revision, efforts for which Shaw seems seminally responsible, have only served to reveal and reenforce the logic behind the second ending.

When not actually rewriting or rescinding Dickens's revised ending, normally reliable critics have often made it happier than it is—financially securer and more hymeneal. J. Hillis Miller, although he prefers the second ending, has concluded: "Pip now has all that he wanted, Estella and her jewels," as if he deserved one or the other but not both. Yet Estella's "personal fortune," mentioned briefly in the first ending, does not survive into the second; she informs Pip that she only owns "the ground" upon which the ruined Satis House stands; it is, she declares, "the only possession I have not relinquished." Drummle's "avarice," no factor in the first ending, has virtually beggared her; so Pip, who accepted the expiring Magwitch's claims upon him after the latter's fortune had been confiscated, is also prepared to take Estella without the prospect of material gain. Butt and Tillotson would have welcomed a different parallel: it was "more appropriate," they felt, that Pip, "who had lost Magwitch's money, should also lose his daughter, than that he should marry her in the end."

John Forster, the earliest advocate of the original ending, refused to condone the "too great speed with which the heroine, after being married, reclaimed, and widowed, is in a page or two made love to and remarried by the hero." Similarly, Christopher Ricks expressed "dismay that Dickens changed his original ending and allowed Pip to marry Estella," while T. W. Hill incorrectly computed Pip's age to be "thirty-six when he married Estella." Going further, G. W. Kennedy linked domestic redemption in the novel to "the pure and undifferentiated potential of the unbuilt house that will arise on the site of Satis House," a domicile which he presumed the soon-to-be-married Pip and Estella will erect and inhabit. Forster, Ricks, Hill, and Butt and Tillotson are typical commentators on the second ending in that they treat the potential wedding of Pip and Estella as an actual event in the revision. Shaw may again be the instigator. When he demoted the revised ending to an "Editor's Postscript" for the 1937 edition of *Great Expectations*, he appended this snub: "Sentimental readers who still like all their stories to end at the altar rail may prefer this. They have their choice."

Were Pip's marriage to Estella to take place, it would be more of a continuation than a departure. The tone of the final pages emphasizes acceptance and reconciliation; their momentum throughout is definitely matrimonial. In the fifth paragraph of chapter 59, Biddy insists to Pip: "You must marry," and despite his demur, Pip discovers "a very pretty eloquence" in the "light pressure of Biddy's wedding ring" whenever her "matronly hand" brushed him. Once Dickens decided on revision, he apparently combed his text for hints that facilitated the new ending he had in mind. Given Biddy's question and the magic in her ring, Pip's subsequent actions are no surprise. Even as the revised Pip tells Biddy that he has "quite forgotten" Estella, he "secretly" intends "to revisit" Satis House "for her sake"—that is, he behaves like a man on a mission.

It is never a question of Estella "being married, reclaimed, and widowed" and then courted and remarried in "a page or two," for she told

Pip of her intention to wed Drummle in chapter 44, eleven years and fifteen chapters ago. Instead Dickens used the revised ending to demonstrate that larger patterns continue to unfold. In a tragicomic universe, where it takes years for long-term plans fostered by greed and revenge to go awry, Dickens reconciles his readers to the workings of a deliberate providence; he offers a bit of solace to individuals who, like Pip, learn to forgive or who, like Estella, although "bent and broken," are remade through remorse.

A wedding for Pip and Estella would augment the unions of Joe and Biddy and of Wemmick and Miss Skiffins, which gave chapters 55 and 58 a connubial aspect. Dickens seems ultimately to have sought a sense of redress extending beyond Pip and Estella: a novel that began with a non-wedding—the earliest event in the plot is the jilting of Miss Havisham twelve years or so before the narrative actually commences—would conclude with the intimation of nuptials-to-come after the story has ended. To the extent that Pip is Magwitch's creature while Estella is Miss Havisham's (i.e., to the extent that each creator has tried to live vicariously through his or her creation), the prospect of union for Pip and Estella is doubly efficacious: it not only signals their spiritual survival, but also imparts a modicum of recompense to Magwitch and Miss Havisham, both of whom perished rather ignominiously as social outcasts.

If Pip and Estella are altar-bound, as Shaw put it, theirs will hardly be the conventionally happy union that critics opposed to the event regularly imagine. Practical difficulties are bound to intrude. For example: Pip has sworn before Jaggers and Wemmick not to divulge Estella's true parentage. The marriage bond would put great pressure on this promise, particularly when Mr. Philip Pirrip, Esquire, writes his lifestory. Also, in chapter 59 Pip is only home on furlough. Estella notes: "you live abroad still," and Pip replies, "Still." So at least a temporary separation must ensue while Pip returns to Egypt to settle his affairs. Pip's refusal to see "no shadow of another parting" from Estella may become problematic almost immediately.

Pressure on Pip, some might argue, is already evident in the revised ending where, contrary to the novel's prevalent tone, Pip is no longer the ironic, self-deprecating, yet reliable adult commentator who began the narrative. Instead, as he becomes unusually reticent, subdued rather than passionate, Estella does most of the work; she speaks nearly three times as many words in the revision as Pip does. Not until her confession that she has often "thought of " Pip and given the "remembrance" of his devotion "a place in [her] heart" does he talk at length. When he speaks, however, he assumes control of the conversation; he responds ironically to the ambiguity in Estella's remarks, which sound as if she is "very glad" to be "taking leave" of him, too, not just of Satis House. Surely Pip would not risk this rejoinder if Estella's comments and the romantic possibilities increasingly present in the occasion did not encourage him. In reminding Estella how "painful" he found their "last parting" (in chapter 44), Pip also implies that it will, indeed, prove to have been their "last." Furthermore, the emphasis Pip places on "friends" in his statement "We are friends" seems quite amatory. To preserve an ironic Pip and lessen, without forfeiting, the ambiguity in the novel's final sentence, one need only see him in a marital light potentially rather than actually—i.e., gently but ironically revising Estella's use of "friends" and "apart."

Not just the return to the ruined garden, where Pip and Estella have walked together before, constitutes a repetition with a meaningful variation. The "evening mists" also rise in chapter 59 the way the "morning mists" rose "long ago" at the end of the First Stage. The Miltonic echo from the last sentence of chapter 19, which reminded one of Adam and Eve facing a lifetime of effort in a brand new world, can thus be heard again but without as much irony now, for Dickens suggests that Pip and Estella are beginning the world a second time and are doing so promisingly.

One may argue that the allusion to Milton fits much better in chapter 59 than it did previously, and that Dickens modifies the earlier ironic usage with this straightforward application. As Pip's coach sped toward London, the eighteen-year-old observed that "the mists had all solemnly risen now, and the world lay spread before me" (ch. 19), just as Milton wrote of Adam and Eve upon their expulsion from Eden: "The World was all before them." Innocent, untested Pip was surely rash to compare his London prospects, glowing at the time, with Milton's depiction of the fall as a fortunate occurrence that exposed our first parents to a temporal existence of sweat and sorrow. If the "Second Stage of Pip's Expectations" deflates the First Stage, the Third Stage's reuse of Milton enabled Dickens to reconsider the Second; the original ending, in contrast, seemed unconnected, self-contained.

On the other hand, the allusion in chapter 59 is not entirely devoid of irony: potential newlyweds rarely see themselves as Adam and Eve, formerly of Paradise. Unlike the Miltonic echo in chapter 19, where the easy target is Pip's naivete, this one is subtly tragicomic: it affords a second chance to two people who have already paid heavily for it. The garden at Satis House was a false and perverse Eden; emergence from it—an exit that is symbolic as well as actual—gives Pip and Estella their first real opportunity to work out their salvation. Their prospects, no matter how tenuous, are truly brighter than they ever could have been in the past they leave behind. The original ending, Dickens may have realized, neglected the aesthetic and philosophical opportunities in Milton and the mists. "The lady and I looked sadly enough on one another," the Piccadilly Pip reports, but a comfortably remarried Estella, living "on her own personal fortune," and an avuncular Pip, willing to pass off Biddy's child as his own, seem excused from further effort.

Hand imagery in the revised ending better underscores the themes of remorse, softening, and forgiveness. In the original, Estella merely offered "to shake hands" with Pip, just as she offered to do at least twice before— once when they were traveling to Richmond (ch. 33) and again at Satis House when she announced her resolve to marry Drummle (ch. 44). Although Pip kissed Estella's hand both times, he was unable to retain it— unable, consequently, to convert their friendship into love. But in the second ending, says Pip, "I took her hand in mine." Having seized the initiative, he appears to have bound their fates together. Evidently, they leave "the ruined place" not just together but still, like Adam and Eve, "hand in hand," proof of a permanent reconciliation. Estella's desire to "continue friends apart"— her last words in the novel—does not count, for Pip's actions have superseded it. His final line, in which he foresees no additional partings, challenges Joe's definition of life as "ever so many partings welded together" (ch. 27); it would not have been so contrary, however, had Dickens retained the "but one" that appears in the earliest manuscript reading. Like rising mists and Miltonic echoes, clasped hands are "touching" and "exactly right" but have not enriched Pip and Estella or swept them as yet to the altar.

Edgar Rosenberg's fondness for the Piccadilly encounter, his reservations regarding the logic of the second ending, are based on what he felt may have been Dickens's implicit preference for the original conclusion. In Rosenberg's opinion, the argument that the second ending has superior retrospective weight—i.e., that it successfully reuses mists, Milton, and hand imagery—creates the impression that Dickens did not know what he was doing before he talked to Bulwer at their Knebworth conference. Moreover, calling the Piccadilly meeting an "accident" struck Rosenburg as absurd; the one at Satis House truly is coincidental, he added, because Pip finds Estella on the very spot from which they have been separated for years, after having had numerous childhood encounters there—and they meet fortuitously on what Estella confesses was to be her last visit.

Nevertheless, providential meetings and fateful returns are staples of Dickens's melodramatic realism; by 1860, they had become central to his conception of the life process. The novel begins with Pip's unplanned meeting with Magwitch in the churchyard and pivots on its startling repetition when Magwitch, newly returned from Australia, suddenly materializes in Pip's chambers (ch. 39). Magwitch grapples with Compeyson in the Thames (ch. 54) just as they struggled on the marshes in chapter 5. Pip imagines Miss Havisham hanging from a beam in chapter 8, and the hallucination recurs in chapter 49. Unlike the carriage scene in Piccadilly, which has no antecedents in the text, the final encounter in the ruined garden balances the opening confrontation in the churchyard; although Pip's return from Egypt is not terrifying, it proves as unexpected and momentous for Estella as Magwitch's return from Australia was for Pip.

Thanks to Pip's rediscovery of Estella as the "solitary figure" in the gloomy garden, reuse of mists and Miltonic echoes seems entirely in keeping with the novel's pattern of repetition through variation—i.e., its interest in unexpected encounters that lead to equally dramatic re-encounters, which, of course, are necessary for both revenge and reconciliation, two primary thematic concerns that are also variations on each other. An unexpected re-encounter may be said not to violate expectations if it can be seen as part of a pattern in the novel, one which the novelist claims to have copied from providence's practice in real life. The second ending is less of an accident in that it describes a meeting which, like those between Pip and Magwitch or Magwitch and Compeyson, is not one of a kind; moreover, it transpires without such accidentals as a "little Pip" to confuse Estella or an extraneous "Shropshire doctor" to benefit from the softening of her heart.

Revising the conclusion of *Great Expectations* may have seemed palatable to Dickens because he had already altered the first ending *before* Bulwer-Lytton allegedly objected to it. In the manuscript version, the Piccadilly encounter took place "four" years after Pip's return from Egypt, not "two" as in the proofs that Bulwer read. Admittedly, the new ending exiles Pip for eleven years, not eight, so the overall separation is about the same in the manuscript version and the revision, but the latter moves the garden meeting, as opposed to the reunion in Piccadilly, from two years after his return to within twenty-four hours. Dickens may have been amenable to revision because he approved of an additional contraction of the time process; stepping up the pace may have appealed to him as something he had already begun.

With Pip staying abroad longer (eleven years instead of eight), Estella's reformation through suffering became more credible; her release from her husband "two years before"—during Pip's ninth year of absence—may be a sub-conscious factor behind his otherwise unexplained return. If one allows for the requisite period of mourning, Pip could hardly have spoken of marriage to Estella sooner than he does. He is careful to relate that he "had heard of the death of her husband" but not whether she has remarried. Pip's propulsion toward Estella is thus quite remarkable: in manuscript four years after his return, shortened to two in the original ending, then to less than a day after his return in the second ending.

In contrast, the Piccadilly meeting seems to take forever to happen: although Pip may have been home for the "two years" during which

Drummle died and Estella remarried, he has never attempted to see her. On the other hand, Pip says "I was in England again," so he may have been back and forth to Egypt for some or all of the time between his visit to the forge at the start of chapter 59 and the chance meeting in Piccadilly. In that case, it is highly coincidental that Pip is both back and not at the forge but "in London" and Piccadilly on the very day that Estella, who presumably resides in Shropshire, drives past. Only her sending a servant after Pip finally brings them face to face. Given her less than full-bodied apology—Estella merely offers Pip the "assurance" that she now comprehends his former miseries— one is surprised that he is "very glad afterwards to have had the interview." If Estella is already out of Pip's system, as his lack of initiative in meeting her implies, the interview becomes superfluous; if it sets his heart at rest, why has he waited so long, relying on luck to arrange things?

Dickens permitted four chapters of *Great Expectations* to reach print either during the Knebworth conference or shortly thereafter. He conferred with Bulwer-Lytton until Tuesday, 18 June. Three days earlier, chapters 47–48 (installment 27) had appeared. During the week in which Dickens worked on his revision (18–24 June), chapters 49–50 were published (22 June). Even if Dickens had wanted to, he could not have undone more than the last nine chapters, and he probably could not have moved quickly enough to retouch chapters 51–52 (29 June). Still, he elected not to tamper with the first six of his last seven chapters (i.e., 53–58). Only the very end of the entire book underwent substantial revision, and not a word elsewhere—besides the last chapter's opening line—had to be altered as a result of Bulwer's so-called intervention. The problem, Dickens apparently decided, was serious but local.

As Dickens wrote Bulwer on 24 June 1861 when sending him the revision: "My difficulty was to avoid doing too much. My tendency, when I began to unwind the thread that I thought I had wound for ever, was to labour it and get it out of proportion." Consequently, he continued in the next paragraph, "I have done it in as few words as possible." If Dickens felt that the original ending needed an adjustment that would not appear out of proportion, he may have found the Piccadilly scene, upon reconsideration, too short, too final, and too much of a letdown. Compared with Miss Havisham's incineration, Pip's discovery of Estella's parentage, Orlick's attack on Pip, and the abortive escape attempt resulting in Magwitch's capture and death, Pip's reunion with Estella was bound to seem anticlimactic, an obligatory scene to tie up a loose end rather than an ending that would contribute to a crescendo.

One may interpret the letter to Bulwer to mean that Dickens wanted a slightly longer, livelier, less dismissive final encounter, one that would involve no changes prior to chapter 59. Instead of seeming flatly un-Dickensian, the final scene would have to be suspenseful and tragicomic, a mixture of happy and sad. Working backward from the last word, Dickens sought to locate the latest possible point at which his story had gone wrong; when he got as far as the eleventh paragraph of chapter 59, the spot Millhouser also pinpointed, he stopped and began to revise. To his credit, Dickens hit upon a twilight reunion scene in a graveyard-like garden, a scene at once as surprising and fortuitous as the novel's opening and possibly as providential in its ramifications. Although this reunion is hymeneal by implication, Dickens probably surmised that Pip's intriguing observation in the last line would keep readers speculating about his future with Estella, much as purchasers of the weekly installments had wondered about the identity of his secret benefactor.

It is no insult to Dickens's art to imagine him bothered by the ending to *Great Expectations*. Having penned the original conclusion, he may have begun to feel that the book's complex possibilities had been summarily resolved. In other words, Dickens may have been disturbed by the final scene both before and during the Knebworth conference. George Gissing set a precedent in blaming the revision on Dickens's "unhappy deference to a brother novelist's desire for a happy ending," but an uneasy Dickens may have solicited his fellow artist's approval to make a change; perhaps he asked Bulwer to marshal every reason he could think of in favor of alteration. This was generally the nature of Dickens's conferences: he asked supporters for additional proof in favor of the position toward which he was already leaning.

But did Dickens go so far as to request, then follow, specific directions? Most likely no—or else he would not have had to wait until he returned to Gad's Hill to effect the change. Nor need he have sent his new advisor the result if Bulwer was already familiar with the Satis House alternative. In the letter for 24 June about not extensively unwinding, Dickens's use of a "thread" to symbolize his novel's plot line recalls the all-important "rope" holding aloft the ceiling of Misnar's pavilion when Pip describes the edifice in chapter 38: the rope runs through miles of tunnel before being fastened to a "great iron ring." The well-timed collapsing of the pavilion once the rope is severed is Pip's analogue for the unfolding of his lifestory, a process that builds steadily toward a stupendous downfall upon Magwitch's return in chapter 39. But as greatly as Dickens admired *The Tales of the Genii* and obeyed its influence throughout *Great Expectations*, he implies that his thread is superior material to Horam's rope; it has remained tensile and subject to reuse long after Pip's castles-in-the-air caved in. Having unwound part of the final episode, Dickens was delighted to announce that he had tautened his ending and rewound the thread more tightly than before. The letter to

Bulwer primarily expressed relief, but it also contained Dickens's quiet satisfaction with his own restraint, thanks to which the crisis had been narrowly contained—i.e., in some 36 additional paragraphs, of which over a dozen are only one line long.

Shaw tried to have things both ways: a meddling host and a supplicatory guest. Dickens, Shaw presumed, "must have felt that there was something wrong with this [i.e., the first] ending; and Bulwer's objection confirmed the doubt." One may go further and exonerate Bulwer entirely; he has been made the villain of the endings controversy as undeservingly as Shaw has been hailed as its hero. Presuppose a Dickens unhappy with the novel's resolution yet cognizant of John Forster's satisfaction with the ending as it stood. This Dickens was also less than eager to consult Wilkie Collins because he was hoping to equal, if not surpass, his friendly rival's recent success, *The Woman in White*, which had outsold *A Tale of Two Cities* in *All the Year Round*. In such a combination of circumstances, unique in Dickens's career, why should he not have resorted to a new source of advice: an eminently successful novelist with whom he was on excellent terms and had already planned a meeting?

Impressions of Bulwer's role in the Knebworth conference derive almost entirely from a handful of Dickens's letters to Forster, Collins, and Bulwer himself; these turn out to be very curious documents. The ostensible purpose of the Knebworth gettogether was to discuss *A Strange Story*, the Bulwer novel scheduled to succeed *Great Expectations* in *All the Year Round*, but, strangely, none of the key letters in this exchange so much as mentions it by name. This may indicate which novel lay uppermost in Dickens's mind from mid to late June 1861. To Forster Dickens wrote on 1 July: "You will be surprised to hear that I have changed the end of Great Expectations." Dickens's closest literary advisor was doubtless shocked, not "surprised"— taken aback not just by such an unexpected announcement but also by Dickens's jaunty tone throughout this letter, as if reorienting the lives of one's hero and heroine at the last minute was a minor affair.

In the letter to Forster and when writing to Collins earlier on 23 June 1861, Dickens took pains to portray Bulwer-Lytton as the instigator: "Bulwer was so very anxious that I should alter the end of Great Expectations . . . and stated his reasons so well," Dickens told Collins; later he would inform Forster that Bulwer had "so strongly urged it upon me, and supported his views with such good reasons, that I resolved to make the change." In both cases, one may conclude, Dickens was striving not for accuracy but to placate his regular confidants. He made it sound as if, having gone to Knebworth with no anxieties regarding his novel, he was defenseless when Bulwer questioned the ending. This is the scenario that Forster reported in *The Life of Charles Dickens* and that nearly all commentators since Gissing have accepted, but it depends entirely on two brief passages in Dickens's letters, passages that appear designed to magnify Bulwer's responsibility and pacify Dickens's friends. Twice Dickens referred to Bulwer's "reasons"; regrettably, he never quoted these marvelous arguments, so one can only wonder not merely about their eloquence but also whether they ever existed. From the letter to Forster, it sounds as if Bulwer submitted a detailed recommendation (i.e., "the change"), but Dickens carefully stops short of saying so, and the letter to Bulwer about wanting "to avoid doing too much" implies otherwise.

In sum, Dickens seems to have had his own agenda for the Knebworth conference, one that may have included a revision proposal from the start. He offered Bulwer to Forster, Collins, and posterity as a prime mover rather that what he probably was: a willing accomplice. On 24 June, Dickens sent Bulwer "the whole of the concluding weekly No." so that he could peruse what Dickens flatteringly called an "alteration that is entirely due to you." One may detect a degree of satisfaction in this lavish compliment that absolved Dickens of all responsibility; "alteration" may have been the option that Dickens had stimulated Bulwer to suggest and over which the Inimitable had never relinquished control.

Dickensian diplomacy—keeping himself detached and blameless while manipulating and propitiating others—also accounts for the off-hand manner in Dickens's letter. Addressing Collins, he minimized the extent of the change—if affected only "the extreme end, I mean, after Biddy and Joe are done with." For Forster, too, he downplayed the new ending, characterizing it is as merely, "a very pretty piece of writing" that would prove "more acceptable" but failing to specify to whom. As if to augment the inconsequence of so momentous a decision, Dickens told Collins of his "thorough laziness" now that the deed was done—this became a "desperate laziness" in the letter to Forster. Such convenient lassitude seems designed to excuse Dickens from further self-justification; it helped to explain why Dickens had sent revised proofs to Bulwer but wrote Forster and Collins that they would have to wait. "You shall see the change when we meet," he promised Collins; "You shall have it when you come back to town," he guaranteed Forster.

Keeping Forster and Collins in the dark was Dickens's method of forestalling a counterattack; the change, he implied, was not only minor but also final. The Knebworth conference had run from 15–18 June, work on the new ending followed, and Dickens sent it to Bulwer on the 24th, yet the letter to Collins only went out from Gad's Hill on 23 June, the day before, and Forster's letter, also from Gad's Hill, is dated a full week later than

Bulwer's. Given Dickens's diligence in creating the impression that the second ending came about virtually without his cooperation, an implicit preference for the original ending seems improbable. Defending what he originally wrote would have cost Dickens less trouble. The "too great speed" alleged for Estella's reclamation and so-called remarriage in the revised ending cannot match Dickens's alacrity in dealing with Bulwer's unspecified "reasons" for enacting a change, but it contrasts sharply with Dickens's slowness in bringing Forster and Collins abreast of a major development.

Taken one after the other as they generally occur in post-Shavian editions, the two endings impart an undeserved modernity; they constitute alternative versions of what could have happened. Modern editorial practice has kept *Great Expectations* capable of multi-directional advancement, as though not one but two sequels were called for: the first to work out Pip's life with Estella, and another for life without her. A prescient Dickens appears to have anticipated John Fowles's *The French Lieutenant's Woman* (1969), in which chapters 60 and 61 provide two equally plausible but mutually exclusive conclusions to a story that came to one terminus in chapters 43–44, then took a different tack in chapters 45–60: initially, Charles foregoes the mysterious Sarah and is reconciled with the more traditional Ernestina; then the novel explores what might have happened had Charles pursued Sarah; finally, it supplies two different resolutions for this quest.

But the third and final volume of Forster's *Life* (1874), which first divulged the existence of the original ending, did not come out until thirteen years after *Great Expectations*. Dickens's earliest readers did not have the luxury—or the dilemma—of alternative endings. Besides, Dickens was not trying to be anticipatory; instead, he was interested in appearing more realistic than Collins, Lever, and Bulwer, whose novels surround *Great Expectations* in *All the Year Round*. Since their stories exhibited the kinds of endings familiar to serial readers in 1860–61, *Great Expectations* should be placed in a context of Victorian rivalries, not misjudged as proto-modern because of its double ending. The modernity of Dickens's novel stems from his use of the second ending to outclass his competitors: more imaginatively than he felt they could, he addressed the phenomenology of closure; where they behaved conventionally, he strove to be ambiguous and paradoxical.

Granted, the survival of two endings for *Great Expectations* may have prompted Fowles simultaneously to modernize and parody Victorian fictions, but his novel does not endorse openness and resist closure in Dickens's sense of the terms. Fowles's story may be said to end several times, so that, in effect, it never does or can. The plausibility of each new possibility underlines this predicament until one recognizes the impossibility of stopping with authority before all options have been considered, at which point, however, it still seems bewildering to have to choose. Dickens did not want to subvert closure; his intention was not to unsettle readers by demonstrating that things can always go differently and perhaps should; instead, he wanted to correct abuses of closure in three of his immediate rivals, to discredit what he considered utterly facile closings. The third stage of Pip's maturation would come to an end, yet the sense of the hero's life still in the making would be preserved, as if this three-staged novel could easily expand to a fourth or fifth stage. Each additional segment would modify its predecessor, not substitute for it as Fowles's chapter 61 contradicts chapter 60 or as the original ending raises doubts about the revision it generally follows in modern editions.

Lumping *Great Expectations* with *The French Lieutenant's Woman* as novels with problematic endings, David Lodge used the occasion to celebrate "the great modern works" that acknowledge "ambiguity or uncertainty"; they leave readers with the sense that life goes on. Actually, Dickens does this better than Fowles, whose point is not that life continues but that one chain of events may be no more binding than another. Dickens tacitly conceded Fowles's point when he resorted to an alternative ending, but he devised that ending to confirm the principle of continuation, to keep the future stretching before Pip and Estella instead of permanently consigning each to the other's past. Since marriage is supposedly symbolic of happiness, Lodge decided that Dickens's refusal to tie the knot in the original ending makes it less pleasing, more uncertain, and therefore the truer of the two, whereas Dickens presumably thought just the opposite.

What happens if one measures the revision against the endings of Wilkie Collins's *The Woman in White*, Charles Lever's *A Day's Ride*, and Bulwer-Lytton's *A Strange Story*? To the embarrassment of all three, Dickens's point seems to be that conclusions have become increasingly difficult in a universe he considered tragicomic—one lacking the definitiveness common to both tragedy and comedy, wherein the hero either succeeds or fails. Unlike Fowles, who spells out different possibilities, Dickens leaves the matter unresolved: on the one hand, Pip and Estella appear to be on the threshold of an extended period of wedded bliss; on the other hand, perhaps they are not. It is not possible to be absolutely positive. Either way, the sense of wasted lives persists, for Pip and Estella cannot recover the past eleven years or erase the scars they carry from their respective childhoods; there can be no conventional ending when the prospective marriage partners are so badly damaged that their life together must include a fair amount of reparation and repair.

Mr. Pirrip has learned that the expectation process—one's ability to formulate what one wants from the future—is a major reason the human situation remains ironic and unsatisfactory: not only are one's hopes regularly frustrated, but their attainment can be demanding, if not disastrous. To be expectant, although part of being human, is vastly inferior to the self-understanding that an older Pip and a "bent and broken" Estella now realize comes only through hindsight. One must continually expect before one is qualified to evaluate the worth and consequence of one's expectations—i.e., before one knows what to expect. In other words, Pip has had to look forward in hopeful but ignorant expectation and backward with comprehension and regret.

Endings, it follows, never really happen because events are always subject to continuation and review, both of which are modifiers but not in Fowles's sense of doing things over, of replaying them differently. Pip and Estella can never totally dismiss each other. Thus Shaw's imaginary "perfect ending," so resoundingly final, merely exposed the weakness in Dickens's original: both absolve Pip and Estella (and the reader) from expecting anything further. In allowing Pip and Estella the belated possibility for a modest but mutually restorative life together, Dickens revaluated the permanent separation in his original conclusion, finding it as false to the nature of things as the static felicity that heroes and heroines achieve in the novels of his immediate rivals. He countered such artificiality with a semi-resolution that seems open-ended in comparison, hence, he implied, truer to life.

The revised *Great Expectations* can be said to end paradoxically with a beginning, just as *Paradise Lost* does. Trying times lie ahead for Pip and Estella even if they become Mr. and Mrs. Pirrip. Not for them the complacent future that awaits David Copperfield and Agnes Wickfield in Dickens's earlier bildungsroman. The situation for Pip and Estella more closely resembles that of Candide and Cunegonde, who are resigned to cultivating their garden at the end of Voltaire's story. Estella's beauty has lost its bloom; Pip has lost a fortune. The challenge facing them is to discover how much can be made of what is left. Can her battered spirit and his long-disappointed hopes be assuaged?

Pip clearly thinks so, but it may be to Mr. Pirrip's credit, as he puts down his pen in 1861, not to have told us for certain if Pip is correct, so that, strictly speaking, the exact nature of the new beginning remains ambiguous. If one of the lessons of *Great Expectations* is to discipline but not abandon one's expectations, then readers desirous of knowing the future (Pip and Estella's, that is) should not expect to have it handed to them. If Pip and Estella have long since parted, it may be dishonest in Mr. Pirrip to be less than conclusive, but otherwise he is free to tantalize us. A chastened Pip, however, is understandably cautious: he states that on a specific evening in a specified place, he was unable to foresee another parting—a statement one must certify as truthful regardless of subsequent events. Pip divulges all he knew or could have known at the time.

The rest, Mr. Pirrip seems to say, is not history but another story, the sequel he should perhaps proceed to write. If one decides that Pip has grown sufficiently in judgment and self-awareness to become a reliable prognosticator, a better expectant, then the positive implications pervading the revised ending can be taken as a warranty. Yet Pip's decision not to be retrospective in the novel's final line, his failure to add "and I was right" (or "I was mistaken") must be defended: such a phrase would have been the equivalent of Jane Eyre's "Reader, I married him." It would have created the impression of a couple living happily ever after, their tribulations brought to an end with the stroke of a pen. Dickens would have falsified the complexity of their struggle, which should either be told in detail, with the same degree of reflection used in chapters 1–59, or left to the reader's imagination, which Mr. Pirrip evidently preferred.

None of Dickens's immediate rivals exhibited a similar restraint. A hard-working Pip and a much-diminished Estella should be interpreted as downward modifications of the hero and heroine in Collins's *The Woman in White*. Walter Hartright aspires to wed, and eventually claims the hand of, an heiress—but only after returning from abroad (Central America in this case) to discredit the man Laura Fairlie felt obligated to marry instead of him: Sir Percival Glyde, a brutal baronet even less scrupulous than Drummle. Pip's detective work—the uncovering of Estella's sordid parentage and the ironic realization that his beloved and his gentility both originate from a convict—deflates Hartright's more lucrative investigations on behalf of Miss Fairlie. Sir Percival and Count Fosco have cruelly dispossessed her of fortune, position, and even identity by installing a look-alike, Anne Catherick; although Anne dies in the process of taking Laura's place, she is buried as if she were Laura, who has been institutionalized as Anne. Miss Fairlie's complete recovery, not just of wealth and status but also of bodily health and presence of mind, exceeds one's hopes for a battered and jewel-less Estella. Walter and Laura's son, it turns out, will inherit Limmeridge House, her family estate, whereas Pip and Estella, both in their mid-thirties, will probably remain childless and in moderate circumstances even if they marry.

Pip's daydreams, all destined to be frustrated, became facts of life for Hartright, blessings he is said to deserve or feats he was able to perform. Ineffectual as Estella's would-be knight, Pip is equally ludicrous as a male Cinderella or as Prince Charming. Although he imagines himself marrying

Estella and restoring Satis House to daylight splendor, he accomplishes neither. Collins's ending is not false to its antecedent events but does resemble a fairytale. In contrast, the revision Dickens did for *Great Expectations* presents a middle-class hero and a faded heroine who seems mellow, even melancholy; the second ending parodies fairytale elements in Victorian fiction, exposing their falsity by substituting a sobering reality.

Collins's final chapters are given over to revenge, exoneration, and triumphant reinstatement. The late Sir Percival and the Count, a fugitive on the continent, are made to stand trial *in absentia*; legal proceedings in *Great Expectations* are unfairly reserved for Abel Magwitch, whose hardearned wealth is confiscated by the government. Contrary to anything Pip can do for Miss Havisham, Walter in effect turns back the clock to the time before Laura's calamitous first marriage. From that point, now that he is considered good enough for her, they resume normal lives, seemingly unscathed by recent events. Dickens puts his emphasis on remorse, resignation, and forgiveness; Pip's rise from blacksmith's apprentice to London gentleman parallels Walter's from drawing master to father of the next master of Limmeridge House—except that the former's rise proves unreal and shortlived. Thanks to its collapse, Pip then ascends from false and demeaning attitudes to a true but not affluent gentility.

If one compares *Great Expectations* with *The Woman in White*, which it followed in *All the Year Round*, it seems plausible that Dickens had "reasons" other than Bulwer's for making a change: the revised ending furnished "an opportunity to enlarge upon his parody of the success story so crucial to *The Woman in White*." Both endings undermine Collins's, but the second does so on a point-for-point basis. The revision better suits what Forster called the story's "drift" because it is a conscientious elaboration on Dickens's parody of Collins. One can only marvel at an outraged Shaw accusing Dickens of inflicting "the conventionally happy ending" on his novel, for the second ending becomes less happy the more closely it is compared with Collins's conclusion.

As late as May 1861, before most of the final stage of *Great Expectations* had seen print or either of its endings was on paper, Bulwer-Lytton told Dickens that he planned to kill Lillian, the clairvoyant, semi-mystical heroine of *A Strange Story*, and to allow the novel's husband-hero, Allen Fenwick, to fade unhappily into old age. But in chapter 82, things work out differently. Having relocated with his ailing wife to, of all places, Australia, Dr. Fenwick returns home from an all-night struggle in the goldfields; he has prevented the mysterious, wizard-like Margrave and his evil forces from conjuring up the elixir of life, the "life renewer." Thanks, it seems, to his successful exertions, he finds Lillian fully recovered from a long, trance-like illness which was likely to prove fatal, despite her husband's medical expertise. Fenwick then concludes the novel that succeeded *Great Expectations* in *All the Year Round* by summarizing the uneventfully blissful years he and his wife have since enjoyed. He connects Lillian's wifely greeting the morning of her recovery with her continuing love and support for him as he completes his narrative many years later: "Again those dear arms closed around me in wife-like and holy love, and those true lips kissed away my tears,—even as now, at the distance of years from that happy morn, while I write the last words of this Strange Story, the same faithful arms close around me, the same tender lips kiss away my tears."

The ending of *A Strange Story* is a placebo of the conventional sort that Dickens had employed for *David Copperfield* a decade earlier. Sameness, the unbroken serenity of married life, is the point of Fenwick's final sentence. The story's happy resolution and the moment of retelling long afterward become identical because, apparently, they have been; reality to the contrary, no changes or problems have arisen in the meantime. Given the way life after marriage has stood still, Fenwick can simultaneously recall and duplicate the kisses and tears that sealed his wife's recovery.

As happened when Collins's novel was the referent, the alteration Dickens made in chapter 59 becomes less optimistic, less unambiguous, the minute it is compared with the conclusion Bulwer finally adopted. A narrator who claims that he foresaw no indication of a parting from Estella is tantalizingly similar to, yet parodically different from, one who is busily demonstrating through a timeless embrace, that no separation from Lillian has taken place. Evidently, Bulwer's usefulness did not end at Knebworth; his cooperation in revising the outcome of *Great Expectations* did not spare him from becoming one of Dickens's targets. After the conference, Dickens was presumably armed with foreknowledge of Bulwer's ultimately benign intentions for Lillian and Allen. Consequently, he increased his own credibility at Bulwer's expense—that is, first by soliciting Bulwer's objections to the original ending, then by not following the example of *A Strange Story* in his revision.

Prior to marriage to Laura in Hartright's story and immediately after marriage to Lillian in Fenwick's, a crisis arises; once it has been met, years of tranquility follow. Such, of course, was not the case for Dickens, whose unhappy marriage had collapsed in 1858 after twenty-two years. All the more reason why he may have used the revision process to satirize the complacent finality in the endings of both *The Woman in White* and *A Strange Story*—not to mention the absence of lasting wear and tear on their respective heroes and heroines.

Shaw opined that Dickens listened to Bulwer because the latter showed him how closely the first ending resembled Lever's *A Day's Ride*, the fiasco with which the first seventeen installments of *Great Expectations* had run concurrently in *All the Year Round*. "Note, by the way," Shaw wrote, "that the passing carriage in the Piccadilly ending was unconsciously borrowed from A Day's Ride: A Life's Romance . . . but in Lever's story it is the man who stops the carriage, only to be cut dead by the lady. That also, was the happiest ending both for Potts and Katinka, though the humiliation of Potts makes it painful for the moment. Lever was showing Dickens the way; and Dickens instinctively took it until Lytton moidered him from fear for its effects on the sales."

As usual, Shaw's comments are provocative but badly skewed. Bulwer would not have been concerned about the impact on sales from the thirty-sixth of thirty-six installments. Nor can one argue that Dickens would have retained the Piccadilly ending had it not resembled a scene in Lever. He blamed *A Day's Ride* for lowering the circulation of his new periodical and had introduced *Great Expectations* to counteract the drop in sales, so he would never have copied a resounding failure. Shaw was wrong to raise the specter of unconscious plagiarism from a novel that Dickens had kept an eye on constantly, hoping for its popularity to improve.

Instead, one ought to credit Dickens with a deliberate—not an instinctive—redoing of Lever, a satiric reworking or revaluative parody. Indeed, *Great Expectations* revalues Lever's novel throughout in that it is more truly a snob's progress, charting not only Pip's unmerited elevation but the more demanding moral climb he undertakes after his false rise is justly reversed. Dickens's first ending was designed to invalidate Lever's carriage scene, but the second, he must have seen, works even better to expose a rival's unrealistic conception of character growth and plot resolution.

The descendant of a humble line of apothecaries, Algernon Sydney Pottinger (nee Potts) travels across Europe from one misadventure to another after a lackluster first year at Trinity College, Cambridge. Cherishing "grand aspirations," Potts excels at "castle-building" and imposture; his dreams of overthrowing "miserable class distinctions" do not preclude passing himself off as the greatest swordsman in Europe or a royal prince traveling incognito. Despite a minor character's description of him as "the most sublime snob I have ever met," Potts remains a likeable cockney reincarnation of the picaro; the more he desires gentility, the more prone to embarrassments he becomes.

In the original ending, Dickens changed the tone of Lever's carriage scene so that it suited his own novel's tragicomic treatment of snobbery and its consequences, subjects he implied that *A Day's Ride* had trivialized. A Pip and Estella who gaze "sadly enough on one another " must savor the bitter results of their snobbishness—his wanting to be good enough for someone who is actually a convict's daughter has left him expatriated and alone; she has suffered "outrageous treatment" for preferring Bentley Drummle, whose only merit when he is introduced in chapter 23 is being "next heir but one to a baronetcy." Pip and Estella must also pay for the vindictive snobbery of Magwitch and Miss Havisham: his vendetta against gentlemen, hers against all men; both dedicated their lives to punishing their allegedly superior victimizers.

Unlike the saddened Pip, the Potts whom Catinka cuts "dead" seems terribly shallow, not much different from the foolish young man in Lever's opening chapters; not is he seriously stunned by Catinka's disregard. Despite marrying far above her rank, she has experienced none of Estella's misfortunes. In short, the Piccadilly encounter made the carriage scene in Lever's comic novel on snobbery seem frivolous. Dickens exhibited a regenerate hero whose forté is now humility, not being humiliated, which is the upstart Pott's fate from the start to finish.

But Lever's novel does not actually conclude with the scene Shaw described. Instead, *A Day's Ride* may be said to end twice. First, Potts receives his comeuppance from Catinka. He was ashamed of his attraction to this untutored gypsy-child, a laid-off circus performer, when they were both vagabonds in Germany; now, having eloped with a Bavarian prince, Catinka travels the Parisian boulevards in style and awards Potts the snub he deserves when he attempts to renew their acquaintance. Then comes, as it were, a revised or happier ending. At the police department, Potts finds a letter that has been waiting for him for over a year from Kate Whalley, his true love, whom he has not seen since he set off to locate her outlawed father, a mission completed two years ago in Sebastopol. A grateful Kate and her father request the hero's presence in Wales (Sir Samuel, whom a suddenly capable Potts nursed back to health, has long since recovered wealth and reputation). The novel's one-sentence final paragraph foreshadows Pip's ban on future partings: "I set off for England that night—I left for Wales the next morning—and I have never quitted it since that day."

In the original ending, Dickens stopped his novel at the point where he implied Lever's should have (i.e., Potts' encounter with Catinka). In the second ending, he parodied the gloating in Potts's final paragraph with Pip's calm hope confidently expressed. Pip's ambiguity sounds genuine and appropriate in comparison; it replaces Pott's disingenuous ambiguity, which is really facile certainly in disguise. Pip finds Biddy married to Joe, a truer prince than Catinka's Bavarian. The newlyweds do not snub Pip who then asks their forgiveness for having considered himself above them. Whereas Pip opts for self-exile, the recourse in *David Copperfield* only for fallen women and the unemployable, Potts lives idly on an inheritance from his father; he is recalled to Kate after a separation of a year or two and immediately following the snub he receives for presuming to address a prince's lady. In contrast, eleven years are required to reunite Pip and Estella, Pip must press his suit, and it remains uncertain if he has succeeded.

Perhaps Bulwer, like Shaw, mistook the original ending for a straightforward "borrowing" from Lever. More likely, Dickens felt that the original revaluation was insufficient: thanks to the auxiliary ending in which Potts tells of hastening to Wales, *A Day's Ride* might appear to survive Dickens's Piccadilly put-down. Lever's second ending, the summons from Kate and her father, is the real false note, a *deus ex machina*, as Dickens probably realized upon reflection. In addition to rewarding an unchanged Potts unduly, it guaranteed him a lifetime of the same kind of artificial uneventfulness that Collins had bestowed on Hartright and that Dickens knew Bulwer planned for Fenwick. Shaw was right to see Lever's carriage scene as "the happiest possible ending both for Potts and Katinka" but not just because they are as ill-suited to each other on a Paris boulevard as they were in a German forest; a stronger reason for calling this the "happiest" eventuality and also the least credible is that Catinka's triumph over Potts leads, illogically and unfairly, to his apotheosis.

That the mature Dickens constructed "far better conclusions than literary convention might demand or than superficial reading might suggest" is itself a commendable conclusion. The alternative Dickens invented for *Great Expectations* is so versatile that the idea of a revised ending applies just as readily to the endings Dickens found unacceptable in the works of three rivals, whose conclusions he therefore rewrote. Answering Lever as well as Collins and replying in advance to Bulwer, Dickens refused to equate *closure* with *stasis*, as if novels, unlike life, ever reach a point after which nothing else occurs although time still passes.

Hartright and Laura, Potts and Kate, and Fenwick and Lilian luxuriate in final paragraphs that seem to have struck Dickens as dispensations from the human condition. "In writing these last words," declares Walter Hartright, having just learned of his son's good fortune, "I have written all. The pen falters in my hand. The long, happy labour of many months is over." Walter confesses that he has enjoyed not only happiness with an attractive though ineffectual Laura but also sensible advice and protection from Marian Halcombe, who has been their "good angel," just as Agnes Wickfield is Copperfield's but only after he is deprived of Dora. All that can be said of Potts is that the former wanderer has stayed put, he has never quit Wales or Kate, and the Fenwicks have locked themselves into a lifelong embrace. None of his immediate rivals, Dickens implied, had dramatized the process of individual growth and responsibility convincingly enough for readers to imagine its continuation, yet that is precisely what the revised ending to *Great Expectations* compels one to envision.

Presumably therapeutic, Mr. Pirrip's novel-writing is certainly instructive, even cautionary, but was never intended to be exhaustive. No matter how fine a sense of irony he has cultivated, Mr. Pirrip's recollection process cannot have been, like Hartright's, a "happy labour." The last thing Pip describes is a "broad expanse of tranquil light," but night is falling and Mr. Pirrip purposely breaks off before he has "written all." That Pip and Estella hold hands is a positive development when compared to their earlier meetings; it becomes less so, however, when the comparison involves Potts cleaving to Kate or the Fenwicks clasping each other.

Even if Pip persuaded Estella to share his future, it is conceivable that she has recently died when Mr. Pirrip finally picks up his pen to write *Great Expectations*, her death being the "but one" parting foreseen in the first version of the revised ending's final line. That would explain why the Satis House encounter in chapter 59 took place about 1840, whereas Mr. Pirrip is publishing his lifestory in *All the Year Round* twenty years later. Only after Estella's demise would he be free to relate his tale without paining her by proclaiming her true parentage and youthful coldheartedness. Unlike Potts, Hartright, and Fenwick, all of whom attain a conventional unbroken happiness because they continue to receive strong female support, Mr. Pirrip, at about 56, may be toiling over his manuscript and facing old age alone. In any case, Hartright's regret that his storytelling days are over seems unrealistic in comparison, a formulaic declaration in keeping with the untroubled existence he now shares with Laura; and Fenwick's decision to wait a "distance of years" before he wrote his novel, Dickens suggested, is simply tardiness.

As did Greenberg and Millhouser before him, Peter Brooks identified "Pip's recognition and acceptance of Magwitch after his recapture" as the novel's "ethical denouement." In view of Dickens's revaluation of his rivals, however, Brooks's reason for cutting everything after chapter 58 is unique: from that point, Pip has allegedly learned to stop reading the events in his life as an adventure story with him as the central figure. The true act of "acceptance," therefore, does not just involve kinship with Magwitch but also Pip's "continuing existence without plot, as celibate clerk for Clarriker's," the rest (i.e., chapter 59) being "obiter dicta." Yet it is specifically the sudden cessation of plot, the subsidence into sameness or plotlessness, that Dickens deplored in Lever, Collins, and Bulwer. Although Dickens's novel may be called a satire against the entertaining or arousing of unrealistic expectations, Brooks's call for a clerkly, celibate Pip would deprive him of Estella yet still produce the same sort of artificial termination that keeps Potts without incident in Wales and the Fenwicks in each other's arms, such fiction-free permanence being the falsest expectation of all. Brooks's implicit perfect ending would impose Shaw's demand for finality much sooner: Pip would still say, "I went out and joined Herbert. Within a month I had quitted England, and within two months I was clerk to Clarriker & Co." Then he might add a new last line to chapter 58: "I have never quitted Herbert, Egypt, or Clarriker's."

To deconstruct Dickens's novel, Brooks discounted the second ending by pitting the storyline Pip thinks he has been enacting against the actual direction events have been taking. This procedure, an attempt to use the plot against itself, dictates that the novel end where the dichotomy of the illusory or fairytale plot and the official one dissolves—i.e., with the departure for Egypt, at which point Pip has exhausted his expectations. As was Shaw, Brooks seems hostile to the modernist assumption which the second ending anticipates, the sense that resolution, whether through attainment of perfect happiness or the total collapse of one's hopes, is the ultimate illusion because it is always temporary (a stage or phase). As Mr. Pirrip realizes, he can revise his lifestory which he misread as it was unfolding—indeed, such revision is one of the novel's motivating concerns—but as a human being, he cannot stop living and reliving it; nor can he cease trying to foresee occurrences, although both Shaw and Brooks want him to.

As a shopworn literary convention, plot may be the simplification of an agenda actually cluttered with contradictions and irrelevancies. Moderns sound confused when they regret that novels must tell stories but insist that the stories remain open-ended, susceptible to endless continuation. It is the switch to plotlessness, however, that brings a specious clarity which threatens a work with self-contradiction: either the new state of affairs or the one preceding it, the plot-filled chapters readers have avidly consumed, must be deemed perfidious. When Potts, Fenwick, and Hartright lapse into plotlessness, their lives since the conclusion of their adventures contradict all that went before.

Were *Great Expectations* really about Pip's progress from misreading the plot of his life to an acceptance of its plotlessness, there would still be plot enough for him to read, and the final verdict would be that he has finally read it aright. But such an interpretation must ignore Pip's parting ambiguity, Mr. Pirrip's awareness at the close of the narrative that no final stage in Pip's life has yet emerged. Brooks preferred the original ending because the revision reopens the plot; it rekindles expectation, which becomes a synonym for plot. Where Brooks wanted the novel to retract its new beginning, to retreat to the nearest facsimile of a final stage (Pip's quitting England in chapter 58), Dickens sought to do exactly the opposite. He moved back into the narrative only to the latest point at which he could get the plot moving again, the point from which a revision could take Pip and Estella forward. Dickens may have canceled the phrase ruling out all parting "but one" because this reference to individual mortality injected a sense of foreseeable finality, the one thing he especially wanted to avoid.

Closure, Marianna Torgovnick has argued, is the "process by which a novel reaches . . . what the author hopes or believes is an adequate and appropriate conclusion" (i.e., Brooks's "ethical denouement"). On the other hand, she considers a novel "anti-closural" when the author seeks "to end . . . with the sense that it could be continued." Shaw's "perfect ending," Millhouser's cuts in chapter 59, and Brooks's "futilization of the very concept of plot" have a common, anti-modernist denominator: all embrace closure and abhor its opposite. But Dickens's purpose, to accomplish closure while remaining anti-closural, frustrates clear-cut distinctions such as Torgovnick's and eludes common denominators. Paradoxically, Dickens wanted to close without ending, to end without closing, a tactic he considered life-like. Contrary to *The French Lieutenant's Woman*, the ultimate question in *Great Expectations* is not which ending to choose but what happens next. We want to know whether Pip and Estella make a go of it, just as readers would like to learn whether Connie and Mellors, who are separated when *Lady Chatterley's Lover* ends, have been reunited or whether Stephen Dedalus, Paris-bound at the conclusion of *Portrait of an Artist*, ever forges his race's conscience.

According to Alan Friedman, whom Lodge relied upon when comparing *Great Expectations* unfavorably to *The French Lieutenant's Woman*, twentieth-century novels tend to be "open" and therefore truer to life than the "closed" endings of nineteenth-century novels. Everything having become less decisive, modern novelists maintained that new approaches, openness paramount among them, were needed; they launched "an assault on the 'ends' of experience"—that is, on any view of existence that failed to emphasize "continual expansion" or "unrelieved openness." Unless Friedman adhered to chronological determinants, however—nineteenth-century novels must be "closed," only twentieth-century novels remain "open"—he could not highlight "The Transition to Modern Fiction" promised in his subtitle. So he coerced *both* endings for *Great Expectations* into his first category. "The ending in which Pip marries Estella," Friedman argued, "is of course narrow," but "so was the first ending" in its invocation of "an unobtrusive commercial bachelorhood" to "contain" the novel's "disturbingly broad moral situation" (the Pip-Estella-Magwitch-Miss Havisham entanglement). Dickens allegedly substituted the second ending because his public clamored for an even narrower outcome: "readers demanded marriage with Estella" and, Friedman conceded, "perhaps they had a right to suspect that they were not being told the full story."

Like Miller, Ricks, and Hill who made *Great Expectations* unduly hymeneal, Friedman invented a wedding scene for the second ending. Then, compounding Shaw's error, he attributed the revision not to Bulwer's idea of public taste but to popular demand *per se*, as if Dickens's readers actually petitioned for a nuptial sequence. Weakest of all is the presupposition that those readers, conscious of themselves as Victorians, were bound to insist upon a "closed" ending ("the full story"), instead of accepting something more "open" and proto-modern. Dickens's revised ending ought to have fared well by modernist standards. Surely it stands out as the more inconclusive of the two, its implication being that every termination contains a fresh start, the advent of another stage. Oddly, commentators like Friedman, misled by Shaw, have condemned the second ending for exhibiting the finality he mistakenly craved.

The second ending, one must reiterate, does double duty as a reviser of texts besides itself. The "full story" (Friedman's word for plot) turns out to involve the discrediting of three other stories in addition to the original ending. This is the way the revision proves that it is not only "more congruous" (to borrow Shaw's phrase) but *most* congruous. Although concerned about *All the Year Round*, Dickens was not unwilling to capitalize on Lever's failure in order to rival Collins's success and anticipate Bulwer's. Given the relative uncertainty of Pip's future with Estella compared to Fenwick's certifiably uncomplicated years with Lilian or Pott's idyllic bonding with Kate, "the full story" becomes an elusive proposition in Dickens's opinion—in one sense, the Pip of chapter 59 claims to have told one; in another, Mr. Pirrip has conscientiously withheld this satisfaction because Dickens considered it an expectation that Collins, Lever, and Bulwer-Lytton were only pretending to meet.

In discussing the revised ending, one should not contrive a third alternative or put a pox on both endings or incriminate Bulwer. Nor does it help to deny or distort Dickens's proto-modern penchant for openness. Better to underline the second ending as an antidote for the sweeping objections often lodged against Dickensian conclusions in general. Dickens could never resist "tracing the lives of the main characters over the next five or ten years after the proper climax of [a novel's] plot," Humphry House complained; yet the novelist clearly refrained in *Great Expectations*. For Orwell, Dickens typically concluded with an "endless succession of enormous meals" and "Christmas parties," besides which "nothing ever happens," an observation contradicted immediately by Pip's miserable Christmas dinner at the *start* of *Great Expectations*.

If marriage in Victorian fiction is equated with the stopping of time, as though death itself were immanent in weddings, *Great Expectations* begged to differ. Its ending is sufficiently open to compare favorably with the much-acclaimed conclusion to *Little Dorrit* (1855–57). Having exchanged vows in St. George's Church, Amy and Arthur Clennam are required to go "quietly down into the roaring streets"; there they must test their "blessed" inseparability against the world's constant "uproar," a challenge also in store for Pip and Estella as they leave the garden at Satis House. In *Great Expectations*, the jilted Miss Havisham, not the novel's prospective newlyweds, brings time to a stop; her changeless existence serves as a savage caricature of the unruffled serenity relished by the married couples in Bulwer, Lever, and Collins.

Dickens achieved both symmetry and closure through having *Great Expectations* come full circle to another beginning. The novel opens with a terrible apparition in the deserted churchyard; it concludes with a double manifestation in the ruined garden—Pip to Estella/Estella to Pip, apparitions as unexpected as Magwitch's but far more welcome. The parallel of finish to start suggests that Pip's life will be radically altered on the second occasion, much as it was on the first. It suggests further that Pip, having learned the art of benefaction—i.e., of being human—will serve Estella better than Miss Havisham did or that Magwitch benefited Pip himself. In this regard, repetition of the Miltonic echo does its job: in addition to recalling Pip's premature reference to *Paradise Lost* at the conclusion of the First Stage, the emergence of Pip and Estella from the "desolate garden," like that of our first parents from the Garden of Eden, assures readers that this couple must continue to work and grow. In contrast to the couples in the novels of Dickens's rivals that bracketed *Great Expectations* in *All the Year Round* but in keeping with the lot of all children of Adam and Eve, the revised Pip and Estella must "add/Deeds to their knowledge answerable."

CHRISTOPHER D. MORRIS

The Bad Faith of Pip's Bad Faith: *Deconstructing* Great Expectations

The problem of Pip's moral bad faith, both in his actions and in his narrative assessment of his past conduct, has long troubled critics, so much so that in recent years very probing questions have been asked about the depiction of his moral character, even about his self. In this essay I want to extend the direction of this recent questioning by considering Pip's bad faith as an instance of what J. Hillis Miller calls "varnishing," that is, the authorial establishment of some putative center for a work which simultaneously conceals evidence that would invalidate such a center. Pip's bad faith works this way in *Great Expectations*: because we so often attend to the serpentine maneuvers of his conscience, we accept without question that this conscience is functioning within an autonomous, continuous, achieved, created self. And yet analysis of the varnished side of *Great Expectations* shows that it is precisely these assumptions that have been called into question, even in the very attempt to establish Pip's conscience as a center. After a discussion of the general relation between narration and bad faith, I examine, in turn, the novel's famous opening, the allusions Pip makes as narrator, and the letters sent in the novel. The polemical connotations of "deconstruction" are nothing to the purpose here, but I do hope to show the existence of fundamental contradictions in the novel, aporia whose logical reconciliation seems impossible to articulate.

From *ELH* 54, no. 4 (Winter 1987). © 1988 The Johns Hopkins University Press.

I

Pip's relation with all characters is self-serving, even when he claims to be acting altruistically, and in his narration he occasionally covers this seemingly irreducible egotism with a veneer of disingenuous contrition. One example is his relation with Joe. As narrator, Pip claims to have developed a solicitude for Joe, but that claim is everywhere contradicted by his actions. After learning the selfless rationale for Joe's acquiescence in Mrs. Joe's "government," Pip writes:

> Young as I was, I believe that I dated a new admiration of Joe from that night. We were equals afterwards, as we had been before; but afterwards, at quiet times when I sat looking at Joe and thinking about him, I had a new sensation of feeling conscious that I was looking up to Joe in my heart.

But nowhere afterwards are they "equals." On the contrary, at the end of the novel, Pip still condescends to Joe even as he benefits from his ransoming, even as he egocentrically worries what "little Pip," his only posterity, will think of him. Similarly distorted appraisals of his past conduct surface in his comments on Biddy, Estella, Pumblechook, and Magwitch. The pervasive pattern of Pip's distortions raises the question of whether there might be some inherent discontinuity between the narrating and the narrated self. Peter Brooks hints at such a contradiction when he cites Sartre's remark that all autobiographies are obituaries, excluding the margins of experience. But Pip's bad faith runs deeper than that phenomenological *mauvaise foi* described by Sartre: it is not that Pip distorts by reifying the For-Itself in language. Instead, as we will see, there never was an original self apart from language to suffer such distortion. Selfhood has always already been the narrator's fictive construct, and Pip's moral bad faith serves to varnish that fact.

This deeper contradiction within the process of narration is discernible in other retrospective judgments. After concluding the account of his first visit to Satis House and his new perception of Joe's thick boots and coarse hands, Pip writes:

> That was a memorable day to me, for it made great changes in me. But it is the same with any life. Imagine one selected day struck out of it, and think how different its course would have been. Pause you who read this, and think for a moment of the long chain of iron or gold, of thorns or flowers, that would

never have bound you, but for the formation of the first link on
one memorable day.

The admonitory tone of the passage makes it resemble an epitaph on a
tombstone: narration itself may be only the substitution of a new set of dead
letters for old. But in this paragraph, too, Pip struggles to articulate the
determinative value of this first exposure to class, to wealth, to humiliation.
In retrospect Pip speaks as a developmental psychologist, a Piaget, who
believes in formative events and irrevocable stages of development. (We may
note in passing that the metaphor of the chain also serves to exculpate Pip:
after this point, he is not longer responsible for his actions.) Yet even more
important than the passage's self-serving function are its contradictory
metaphors for life. The chain is the privileged metaphor here, implying
absolute continuity, formative events, historical determinism and a narration
that could transparently trace these. And yet a life is also a "course," a
movement through time, that lacks the capacity to "bind." The problem is
not simply one of mixed metaphors. Instead, language seems incapable of
articulating both diachrony and synchrony simultaneously. Words mark the
conversion of the synchronic into the diachronic; to articulate is to be caught
in a signifying chain; what Pip struggles to express cannot be expressed: the
act of narration already excludes it. It is against this background that we
should understand the novel's famous opening, in which Pip reads his name
from the dead letters of the tombstones.

II

The first page of *Great Expectations*, especially the process by which the name
Pip is arrived at, has been the subject of extended critical commentary.
Nearly all agree that the process is alienating and that Dickens emphasizes
the arbitrary nature of language. Brooks's analysis is one of the most astute
in this vein: "This originating moment of Pip's narration and his narrative is
a self-naming that already subverts whatever authority could be found in the
text of the tombstones." Other critics have also noticed this subversion at the
novel's origin; misconceptions may be perpetuated, however, by the use of
the phrase "self-naming" for this process. It is true the narrating Pip says "I
called myself Pip," but his doing so is not a wholly free act, nor should it
presume the existence of some self apart from language. Instead, the name
must be formed—as all names must—out of signifiers that exist prior to and
independent of their subsequent combination. Rightly considered, then,
Pip's action is a trope, a syncope, a substitution of one group of signifiers for

another through the omission of mediate letters. The idea that the process of naming can never be a free act generated out of some autonomous subjectivity is reinforced by the words, less often cited, that follow Pip's assertion: "I called myself Pip, *and came to be called Pip*" (emphasis added). The sentence forces us to understand the Janus-like nature of signifiers, which derive their signifying capacity not from the individual, but from a prior linguistic order of which they form a part.

I stress this point because part of Pip's bad faith throughout the novel is his belief in his own freedom to name—that by naming or narrating he is imparting some truth, defining some center or signified, if only himself. Such is the lure or ruse that has seduced not only Pip, but so many critics of *Great Expectations*, who see its triumph as the construction of a self. Joseph Gold's view is typical: "Pip is made by Pip in the telling . . . By using the first person Dickens eliminates himself and this makes clear his moral-psychological conviction that the remaking of oneself by the confrontation with the past and one's own nature is essential to being fully alive and aware in the present." Brooks's assessment seems more defensible than such a claim because it presumes less: Pip's experience shows us that we are "condemned to repetition, re-reading, in the knowledge that what we discover will always be that there was nothing to be discovered. . . . Like Oedipus, like Pip, we are condemned to reinterpretation of our names."

Brooks is right, too, to emphasize the circularity of Pip's name, a palindrome whose emptiness reflects the futility of his quest for meaning. In general, following Jakobson's distinction between the referential and poetic functions of language, we can distinguish two sets of meanings for that name. The first set is oriented toward the referent: thus, a pip is a seed, a unitary origin whose growth is presumably as continuous as that of the organic world. The narrating Pip fills his story with imagery of gardens and cultivation, language that has been analyzed at length for the light it sheds on Pip's moral and ethical education. But a pip is also a disease or the symptom of a disease, so the semantic values of the word begin to cancel or contradict each other: a seed that is a disease, a growth that is a dying. A pip is also a mark on a deck of cards, distinguishing one value from another. Yet this third message-oriented, or referential, meaning also subverts the first, organic definition: the sequence of numbers is less self-evidently continuous than the growth of plants. In any case, the deck of cards figures prominently in Estella's game of "beggar your neighbor" and other alienating power relations in the novel. The possibility is raised that Pip's self may be but one card manipulated in a game subordinated to some order outside himself.

But if the referent-oriented meanings of the name Pip suggest ultimate aporia, the two "poetic" meanings (in Jakobson's terms)—those that focus on the message for its own sake—yield even more startling contradictions. A pip can, more generally, be any mark, step, or degree that signifies a difference. Here "pip" could be merely sensory evidence of a possible meaning, like an alaphone, which at the same time cannot mean without the juxtaposition of some other sound or silence. Therefore Pip's name suggests an unrealized potential for signification, truly a deferral, in Derrida's sense. This poetic meaning of the word further calls into question the already problematic semantic meanings. And the final referent of "Pip" is its allusion to *Sartor Resartus*. Given the chronology of *Great Expectations*, neither the narrating nor the narrated Pip could be aware of Carlyle's use of the word to denote an inarticulate cry. Therefore, this sense of the protagonist's name can only call attention to Dickens, to his readers in and after 1860, and ultimately to the fictitiousness of the novel *Great Expectations*. There is one other such self-reflective device in the novel—the capitalized words that conclude each third of the book. The importance of these legends, which almost resemble intermittent epitaphs for the novel itself, will be more fully analyzed later. But here we can observe that the novel's opening is more complex even than Brooks allows. Pip's "self-naming" conceals a fallacy. It holds out hopes for signification in general and for some continuously stable self in particular, but it simultaneously denies these hopes by emphasizing the arbitrary and fictive nature of its language and of language in general.

III

Pip's allusions continue the double play of language noted in the aporia of his "self-naming": they reflect the narrating Pip's desire to stand outside his narration, to make his words objective, independent tracings of an autonomous self, a continuous life; at the same time, however, they undermine these very expectations by exposing the narrated Pip as merely a fictive entity constructed from discontinuous signs. The allusions, then, serve that "varnishing" purpose that J. Hillis Miller finds at work in narrative since Oedipus.

At first glance Pip's allusions show mild urbanity: his knowledge of the Bible, of the classics, and of recent literature confers upon his narration a veneer of sophistication in keeping with his ostensible "maturation" from blacksmith's apprentice to clerk at Clarriker's. Yet the status of any such maturation is immediately called into question by these allusions: is the clerk who can quote from Collins superior in any way to the world of illiteracy from which he emerged? Has education enabled him to some qualitatively new stage of perception barred to characters without the ability to allude?

That the answer to these questions should be no is implicit not only in the limited range and relative accessibility of the passages to which Pip alludes, but also in his persistent misapprehension of them, which leaves the reader to decide between mutually contradictory interpretations.

An early example is Pip's recollection of a sermon on the morning after he learns of his expectations: "I went to church with Joe, and thought, perhaps the clergyman wouldn't have read that about the rich man and the kingdom of Heaven, if he had known all." The blatant bad faith of Pip's wish to exempt himself from the applicability of New Testament parables is of course in keeping with the morally repugnant condescension he begins to show here to Joe, Biddy, and the townspeople. But more disquieting is the narrating of Pip's failure to correct his earlier opacity. Of course the irony of the passage may be interpreted differently: Pip's silence, his apparent inability to see his own bad faith, may merely be his grimly wry commentary, full of the wisdom of experience, on an earlier egotism too obvious for later remark. The point is not that one interpretation can be shown to be more tenable, but that it is impossible to decide between the two. Both coexist and cancel each other. According to the first, Pip has not learned and persists in his folly. According to the second, Pip's learning, his grasp of the allusion, is complete. The issue ⟨. . .⟩ turns upon the interpretation of a silence, and cannot be decided.

The most extended allusion is Pip's recounting of this episode in which Wopsle and Pumblechook read "at him" George Lillo's *The History of George Barnwell*. Several elements of the scene show that Pip as retrospective narrator uses this literary work to protest his innocence even as he misinterprets its purport. Traditionally the play had served as a cautionary role for apprentices, warning them of the evils of rising up against masters. Pip protests against the application of this theme to his own case: "What stung me, was the identification of the whole affair with my unoffending self." Yet Pip's claim to innocence is belied by the undeniable fact that he *has* grown restive with his apprenticeship to Joe, ever since his first visit to Satis house. But even more disingenuous is his response to Pumblechook's admonition "take warning!" which prompts Pip to observe sarcastically: "as if it were a well-known fact that I contemplated murdering a near relation, provided I could only induce one to have the weakness to become my benefactor." But quite clearly, Pip has resented a near relation (his sister); he has also contemplated murdering a benefactor (his surreal vision of Miss Havisham hanging from a wooden beam). Pumblechook and Wopsle are of course in error to interpret the play as applying exclusively and directly to Pip; but Pip is in error (and as narrator compounds this error by refusing to correct it) by assuming that the allusion is without any application to him.

And it never occurs to either the narrated or narrating Pip to forge the obvious parallel between the prostitute Millwood (seducing Barnwell and exacting her revenge on men) and Estella.

Our confidence in the narrating Pip's perspicuity in allusion may also be shaken by his idiosyncratic adaptation of the parable known as "The Pharisee and the Publican." At Magwitch's death Pip "thought of the two men who went into the Temple to pray, and I knew there were no better words that I could say beside his bed, than 'O Lord, be merciful to him, a sinner.'" The point of the parable in Luke is that the Publican's simple confession of his own unworthiness is preferable to the Pharisee's lengthy self-justifications. But Pip's twist of the parable into a prayer for Magwitch rather than a confession of his own unworthiness disingenuously allows him to preserve an altruistic sense of his own selfhood. In fact it is always impossible to separate Pip's apparent solicitude for Magwitch from his own self-interest. For example, he has much to gain from Magwitch's escape from England, since it would prevent the convict's wealth from escheating to the crown. And even after Magwitch's imprisonment Pip's actions remain self-serving, especially his withholding from Magwitch until the moment before he dies the news that Estella lives. In short, it is Pip, not Magwitch, who continues to be a "sinner" up to the very moment their relationship ends. Pip's inversion of the parable's applicability is another instance of the persistent misreadings by which he surreptitiously affirms his own selfhood.

Two other allusions may deepen our sense of Pip's narrative duplicity. As he read in foreign languages to an uncomprehending Magwitch, he compares his situation to Victor Frankenstein's: "The imaginary student pursued by the misshapen creature he had impiously made, was not more wretched than I, pursued by the creature who had made me, and recoiling from him with a stronger repulsion, the more he admired me and the fonder he was of me." In this allusion Pip once more exonerates himself as he interprets a text. The allusion first claims Pip is more wretched than Victor Frankenstein. But the second comparison contradicts the first: Pip is pursued by the "creature who had made me," thereby aligning himself with the creature and Magwitch with Victor. Pip finds in Shelley's text the idea of the "double": especially in view of the final evocation of Victor brutalized by his need for revenge, Pip's oxymoron—that the creature created its creator—makes sense. But by making himself parallel to both characters, Pip takes on only the sympathetic attributes of each: like Victor he is made "wretched" by the pursuit, the existence, the reappearance of the misshapen Magwitch; and like the creature, his life is threatened in the pursuit. Pip's dual roles serve his purposes: whether maker or made, possessor of free will or determined by the action, the narrated Pip is given the status of a pure object of sympathy, independent of his "true" creator, the narrating Pip. Through the allusion to Frankenstein, Pip attempts to establish his own innocence as both character and narrator.

The allusion that most explicitly indicates the narrating Pip's varnishing duplicity is the long comparison, just before Magwitch's return, between the peripeteia of his story and the "Eastern story" he paraphrases from "The History of Mahoud" in Sir James Ridley's *Tales of the Genii*. In that story a Sultan cuts a rope which held a slab above the bed of two of his enemies. Pip explains the meaning of this allusion: "So, in my case; all the work, near and afar, that tended to the end, has been accomplished; and in an instant the blow was struck, and the roof of my stronghold dropped on me." For the narrating Pip, the rope is an excellent figure for absolute continuity, from the beginning of his tale until this very moment (though the discontinuities of the novel are everywhere apparent, most conspicuously in the sentences that begin the very next chapter, which allude to a gap of about two years). The severing of the rope makes Magwitch like Sultan Misnar, unaware of the far-off, catastrophic result of his action, and Pip like his two sleeping enemies. In other words, like the reference to *Frankenstein*, this allusion depicts Pip as pure victim and Magwitch as destructive avenger— albeit, problematically, an unconscious one—of his enemy's illusory triumph. That assignment of roles varnishes Pip's responsibility for his own misinterpretation of events. This allusion, like the others, attempts to cover previous misinterpretations with new signifiers.

But the varnishing function here is also evident in the allusion's placement just prior to the narration of Magwitch's return. The narrating Pip is in a hurry to fix the significance of this episode even before narrating it. Pip's haste betrays his desire to be the sole interpreter, the master interpreter, of his narration. But the novel shows us many times that such a wish is a delusion. For example, a dumbfounded Pip listens to his own story being told by the innkeeper, who sees in it Pip's ingratitude to Pumblechook; Pip of course rejects the innkeeper's interpretation, but doing so leads him to a new interpretation of his own: "I had never been struck at so keenly, for my thanklessness to Joe, as through the brazen imposter Pumblechook. The falser he, the truer Joe; the meaner he, the nobler Joe." The innkeeper's "false" narration changes Pip's interpretation of his own life, thereby demonstrating the deficiencies of his prior narration. Surely Pumblechook is not the only "brazen imposter." Such an incident subverts the notion of some privileged or master interpretation that will fix the course of a life; instead, interpretation in the book is interminable, constantly modified by new interpretations.

This survey of Pip's allusions shows that they work in the same way as his putative "self-naming." Both are, in fact, renamings, substitutions of one set of signifiers for another. The texts to which Pip alludes precede him, just as do those other "dead letters" in the graveyard. And, of course, allusions create an initial effect of enhanced versimilitude: the created life of Pip seems more real when it is interpreted next to lives described in parables, novels, and tales. Yet as we have seen, instead of validating Pip's claims to autonomy, continuity, and moral innocence, his allusions expose the groundlessness of these expectations: no assertion is completely explicit or unfoided; all unfold some hollow; narration is Ariadne's thread.

IV

Many letters are sent and received in *Great Expectations*, and their equivocal status has often been remarked. Murray Baumgarten, crediting John Jordan and Garrett Stewart, notes that in Pip's first letter, to Joe, the complimentary close "inF xn" can mean either "in affection" or "infection" or "in fiction." Thus, like the meaning of the word "Pip," the letters in *Great Expectations* may be understood in both of Jakobson's senses—they convey some content from sender to recipient, and they refer to themselves, to other letters, to the signifying chain.

Like most readers, Pip attends to the first sense. For example, in his letter insisting that Pip meet him at the lime kiln, Orlick writes "bring this letter with you," perhaps to ensure that Pip will come alone. But Pip forgets this self-referential part of the letter; ironically, his negligence is rewarded when he is rescued by Herbert.

Beyond its plot function, Pip's indifference to the second sense of letters perpetuates his bad faith, a cover-up that can be seen in his reaction to Biddy's letter, in which she asks Pip on behalf of Joe if he will receive him on the following Tuesday (chapter 27). The letter's content is simple, yet there is a subtext, created by Biddy's treatment of the letter as letter, Pip gives no indication of comprehending. (More accurately, as in his reaction to the parable of the rich man, this issue is undecidable, since Pip doesn't in retrospect correct his prior silent misreading.) Biddy tells Pip in a postscript that she had read to Joe "all excepting only the last little sentence" in which she had expressed her own hope that "even though a gentleman" Pip will receive Joe. Both contents of the letter are important, but Pip grasps only the first, the semantic content concerning Joe's imminent arrival. The second—Biddy's growing perception of Pip's inhumanity and her resolve to protect Joe—is expressed through her ellipsis, which Pip does not read. This instance of misunderstanding may serve as a template for Pip's bad faith: attending to the diachronic, semantic content of *parole* and forgetting that letters are arbitrary signifiers, Pip assumes the existence of a unitary, necessary connection between signifier and signified. His missing Biddy's delicate criticism is only a local instance of that universal misapprehension—great expectations—which finds its major manifestation, of course, in Pip's assumption that Jaggers's signifiers must correspond to Miss Havisham.

On the one occasion Pip does attend to the self-referential component of language, he is nearly driven mad. Approaching his room at the Temple after leaving Estella for what he believes is the last time, Pip is given a message with the superscription, "Please Read This Here." The message itself, from Wemmick, is "Don't Go Home." This message leads Pip to spend the night in Hummums, where he experiences a kind of dark night of the soul: "What a doleful night! How anxious, how dismal, how long!" In this anguish he is led to perceive Wemmick's message only in its self-referential sense. The result is the conversion of the physical world into a meaningless prison house of language:

> When I had lain awake a little while, those extraordinary voices with which silence teems, began to make themselves audible. The closet whispered, the fireplace sighed, the little washing-stand ticked, and one guitar-string played occasionally in the chest of drawers. At about the same time, the eyes of the wall acquired a new expression, and in every one of those staring rounds I saw written, DON'T GO HOME.

In a nightmare frenzy, Pip comes to his closest experience of language as some order independent of the self, prior to the human. Far from being a neutral or transparent medium with which to capture or define reality, words finally come to suggest that Lacanian discourse of the Other. Pip refers to Wemmick's message as "this" or "it":

> Whatever night-fancies and night-noises crowded on me, they never warded off this DON'T GO HOME. It plaited itself into whatever I thought of, as a bodily pain would have done.

Of course there is semantic content to Wemmick's message, and when morning comes Pip will be ready to act on it. Yet in the light of Pip's extraordinary meditation on these words, the semantic value of the message may be considered apart from its function in the plot. This is the effect of Pip's falling to sleep by conjugating the "vast shadowy verb" in the imperative mood, present tense:

> Do not thou go home, let him not go home, let us not go home, do not ye or you go home, let not them go home. Then,

potentially: I may not and I cannot go home; and I might not,
could not, would not, and should not go home; until I felt that
I was going distracted, and rolled over on the pillow, and I
looked at the staring rounds upon the wall again.

Pip's conjugation of Wemmick's message converts its meaning into a
statement of pure exclusion. The ultimate meaning of the words, in both of
Jakobson's senses, suggest inexorable separation, apartness, exile, lack of
connection. Pip as narrator has shown us, despite himself, that such exclusion
is inherent in his acts of articulation. In order to proceed with life—to obey
the message, to help the convict, to fall in love, to rectify wrongs—we must,
like pip, ignore the insoluble, inescapable contradictions woven into
"plaited" or folded language. Terrified, Pip remembers that a gentleman had
recently committed suicide at Hummums, and that nightmare place, also a
word that resembles "humans," may provide the only alternative to life amid
the contradictions of *Great Expectations*.

V

Each volume of *Great Expectations* ends with a legend capitalized, like "DON'T
GO HOME"; these legends refer to Pip in the third person and, twice, to the
"stages" of his expectations. The voice of the omniscient narrator thus writes
epitaphs for his fiction in the very act of envisioning his protagonist's life
developmentally. As if in some recognition of the novel's aporia, the legend
that ends the third volume attempts to terminate both the novel and the
metaphor of stages: "THE END OF GREAT EXPECTATIONS." The
syntactical ambiguity here—whether misinterpretations end only with the end
of language—is in keeping with the contradictions elsewhere in the novel,
seams in its texture whose existence could only with difficulty be regarded as
deliberately created or even foreseen. And yet not even this conclusion could
end interpretation.

　　Dickens's revision of the ending of *Great Expectations* ensured that
doubleness of interpretation would remain the novel's legacy. Such
doubleness, summarized in the notes below that recount the two
contradictory traditions of critical reaction to the novel, marks the
persistence of authorial bad faith intertextually, that is, beyond even the
expected limits of the three-volume novel: to the extent that interpretation
of *Great Expectations* follows one of its major critical traditions or chooses one
of the two endings, it has already succumbed to the lure through which
Dickens, by unfolding language and varnishing its contradictions, seeks to
sustain the illusion of a signified.

JAMES PHELAN

Progression and the Synthetic Secondary Character: The Case of John Wemmick

[M]y approach to the analysis of narrative progression claims to be an advance over other discussions of plot and structure because it pays attention to the temporal dynamics of the authorial audience's experience of narrative. In the discussions of thematizing so far, I have been illustrating that conception of progression, and as particular occasions such as the discussion of Scholes have allowed, I have been taking small steps to substantiate the introductory claim. I turn now to focus explicitly on the concept of progression and its explanatory power. I will compare the ideas about progression, both implicit and explicit, that I have drawn upon to this point, with the ideas about "reading for the plot" advanced by Peter Brooks in his attempt to account for the dynamics of narrative. Brooks's model provides a good test of my own not only because it is the most powerful model recently advanced but also because, like mine, it wants to consider how the reader's experience is directed by the text. Rather than being a rhetorically based theory, however, it is a psychoanalytically based one.

I will compare the models for analyzing narrative dynamics in connection with Dickens's *Great Expectations*, a narrative that Brooks also analyzes and that raises questions about the synthetic component of character—especially through Dickens's use of Wemmick. Indeed, Wemmick provides us with an occasion to consider the potentially problematic

From *Reading People, Reading Plots: Character, Progression, and the Interpretation of Narrative.* © 1989 by The University of Chicago.

relationships among the three functions of character, because his outlandish mimesis foregrounds his synthetic status and has consequences for both our sense of Dickens's thematic intentions and our own understanding of Pip's mimetic function. Moreover, the variety of Wemmick's functions also illustrates some important general principles of progression that are highlighted by the comparison with Brooks's model.

Brooks offers an initial definition of plot that coincides with much of my own definition of progression, especially in its twin emphases on the temporality and centrality of plot: "Plot . . . is not a matter of typology or of fixed structures, but rather a structuring operation peculiar to those messages that are developed through temporal succession, the instrumental logic of a specific mode of human understanding. Plot . . . is the logic and dynamic of narrative, and narrative itself is a form of understanding and explanation." From this definition, Brooks sets out to develop a model for discussing the experiential dynamics of reading for the plot, a model that he labels an "erotics of art." As I examine that model and its application to Dickens's novel, I shall argue that despite Brooks's success in moving beyond the essentially static conceptions of structure proposed by other narratologists, he nevertheless fails to offer an adequate theory of reading for the plot.

As noted briefly above, Brooks depart from much previous psychoanalytic criticism by focusing not on the unconscious of the author, reader, or characters, but rather on the psychodynamics of the text: he wants, in his words, to "superimpose psychic functioning on textual functioning" in order to discover "something about how textual dynamics work and something about their psychic equivalences." His method privileges psychoanalysis as the way to explain how texts operate, but the method also respects textual functioning: in reading Brooks, one typically feels that narrative structure is being illuminated rather than made to lie on a bed fashioned by Procrustes for Freud.

Brooks begins with narrative, not psychoanalysis, and comments on the paradox of endings. The end always acts in some influential way on everything that precedes it, since the ending is what the beginning and the middle are preparing us for. Furthermore, "it is at the end—for Barthes as for Aristotle—that recognition brings illumination, which then can shed its retrospective light." Thus,

> if in the beginning stands desire, and this shows itself ultimately to be desire for the end, between beginning and end stands a middle that we feel to be necessary . . . but whose processes, of transformation and working-through, remain obscure. Here it is that Freud's most ambitious investigation of

ends in relation to beginnings may be of help, and may contribute to a properly dynamic model of plot.

That most ambitious investigation is *Beyond the Pleasure Principle*, and Brooks focuses first on what help it might be in thinking about repetition in narrative. "Narrative always makes the implicit claim to be in a state of repetition, as a going over again of a ground already covered: a *sjužet* repeating a *fabula*, as the detective retraces the tracks of the criminal." In addition, repetition is the stock in trade of literary discourse: "rhyme, alliteration, assonance, meter, refrain, all the mnemonic elements of literature and indeed most of its tropes are in some manner repetitions that take us back in the text, that allow the ear, the eye, the mind to make connections, conscious or unconscious, between different textual moments, to see past and present as related and as establishing a future that will be noticeable as some variation in the pattern." In Freud's text, repetition is first introduced as a compulsion directed toward the assertion of mastery, as in the *fort-da* game, and then it becomes a compulsion directed at "binding" the instinctual drive for immediate gratification. Thus, Freud views repetition as making possible both the attainment of mastery and the postponement of gratification.

Similarly, Brooks argues, repetition in narrative functions as a "binding of textual energies that allows them to be mastered by putting them into serviceable form, usable 'bundles,' within the energetic economy of the narrative;" "repetition, repeat, recall, symmetry, all these journeys back in the text, returns to and returns of . . . allow us to bind one textual moment to another in terms of similarity or substitution rather than mere contiguity." In this respect, repetition is a key to our mastery over—and hence, pleasure in—the text; at the same time it will frequently involve postponement of that pleasure. "As the word 'binding' itself suggests, these formalizations [i.e., elements of the text that cause us to recognize sameness in difference] and the recognitions they provoke may in some sense be painful: they create a delay, a postponement in the discharge of energy, a turning back from immediate pleasure, to ensure that the ultimate pleasurable discharge will be more complete."

Brooks next follows Freud through his examination of the relation between the repetition compulsion and the instinctual drives, and his conclusion that instincts are not drives toward change but toward stability, or indeed, toward the restoration of an earlier state of things. This conclusion in turn leads to the concept of the death instinct, a concept that stresses not just an organism's drive toward death but also its drive to follow the path to death in its own way. Brooks summarizes the point this way: "'the organism wishes to die only in its own fashion,'" and therefore, it will "struggle against events (dangers) that would help it to achieve its goal too rapidly—by a kind of short circuit." Repetition in narrative, then, says Brooks, works first to allow the operation of the death instinct, the drive toward the end as it is manifest in the text's attempt to return to an earlier state. But repetition also works to "retard the pleasure principle's search for the gratification of discharge" which will occur when the end is reached. Thus, if we begin in an initiation of tension that seeks its own release and generates a desire for the end, the middle must be the place where the narrative seeks that end in the appropriate way, avoiding short-circuit even as it inexorably moves toward a return to the quiescent state before the beginning. The middle is a kind of detour between two states of quiescence at either end of the narrative.

Brooks offers the following succinct summary of his model.

> [Plot] structures ends (death, quiescence, nonnarratability) against beginnings (Eros, stimulation into tension, the desire of narrative) in a manner that necessitates the middle as detour, as struggle toward the end under the compulsion of imposed delay, as arabesque in the dilatory space of the text. The model proposes that we live in order to die, hence that the intentionality of the plot lies in its orientation toward the end even while the end must be achieved only through detour. This re-establishes the necessary distance between beginning and end, maintained through the play of those drives that connect them yet prevent the one collapsing back into the other. . . . Crucial to the space of this play are the repetitions serving to bind the energy of the text so as to make its final discharge more effective. In fictional plots, these bindings are a system of repetitions which are returns to and returns of, confounding the movement forward to the end with a movement back to origins, reversing meaning within forward-moving time, serving to formalize the system of textual energies, offering the pleasurable possibility (or illusion) of "meaning" wrested from "life."

Brooks's model is, I think, very attractive. It not only focuses on the temporal, experiential dimension of reading, but also offers strong accounts of beginnings, middles, and ends. It offers a sensible account of the beginning as the introduction of some tension which produces desire for resolution; a suggestive analysis of the paradoxical drives of the middle, toward both continuation and closure; and a powerful account of the end as the dominant position of the narrative, one which exercises control over both the beginning and the middle. As in his definition of plot, there is considerable overlap here with my discussions of the introduction of instabilities and tensions, their complication in the middle, and their resolution at the end. At the same time, his discussion indicates that there are significant disagreements between us.

II

First, my conception of progression does not give so much dominance to the ending. Where Brooks sees the beginning and the middle as determined by the end, I see the three parts as more mutually determinative. When we read for the progression, we experience the ending as determined by the beginning and the middle, even as it has the potential, in providing both completeness and closure, to transform the experience of reading the beginning and the middle. This difference about the relation between the three stages of narrative is related to a larger difference based on a principle that I have been working with only implicitly to this point. This principle begins to emerge when we ask if there is anything beyond beginning, middle, and end that determines all three, or perhaps better, determines the way in which they are mutually determinative of each other. Can we extend our rhetorical (as distinct from our biographical or sociohistorical) analysis and explain why a particular beginning is chosen or why one out of many possible paths through the middle of the narrative is taken or why a particular kind of resolution might be better than another one? Answering these questions depends on our developing some working hypotheses of an overall design, some principle of a whole that is greater than the sum of the parts.

Austen's choice to begin *Pride and Prejudice* with the conversation between the Bennets not only has significant consequences for the middle and the end but is itself a consequence of a larger design, the development of a comic action that incorporates the narrator's norms and judgments about the marriage market as part of the comic satisfaction to be associated with the ending. Perhaps even more telling are Austen's choices in the middle. To have Darcy's first proposal occur at Rosings, a setting permeated by the values of Lady Catherine, Collins, and to a lesser extent of Charlotte; to have Elizabeth drawn to Darcy first through the intersection of his letter and her own sense of justice, then through what she sees and hears at Pemberly, and then finally through her own gratitude for his intercession in the Lydia-Wickham affair; to have the second proposal come about in part through the meddling of Lady Catherine: all these turns of the progression, which could have been managed in other ways, are in some nontrivial sense determined by the overall design. All these turns not only work to complicate and resolve the instabilities along the track established in the first half of the narrative but they also develop the nuances of the narrator's norms and thus significantly define the kind of satisfaction offered by the final resolution.

Similarly, although Fowles might have ended *The French Lieutenant's Woman* in many ways—Charles and Sarah might have been reunited and sent to an uncertain future in America—the ending is determined not just by what the beginning and middle allow but also by what the principle of design revealed in those parts allows. Given that design of explaining the shift from the Victorian Age to the modern, his ending, with its choice of closures, is more appropriate than the one suggested above. The reasoning may appear circular here but the circularity is more apparent than real. The notion of the whole is, to be sure, developed from reading the parts, but since developing that notion is always part of the reading for the progression—since our sense of the whole is itself always in motion—it is also always corrigible. When we read the first chapter of *Pride and Prejudice*, we make inferences about the whole of which it is a part, and our sense of that whole does influence our reading of new parts. But as the analyses of the ending of "Haircut" and of Chapter 13 of *The French Lieutenant's Woman* indicate, the new parts are also capable of radically reshaping our sense of the whole.

Perhaps the most useful way to illustrate the differences between Brooks's model and mine is to consider the different ways they would deal with the relations between beginning, middle, and end in works with flawed endings. Within Brooks's system there are two ways an ending can go wrong: it can come too soon, and thus short-circuit the working out of the desires aroused by the beginning and the middle; or it can unbind textual material that has been bound by the pattern of repetitions and thus fail to leave the reader in a state of quiescence.

In my terms, the first kind of flaw would be the production of an arbitrary resolution, one in which an author substitutes the imperative to provide a resolution for the greater imperative to work out the possibilities for resolution inherent in the introduction and complication of instabilities and tensions. The second kind would be the reintroduction of—or the failure to resolve—instabilities of the beginning or middle. Although I would be more concerned than Brooks with relating these flaws to some conception of a developing whole for each specific case, the differences between the models at this point are as much terminological as they are conceptual. A close look at the problems raised by a case such as the Phelps farm episode at the end of *Huckleberry Finn* will indicate that Brooks's two explanations of how endings can go wrong are insufficient. This conclusion in turn suggests that his model does not do full justice to the ways that endings can relate to beginnings and middles.

The trouble with the Phelps farm episode is certainly not one of short-circuit; the whole business is unduly protracted. In part, however, the trouble may be that as Twain tries to bind some early textual material through the return of Tom Sawyer, he unbinds some material about Huck's relation to Jim that has been apparently bound for good in Huck's decision to go to hell: The intuitive sense of Jim's humanity that resides behind Huck's decision does not lead him to resist some of Tom Sawyer's inhumane plans for Jim in the Evasion. Yet the whole problem with the ending is more complicated than that, as a look at the tasks Twain sets for himself in the narrative makes clear.

In brief, Twain's narrative progresses by intertwining the two logically independent stories of Jim's quest for freedom and Huck's more intuitive, reactive attempt to find his niche in the world (calling Huck's efforts a "quest" would overstate his sense of direction) by working out his relationship to his society. The dominant focus, of course, is on Huck, and we see him in the beginning unable to enter fully into the world of Miss Watson and the Widow Douglas, or that of Tom Sawyer and his romantic fancies, or that of his Pap. Life on the raft with Jim presents a refuge from the larger world and its problems, but that life is itself provisional and unstable as both the steamboat and the King and the Duke dramatically prove. Twain nevertheless gives his audience enough of their undisrupted life to show the developing bond between the white boy and the black man. He then uses the shore episodes both to portray Huck's intuitive education in the hypocrisy and corruption of "sivilization" and to make his audience even more aware of those features. That development in turn makes the decision to go to hell a kind of resolution to Huck's hitherto unstable situation: he decides he must live outside the professed morality of his society, even if it means suffering the worst consequences the society predicts for such outsiders. What Twain needs at this point is not so much a device of completeness for Huck but a device of closure: a major part of the developing whole, the story of the moral implications of Huck's attempts to define his relation to his society, is essentially complete. If Twain could find a way to have Huck decide to light out for the territory at this point, he would be well on his way to a satisfactory ending.

The problem he faces, however, is how to end Jim's quest. Having intertwined Huck's story with Jim's, Twain cannot conclude Huck's until he also concludes Jim's. And the options he has open are not many: Jim is now in the Deep South where he will be regarded as the rightful property of some one or other of the white folks. The most logical thing to do is have Jim be

set free by his owner, but given the way Miss Watson has already been
portrayed, to do that would be to create a deus ex machina effect. So, falling
back on his skills as a humorist, satirist, and scene writer, Twain gives us the
Evasion, his way of trying to hide the deus ex machina behind a cloud of Tom
Sawyer's romantic dust. But creating the cloud causes more problems than
unbinding the material about Huck's relation to Jim. It introduces material
that is largely extraneous to the instabilities that have moved the plot until
this point and it develops that material at great length. Although the scenes
of the Evasion are funny in themselves, their irrelevance to what has gone
before makes them as annoying as they are humorous.

The more general point here is that the beginning and the middle of
Huckleberry Finn get developed in such a way that Twain has an unsolvable
problem on his hands: given that beginning and middle, he cannot write a
satisfactory ending. The ending in this case is not determinative of the
beginning and the middle, and I would suggest that no ending could be.
Furthermore, the ways the ending goes wrong exceed the ways predicted by
Brooks's theory. One could perhaps say that had Twain initially chosen a
better ending, he could have made it determinative of the beginning and the
middle. But such a move would have required him to write a different
beginning and middle, and who would want to give up the beginning and
middle that Twain has created?

The corollary of this point about Brooks's overemphasis on the power
of the ending is that he underestimates the power of the middle. Although
he attributes to middles the important role of appropriately guiding the
desires aroused by the beginning, the middle remains a means subordinated
to the end of reaching resolution. It is a place of detour, of deflected
direction, of arabesques. As *Huckleberry Finn* and *Pride and Prejudice* show, it
is all those things—but can be much more as well. In Twain's novel, the
middle creates the impossibility of satisfactory ending, while in Austen's it is
the place where many of the thematic functions of Elizabeth's character—
especially those surrounding her own pride—are realized.

A second significant difference between Brooks's model and my own
is what each one implies about the reader's activity—and thus, ultimately
what each implies about the nature of the narrative text. Brooks's discussion
of the dynamics of reading becomes finally a description of a sequence of
drives and reactions—the beginning establishes an initial tension that
produces desire for ending, the middle produces the detour or arabesque
leading eventually toward the end, and the end produces the discharge of
pleasure with the release of the tension. This account is very consistent
with Brooks's announced intention of imposing "psychic functioning on
textual functioning." The problem is not with its consistency but with its

adequacy as a description of the reader's activity. In Brooks's account, the dynamics of the plot itself merge with the dynamics of reading that plot. To give an account of reading for the plot is to give an account of the structure of the plot. In this respect, Brooks is working with a model of a single-layered text.

By contrast, the model of the text implied in my account of progression is double-layered. On this account, the text contains not just the patterns of instabilities, tensions, and resolutions but also the authorial audience's responses to those patterns. In other words, the concept of progression assumes that the narrative text needs to be regarded as the fusion of two structures: (1) the narrative structure per se—essentially the structure that Brooks describes in his model, or what I call the pattern of instabilities and tensions; and (2) the sequence of responses to that structure that the text calls forth from the authorial audience. In still other words, we might say that progression involves not only the developing pattern of instabilities and tensions but also the accompanying sequence of *attitudes* that the authorial audience is asked to take toward that pattern. This conception has been operating throughout my analysis so far, perhaps most obviously in the discussion of Scholes's model and my arguments about the importance of the authorial audience's involvement with the mimetic component of character. The pattern of judgments, fears, hopes, desires, expectations, and so on that typically but not exclusively cluster around the mimetic component is as much a part of the dynamics of reading as the sequence of actions in which the character participates. I will return to this point shortly because it has consequences for a third difference between Brooks's model and mine, but there is another side to this present difference that needs to be illuminated.

In the discussion of "Haircut" in the introduction, I noted that the final sentences help resolve the instabilities by contributing to the completion of the narrative through the alteration of the authorial audience's understanding of the resolution that has already been narrated. In the discussion of *Pride and Prejudice*, I claimed that although Charlotte Lucas's marriage to Collins does not complicate the instabilities of the main narrative line it nevertheless had a significant influence on the authorial audience's understanding of that line, and indeed, played an important role in Austen's development of the thematic function associated with Elizabeth's attribute of independence from the marriage market. Such conclusions about the dynamics of reading these narratives are, I think, simply not available if one is operating within Brooks's system. When the dynamics of reading are merged with the dynamics of plot structure, the reader's role is implicitly limited to responding to the movement of the instabilities.

Both consequences of this second difference between Brooks's model and my own are related to the third difference. Because Brooks conflates the dynamics of reading and the dynamics of plot, he must find the key to reading for the plot not in the reader's affective experience of the text but in formal features of the text, and as we have seen, his psychoanalytical framework leads him to repetition as the identifiable key. In order, however, to account for the significance of repetition within the limits of his way of talking about the reader's experience, he must resort to talking about the thematic importance of the repetitions. The problem again is not so much that this is wrong, but that it is inadequate. When repetition gets linked to theme, then reading for the plot becomes reading for the themes in motion.

III

These last two differences between the models should become clearer as we examine Brooks's analysis of *Great Expectations*, a novel that he chooses in part because it "gives in the highest degree the impression that its central meanings depend on the workings-out of its plot." Furthermore, the novel is "concerned with finding a plot and losing it, with the precipitation of the sense of plottedness around its hero, and his eventual 'cure' from the plot. The novel imagines in its structure the kind of structuring operation of reading that plot is." Note here that in the very act of setting up his analysis Brooks implicitly makes reading for the plot reading about plot. Brooks's model is already committing him to read about themes in motion, but that model leads him away from such standard themes as the individual and society toward this more reflexive one.

Brooks begins his account with an analysis of the novel's famous opening paragraphs, where Pip discusses his acquisition of his name and his "first most vivid and broad impression of the identity of things." This impression occurs on the day in the churchyard when he became fully conscious of his environment and his own place in it as an orphan, a consciousness that in turn leads to his tears that are then interrupted by a "terrible voice," crying out "Hold your noise!" Brooks has many insightful things to say about this passage, some of which I shall return to, but his main conclusion stresses what the passage suggests about the role of plot in the novel. "This beginning establishes Pip as an existence without a plot, at the very moment of occurrence of that event which will prove to be decisive for the plotting of his existence, as he will discover only two-thirds of the way through the novel." In the first part of the novel, Brooks argues, Pip is in search of a plot and the novel recounts how a plot seems to gather around him. In fact, Brooks identifies four lines of plot moving around Pip before the declaration of his experiences:

1. Communion with the convict/criminal deviance.
2. Naterally wicious/bringing up by hand.
3. The dream of Satis House/the fairy tale.
4. The nightmare of Satis House/the witch tale.

Brooks argues further that the four plots are paired as follows: 2/1=3/4. "That is, there is in each case an 'official' and censoring plot standing over a 'repressed' plot." Pip himself favors plot 3, and when Jaggers comes with the news of Pip's Expectations, it appears that reality is conforming to his desire, and that the question of plot is now taken care of. But of course the Expectations "in fact only mask further the problem of the repressed plots."

The relation between the official and the repressed plots is perhaps best illustrated by the relation between the official, public events of Pip's life and both the continual return of "the convict material" and the repetitive features of Pip's experience in Satis House. After Pip is "bound" as an apprentice to Joe, the plot is all but suspended as the narrative recounts what Brooks calls a "purely iterative existence" in which the romance of life appears to be shut out. After the announcement of the expectations, Pip thinks that he need only wait for the next turn of the plot that is now happily controlling his life. Yet for the reader neither binding is sufficient to contain the energy discharged by the initial graveyard scene and the initial visits to Satis House. Moreover, the reappearance of the convict's leg-iron, and of Joe's file, as well as the "compulsive reproductive repetition that characterizes every detail of Satis House," including the trips by Pip and Miss Havisham around the bridal cake, signal the important presence of the repressed plots.

The middle of the narrative is, according to Brooks, "notably characterized by the return," specifically Pip's returns from London to his hometown, ostensibly to see and make reparation to Joe Gargery, and perhaps to find something of Miss Havisham's intentions for him, but deflected always to a reminder of the nightmare of Satis House and his association with the convict. "Each return suggests that Pip's official plots, which seem to speak of progress, ascent, and the satisfaction of desire, are in fact subject to a process of repetition of the yet unmastered past, the true determinant of his life's direction."

Pip comes face to face with this determinant in the novel's recognition scene, which Brooks sees operating "for Pip as a painful forcing through of layers of repression, an analogue of analytic work, compelling Pip to recognize that what he calls 'that chance encounter of long ago' is no chance, and cannot be assigned to the buried past but must be repeated, reenacted, worked through in the present." Pip's "education and training in gentility turn out to be merely an agency in the repression of the determinative convict plot. Likewise, the daydream/fairy tale of Satis House stands revealed as a repression, or perhaps a 'secondary revision' of the nightmare." The "return of the repressed shows that the story Pip would tell about himself has all along been undermined and rewritten by the more complex history of unconscious desire, unavailable to the conscious subject but at work in the text. Pip has in fact misread the plot of his life."

The resolution of the plot for Pip occurs after he comes to accept Magwitch, which also means accepting his past as both "determinative and *past.*" Once Pip is able, through the repetitions of the aborted escape, to work through the material from his past, he is in effect able to escape from plot. In this respect, Dickens's original ending to the narrative is superior to the amended ending in which Pip's reunion with Estella may undercut the extent of his escape. Brooks offers the following summary of his conclusions:

> *Great Expectations* is exemplary in demonstrating both the need for plot and its status as deviance, both the need for narration and the necessity to be cured from it. The deviance and error of the plot may necessarily result from the interplay of desire in its history with the narrative insistence on explanatory form: the desire to wrest beginnings and ends from the uninterrupted flow of middles, from temporarily itself; the search for that significant closure that would illuminate the sense of an existence, the meaning of life. The desire for meaning is ultimately the reader's who must mime Pip's acts of reading but do them better. Both using and subverting the systems of meaning discovered or postulated by its hero, *Great Expectations* exposes for its reader the very reading process itself: the way the reader goes about finding meaning in the narrative text, and the limits of that meaning as the limits of narrative.

As even this somewhat truncated summary of Brooks's reading indicates, he is an impressive reader, one who uses his model with appropriate flexibility to produce an interpretation that is in many ways both compelling and original. My quarrel is less with the particulars of that reading than with its adequacy as an account of the experiential dynamics of *Great Expectations.* Brooks's theoretical conflation of plot structure and the reader's experience has its corresponding practical conflation here. The affective component of reading for the plot is nowhere present in Brooks's analysis. The reader's activity is exclusively cognitive: "The desire for meaning is ultimately the reader's who must mime Pip's acts of reading but do them better." Brooks's reading in effect collapses the question of the experiential dynamics of the narrative with the question of how Pip's narrative can itself be seen as about plot. If one wants to know an answer to this second question, then Brooks is the man to see, but if one wants to know the answer to the first question, one better look somewhere else. In short, Brooks's conflation of the question of experiential dynamics with a question about a theme in motion fails to do justice to the complexity of the response built into Dickens's narrative. I shall now try to substantiate these brave words by offering a contrasting analysis of the progression. In order to build the contrast with Brooks's reading, I shall focus first on material he does discuss— the opening chapters—and then on material he does not discuss— the functions of Wemmick. Considering Wemmick will also add to the general movement of this part of the book, because he is a good example of how a character with a foregrounded synthetic component can affect both the mimetic and thematic levels of our reading.

IV

If we are not asking how *Great Expectations* is itself about plot, then we will respond more directly to the literal level of the opening paragraphs, and thus can recuperate some of Brooks's shrewd, specific insights. Rather than noting that these paragraphs characterize Pip as an existence without a plot, we note instead that they establish a specific instability that becomes the generating moment for the whole narrative. With Pip's description of his "first fancies" about his parents on the basis of the shapes of the letters on their tombstones, the narrative introduces the important idea that at this stage Pip is not the best reader of signs. Thus, later when Pip concludes that Miss Havisham is the agent behind his Expectations, we have cause to recognize that the tension of unequal knowledge between Dickens and the authorial audience is nevertheless maintained. More germane to the opening itself, the way in which Pip is wrong—imagining appearances from the shapes of the letters on tombstones—emphasizes the force of the initial instability, as it emphasizes his distance from and ignorance of his parents.

In the passage recounting his "first most vivid and broad impression of the identity of things," Pip tells us, as Brooks points out, how in effect he has become certain of his own difference from and aloneness among everything else. He concludes his litany of what he knows ("this was the churchyard, there were the graves of my dead parents and brothers, that was the marshes, that over there was the river, and beyond that was the sea") with his conclusions that "the small bundle of shivers growing afraid of it all and beginning to cry, was Pip." Because Pip's acquisition of self-consciousness is accompanied by his fear and grief, the narrative identifies the initial instability as one involving Pip's own identity and place in the world. In this respect, the omission of Pip's situation as the adopted son of Joe and Mrs. Joe is significant: that situation is less a part of his identity than his awareness of himself as orphan. Furthermore, the information of the first paragraph—Pip's account of how he got his name—now functions to emphasize his aloneness: he has not only lost his parents and brothers but also the name he shared with them. The narrative, then, gets its initial movement from the problem of whether and how this orphan will achieve an identity that will enable him to overcome his fear and anxiety. This question gets modified in different ways as the narrative progresses (when Pip the narrator speaks from the time of narration we worry less about whether and more about how) and redefines and resituates Pip's fear and anxiety, but it remains a significant issue until the very end of the narrative.

Again if we are not asking about how Dickens's novel is itself about plot, but rather what its temporal dynamics are, then we will redescribe Brooks's four plot lines in the opening chapters as three, because there are three distinguishable tracks along which the instabilities operate, all three of which are related to the initial instability of Pip's anxiety about identity. These three are what we might call the convict plot, the home plot, and the Satis House plot. In addition, the initiating moments of the convict plot and the Satis House plot establish some significant tensions that suggest an expansion of the scope of the narrative beyond Pip's struggle; the early moments of the convict plot establish a tension about the relationship between Pip's convict and his hated counterpart, and the introduction of Miss Havisham immediately introduces a tension about her past as well as about the presence of Estella in her house. Although the resolutions of these tensions, like the development of the instabilities along three different tracks, does place Pip's story in a much broader thematic context, those resolutions are more striking for the way in which Dickens skillfully links them to the pattern of instabilities surrounding Pip. But that is getting ahead of ourselves.

As we move into the middle of the narrative we see that the chief (though by no means only) source of the complication of the instabilities is Pip's resistance to the identity offered by his home: he can be an honest blacksmith like Joe. At the same time, we recognize that the way in which Dickens has intertwined the plots makes Pip's acceptance of that identity virtually impossible. He begins with the convict plot, immediately interlaces it with the home plot, and then further entwines them both with the Satis House plot, first covertly, then overtly. More specifically, Pip's association with the convict not only complicates his life with Mrs. Joe by making him steal from her, but for him it also increases his tendency to internalize her treatment of him as "naterally wicious." With this sense of his identity firmly established by the time he goes to Satis House, he is of course easily stung by being regarded as "common" and his desire to escape the scenes of his identity as criminal is understandably strong. At the same time, however, the home plot shows us that another side of his identity, the one that develops in his relationship with Joe, has made him unfit for the role he tries to play when the Expectations arrive. He goes on miserably caught between these two sides of his identity until Magwitch makes himself known, a resolution of a tension that sets in motion a major shift in the development of the instabilities. In short, Magwitch's return sets in motion a chain of events in which Pip works through his anxiety and fear about his identity by working back through the instabilities of the now fully interconnected plots and coming finally to accept and appreciate first Magwitch, then Joe, and finally himself.

In the course of these events the main tensions of the Satis House plot and the convict plot are also resolved in a way that signals the success of Pip's working through. Magwitch gives Pip part of the story about Compeyson, Herbert gives him part of the story about Miss Havisham, and he—and the authorial audience—learn of the connection between Miss Havisham and Magwitch through Compeyson. Jaggers and Wemmick give Pip part of the story about Molly, he makes the connection between Molly and Estella, Magwitch tells Herbert about the woman in his past, and Pip puts all the pieces together, even going so far as to startle Jaggers with his conclusions. When Pip is able to tell Magwitch on his deathbed that his daughter is alive and that he, Pip, loves her, the working through is essentially complete. It then remains for Pip to reestablish his relation with home first, through his reunion with Joe in London when Joe comes to nurse him through his illness and then through his being appropriately chastened for his dream of marrying Biddy by arriving home on the day of her wedding to Joe.

This sketch of the progression overlaps to some extent with Brooks's account of the plot but from this overlap our analyses move in two different directions—his toward the way in which the narrative is itself about plot, mine toward the affective structure of the progression, including the way it defines the relations among the mimetic, thematic, and synthetic components of character. Let us return then to the first chapter.

Even as the first chapter identifies the initial major instability of the narrative and sets in motion the convict plot, it also induces the authorial audience to adopt a set of attitudes that are crucial to our experience of the whole narrative. Dickens handles the style of the first-person narration to convey Pip's discovery of his own misery with a combination of wit and matter-of-factness that results in our responding to the discovery with full and deep sympathy rather than seeing in it a sign of Pip the narrator's own unattractive self-pity. In fact, the humor of Pip's misreading of his parents' tombstones and of the "five little stone lozenges" marking the resting place of his brothers all but deflects our overt attention from Pip's situation as an orphan. As we have already seen, when Pip declares his own discovery of self-consciousness, it comes both matter-of-factly and wittily, at the end of a series of discoveries (this place was the churchyard, etc. down to "the small bundle of shivers growing afraid of it all and beginning to cry, was Pip"). With this arrangement and the shift to the third person, we register the narrator's own distance from the scene and so give our sympathy without reservation. Because Dickens establishes this initial sympathy at the time he establishes the initial instability, he has almost irrevocably established the authorial audience's positive attitude toward Pip. He then takes advantage of this firm foundation of sympathy later in the narrative when he shows how egregiously Pip wrongs Joe. At these points our foundational sympathy—as well as Dickens's recourse to letting the mature Pip comment on his former self—moves us to be pained not just for Joe but also—and perhaps even more—for Pip. The importance of this element of the dynamics will become clearer when I turn to discuss the functions of Wemmick; for now I want to emphasize that initially at least this pattern of judgments is developed in a context where the mimetic function of Pip is given more emphasis than any other. Indeed, the very presence of so many psychoanalytic readings of Pip's character is itself a sign of the strong mimetic signals being sent by the text.

Following hard upon the initial instability, the arrival of the convict (whom Pip describes as a man "in coarse grey, with a great iron on his leg") plays a crucial role in the development of Pip's identity. Through Dickens's alternation between Pip on the marshes with the convict and Pip at home with Joe and Mrs. Joe in the first four chapters, he establishes the interpenetration of the convict plot with the home plot. Forced to act to aid the convict, and being told in countless ways by Mrs. Joe that he was no better than a convict, Pip identifies very deeply with him, an identification that propels much of his behavior in the novel until the very end. At the same time, Dickens shows us that Pip also identifies with Joe, though not nearly as deeply. Indeed, the way the convict plot intertwines with Mrs. Joe's reminders of Pip's "nateral wiciousness" itself hinders the full identification: Pip thinks of Joe as an innocent child, himself as a wicked offender. Yet again

Dickens's narrative technique complicates the audience's understanding of Pip's identification with the convict. In the second part of Chapter 1, Dickens restricts us to Pip's vision at the at the time of the action, and the overt comments focus, as we might expect given what we've just read about Pip's anxiety, on his growing terror. Yet what comes through the vision is Pip's intuitive sense of the convict's own misery:

> A fearful man, all in coarse grey, with a great iron on his leg. A man with no hat, and with broken shoes, and with an old rag tied round his head. A man who had been soaked in water, and smothered in mud, and lamed by stones, and cut by flints, and stung by nettles, and torn by briars; who limped, and shivered, and glared, and growled; and whose teeth chattered in his head as he seized me by the chin.
>
> At the same time, he hugged his shivering body in both his arms—clasping himself, as if to hold himself together—and limped towards the low church wall. As I saw him go, picking his way among the nettles, and among the brambles that bound the green mounds, he looked in my young eyes as if he were eluding the hands of the dead people, stretching up cautiously out of their graves, to get a twist upon his ankle and pull him in.

First and most obviously, such passages (there are similar ones in Chapter 3) generate our own sympathy for Magwitch, and thus give us a vision of him that is considerably softer than Pip's conscious one, a vision later confirmed and expanded on by his "confession" of having stolen from the blacksmith's. Second, these passages lead us to recognize a subtler motive in Pip's own desire to carry out his promise to the convict: not only will he do it to avoid the terrible young man but also to give the convict some relief. This subtler motive becomes more obvious in Pip's extra effort to take along the pork pie that his sister had tucked away in the corner of the pantry. Despite his emphasizing that "I had no time for verification, no time for selection, no time for anything," he takes extra time for the pie. "I was nearly going away without the pie, but I was tempted to mount upon a shelf, to look what it was that was put away so carefully in a covered earthenware dish in the corner, and I found it was the pie, and I took it."

The motive is further reinforced as it is essentially echoed in Joe's response to the convict's apology for having eaten the pie, which in turn reminds us of the essential similarity of Pip and Joe: "We don't know what you have done, but we wouldn't have you starved to death for it, poor miserable fellow-creatur.—Would us, Pip?" The force of all these effects is of course felt later in the narrative when Dickens returns to the convict plot and Magwitch is revealed to be Pip's benefactor. Pip's initial revulsion at that point seems not only unjust to Magwitch, but also untrue to his own earlier self, and thus a further sign of how his expectations have hindered rather than helped him.

But even at this early juncture of the narrative, the effects have their force. Although Pip feels that his behavior justifies his sister's many references to him as guilty and deserving of punishment, passages such as these enable us to recognize both the strength of Pip's feelings and the great error he is making—in this sense we have a much broader view of Pip than he does of himself. As we see Pip moving further and further away from Joe, a movement that begins in this opening section and gets accelerated once the Satis House plot begins, we also see him moving further and further away from the best and truest part of his own developing identity.

But of course that is not all that is accomplished by these opening chapters. More than anything else, they establish the depth and strength of Pip's identification with the convict and thus his conviction of his own guilt. In recognizing the strength of his feelings, we also recognize the important beginnings of what I might call the psychoanalytical side of the narrative: the set of associations that is set up here between Pip and Magwitch as father and son; the cluster of devices of setting—the wet, cold, misty weather in the early evening—that always recalls by association this first meeting, and Pip's subsequent guilt, e.g., when he first learns of his sister's being injured, and when Magwitch himself makes his return. Pip's identity, we feel, is not of his own making. When that identity is further confused by his visits to Satis House, we see him more and more in the grip of forces beyond his control. This background then enables Dickens to develop the home plot in such a way that Pip continually seeks to deny that home, even as he is never able to kill entirely his attachment to it. And as Dickens undertakes that development, he takes Pip to a very low point in that plot without seriously threatening our fundamental sympathy with the character.

Now while all that is going on in the mimetic sphere, the progression is creating multiple developments in the thematic sphere. Although the narrative itself is complicated with many more turns than *Pride and Prejudice*, the principles governing thematization are essentially the same in the two works: we have multiple characters with multiple attributes, many of which are converted by the turns of the progression into thematic functions, without there being a single dominant function acting as the central point of the progression. We can nevertheless identify an especially significant group developed from the actions of the main characters: both Magwitch and Miss

Havisham function in part to exemplify the dangers of making others conform to our own images of what they should be; Joe functions as the exemplification of simple, honest dignity, while Estella exemplifies the absence of feeling. Pip, like Elizabeth Bennet, has multiple thematic functions. His responses to his expectations exemplify the consequences of a false pride. His responses to Estella offer a picture of irrational love. His susceptibility to the convict, Mrs. Joe, and Satis House all exemplify the difficulty of forging a strong identity in the world of this novel. This list is neither exhaustive nor impressive for the subtlety of its inferences about thematic functions. But lack of subtlety in the thematic sphere is, I think, a characteristic feature of Dickens's work. It is in the ingenious working out of those thematic elements in both the mimetic and synthetic spheres that his strength and distinctiveness are to be found.

Indeed, we are often led to pay attention to the thematic sphere of his works not only by the turns of the progression but also by his occasional foregrounding of the synthetic sphere. As a result, the reading of a Dickens novel typically involves a more fluid movement by the authorial audience among the spheres of meaning than occurs in the reading of a narrative by, say, Austen or James where the synthetic remains covert. One of the features of *Great Expectations* that contributes to this fluidity of movement—and to the ingenious working out of thematical material—is Dickens's handling of Wemmick.

V

After even a quick consideration of Wemmick's function in the narrative, we ought not be surprised that Brooks does not discuss his character at any length. Not only does Wemmick not fit into the pattern of repetition and return that Brooks identifies as the central part of the narrative's middle, but he also plays no main role in the working out of the resolution. If he were not in the novel, Dickens would have to find another means to accomplish such tasks as informing Pip about the best time to make his escape, but I daresay that none of us would feel that there was a big hole in the narrative, that Dickens just ought to have invented a virtually schizophrenic character whose life was as sharply divided between home and office as Wemmick's. Our first question then is whether Wemmick actually makes a contribution to the progression that is consonant with the attention that the narrative gives to his character, and if so, what precisely the nature of the contribution is. Our second question will be about the relation of the components of his character and the influence of that relation on the progression as a whole.

I shall begin with the relation between Wemmick's peculiar mimetic status and the variety of synthetic functions that he performs in the novel. Wemmick is a character with multiple mimetic dimensions and a doubtful mimetic function. This mid-fortyish man has two distinct personalities—Walworth Wemmick and Little Britain Wemmick. The first is a gentle, caring, sensitive soul who takes devoted and patient care of his Aged Parent and who dotes on Miss Skiffins. He also exercises his imagination, as we see in the way he has done up Walworth like a fort. The fort motif is of course symbolic: his private self is hidden behind that fort—so much so in fact that even when he ventures outside of it in his private mode he hides his intentions, as we see in the appearance of serendipity he tries to put upon his marriage to Miss Skiffins. As a rule, once Wemmick moves to the Little Britain side of the "moat," his character gradually hardens until he becomes the man with a mouth like the slit in a post office box, and with dints instead of dimples in his chin. His values undergo a corresponding change: he is almost as hard as Jaggers himself and his raison d'être becomes the acquisition of portable property.

In the Wemmick of Little Britain, Dickens gives us a character who is part of the convict plot, and he takes advantage of the character's mimetic dimensions to accomplish certain synthetic functions. Wemmick shows Pip the importance of portable property in their tour through Newgate and at other times keeps Pip in contact with the "soiling consciousness" of his own identification with the convict, a contact that encourages his repression of the connection between Estella and Molly until after he has worked through his own relation to Magwitch, and that also contributes to his neglect of Joe. In Walworth Wemmick, Dickens gives us a character who invites reflection on the instabilities of the home plot. Wemmick performs the synthetic function there of providing a contrast between his treatment of his Aged P. and Pip's treatment of Joe. To that extent, the synthetic function reinforces the authorial audience's and the mature Pip's own judgments about Pip's treatment of Joe.

Yet the predominant effect of Wemmick's presence on the affective structure of the text is quite different from the function of either the Little Britain or the Walworth Wemmick alone. The very facts that foreground Wemmick's synthetic component—the sharp division and exaggeration of his two sides—give him a thematic function that in turn has consequences for our response to the mimetic function of Pip. Wemmick's extreme self-division exemplifies the difficulty of living satisfactorily in two different spheres, among two very different sets of people. Consequently, Wemmick's very presence in the novel works to generalize Pip's difficulty in honoring his own lower-class background as he embarks upon his expectations. The problems we see Pip face are not just ones of his own reactions but ones endemic to living in a society where social mobility is becoming more common and where the separation between public and private spheres is becoming more and more pronounced. At the same time, Wemmick's situation indicates one kind of solution to that difficulty. Although Wemmick is more successful that Pip in living in both spheres, the very division of his personality indicates that his solution is less than ideal. Despite the charm of the Walworth Wemmick, Dickens's point is clear: Pip needs to work through to an integration of his different spheres that Wemmick never attains.

In these ways, then, Dickens uses Wemmick to complicate our judgments about the instabilities of the home plot, especially Pip's relation to Joe. Even as the mature Pip is appropriately severe in his judgments of his earlier self's treatment of Joe, Dickens's elaboration of Wemmick's character puts his behavior in a broader context, which allows a greater understanding of Pip's problem and a softer judgment of his failures to solve it until so late in the narrative. Dickens also uses Wemmick to complicate our judgments in the convict plot, which of course is tightly wound together with the other plots in the latter stages of the narrative. Wemmick's self-division functions to deepen our sense of what it is that Pip must overcome as he slowly comes to accept Magwitch. If Wemmick shuts out his private self from his public life, if Pip experiences a difficulty acknowledging Joe once he comes into his expectations, then how much more difficult is his task of acknowledging and accepting the fact that the source of those expectations is the convict. Consequently, Wemmick's presence substantially increases our sense of what Pip eventually achieves in working through to that acceptance. Thus, despite being "compartmentalized" in both Little Britain and Walworth, Wemmick functions to influence significantly the authorial audience's responses to the main narrative line. At the same time, the way in which his fore-grounded synthetic component leads to an emphasis on his thematic function, which in turn influences our response to the mimetic sphere of Pip's story, illustrates my earlier claim about the fluidity of movement among the three spheres of meaning in Dickens. When Pip and Wemmick interact, the authorial audience has an overt awareness of all three components of their characters. In one sense, this simultaneous overt awareness makes *Great Expectations* less strictly realistic than, say, "The Beast in the Jungle," but it does not lead either to a rejection or even a subordination of the mimetic level of reading.

There is more to the story of Dickens's handling of Wemmick, but it is worth pausing here to reflect on the nature of the claims just made. In effect, I am arguing that Wemmick functions the way Charlotte Lucas does in *Pride and Prejudice*, only on a larger scale. Just as Charlotte's marriage to Collins influences the authorial audience's affective response to (and thematic understanding of) Elizabeth's rejection of Darcy's first proposal, so too does Wemmick's presence influence the authorial audience's affective response to and thematic understanding of many of Pip's actions. The question the analysis raises is one of limits: if the connection between the main and the secondary characters is to be found in the thematic sphere, can't one always find a thematic connection—if only by making a thematic leap of the kind that Levin has justly criticized?

The answer is that the thematic connection is not itself sufficient to justify the relevance or explain the contribution of the secondary character. (If it were, all narratives could be elaborated endlessly.) The connection in the thematic sphere needs to be tied not only to an affective result but also to the specific narrative means for achieving that effect. In *Pride and Prejudice*, Austen largely restricts herself to Elizabeth's point of view and commits herself to a mode of presentation that limits her own role as commentator and thus leaves much to her readers' inferences. By rendering Charlotte's decision within this largely dramatic mode of presentation, Austen gives the thematic point a force that would be impossible through the narrator's overt commentary on the pressures of the marriage market. In *Great Expectations*, Dickens's use of Wemmick works wonderfully well with his decision to have the mature Pip tell his own story. Dickens can then guide his audience's judgment by having Pip judge his treatment of Joe in the harshest possible terms, while also directing that audience to see the difficulty of Pip's position in relation to both Joe and Magwitch through the presentation of Wemmick. In that sense, Dickens's handling of Wemmick can be seen as the consequence of his decision to write the novel as a retrospective first-person account.

Another aspect of this same general point concerns some of the specific actions that Pip performs in his association with Wemmick. When Pip stays with the Aged P. and not only takes care of him but enjoys taking care of him, we see that side of his own character that has only intermittently appeared since the bestowal of his expectations. Because we see Pip still able to act from the better side of his character, that side associated with Joe, we remain sympathetic to him and indeed strengthen our desires that he will correctly resolve the instabilities about his own identity, especially as these relate to Joe and Magwitch. Dickens's treatment of Wemmick is, in short, very well integrated with the progression of the whole narrative.

Consider, by contrast, Dickens's handling of Pip's visits to Matthew Pocket's household. This material, which emphasizes the way in which the Pocket children "were not growing up or being brought up, but were tumbling up," can be seen as thematically related to Pip's own experience of being brought up by hand. Significantly, however, that thematic connection is not sufficient to give it any significant role in the progression. As far as I can see, it does not materially alter our understanding or judgment of Pip or his actions. It does indicate some of the difficulties and ironies of his situation—with his great expectations comes this environment—and it does increase Pip's desire to help Herbert, but the extended focus on the family is much less a functioning part of the progression than the material on Wemmick, if in fact it is not altogether extraneous. Dickens's depiction of the Pocket family is funny in the way that Dickens is often funny, but the humor lacks the punch accompanying his depiction of Wemmick because the depiction itself is finally digressive.

Let us return then to Wemmick and Dickens's development of his mimetic dimensions into a function or at least a quasi-function. In effect, what Dickens does here is elaborate a mini-plot about Wemmick, one based on the tensions about the relations between his two selves, and complicated by the resolution of that tension in such a way that we can posit him as having at least a quasi-mimetic function, which makes possible a kind of satisfaction for the authorial audience in the last event of this mini-plot, his so odd ("Halloa! Here's a church!" "Halloa! Here's Miss Skiffins!" "Halloa! Here's a ring!") but so characteristic wedding. For a time our awareness of Wemmick's synthetic function is heightened by our uncertainty about how aware Wemmick himself is of the difference between the two sides of his personality. Then, after he refers to the difference, we remain unsure whether one side or the other is in effect the "real" Wemmick. This question does not get resolved until after Pip himself has come to accept Magwitch, has worked out the solution to the mystery of Estella's parentage, and desires confirmation from Jaggers at his office in Little Britain. When Jaggers initially tries to put him off, Pip successfully appeals to the Walworth Wemmick, and thus we know for certain that it is that side of his personality that is the real Wemmick: the Little Britain twin is a creation of the Walworth character, a creation that has become a second nature, but a creation nonetheless. It is striking, I think, that it is only after this event that Dickens shows us Wemmick's marriage to Miss Skiffins, as if this alteration in Wemmick's situation could not occur until the question of the relation between the two sides of his character were settled.

At this point in the progression, the effects of Wemmick upon Pip's story that I described above have already occurred. Wemmick's marriage adds one small additional effect, even as it predominantly makes a different contribution to the whole. As the Walworth Wemmick functions to offer an alternative reading of the home plot, his marriage to Miss Skiffins raises questions about Pip's own eventual marrying. At first, the event may seem to suggest that Pip ought to marry Biddy. But a little reflection shows that Wemmick's marriage is working by contrast. Wemmick has a claim, while

Pip has none. More importantly, however, the marriage itself adds another positive note to the ending of the book. It occurs right after Magwitch's trial and right before his death. We take a kind of pleasure in Wemmick's marriage that carries over and lightens the potentially dolorous emotions associated with Magwitch's death. This chain of effects could not have been possible without Dickens's gradual movement of Wemmick toward the mimetic. Again, Dickens proves to be a master of using the secondary characters to influence the affective structure of the progression, even as that use depends on the rather fluid movement among spheres of meaning.

Wemmick's marriage to Miss Skiffins also, I think, has the effect of making Dickens's revised ending, in which Pip sees no shadow of a further parting from Estella, less problematic. There is certainly no necessity for such an ending: the major instabilities of the narrative are resolved—Pip has worked through the issues of his identity, his relation to his own home, to his expectations, and to his past—in both the first and the second endings. Furthermore, unlike the situation in *The French Lieutenant's Woman*, the completeness of this narrative does not require two closures. To have closure Dickens does need to bring Pip into contact with Estella one last time, but since completeness has already been achieved, he has some latitude in choosing the outcome of the final meeting. In any representation, he must show that Estella is as altered as Pip or else Pip's feelings for her won't be in keeping with his present state; that stricture in turn means that any indication of their facing the future together must itself be muted, accompanied as it will be by their mutual knowledge of the unhappy past. Thus, regardless of the details of the closure, its emotional quality is already determined by the progression to this point. The ending can be hopeful, indeed, it should be hopeful, but it cannot signal a fulfillment: too much painful education has preceded it; to make the ending triumphant would be to deny the validity of the middle. Within those limitations, Dickens can choose to unite Pip and Estella or to have them meet and pass on.

My own preference is for the original ending because I prefer the idea of Pip living independently now that he has achieved his peace with himself and his acceptance of who he is. Nevertheless, Wemmick's recent marriage is a reminder that the narrative has been concerned from the very beginning with questions of identity as they relate to family and, to some extent, to marriage. Consequently, the impulse to see Pip with his newly forged identity end, like Herbert and like his older allies Wemmick and Joe at slightly earlier stages, in a relationship that will lead to marriage and family is rather strong. It is that impulse that Wemmick's marriage strengthens and that Dickens's revised ending is responding to.

VI

A final note about the relation between Brooks's model and my own. In emphasizing the differences between the two models, I have shied away from any claim that the trouble with Brooks's model is its commitment to psychoanalysis. I locate that trouble rather in Brooks's limited conception of the nature of the narrative text, a limit that stems more from the heritage of the New Criticism (reading for the plot must be reading the structure of the plot) and the whole Anglo-American critical habit of equating interpretation with thematizing. One consequence of this approach to Brooks is that he—or more likely another theorist committed to psychoanalysis—could come along and recast my whole rhetorical approach to progression in a psychoanalytical frame. That is, such a theorist could situate my interests in the sequential and affective structure of narrative in a psychoanalytical framework, one that would among other things psychoanalyze the responses of the authorial audience. I would have no great objection to such a procedure provided that no strong claims were made about that recasting being a superior (rather than an alternative) form of explanation.

The reason I would object to any claim for superiority is connected to the one way in which I would fault Brooks for his turn to psychoanalysis. Such a move presupposes that to explain the surface structure of texts, to explain the experience of reading, we need to move away from that surface and propose a model of its deep structure. The trouble with that assumption is that it immediately causes one to work at some distance from the details of texts, as one tries to find a model that will be applicable to all texts. In Brooks's case, we see him going to psychoanalysis, which gives him the concept of the death instinct, which in turn gives him the idea of the dominance of endings, which in turn causes him to underrate the importance of beginnings and middles.

The moral I draw at this point is that we need to do more work with the details of the surface structures before we are ready to consider different models of deep structures. My concept of progression commits its user to very little in the way of conclusions about the nature of any narrative to be read and interpreted. Instead, it seeks to posit categories and principles of analysis that correspond to the experience of reading, categories and principles that are specific enough to lead to detailed insights into individual narratives but flexible enough to be useful across the wide variety of surface structures that narratives offer us.

JEREMY TAMBLING

Prison-bound:
Dickens and Foucault

G_{reat} *Expectations* has been called an analysis of 'Newgate London,' suggesting that the prison is everywhere implicitly dominant in the book, and it has been a commonplace of Dickens criticism, since Edmund Wilson's essay in *The Wound and the Bow* and Lionel Trilling's introduction to *Little Dorrit*, to see the prison as a metaphor throughout the novels. Not just a metaphor, of course: the interest that Dickens had in prisons themselves was real and lasting, and the one kind of concern leads to the other, the literal to the metaphorical. Some earlier Dickens criticism, particularly that associated with the 1960s, and Trillings 'liberal imagination', stressed the second at the expense of the first, and Dickens became the novelist of the 'mind forg'd manacles' of Blake, where Mrs Clennam can stand in the Marshalsea 'looking down into this prison as it were out of her own different prison'—*Little Dorrit* pt. 2 ch. 31. This Romantic criticism became a way of attacking the historical critics who emphasised the reformist Dickens, interested in specific social questions: Humphry House and Philip Collins, the last in *Dickens and Crime* and *Dickens and Education*, (1962 and 1964). With Foucault's work on the 'birth of the prison'—the subtitle of his book *Discipline and Punish*, (1976)—it may be possible to see how the physical growth of the modern prison is also the beginning of its entering into discourse and forming structures of thought, so that the literal and the metaphorical do indeed combine, and

From *Essays in Criticism* 36, no. 1 (January 1986). © 1986 Oxford University Press.

produce the Dickens whose interest is so clearly in both ways of thinking about the prison.

Discipline and Punish is the first of Foucault's books about modes of power operating in western societies, and it succeeds his inaugural address at the Collège de France in 1970, the 'Discourse on Language', where his interest is in showing the way that knowledge is a form of manipulation, and must be thought of in the same breath as the word 'power'. Power in the absolutist state takes its bearings on the body, illustrated in the first part of the book, but the 'gentle way in punishment', associated with late 18th century enlightenment thought, leads to a change in the way power is exercised—from 'a right to take life or let live to a form of power that fosters life, the latter being described as a power over life, in contrast to the former sovereign power, which has been described as a power over death'. At the end of the 18th century, penal codes were drawn up which addressed themselves to the mind of the criminal, not defined as such, nor as an offender, but as a 'delinquent'. A personality type is thus created: the change Foucault marks is one towards the creation of an entity: a mind to be characterised in certain ways, (whereas earlier the body was directly marked), to produce the 'docile body'—'one that may be subjected, used, transformed and improved'—and thus fitted for new modes of industrial production. A 'technology of subjection' comes into use: Foucault refers to Marx's discussion of the division of labour in this context. The arrangement of the bodies of individuals for productive and training purposes is facilitated by the renewed attention given to the mind, to the prisoner as personality.

Foucault's subject is thus the 'disciplinary technology' engineered in western societies, but perhaps the most compelling image in the book is the very utopist idea of the Panopticon—that which would have been the appearance of the superego in time, if it had been realised, not merely been left on paper by Bentham. The Panopticon, with its central tower where the unseen warders may or may not be looking at the several storeys of individually divided-off prisoners, who can see neither their controlling agency, not the others in the cells, but are arranged in a circle around this surveillance tower, presents the possibility of total and complete control being exercised over the prison's inmates. Philip Collins discusses it in *Dickens and Crime*—a book still useful for its donkey work, though very undertheorised, and not able to question the role of the prison in western society—and Collins stresses that the Panopticon, while it was itself not to be recognised as a project, was to provide the model for all other types of institution: the birth of the prison means the birth of all kinds of normalising procedures, carried out in buildings still very familiar today, that all look exactly like the exterior of the 19th century prison. Collins quotes Bentham:

'Morals reformed, health preserved, industry invigorated, instruction diffused, public burdens lightened, economy seated, as it were, upon a rock, the Gordian knot of the Poor Laws not cut but untied—all by a simple idea of Architecture!' Something of the Panoptical method is at work in *Hard Times* too: the idea being thought suitable for schools and factories. In Gradgrind's school, the pupils are so raked that each can be seen at a glance, and each are individuated, though with a number, not a name. Leavis's influential account of this book stresses how Benthamism in Coketown stifles individuality, and life and emotions, but Foucault's argument implies that the Panopticon idea stressed individuality, though not in the idealist manner that the Romantic poets, themselves contemporary with this 'birth of the prison', saw that concept of the individual. The Panopticon's rationale was the sense that each subject of care was to be seen as an individual mind. Alongside this creation of separate sentiences, goes a discourse to sustain it—in the formation of the 'sciences of man . . . these sciences which have so delighted our 'humanity' for over a century . . . (which) . . . have their technical matrix in the petty, malicious minutiae of the disciplines and their investigations'. The social sciences emerge out of what Foucault calls the 'constitution' of this individual with an individual mind, as 'a describable, analysable subject', the origins of the sciences of man may have their origin, Foucault suggests, in the files of prisons and institutions, 'these ignoble archives, where the modern play of coercion over bodies, gestures and behaviour has its beginnings'. This new carceral framework 'constituted one of the armatures of power-knowledge that has made the human sciences historically possible. Knowable man, (soul, individuality, consciousness, conduct, whatever it is called) is the object-effect of this analytical investment, of this domination-observation.' It is a retreat from this positivist conception that stresses 'man's unconquerable mind'—the conclusion to a poem significantly written to a man in prison—and that invests the mind with unknowable, unfathomable qualities—as both Dickens and Leavis-like criticism do. The two stresses run together.

Bentham, more than just the inspirer of Mr Gradgrind, is a voice behind a whole new 'disciplinary technology', then, and the Panopticon becomes a metaphor, or, to quote Foucault,

> the diagram of a mechanism of power reduced to its ideal form;
> its functioning, abstracted from any obstacle, resistance or
> friction, must be represented as a pure architectural and optical
> system: it is, in fact, a figure of political technology that may
> and must be detached from any specific use. It is polyvalent in
> its applications; it serves to reform prisoners, but also to treat

patients, to instruct school children, to confine the insane, to supervise workers, to put beggars and idlers to work. It is a type of location of bodies in space, of distribution of individuals in relation to one another, of hierarchical organisation, of disposition of centres and channels of power, which can be implemented in hospitals, workshops, schools, prisons.

As a metaphor, what is implied is that the prison will enter, as both reality and as a 'type' that will form the discourse of society. Trilling's discussion of the prevalence of the prison motif in 19th century literature finds its explanation here: the sense that metaphysically the prison is inexcapable,—reaching even to a person's whole mode of discourse, and creating even Nietzsche's 'prison-house of language', so that nothing escapes the limitations of the carceral,—is objectively true in the domination of the prison in other 19th century forms of discourse.

What is in question is normalising delinquent mentalities and preserving them as abnormal, for Foucault makes it clear that normalising powers succeed best when they are only partially successful, when there can be a marginalisation of certain types of personality, and the creation of a stubborn mentality that resists educative and disciplinary processes. 'The prison, and no doubt punishment in general, is not intended to eliminate offences, but rather to distinguish them, to distribute them, to use them. . . .' On such bases, the vocabulary of power is sited, where, for additional prop, not the law, but the norm is the standard, and where not acts, but identities are named. The law was however involved as well: police surveillance grew especially in the 1850s, with as a result the nearly inevitable criminalising of so many sections of the population, due to the growth of number of penal laws. In the Panopticon, that 'mill grinding rogues honest and idle men industrious', identity is created and named: while the model prison (i.e. solitary confinement, either partial, and belonging merely to the prisoner's leisure time, or total, as in Philadelphia) is discussed by Foucault in terms of the way isolation becomes a means of bringing prisoners to a state where they will carry on the reform work of the prison in their own person, where the language of the dominating discourse is accepted and internalised.

To come with these insights of Foucault to *Great Expectations* is to discover two things. It is to see how far a 19th century text is aware of this creation of power and of oppression that Foucault has charted so interestingly: to examine the text's relation to this dominant ideology as Foucault has described it. It is also to read the book, as having itself to do with 'the power of normalisation and the formation of knowledge in modern society', which is how Foucault describes what *Discipline and Punish* is concerned with. The issue of seeing the prison as an essential condition of Victorian society, as also of the generation that was pre-Victorian, turns on the libertarian notion of the prison as inherently oppressive; that much is clear in the novel, with its Hulks, Newgate, and transportation, and prisonous houses, such as Satis House and even Wemmick's castle. It also has to do with Dickens's registering of the prison being bound up with questions of language and the control of language—which, of course, entails ways of thinking, a whole discourse. In other words, the book shows an awareness of the fact that to learn a language is connected with the control of knowledge. In the Panopticon, the knowledge of a person is both coloured and colouring, and to acquire knowledge, by entering into the dominant discourse, is to learn the language of oppression.

In Dickens there is a move from literal treatment of the prison from *Sketches by Boz* onwards, including the visits to the isolation penitentiaries in the United States in 1842, where he saw the 'Auburn system' at work—based on the prison at Gloucester (which Foucault refers to) at both Boston and Connecticut; his accounts of both appear in *American Notes*, chs. 3 and 5. The 'silent association' system there—partial solitary confinement only—he preferred to the Eastern Penitentiary at Philadelphia. It is not hard to see both systems as relations of the Panopticon dream. Dickens found what he saw distasteful. He questioned, in a letter to Forster, whether the controllers 'were sufficiently acquainted with the human mind to know what it is they are doing': while *American Notes* finds 'this slow and daily tampering with the mysteries of the brain to be immeasurably worse than any torture of the body'. The person must be returned from this state 'morally unhealthy and diseased'. It is halfway to Foucault's gathering of criticisms of the prison that were made in France between 1820–45: indeed, Dickens's comments are sited within those criticisms, commented on in *Discipline and Punish*.

But, as criticism, it isn't free from the point that the thinking about the nature of the prison has not gone far enough to question its rationale, as a social fact, as the product of a type of thinking. The point may be made from *Great Expectations*, at a moment where Pip (the moment is almost gratuitous—Dickens is moving away from treatment of literal prisons), is invited by Wemmick to visit Newgate:

> At the time, jails were much neglected, and the period of exaggerated reaction consequent on all public wrongdoing—and which is always its heaviest and longest punishment—was still far off. So, felons were not lodged and fed better than the soldiers (to say nothing of paupers) and seldom set fire to their prisons with the excusable object of improving the flavour of their soup.

Collins links this observation to the riots that took place at Chatham Convict prison early in 1861, and makes it clear that Chatham represented a heavily reactionary kind of discipline, certainly no 'better' than the Newgate Pip is describing. I put 'better' in quotation-marks to suggest that the concept of progress in prison discipline and order cannot be assumed: in Foucault's terms, the more enlightened the prison, the more subtle its means of control, that is all. Can much be said in favour of this passage? Many readers of Dickens will assume it to be part of the dominant mode to be noted in Dickens's speeches and letters: the voice of the liberal consensus, wanting prisons as simply neither too hard nor too easy. But the quotation also gives the register of Pip, who is historically at the moment when he is furthest away from his knowledge about the criminal basis of society; most alienated from his own associations with criminality—hence, of course, the irony that the chapter closes with the facial resemblance that Estella has to Molly. In terms of writing, he is looking back ('at that time') and seems to have learned nothing: at least he still wishes to place prisoners as below soldiers and paupers, not seeing that both these groups endure the same oppression that makes people prisoners—a conclusion that the novel often comes to, not least in giving Magwitch the significant name of Abel and so making him the original innocent and hunted down figure. Pip's language, then, is still part of that of a 'brought-up London gentleman': it belongs to a Victorian dominant discourse. (And 'brought-up' also suggests 'bought-up' and goes along with the equations of property and personality that go on throughout; compare Havisham—Have-is-sham, even Have-is-am; the last the latest development of the Cartesian cogito. The dominators, no less than the dominated, receive their individuality from their position in the carceral network.)

Those who identify Pip's attitude with Dickens's assume there is nothing in the text to qualify what is said here, or else that a plurality in the text allows Dickens to engage in a journalistic point in the middle of Pip's narration. Either may be right, but I would rather regard the utterance as being ironic rather than sincere—a disavowal, in this most confessional and disavowing of books, of a way of thinking once held. Pip's mode is autobiographical and confessional almost in the Catholic sense of that last word: the book reveals Dickens's autobiography and self-revelation of disgust in the same way. The reader of *Great Expectations* is able to reject the opinions expressed at the start of chapter 32 in the light of the reading of the rest of the book. Behind the narrator, the author asks for a similar dismissal. Behind Pip's confession, lies Dickens's own: or Dickens's as the representative of a precisely positioned class, of the liberal petit-bourgeoisie. The novel distances itself from Pip's confessions perhaps in order to listen to

Dickens's. But then that one—Dickens's—may itself be refused, be shown to be as relative as the one that it shadows.

What is clear is the prevailing confessional note of *Great Expectations*. TO BE READ IN MY CELL is apt metalinguistically. That is to say, it comments on the text's sense of the way it should be read, and what Pip thinks it is about. This is not the fictional Augustinian mode of confession, though a 'cell' would well suit the Catholic form of confession: it is rather that the mode of autobiography fits with Protestant thought. Trilling comments on the late 18th century 'impulse to write autobiography' and says that 'the new kind of personality which emerges . . . is what we call an individual: at a certain point in history men become individuals'. The ability to confess in autobiography is constitutive of the subject for him-herself—but as Foucault would add, it would be 'subject "in both senses of the word"', for confession would be the means whereby the dominant discourse is internalised. Foucault continues: 'The obligation to confess is now relayed through so many different points, is so deeply ingrained in us, that we no longer perceive it as the effect of a power which constrains us; on the contrary, it seems to us that truth, lodged in our most secret nature, "demands" only to surface'. *The History of Sexuality* is the continuation of that theme of power as constitutive of knowledge that runs through *Discipline and Punish* and it is a keypoint of the novel that Pip is ready always to confess: such is his autobiography, a disavowal. The interest in the prison and the interest in autobiographical confession: these two things converge.

For *Great Expectations* certainly recognises itself to be about the creation of identities, imposed from higher to lower, from oppressor to oppressed. From the first page there is the 'first most vivid and broad impression of the identity of things', where a considerable amount of naming goes on—'I called myself Pip and came to be called Pip'; where the 7-year-old child names 'this bleak place overgrown with nettles' as 'the churchyard' and similarly characterises the marshes, the river, the sea, and himself as 'that bundle of shivers growing afraid of it all and beginning to cry' who 'was Pip'. The phrasing of the last part suggests that the act of naming the self and nature is a rationalisation, an incomplete and unsatisfactory way of labelling what resists formulation. It fits with that pejorative way of describing the self just quoted: that too fits the confessional position. The self is mis-named from the beginning, minimised; and gross acts of naming take place thenceforth, from Mrs Hubble's belief that the young are never grateful, not to say 'naterally wicious' to Jaggers saying that boys are 'a bad set of fellows'. Wopsle and company identify an accused with the criminal, Pip sees him as George Barnwell, and receives a number of descriptions and names—Pip, Handel, 'the prowling boy', 'you young dog', 'my boy', 'you boy', 'you visionary boy'. Anonymity, though not the absence of naming, hangs over Mrs Joe (defined, absurdly, through the husband), Orlick, whose name Dolge is 'a clear impossibility'. Magwitch—Provis at all times to Jaggers, Trabb's boy, Drummle—the Spider—, the Aged P and Mr Waldengalver. The power of naming confers identity: Q. D. Leavis's analysis sees the power as one that implants guilt. That guilt-fixing belongs to Foucault's Panopticon society, and indeed the sense of being looked at is pervasive—whether by the young man who hears the words Pip and Magwitch speak, by the hare hanging up in the larder—an early execution image—or by the cow that watches Pip take the wittles on Christmas Day. Pip expects a constable to be waiting for him on his return; has the sensation of being watched by relatives at Satis House, has his house watched on the night of Magwitch's return, has Compeyson sit behind him in the theatre (where he himself is watching), and is watched by the coastguard and the river police in the attempt to take off Magwitch (none of the friendship here with the police implied in the 1853 article 'Down with the Tide': the Dickensian hero is shown here as in flight from the agents of law). Where such spying is an integral part of the book, the sense of being someone constituted as having a secret to hide is not far away. Pip feels himself a criminal, early and late; and Orlick tells him he is: 'It was you as did for your shrew sister'—this coming from the man who has tracked Pip constantly, and shadowed Biddy, too. Reflecting the first chapter's growth of self-awareness,—where the child is crying over his parents' grave, as though not just feeling himself inadequate, but as already guilty, already needing to make some form of reparation—Magwitch says that he 'first became aware of himself down in Essex a thieving turnips for his living'. Jaggers identifies Drummle as criminal—'the true sport'—and encourages him in his boorishness and readiness to brain Startop. His method of cross-examination is to criminalise everyone, himself resisting classification, no language being appropriate for one as 'deep' as he. 'You know what I am, don't you?' is the last comment he makes after the dinner party where he has hinted that Molly (whom he seems to own) is a criminal type. The question is to be answered negatively, for he is like the unseen watcher in the central tower of the Panopticon, naming others, but not named himself (his centrality is implied in the address of his office), in the position, as criminal lawyer, of power, conferring identities, controlling destinies—not for nothing are those criminals in Newgate compared to plants in the greenhouse, and regarded with the scientific detachment that for Foucault is part of the 'discourse of truth' of nineteenth century positivism.

Identities all become a matter of social control and naming: Estella might have turned out one way as one of the 'fish' to come to Jaggers's net, yet she is constituted differently (though almost as nihilistically) by the identity she receives from Miss Havisham's hands. Pip remains the passive victim whose reaction is to blame himself for every action he is in: his willingness to see himself as his sister's murderer (chapter 16) is of a piece with his final ability to see himself characteristically unjust to Joe. Q. D. Leavis's account works against those which see the book as 'a snob's progress'; her emphases are useful in suggesting that it is *Pip* who sees himself thus; and that now he is 'telling us dispassionately how he came to be the man who can now write thus about his former self '. The 'us', by eliding the 1860s readers of the text with these who come a century later, implies that there is a central, ahistorical way of taking the text: a strong liberal-humanist ideology underwrites this assumption which also implies that there is some decent norm Pip could approximate to, which would untie all his problems. It thus assimilates all historical differences, at the least, to the notion of the free subject, who is at all times accessible to decent human feelings—and capable of reaching a central normality.

If what Q. D. Leavis said were the case, it would mean Pip had reached some degree of 'normality' by the end of what has happened to him, before he starts narrating. He is not a central human presence, but a writer whose text needs inspection for its weakness of self-analysis; for he never dissociates himself from the accusations he piles on himself at the time of the events happening, and afterwards. In Wemmick's and Jaggers's character-formulations of people as either 'beaters or cringers' he remains a cringer, and unable to recognise himself in Herbert's genial view—'a good fellow, with impetuosity and hesitation, boldness and diffidence, action and dreaming, curiosity mixed in him'. That positive evaluation, binary nonetheless in its terms, in the same way as the Panopticon system lends itself to an extreme form of binary division, is beyond him: his self-perception makes him oppressor, while, more accurately, he is victim. Foucault stresses how the healthy individual is defined in relation to that which has been labelled as delinquent, degenerate or perverse; and his studies of madness, of the birth of the clinic and of the prison all meet in this: 'when one wants to individualise the healthy normal and law-abiding adult, it is always by asking him how much of the child he has in him, what secret madness lies within him, what fundamental crime he has dreamed of committing' (*Discipline and Punish*). On this basis, Pip might be said to be the creation of three discourses that intersect: he remains something of the child—his name, a diminutive, establishes that; he is never in a position, he feels, of equality with anyone else; his dreams of the file, of Miss Havisham hanging from the beam, of playing Hamlet without knowing more than five words of the play, his nightmarish sense of phantasmagoric shapes perceived in the rushlight in the Hummums, and his sense of being a brick in a house-wall, or part of a machine, 'wanting to have the engine stopped, and my part in it hammered off'—all proclaim his 'secret madness'. His sense of criminality is fed by virtually each act and its consequences that he undertakes.

A victim of the language system, only on one or two occasions does he reverse the role and become implicitly the accuser; one is where he prays over the head of the dead Magwitch: 'Lord be merciful to him a sinner' where commentators such as Moynihan have found something false. It is inappropriate, but it seems to belong to the Pip whose sense of himself is not free enough to allow himself to deconstruct the language system he is in. The odd thing is not that he fails to see himself as the sinner, as in the parable (*Luke* ch. 18), but that he should want to name Magwitch as such. But that act of naming is a reflection of the way the dominated have no choice but to take over the language of their domination—to continue to beat, as they have been beaten, to continue to name disparagingly, as they have been named. That act in itself continues to name Pip—implicitly, as the Pharisee, of course. The question the novel asks is what else he might do: he seems caught. The self can only retreat from that dominant discourse through schizoid behaviour, as happens with Wemmick and his dual lifestyles, yet does not the 'Castle's' existence betray the prison's presence still in Wemmick's thinking? He, too, has not got away.

A second time when the language of Pip's oppression becomes one to oppress another is at the end of the book where he meets the younger Pip and suggests to Biddy that she should 'give Pip to him, one of these days, or lend him, at all events'. To this Biddy responds 'gently' 'no', but her answer might as well have been a horrified one in the light of what surrogate parents do to their children in the book: Pip is offering to play Magwitch to Biddy's child. He has learned nothing: is indeed a recidivist, unaware of how much he has been made himself a subject of other people's power and knowledge. Magwitch, similarly 'owns' Pip as he says with pride: it is well-meaning as a statement, but with Foucault's aid it may be seen that Magwitch as a member of the class marginalised and set apart by the Panopticon society, has had to take on those dominant oppressive values, and talks the same language of property. His attitude is not inherently selfish, but it is a mark of his social formation which conditions him to speak as he does. In this most sociologically interactionist of novels, it is recognised that the self can use no other language than that given to it. What liberty there is is suggested by Orlick, who cringes after Joe beats him, beats Mrs Joe and secures her cringing—which, indeed, as 'a child towards a hard master' she seems to enjoy, as she continues to draw the sign of his power over her: such is the token of her self-oppression. (The contrast with Rosa Dartle, also the victim of a hammer-blow, is worth attention: Rosa's whole position as poor relation is self-oppressive.) Orlick, through a certain upward mobility, derived from his association with Compeyson, changes from the cringer himself (paid off by Jaggers from service at Satis House) to the accuser of Pip in the sluice-house. He perceives he has been marginalised, in some ways defined as delinquent, but it is an insight that could not be the source of social action or improvement, for it never extends beyond himself: as he says to Pip, 'you was favoured and he (Orlick) was bullied and beat'. Out of that crazed imperception, he lashes out at Pip: the reverse action to Magwitch's, who almost equally arbitrarily identifies Pip with himself. (The novel wishes to close the gap between the convict and Pip, so Herbert says that Pip reminded Magwitch of the daughter he had lost.) Orlick and Magwitch go in opposite directions: what unites them (as it links them with Pip) is their sense that they are the watched, the ones under surveillance. Orlick's reactions to Pip look like Nietzsche's *ressentiment*, that quality that Foucault has made much use of in discussing the origins of the impulse towards power. Dickens's 'cringer' is like Nietzsche's 'reactive personality': for Nietzsche, it is characteristically this type that, fired by resentment, tries to move into the legislative position. Orlick's rancour is born out of the inability that those watched in the Panopticon society have (since they have been put in individual cells, they cannot see each other) to read their situation as akin to that of other marginalised figures.

Thus the production, and reproduction, of oppression is what the book charts. Orlick attempts to move over to the other side in the Panopticon, and from the attempted assumption of that position, turns against Pip. Magwitch's acquisition of money is his attempt to move to the other side, to create a Pip, whom he surveys. In fact, he remains the criminal in the way he is named. Nor can Orlick change, and though he is in the county jail at the end, the replication of the book's past events seems safe with him when he is released: he really has no alternative, and as such he remains an apt commentary on the course an oppressed class must follow. Pip, in terms of status, moves over to the other side, in Panopticon terms, but his social formation is already firm, and basically he cannot change either: the events in the second part of his 'expectations' are an aberration from what he is in the first and third parts. Ironically, since he is cast there as guilty, what he is at those points is preferable to what he becomes in the second part.

As the recidivist, he wishes to be given Biddy's child, which would start again the whole cycle of oppression, and self-oppressive to the end, he writes out his autobiography—one that remains remarkably terse as to its intentions and its status as writing and which rolls out as though automatically, the product of a consciousness that remains fixed. Comparisons with the modes of David Copperfield's, or Esther Summerson's, or George Silverman's narratives would bear out this frozen, and at times almost perfunctory, manner. Miss Wade begins her account of herself sharply with the statement that she is 'not a fool'. Pip says nothing about himself as he is at the time of writing. He remains as someone who seems not to have gone beyond the emotional state documented in the writing, so that there is nothing cathartic about the confession, and no release is gained, just as Dickens's revised ending remains as ambivalent as the former, much more telegraphic one. For 'I saw no shadow of another parting from her' allows the ambiguity that they did or did not separate, and the narrator shows how his mind is closed now: what follows is not known. Writing about himself and his childhood experience, Dickens said 'I know how all these things have worked together to make me what I am' in a confidence belonging to the *Copperfield* period and akin to that expressed so often in Wordsworth's *Prelude* of 1850. The distance from *Great Expectations* is pronounced: the very dryness of the narrative is an ironic comment on the book's title. The more buoyant, earlier statement may have its optimism unfounded as far as its belief in development goes, but the mode of writing in Pip's case may been seen as carceral: it belongs to the prison in its sense of giving automatic, unstopping confession, which pauses not at all in its recounting of events and its self-accusation.

Foucault's 'birth of the prison', the concept of the individual, the privileging of the autobiographical mode—these related ideas are intrinsic to the novel, and while there is the creation of the human subject through a relaying of oppression and through a dominant discourse that he/she is within, there is also, in *Great Expectations*, implicit commentary about the mode of autobiography. Autobiography defines the subject confessionally; it puts upon it the onus of 'explanation', makes it prison-bound: a state that proves naturally acceptable to so much Romantic writing, where the tragic intensity of those who have to inhabit alienating spaces or constrictions can be defined as the source and inspiration of their reality. 'We think of the prison'—Eliot's reading of F. H. Bradley in *The Waste Land* proves comforting as it suggests that the essence of humanity is that it is confined, this is its common condition. In contrast, Foucault's analysis is precisely useful in its stress on the prison as the mode that gives the person the sense of uniqueness, the sense of difference from the others. In that sense, autobiography becomes a mode that assists in the reproduction of the discourse that the Panopticon society promotes. And in Pip's case, subjugated as he is by these discourses, the mode becomes a vehicle for 'self-reflection'—and for nothing else. Not, that is, the self thinking and moving from there into an area of thought where it can question the terms of its language, but the self continuing to reify its own status, to see it as an isolated thing. It continues a divisive trend. Not only is Pip's autobiography one that is markedly end-stopped in the sense that there is no feeling for a future, no way in which there can be a further development of the self, so that experience seems to avail nothing; but that cut-offness exists too in Pip's relations with others, in his inability to see other's complicity in the events surrounding him, save perhaps with Pumblechook, and there it is hardly difficult to see. It is appropriate that Miss Havisham should say to him 'You made your own snares. *I* never made them.' It is manifestly untrue as a statement; and especially as far as the second sentence goes, as Miss Havisham's own confession suggests, finishing as it does with her self-condemnatory immolation and her entreaty, 'take the pencil and write under my name, I forgive her'—Miss Havisham is the 'cringer' here, as so often. What is interesting is that Pip seems to receive this analysis and can't see that to individualise the issue in this way won't do. *Great Expectations* comes close to suggesting that in an understanding of a society, the concept of the individual is unhelpful, that what is important are the total manipulations of power and language by whatever group has the power of definition and control. Autobiography provides an inadequate paradigm.

Is that the final irony of *Great Expectations*, that it displays the bankruptcy of Pip's efforts to understand what has happened to him? That he speaks throughout in a language that has been given to him, and that includes the language of his perception of himself as a particular kind of being? If that is so, discussion might move at this point from what Pip might do with regard to his own inarticulateness in face of the dominant discourse, to what the text might do. The post-structuralist in Foucault displaces human consciousnesses for larger historical processes: Dickens as a 19th century novelist is marked by more confidence in individual sentience. It might be possible to find in *Great Expectations* a modernity of attitude which means that its parabolic kind of narrative is open-ended; that the title hints at the space within it for the reader to construct his/her own sense of how to take it; that, unlike the warder at the heart of the Panopticon, the author is not felt to be directing and encouraging a labelling; that the text resits single meaning. The ambiguity of the ending, already discussed, is relevant here, and so too is the sense that the reader has only Pip's text to work upon, and that this is certainly not final or necessarily authoritative. At the same time, however, the bourgeois Dickens has been located often enough within the book: for example, what do we make of Herbert's reporting of his father's principle of belief that 'no man who ever was a true gentleman at heart ever was, since the world began, a true gentleman in manner . . . no varnish can hide the grain of the wood, and . . . the more varnish you put on, the more the grain will express itself'? Is not this like the voice of the conscious novelist, and if so does it not express a different, more essentialist view of humanity than the very relative one formed through the whole pattern of the book with its insistence on the social construction of identities? Herbert's decent liberalism of attitude, which is intended to cut through class distinctions, both in relation to the upwardly mobile and the aristocratic-snobbish, is tactfully put, but it represents a trans-historicalsim, in its view of human nature 'since the world began', an 'essentialist' view of humanity.

I give this example as one of the many that might be cited to suggest that the novel resists the irony of its form—which, in its radicalness, is where Raymond Williams finds 'Dickens's morality, his social criticism'; and that it might allow for a basic human nature, which would stand against Foucault's account, since for the latter there can be no cutting through a statement which is not framed within the limits of a particular discourse. The passage quoted from the opening of chapter 32 has been similarly seen—as the authorial voice, as part of the classic realist text, as that where 'bourgeois norms are experienced as the evident laws of a natural order'. But in response to this view that the novel does invest time and space in a 'decent' common-sense attitude, several points might be urged. The first would be that it was no more necessary to take the comment in chapter 32 as authorial than to assume that Herbert's views are purely normative. And even if they were, and Mr Pocket's views about what constituted a gentleman coincided with Dickens's, the statement might still be situation-specific, having to do with what a gentleman might be in a society that laid so much stress on this bourgeois title. But in any case, Mr Pocket's views themselves are not beyond criticism: chapter 23 where he appears presents him wittily as the liberal whose 'decent' attitudes are themselves subverted by his wife's tyrannies—he is nearly as helpless as Joe, and that ineffectuality itself invites criticism, is indeed even part of a self-oppression. Moreover, although the concept of a true gentleman may be a mirage pursued through the book (cp. Pip's uttering 'penitently' at the end about Joe—often seen as the ideal—'God bless this gentle Christian man', as though here at last disinterested, decent qualities were being displayed), as a term it is itself not allowed to stand by the novel.

Joe drops out again of the London scene after Pip has recuperated: Pip's terms for him are part of the vocabulary he has learned to deploy from Satis House—and from exposure to Estella's power, which makes him tell Biddy that he wants to be a gentleman. The term—even in Mr Pocket's oppositional formulation about it—is not one that fits Joe, even in Pip's modified way of putting it. Joe needs to be seen in another set of relations, and what Pip says about him is inappropriate because it bears more on Pip's sense of his own deficiency; Joe is what *he* is not; he has not succeeded in living up to the terms of his cultural formation that have been dictated to him, so he believes. What Joe is in rescuing Pip requires a set of terms that do not involve assimilation of him into the power relations and language of middle-class society, from which he is nearly totally excluded, save when he has to wear holiday clothes, and which are supremely irrelevant to him.

It is the cruellest irony for Pip that he must disparage himself and praise Joe so constantly in his narration. Joe does not require any setting down, but Pip has no means of assessing the forge and the village life independent of his own given language: under the influence of Satis House and its language he feels ashamed of home. Nothing more is given of the forge in the novel apart from Pip's perception of it, and the absence of such a thing makes the torture for Pip, the prisoner in the Panopticon societal prison, the more refined. For it remains as a deceptive escape for him, although one that he cannot endorse (so that his intention to go back and marry Biddy has something masochistic and self-oppressive within it), and any step that he takes, either of accepting or rejoicing it, remains a compromise. The split is caught finely in the scenes leading to his going to London in the first instance, and a compromise is dictated to him by the dividing nature of the society as prison. For Foucault argues that there is no 'knowledge that does not presuppose and constitute at the same time power relations' (*Discipline and Punish*). That is, the birth of the prison—that most divisive of institutions—is an instrument not only to create Man as individual, to be known thus, but also ensures that there is no common language—no means of making a value-judgment which is outside the terms of a particular set of power-relations. Foucault is opposed to totalising interpretations of society precisely because of the way they ignore the endless replication of modes of oppression, of imposition of languages. The methods of deployment of power are various, as are the social groupings; indeed *Great Expectations* displays something of that variousness. What Pip finds to be true of himself is the result of the way he has been set up; at the same time, he does not possess a set of terms to think about a different way of life—the forge—that are not themselves instrumental for control over that way of thinking. Difference is not allowed for. Pip is bought up completely. The illusion he is given is of seeing things whole, but to the very end he cannot see the forge way of life as something different from his, and one that his own language formation cannot accommodate, from the moment he got to Satis House.

The modernity of the novel lies in this area: Dickens commits himself to no view about Joe or Biddy, or Pip, but writes rather a *Bildungsroman* where the expectation that the hero will learn through experience is belied, and not only by the title. Readerly assumptions generated through the lure of the narrative are set aside, for the central figure can only proceed on the language assumptions given to him. *David Copperfield* was the standard kind of *éducation sentimentale*; *Great Expectations* questions the ideological assumptions inherent in the earlier book, by presenting (with the earlier novel consciously in mind, re-read just before embarking on it) a development that can be no development. If the hero learns at all, it is only within his terms of reference, so there is no breaking out from the obsession with the self. The mode of the novel is ironic (it is noticeable how Dickens emphasises what is 'comic' about it to Forster, as Forster relates in the *Life*): 'comic,' in spite of the comedy within it, seems inappropriate, but perhaps it may draw attention to what is subversive about the book. And Dickens's absence of explanation about it only emphasises the extent to which he as author has receded: the novel stands alone, open-ended, marked out by the lack of 'closure' within it supplied by the moralist Dickens.

Whatever liberalism affects the book—as in the 'poor dreams' that nearly save Mr Jaggers in spite of himself, or in the way that Pip seems to enjoy a reasonable bourgeois existence in the Eastern Branch of Herbert's firm, or in its casualness about dates and historical positioning—is not central: the book has little faith in human nature considered as a Romantic, spontaneous and creative thing; no sense that the issues it addresses may be met by the middle-class values that commonly sustain the 19th century novel. The interest in character here—which still so often forms the basis of Dickensian criticism—does not sanction belief in the individual as ultimately irrepressible. Rather, the idea of the Panopticon as the chief model for the formation of any individuality in 19th century Britain makes for something much more complex and gives rise to the sense that the formation of individuality is itself delusory as a hope. It is itself the problem it seeks to solve—through its way of dividing a society and separating it. The prison is not the 'human condition' in a trans-historical sense, as Denmark was also a prison for Hamlet, but is the apt symbol for enforcing models of helplessness: the more aware the self is of its position, the more it confirms the prison, and thus cuts itself off further. To that diagnosis, which demands a consideration of power structures in society such as Foucault gives, and which draws attention to language as a way of making the person prison-bound, the autobiographical mode of *Great Expectations* bear witness. In itself the mode works to keep the narrator in prison. Just as Wemmick's father and his pleasant and playful ways, and the possibility that Jaggers himself might one day want a pleasant home, also ensure that the prison's durability is not in question: these individual escapes, simply by staying within the limits of the individual idea, address, effectively, no problem at all.

WILLIAM A. WILSON

The Magic Circle of Genius: Dickens' Translations of Shakespearean Drama in Great Expectations

> Carlyle took his glass and nodding to Dickens said: "Charley,
> you carry a whole company of actors under your own hat."
> —Amy Woolner, *Thomas Woolner, R.A.*

When *Nicholas Nickleby* accompanies Miss Snevellicci through Portsmouth on her "bespeak," he encounters Mr. Curdle, a self-described drama critic. When not adding to the store of criticism, Curdle joins his wife bemoaning the death of the tragic hero:

> "What man is there now living who can present before us all those changing and prismatic colours with which the character of Hamlet is invested?" exclaimed Mrs. Curdle.
> "What man indeed—upon the stage;" said Mr. Curdle, with a small reservation in in favour of himself. "Hamlet! Pooh! ridculous! Hamlet is gone, perfectly gone."

Without the historical imagination to appreciate Shakespeare's presence on the stage, the Curdles so praise the bard that they bury him. Shakespeare appears in their world only on the occasions when Mr. Curdle exhumes the corpus in order to inflict critical injuries upon it. His reputation stands, we are reminded, on a speculative monograph on the Nurse's deceased husband

From *Nineteenth-Century Fiction* 40, no. 2 (September 1985). © 1985 by The Regents of the University of California.

in *Romeo and Juliet* ("sixty-four pages, post octavo") and on his proof "that by altering the received mode of punctuation, any one of Shakespeare's plays could be made quite different, and the sense completely changed."

While amused by the impotent hagiolatry of Mr. Curdle, Nicholas is infuriated later in the narrative by the presumption of a plagiarizing "literary gentleman," who claims that since "human intellect . . . has progressed since [Shakespeare's] time," one best view "Bill [as] an adapter." Admitting that Shakespeare "derived some of his plots from old tales and legends in general circulation," Nicholas defends Shakespeare's apparent lack of originality:

> "He brought within the magic circle of his genius, traditions
> peculiarly adapted for his purpose, and turned familiar things
> into constellations which should enlighten the world for ages."

Both Curdle and the pirate consign Shakespeare to the dead past; that is to say, they commit the fallacy of radical historicism. But Nicholas, neither fetishist nor iconoclast, keeps Shakespeare alive in his mind by viewing him historically, both as the shaper of literary tradition and as the major figure in the tradition he himself inherits.

It is not at all surprising that Dickens should defend Shakespeare's contemporaneity early in his career, for the figure of Shakespeare was a constant presence within the literary consciousness of the nineteenth century. Artists of various cultures and sensibilities—Coleridge, Keats, Schiller, Berlioz, Stendhal, Pushkin, Hugo—all attested to his influence upon them. However, of all the geniuses of the last century, perhaps Dickens comes closest to approximating Shakespeare's scope and achievement. Dickens was sparked by the example Shakespeare set, and he thus escaped the unhappy fate of others, like Curdle, who were smothered by it. Dickens saw much in Shakespeare that spoke to his own sense of "familiar things" as the raw stuff of literature. He also found much in Shakespeare to reverently imitate, some things to parody, and, like the "literary gentleman," a few things to adapt. These correspondences have been well documented. Yet beyond these incidental connections lies a remarkable range of influence and intertextuality—the magic circle of genius—that cannot be plotted by scholarly annotation alone.

This area of Dickens' genius is drama, which, perhaps more than London itself, is his native ground. Dickens believed that "every writer of fiction . . . writes in effect for the stage. He may write novels always, and plays never, but the truth and wisdom that are in him must permeate the art of which truth and passion are the life, and must be more or less reflected in that great mirror which he holds up to nature." As a young writer, he defended the "absurd [and] . . . violent transitions and abrupt impulses of passion or feeling" in *Oliver Twist* by citing a precedent in the "streaky, well-cured bacon" of popular stage productions. Throughout his career Dickens created characters whose lives, often derived from the theater and other literary forms, all strive for dramatic richness and coherence—the "prismatic colours" and "universal dove-tailedness" prized by Mr. Curdle. Dickens' excessive reliance upon such melodramatic plots and modes of characterization—upon what Martin Meisel calls "the art of effect"—has been faulted by many readers. Yet, as Stephen Dedalus says in defense of Shakespeare's creation of the hesitating Prince, "a man of genius makes no mistakes. His errors are volitional and are the portals of discovery." The truth and passion of Dickens' genius lead him beyond the theatricality in his early works to a mature dramatic power that informs his plots, his themes, as well as his memorable characters. Its energy proceeds in great part from the resistance that the realities of middle-class life offer the literary identities and aspirations of his characters. Indeed, "the great mirror" Dickens holds up to Victorian life reflects an essential conflict between dominant social and economic institutions and his characters' fanciful visions of heroic justice and love derived from the popular stage.

To describe the ramifications of Dickens' discovery, it is helpful to regard Nicholas's defense of Bill the Adapter as heuristic; that is, it is an indication that Dickens consciously imitates Shakespeare's method of transforming familiar things—Shakespeare's plays included—into art. Begun as early as *Nicholas Nickleby* (1839), this creative process does not, however, reach its fullest expression until *Great Expectations* (1861). Of particular interest in this later novel is Dickens' fascination with Shakespeare as the father of comedy and tragedy, the artist who writes in both genres with equal facility, often blurring the distinction between them. Dickens shapes the themes and structure of *Great Expectations* within this particular Shakespearean context by developing his own comic and tragic vision through two remarkably complex acts of generic translation. In the first, Dickens violently and humorously wrenches the characteristic form of Elizabethan revenge tragedy—*Hamlet* is the major text—and attempts to reshape it into a Victorian comedy of foregiveness. In the second, he transforms the happy conclusion of the typical New Comedy and Victorian melodrama into a bittersweet Dickensian fruit, neither purely comic nor tragic. The ambiguous conclusion of *Great Expectations* is the result of slightly corrected vision and resigned compromise. It is one in which few losses are restored; and if sorrows end, they end in self-reproach, alienation, and ambiguous prospects, not in triumphant justice or happy marriages.

These Dickensian translations are likewise anticipated by Shakespeare's generic metamorphosis in *Midsummer Night's Dream*. There Peter Quince and company translate *Pyramus and Thisby*, a tragedy of misprision and suicide, into "tragical mirth." Tragedy is made comic as the mechanicals' misreadings and thespian ineptitude destroy dramatic distance; meanwhile, over the course of the play the generic distinction between a comedy of love and its tragic counterpart is nearly eradicated by the misperceptions of fairies and nobility alike. Although *Midsummer Night's Dream* and *Hamlet* inform *Great Expectations*, as the *Odyssey* underlies *Ulysses*, Dickens does not circumscribe his genius with these works alone. Indeed, the novel's intertextuality also includes *King Lear* and *Frankenstein*, two other works of revenge and transformation. Regardless of the specific texts, however, Dickens welds together, as Joe Gargery would have it, the "diwisions" between the classical genres. The product of this literary forgery is a novel that reveals, perhaps better than any other Victorian work of fiction, why major representations of middle-class experience resist the aesthetic resolutions of these traditional genres, why modern audiences feel put on or put off when bourgeois life is portrayed as a traditional tragedy or comedy.

> There are characters which are continually creating collisions and nodes for themselves in dramas which nobody is prepared to act with them. Their susceptibilities will clash against objects that remain innocently quiet.
> —George Eliot, *Middlemarch*

At the end of the second stage of Pip's great expectations, Abel Magwitch returns to London from Australia. Like a ghost lately returned to the world from the infernal antipodes, the convict haunts Pip's rooms while he unfolds a tale that binds their lives together in mutual dependency and mortal fear. Although Pip's reaction to his second father is complex and hurried in its development, its pattern is nonetheless clear. At first, he fears the old man as ripe pickings for the gallows. But his fear soon softens into pity as he hears Magwitch's history of orphanhood, abuse, and neglect, all leading to a pathetic desire for revenge.

Pip's initial pity and fear are, of course, the tragic emotions, which are grounded in the old man's woeful tale. Dickens' use of drama, however, is more specific and subtle here, for he intends the reader to see that Pip's reaction is also grounded in *Hamlet*, the revenge tragedy that is fused with the novel at major points in the narrative. Dickens prepares us for the Shakespearean parallel by having Pip dream in chapter 31 of playing Hamlet to Miss Havisham's Ghost, a nightmare uncannily prompted by Wopsle's humorous attempt at the Dane earlier in the evening. We are presented with surface similarities between the two texts that are as remarkable as they are obvious. For example, both fathers are doomed to walk the night. Like the Ghost in *Hamlet*, Magwitch swears young men to secret complicity in a revenge plot. Holding out a testament to Pip and Herbert, Magwitch says to the latter: "Take it in your right hand. Lord strike you dead on the spot, if ever you split in any way sumever!" In both works impotent fathers bind their sons to will-less instrumentality, for the satisfaction they seek can only be accomplished through an agent appropriated for the purpose. And significantly in each, the son sees the return of the father as a confirmation of his presentiments of crime, guilt, and unworthiness.

These allusions certainly add depth and dignity to Magwitch, a principal character Dickens has kept from the narrative for over thirty chapters. Yet Dickens does not add these analogues to his work the way Vincent Crummles adds a water pump or washtub to his. Indeed, these incidental allusions point to significant differences between *Hamlet* and *Great Expectations* that more clearly indicate how Dickens adapted Shakespeare's tragedy and methods for his own purposes. The most telling difference is simply noted: the Ghost of Hamlet's father appears in Elsinore to begin a revenge tragedy, while Magwitch's return to London effectively ends the one he himself authored. For the remainder of his life Magwitch must play the fugitive from the society epitomized by Compeyson, the society of forgers, impostors, and self-swindlers he hoped to defeat by creating an honest gentleman of Pip. Although Magwitch returns to London to witness his triumph, he only hastens his own demise. As he tells Pip, "it's Death."

The complex dynamics of Magwitch's secret plot are self-destructive, his intentions to the contrary notwithstanding. But before the reader can trace the causes of Magwitch's defeat, Pip halts his own narrative in chapter 38 and becomes a spectator at the collapse of the most obvious and most richly described plan of revenge in the novel, Miss Havisham's. It is as if a knowledge of the one was a prerequisite for understanding the other. Specifically, it is as if Pip is preparing us to read the plot of his own life through the old woman's failure. Why her revenge plot fails is best seen in an analysis of its instruments, object, and method.

The course of Havisham's revenge is not a smooth one. To repair the injuries of her wedding day, she slowly transforms the innocent Estella into a well-tempered instrument, a heartbreaker. Since Estella is "stock and stone"—even the amorous Pip speaks to her as if she were an object, calling her "*the* Estella" (emphasis added)—Havisham need not fear that sentiments of fanciful attachments will soften her purpose.

Although Estella is the perfect instrument for revenge (she is absolutely unpossessed of self-interest), Havisham's object is so ill-conceived that it frustrates her desire at the outset. Compeyson is the malefactor, of course, but he escapes the justice of her cause as she takes scattered aim at the entire class of gentlemen, nameless and faceless though they be. Unable to destroy the shadowy Compeyson, Estella eventually marries Bentley Drummle. This act of mutual misery does not signal Havisham's success. Indeed, Jaggers considers the "question of supremacy" in Estella's marriage a "toss up." Compared to Compeyson, Drummle is a minor villain, at most a bullying snob, albeit of the "true sort." But in the end Drummle seems little more than a trope in the novel, as he takes much of his thematic identity from one of Dickens' major symbols. He is, as Jaggers dubs him, "the Spider," the "blotchy" fellow who properly resides with the other "blotchy bodies" in the "spider community," the social pyramid symbolized in the remains of Havisham's wedding cake. To seek revenge upon Compeyson through the metaphorical Drummle is to receive scant satisfaction because the desire for revenge is mediated through a petrified and unshakable class structure that conceals the actual villain.

Havisham's failure is melodramatically staged before Pip as Estella and her maker act out the contradictions of this revenge plot. Completely heartless, Estella turns against Miss Havisham, and the already dusty atmosphere of Satis House is further thickened with allusions to *King Lear* and *Frankenstein*:

> "I am what you have made me [said Estella]. Take all the praise, take all the blame; take all the success, take all the failure; in short, take me."
>
> "O, look at her, look at her!" cried Miss Havisham, bitterly; "Look at her, so hard and thankless. . . ."
>
> " . . . But what would you have? You have been very good to me, and I owe everything to you. What would you have?"
>
> "Love," replied the other.
>
> "You have it."
>
> "I have not," said Miss Havisham.
>
> " . . . Mother by adoption, I have said that I owe everything to you. All I possess is freely yours. All that you have given me, is at your command to have again. Beyond that, I have nothing. And if you ask me to give you what you never gave me, my gratitude and duty cannot do impossibilities."
>
> "Did I never give her love!" cried Miss Havisham, turning wildly to [Pip]. "Did I never give her a burning love, inseparable from jealousy at all times, and from sharp pain, while she speaks thus to me!"

Like Lear, Havisham has given her daughter all. The old woman suffers, however, not from the rapacity of Goneril and Regan but from the gratitude of a perverse Cordelia who loves according to her bond, no more, no less. Furthermore, like Victor Frankenstein, Havisham is haunted by the inhuman monster she has made: it now undeniably confronts her with the folly of her Promethean ambition, the tyrannous usurpation of a child's life. Havisham's "burning love" was, of course, kindled on her disastrous wedding day; and, fed by hatred and accelerated by intense egotism, it eventually destroys her. Given its instrument, object, and method, Havisham's drive for revenge falls short of heroism and justice. It remains in the end a cry of dementia that echoes Lear's: "Let her call me mad," she says in despair to the thing she has created, "let her call me mad!"

For Havisham the "vanity of [her] sorrow . . . had become a master mania," which twisted charity into revenge. Speaking to Pip after her conflagration, she confesses:

> "My Dear! Believe this: when she first came to me, I meant to save her from misery like my own. At first I meant no more."
>
> "Well, well!" said I. "I hope so."
>
> "But as she grew, and promised to be very beautiful, I gradually did worse, and with my praises, and with my jewels, and with my teachings, and with this figure of myself always before her a warning to back and point my lessons, I stole her heart away and put ice in its place."

In *Hamlet* the Ghost finds the Prince an "apt" instrument of justice, for the Prince was "born to put things right." In *Great Expectations* the conditions of birth may subject one to abuse and neglect, but they alone cannot make an avenging hero. Thus to have her apt instrument, Havisham must create a monster through Frankensteinian egotism. As twisted self-sacrifice becomes self-destruction, *Hamlet* shades into *Lear* and darkens into *Frankenstein*. This confusion precludes the heroism and justice seen in Shakespearean tragedy because Havisham's act of revenge is dependent upon the transformation of an innocent child into a loveless grotesque who embodies the worst of the social class she intended to best.

After witnessing the collapse of Havisham's plans, Pip is prepared to see that Magwitch's revenge is similarly diffuse and flawed. Treating Compeyson only as a synechdoche for a corrupt world, Magwitch in the end seeks to defeat an entire social class. He thus depersonalizes his vengeance, rendering it an occasion of unheroic pathos. When he looks at the fine weapon he has forged in Pip, Magwitch proclaims to all the absent villains of his life:

"Blast you all!" he wound up, looking round the room and
snapping his fingers once with a loud snap, "blast you every
one, from the judge in his wig, to the colonist a stirring up the
dust, I'll show a better gentleman than the whole kit on you put
together!"

There is no more power in Magwitch's hands to defeat his social betters than
there was magic in the crutch that the "fairy godmother" Havisham waved
about Pip on his departure for London. Neither Jaggers' massive forefinger
nor Pip's fervent appeals can save this good man from the injustice of the
gallows. Indeed, the victim himself suggests that a death sentence from
society's most powerful institution deserves more respect than the one God
has given all men: "My Lord," Magwitch addresses the judge, "I have
received my sentence of Death from the Almighty, but I bow to yours." In
the end, the "stern shut-up mansions" of the law that protect the spider
community remain deaf to the cries for justice that reverberate throughout
the narrative.

Significantly, both Havisham and Magwitch confuse the ends and
means of their revenge by conceiving it in purely conventional terms. Estella
is intended for marriage with a "gentleman," while Pip is given fine linens
and thoroughbreds to "'hold [his] own' with the average of young men in
prosperous circumstances." So ideologically bound are both parents to
bourgeois culture that their idea of vengeance is not an heroic putting things
right but social assimilation born of an unconscious identification with their
oppressors. That is, Dickens portrays Havisham and the convict as social
products who self-defeatingly embrace the ideology of the class that has
unjustly destroyed their innocence and happiness. This self-defeating pattern
is set early in the narrative when Magwitch avoids becoming Compeyson's
"tool" again by foiling the gentleman's escape from the Hulks. This act of
self-sacrifice costs Magwitch his freedom and affords him only greater
suffering at the hands of the law.

The contradiction in the revenge plots can be seen emblematically in
the characters' attire, as Dickens' use of drama extends beyond structure to
include costume. Unlike Joe Gargery, whose best self is seen in his "forge
dress" and not in "holiday clothes" and "bird's nest" hat, both Magwitch and
Havisham willingly don costumes that reduce them to burlesques. Havisham
wears the costume of the bride, condemning herself to appear forever as
what she is not, to self-consciously display the indignity dealt her by
Compeyson. She ultimately obtains Pip's forgiveness, but only after a fire
destroys this emblem of her sinful self-mockery. When asked by Pip how he
will avoid capture, Magwitch says, "Dear boy, there's disguising wigs can be

bought for money, and there's hair powder, and spectacles, and black clothes—shorts and what not." Money will allow Magwitch, like Pip, to appear the gentleman and, more significantly, to look as Compeyson did at their felony trial. Further, wearing the powered wig of a jurist, Magwitch apes the forensic injustice that has qualified him for the hangman since childhood. Thus costumed, Magwitch loses much of his dramatic impact and his consequent claim to Pip's sympathy. Asking Pip to read him "Foreign Language," Magwitch, "not comprehending a single word, would stand before the fire surveying [Pip] with the air of an Exhibitor, and [Pip] would see him . . . appealing in dumb show to the furniture to take notice of [his] proficiency." Playing pathetically to an empty house, Magwitch falls through self-consciousness into what Dickens elsewhere condemned as mere theatricality. Pip's second father returns to his authentic self only when he is again placed in prison, where he and the young man are finally reconciled. Misunderstanding that the fundamental injustice of the social structure resists their attempts to engage it dramatically, both Havisham and Magwitch are defeated as they strive to become what they despise.

Since Pip, like Estella, is not a born hero, Dickens also draws *Frankenstein* within Magwitch's plot as well. Like Shelley's mad doctor and like Miss Havisham, Magwitch is obsessed with the "mastering idea" of making a perfect creature. This ambition paradoxically enslaves him to his creation, making his very survival dependent upon his "dear boy." Indeed, when Magwitch first appears at Pip's door, he calls the young man "Master." And later, in the same episode, Pip himself draws the many parallels between Frankenstein's fate and his own, between the Romantic myth of perverted creation and his own transformation from simple apprentice to London dandy. All the tangled connections fall in a lump in Pip's mind:

> The imaginary student [Pip says] pursued by the misshapen creature he had impiously made, was not more wretched than I, pursued by the creature who had made me, and recoiling from him with a stronger repulsion, the more he admired me and the fonder he was of me.

This is a literally confused allusion, for Pip cannot keep the lines of correspondence clear: he at once plays the monster to Magwitch's Frankenstein and vice versa. Moreover, carrying out the galvanic imagery of Mary Shelley's novel, Dickens shows that in a relationship charged by secret revenge, parental love does not attract but repulses.

These ironic uses of Shelley's novel are foreshadowed early in the plot when Pip attempts to create a boy in boots of the refuse of his washerwoman's family. There is no horror here, only laughter. Rather than haunt his maker in a gothic chiller, Pip's monster—The Avenger, as he is called—stalks him among the columns of the domestic accounts. The Avenger, Pip laments, plagues him, for the monster wants a great deal to eat without doing a great deal to earn it. The net effect of the Avenger is to parody the serious acts of creation in the novel, those Magwitch's Avenger sees and those he is ignorant of.

The greatest ironic deflation of Magwitch's revenge tragedy is, of course, the production of *Hamlet* mounted on the boards by Waldengarver né Wopsle. A brilliant satire of nineteenth-century theater, Dickens' description of Waldengarver's *Hamlet* is the best case against a pure translation of revenge tragedy into Victoria's England as portrayed by him. No paraphrase can equal Pip's description of textual mutilation, ludicrous staging, and salvos of nuts and orange peel. What Pip sees is the world of the drama abandoned to the groundlings, the barren spectators, as Hamlet says, who are capable of nothing but inexplicable dumb shows and noise. This is the audience lamented by Walter Scott in his "Essay on Drama"; these are the hoards of the unwashed who flocked to "private theatres," satirized by Dickens in *Sketches by Boz*. Here, the classic ritual of tragedy has degenerated into a form of mass entertainment nurtured by a social groundwork of "lamentable ignorance and boobyism" inimicable to tragic concerns. Like Quince and his fellows in *Midsummer Night's Dream*, Waldengarver and company make tragedy the silliest stuff one ever heard. And Pip, like Theseus in the same play, feels a justifiable distance from those louts who treat *Hamlet* as if it were a slice of their own squalid lives. Indeed, at this stage of Pip's great expectations, the fictional world that translates Wopsle into a Prince, a kitchen table into a throne, and the graveyard scene into a dispute with a waiter is as alien to him as is Bottom's to the Duke of Athens.

But the pride experienced by Pip and Theseus is negated by what we as spectators can see of the world that remains hidden from them. As the audience of *Midsummer Night's Dream*, we know that the magical Puck has already implicated Theseus in the world of Quince and Bottom, for at the highest level of spectation we see Puck watch Theseus watching Bottom attempt a tragedy that closely parallels Athenian life. Dickens completes a similar pattern of spectation with Magwitch's imminent return to London. Here, we watch the outlaw watch Pip play a role in a revenge tragedy already made absurd by Wopsle. Thus, Pip's life is implicated in the squalor of the groundlings, in the heap of boors and criminals, and his pride in his great expectations is reduced to bald snobbery. When seen in terms of audience and players, Magwitch's relationship with Pip has been his attempt to ideally translate *Hamlet* into Victorian England. But the gentleman Pip, like Waldengarver the actor, is a travesty upon the original Prince that no exercise of the imagination can mend.

There are other characters in the novel who do have a claim to heroic powers and virtue, but the spider community, in the main, resists their efforts to control events. Jaggers' hands, obsessively cleaned and perfumed, may keep the riffraff from him, and his forefinger may intimidate the bar. But this hierophant of society's secrets and the "closest approximation of a Providential figure . . . in the public plot of the novel" cannot redeem all who deserve it. Even the one character who can cow Jaggers is not capable of righting the spider community; Joe, a Hercules of strength and weakness, is not an avatar of the Hyperion that Hamlet wishes would save Denmark. Although Joe resists Jaggers' temptation to sell Pip, he does not keep Pip from falling into the world ruled by the "father of lies," nor is he wholly immune from the corruption of society. He keeps Orlick as journeyman, and he lies to Mrs. Joe, albeit in the interest of domestic tranquility, when he first returns with Pip from Satis House. Moreover, Joe's dignity and labor seem irrelevant in the spider community, as is seen most clearly in chapter 15. Since Pip is concerned about expressing his gratitude to Miss Havisham for his apprenticeship, Joe comically catalogs presentable handiwork from the forge—he suggests toasting forks, gridirons, shark-headed door chains for Miss Havisham, but, recalling Pip's account of his first visit there, he cautions that "a set of shoes all four round might not act acceptable as a present, in a total wacancy of hoofs." But these expressions of talent and good will are rejected by Pip as beside the point. It seems no individual can finally shape the course of events. Magwitch dies in prison; Pip, his hands burned by Havisham's fire, remains estranged from the forge; and Compeyson, the man of "fifty hands," dies attempting to destroy Magwitch. In a profound moment on the river, Magwitch acknowledges his hubris and implicitly indicates the limits of individual action in Dickens' world. Speaking to his "dear boy," he says,

> "I was a thinking through my smoke just then, that we can no more see to the bottom of the next few hours, than we can see to the bottom of this river what I catches hold of. Nor yet we can't no more hold their tide than I can hold this. And it's run through my fingers and gone, you see!" holding up his dripping hand.

This is not to say that there is no justice in Dickens' world; but the justice we see does not derive from heroic virtue asserting itself against evil. In Dickens' fiction, as in Hegel's *Aesthetics*, the reader finds an anatomy of a modern world that cannot sustain heroic tragedy. It is a world where work for the common good is divided among the masses and institutions, and where business, trade, and the professions are divided in the most various and class-conscious way. These divisions are essential to Dickens' world and are found both in its overall structure, as in *Bleak House* and *Little Dorrit*, and in its seemingly trivial details. (For example, the barber in *Nicholas Nickleby* will not cut a coal handler's hair, while in *Great Expectations* Herbert tells Pip that a public-house may keep a gentleman, but the reverse is never acceptable.) In a class-ridden world, the cause of justice will not be furthered by the force, insight, and courage of a heroic individual. Since what is important is the stability of the established social order, "the punishment of a crime . . . is no longer a matter of individual heroism and the virtue of a single person; on the contrary, it is split up into its different factors, the investigation . . . of the case, judgement, and execution of the judge's sentence" (Hegel). Thus, whatever justice is to be had is found most readily in the work of a Jaggers or in the detection of a Bucket, not in the individual revenge of wronged heroes.

Even the most famous unmasking scene in Dickens' fiction is colored by this severe qualification upon heroism. Micawber's revelation of Uriah Heep's true character is wonderful melodrama, but Micawber, too self-conscious to be truly dramatic, is at best theatrical and finally ineffective. The villain quickly recovers from this setback. Indeed, it is not Micawber or Copperfield who finally brings the serpentine Heep under heel but a social institution—the Bank of England. Other villains—Compeyson, Steerforth, Drummle, and Bounderby—are undone by Nature, thus escaping both the heroes' cause and the justice of the law. As Dickens' career develops from *Nicholas Nickleby* on, villainy seems to become more and more a product of the class structure and its institutions, and, consequently, it seems increasingly resistant to the virtues of his heroes. As questions of justice and right are relegated to legal institutions, Dickens' heroes become less efficacious in the dramas he creates for them or in those they strive to construct for themselves. The heroic revenge of Hamlet is difficult to realize in a society where private virtue is subordinated to corrupt and inefficient legal systems. It is, as Magwitch tells Pip, not truth but Compeyson's class identity—public school education, club and society associations, successful schoolfellows—that gleans the "gentleman" a light sentence and the judge's sympathy. The just cause of the hero is doubly irrelevant in a world where, as Dickens wrote of the courts: "Suffer any wrong that can be done you, rather than come here!"

We discover the other limits Dickens sees in generic translation when he again uses the levels of spectation gleaned from *Midsummer Night's Dream* to great effect in chapter 47, in which Pip enjoys Waldengarver's second performance. Pip sees two plays that ironically portray the aborted comedy of his life. In the first play, a rich boatswain arrives in Portsmouth and cements a young couple in wedlock with his money, a deed which elevates the humble fellow into civic sainthood. In the second, Waldengarver plays the Enchanter, who arrives from the antipodes to correct acts of misprision so that a stubborn father will permit his daughter to marry the beau of her choice. The parallels with Pip's life and Magwitch's are close and intricately drawn, down to the port of entry for both men, to the magical character of money, and to the Enchanter's necromantic book and Magwitch's worn testament. But these comedies of love and fortune are irrevocably translated by the figure of Compeyson, the perverse Puck who turns conjugal love into a violent confidence game. In Waldengarver's *Hamlet*, the actors were the translators; here, a member of the audience turns the trick.

In addition to concluding the revenge tragedy, then, the presence of Magwitch and Compeyson in London effectively ends what Pip believed to be the comedy of his life, his "great expectations" underwritten by his "fairy godmother," Miss Havisham. Translated from the fortunate gentleman into a guilty fugitive, Pip perforce dismisses these apparently comic plans for Estella and himself as mere illusion. Indeed, rather than being the romantic lead in the drama of Estella's life, Pip finds that he was to be only the first victim of Havisham's revenge upon the male world. It is true, of course, that Pip comes to forgive both Magwitch and Havisham, but his acts of forgiveness do not, as in comic drama, fulfill his wishes. After the deaths of Magwitch and Havisham, we watch Pip recover what is left of his inner life and forge a livable compromise for himself between foiled ambition and hard work, and between a persistent desire for Estella and a benign celibacy.

Thus the arrival of two criminals makes us see that Pip has been a character in a confused drama that is at odds with his sense of identity. He is not the hero or even the "oncommon" man; rather, he is a dupe and a victim. This awareness and his subsequent secret knowledge of Estella's parents place Pip interestingly in a position to seek revenge upon those who deceived him, to be the author of his own revenge tragedy. Before he mounts his production, however, he tries out a plot summary on Jaggers, perhaps the best critic of life in Little Britain. In response, the lawyer draws on a biblical text (Matt. 18:8) and tells Pip that it would be better to cut off his hands rather than to reveal this secret to Estella and her parents. That is, the young man is told that it would only offend himself to give further scandal to the other warped child in the novel. Pip decides to preserve what remains of Estella's innocence and secretly forgives her.

It is precisely these two qualities—innocence and forgiveness—that make Pip's world, on a positive note, incapable of tragedy. Despite Hubble's verdict that all children are "naterly wicious," Dickens puts the opposite case. As children, Pip, Joe, Magwitch, and Estella are all innocent, possessing a Rousseauian virtue that the cruelty of the spider community compromises and often hardens into crime and guilt. The premise of heroic tragedy is precluded by the innocence of all men, even when conceived only as a legal theory. In chapter 18 Wopsle is feverishly reading in the gazette about a famous murder case, and his thespian ambitions are leading him to view the crime as a modern example of *Coriolanus* and *Timon of Athens*. This would-be translation of modern crime into theatrical tragedy is abruptly halted by the massive forefinger of Jaggers. After a deflating cross-examination, the lawyer makes Wopsle agree that every Englishman is innocent until proven guilty. These are strange words from the man who calls himself a fortune-teller, the clairvoyant who sees that all men will eventually go wrong. But Jaggers himself finds the concept of his own innocence necessary for his manipulations of Little Britain. He only feigns innocence, of course; but without the freedom that the illusion allows him, Jaggers could offer the heap no modicum of justice however attenuated and unorthodox.

If innocence makes the origins of tragedy uncertain, then forgiveness is the end that makes it unrealizable. Forgiveness obviates the necessity for revenge since it transcends grievance. Pip forgives Magwitch, Havisham, and Estella; Joe forgives Mrs. Joe, "Sir" Pip, and his monstrous father, whose essence, like Orlick's, is epitomized in the "hammer" he beat his family with. The acts of forgiveness are themselves an acknowledgment of man's essential goodness. Pip can say of his fellow man, as Joe said of his father: "Whatsume'er the failings on his part, Remember reader he were good in his hart." Forgiveness predicted on "knowledge of the circumstances, conviction of the good, and the inner intention" (Hegel) repudiates the princely nobility of revenge and in Dickens' world reduces it to the domain of inept actors and criminal justices. The "totality of the heroic character" (Hegel) is the sine qua non of tragedy, but it cannot prevail against injustice in bourgeois society. Dickens' would-be heroes submit themselves to legal institutions or to the Christian doctrine of forgiveness. Or if they persist in seeking to put things right, they are reduced to impotent rage and bluster, like Boythorn and Gridley in *Bleak House*.

In a Christian world, even one as secularized as Dickens', forgiveness should open the way to salvation, often portrayed in Victorian fiction in marriage. Even a critical realist like Mr. George in *Bleak House* can overlook the distracting gaffs at Astley's Theatre—poor swordsmanship and the Emperor of Tartary waving the Union Jack—if he is "touched home by the sentiments" of lovers united on the stage. It is therefore remarkable to note how forgiveness profoundly thwarts *Great Expectations'* movement toward a sentimental conclusion. Early in the narrative Pip dreams of being forced to play either Hamlet or a middle-class husband. By forgiving those who have offended him, Pip eventually avoids the fate of the one, but his act of forgiveness does not necessarily make him the other. In chapter 58, Pip, resigned to the loss of his "poor dreams" of Estella, returns to the marshes musing of a life with Biddy, his "guiding spirit . . . [of] simple faith and clear home-wisdom." His initial disappointment is compounded when he finds she has married Joe. Pip's indelible bachelorhood—most emphatically present in the original ending—seems necessary for the novel's thematic continuity, for at the core of *Great Expectations* lies the marriage that never took place. Compeyson's betrayal of Havisham is both her obsession and the author's as well. Not only does the presence of the false suitor in the theater translate the comedy of Pip's life, but the hour of Havisham's betrayal is the dead moment around which the characters move: most of the morning hours specifically mentioned in the novel bracket 8:40 A.M.

To be sure, there are marriages in *Great Expectations*, but they do not necessarily signal the triumph of love, since they occur in the wake of deaths or in the shades of secrecy. Herbert marries Clara only after her father, Gruffandgrim, cuts anchor; Biddy's betrothal to Joe is a secret kept from the hero; and Wemmick—half male, half mail box—goes to wed Miss Skiffins poorly disguised as the Compleat Angler. The most anticipated marriage in the novel is without doubt Pip's to Estella, for it would have the effect of triumphantly supplanting hateful revenge with love. Indeed, the mere mention of Pip's love for Estella has a powerful influence for good, notwithstanding the harm it brings him. Late in the narrative, Pip proclaims his devotion to her to the dying Magwitch, and Pip's "I love her!" is a viaticum for the repentant convict. Yet, since Estella is ready to marry Bentley Drummle, Pip's love will not have its desired consequence. Again recalling the original ending of the novel, we see that the hero's marriage is a false anodyne, which the chemistry of the novel cannot easily realize.

Even after Pip has repaired his heart through industry and self-denial, he cannot imagine himself married. At most, he aspires to be a second father, to repeat the role already compromised by Magwitch. Visiting the forge, in chapter 59, Pip speaks to Biddy about her son in terms that darkly recall the convict's "proprietorship": "Biddy, . . . you must *give* Pip to me, one of these days; or *lend* him, at all events" (emphasis added). Finally, faced with the radical ambiguity of the revised ending, we can say that Pip's marriage to Estella, however devoutly wished, is the best-kept secret in *Great Expectations*, since it remains hidden from everyone, including the reader.

Why doesn't *Great Expectations* openly sustain a happy ending? One possible answer lies in the limits of translation in the novel. In Shakespeare's comedies characters are inwardly transformed before they can recover what they have lost. For example, Titania must become aware of her ludicrous attachment to Bottom before she can recover Oberon. This inward metamorphosis is often accomplished by a particular dramatic irony, by an exploitation of the gap in awareness between characters and audience as a heuristic device in the plays themselves. We have already seen how this device successfully operates in Pip's life. Pip saw the structure of his life dramatized, and he knew after the curtain fell that Joe always held the formula for true gentility of character—a constant perception of man's essential goodness. Where does Estella enjoy this restoring irony?

In the concluding pages of the novel Estella confesses that she has suffered and that, like the fool who discarded the priceless pearl, she has ignorantly abandoned Pip and his devoted love. Nonetheless, Estella still seems heartless, self-estranged, and quite prepared to discard Pip once again, to willingly lose the one person who might translate her self-reproach into forgiveness and give her human passion. She has been bent and shaped in the novel, but she has been fashioned by smithies who do not acknowledge the ideal of innocence that, however compromised by bourgeois ambition, can be the pattern of existence in Joe's hands. Indeed, the apprentice who could shape Estella for the good has, contrary to the case put by Jaggers, done her further harm by keeping the secret of her birth. Pip has figuratively amputated his hands by keeping the truth from her. And without the restoring irony of Pip's revelation she has no insight into her own heart, her own inner life. Since Pip keeps her secret, she cannot speak the most eloquent phrase in Dickens' lexicon: she must ask Pip to repeat "God bless you, God forgive you!" because she cannot forgive herself. Without any ideal of love and forgiveness to counter the squalor and violence of life, Estella is without the key to translate her life into a comedy. In *Great Expectations*, as in all works of transformation, something, or rather someone, is lost that no power of the imagination can restore.

Although Dickens rewrote the conclusion of the novel to please readers like Bulwer-Lytton, it is not clear that he completely yielded to their desire for a union of Pip and Estella. When Pip leads Estella from "the ruined place" of Satis House, he pointedly asks the reader to compare this departure with the one that concluded the first stage of his great expectations. There the emphasis was upon Pip's altered life as he leaves the paradise of the forge and moves into the world that "lay spread before" him, just as Milton's Adam accepts the world spread before him upon expulsion from the Garden (see *Paradise Lost*, XII. 646). Indeed, Dickens keeps the concept of change before the reader by repeating that Pip *changed* horses five times within two brief paragraphs. Pip continues to undergo alterations in the narrative—several rebirths, a renaming, and a rough course from common man to "oncommon" and back again. At the end of the novel Pip can find some fortune in his fall from childhood innocence, if only *faute de mieux*: he tells Estella, "I work pretty hard for a sufficient living, and therefore—Yes, I do well."

In the last chapter Estella also speaks of transformation. She says she is "greatly changed" and that Satis House will undergo unspecified changes in her absence. Since change in Estella is synonymous with degradation, neglect, and violence, hers is no *felix culpa*, however diminished. Moreover, because Estella is, as we have already noted, willing to maintain the status quo and leave Pip again, the ambiguity of Pip's last words—"I saw no shadow of another parting from her"—cannot regain what has been lost, cannot restore them to the Victorian paradise of happy wedlock.

Unable to be the comic heroine, Estella leaves Satis House and, one assumes, Pip as well. She reappears in the works of Hardy and Lawrence, where the elements of middle-class life—making a living, love affairs—have finally and violently displaced the ideal of innocence, where the tone of life, like the tone of the last pages of *Great Expectations*, is neither tragic nor comic, but elegiac.

ANNY SADRIN

Oedipus and Telemachus

As the least perspicacious reader will come to realize at the end of the book, the narrator of *Great Expectations*, in choosing such a title for his autobiography, has chosen to express himself in the ironic mode. Having now reached maturer years and given up impossible dreams, he can afford to recollect emotions in tranquility, look at his younger self with amused and sympathetic superiority and take pleasure in misleading all the other fools who are ready to follow in his steps. His readers' delusions are now those that once were his: is it not the prerogative of all ironists to write in bad faith?

But the method entails critical difficulties; as it consists mainly in concealing, at best half-concealing, the truth, postponing revelations, expressing feelings that cannot always be attributed with authority to the 'visionary boy' or to the wise chronicler, it is at times next to impossible to draw the line between deception and sincerity. 'What to believe, in the course of [our] reading' is our 'chief literary difficulty indeed'; and if, like Boffin, we decide 'to compound with half', the question still remains, 'which half'? How, in particular, are we to account for the many outbursts of self-pity that punctuate the book from beginning to end? When he speaks of 'wretched me', of his 'ecstasy of unhappiness', of 'that poor dream . . . all gone by', must we impute the emotion to the narrator's legitimate desire to

From *Great Expectations*. © Anny Sadrin, 1988.

269

recreate the passionate atmosphere of the past or should we understand it as the expression of lasting regrets and undying nostalgia? When he grows lyrical and resorts to personal apostrophes to the reader, 'Pause you who read this', must we dismiss them as pure rhetoric and turn a deaf ear to the pathos of such passages? Sometimes, to be sure, the emotion is cautiously dated as definitely belonging to the past, as in the following instance: 'When I woke up in the night . . . I used to think, with a weariness on my spirits, that I should have been happier and better if I had never seen Miss Havisham's face'; but what are we to make of a remark like this one: 'I washed the weather and the journey from my face and hands, and went out to the memorable old house that it would have been so much the better for me never to have entered, never to have seen'? The pathetic accents of passages like this one ring truer and more heart-felt than the sedate tone adopted at the last minute when, in less than a page, the narrator sums up eleven years of 'happy' industry and frugality:

> Many a year went round, before I was a partner in the House; but, I lived happily with Herbert and his wife, and lived frugally, and paid my debts . . . I must not leave it to be supposed that we were ever a great House, or that we made mints of money. We were not in a grand way of business, but we had a good name, and worked for our profits, and did very well.

We would like to take his word for it that he has given up for good 'those wretched hankerings after money and gentility' that had so disturbed his boyhood and that the Victorian gospel of work, wisdom and contentment is all he goes by now. But should we not rather read this declaration as one more instance of his self-swindling?

The question remains all the more perplexing as we know so little of the man's present life. Some critics, on the strength of the very last words of the revised ending, take it for granted that he has married Estella and lived happy ever after. But this is to stretch unduly the meaning of a purposely evasive sentence and, as far as we can tell, there is no 'dear presence' attending on him as, 'far into the night', he writes his recollections, no dear little heads to confirm such assumptions, no homely scene as in the closing chapter of *David Copperfield*. Other commentators assume that the act of narration is accomplished by one Mr Pirrip; but for all we know, the narrator is still Pip, or more appropriately maybe, Mr Pip, or 'Philip Pip, Esquire', to use Wemmick's form of address, though even this is purely conjectural. It would be fairer in fact to describe him as someone who used to go by the name of Pip and has, in the course of years, dissolved into anonymity and into non-entity, someone who has no present life, just a past to relate and re-live and whose recollections read almost like 'memories from beyond the grave'.

Such reticence is most frustrating. It deprives us of the necessary perspective and referential standpoint from which to make final pronouncements on the hero's progress and the meaning of his life, so that any attempt at aligning him with other Dickens heroes is bound to bring tentative answers.

It is difficult in particular to decide whether this story is, in the long run, a Victorian success story after the *David Copperfield* pattern or Dickens's 'Tale of Lost Illusions' as it has been called; and it is therefore difficult to appreciate the hero's modernity fairly. If we consider with Marthe Robert that modernity in fiction-writing must be understood as 'the self-searching, self-questioning literary movement which uses as subject matter its own doubt and belief in the value of its message', we can with no further hesitation call *Great Expectations* a modern novel, but it does not follow that the hero of this modern novel is himself a modern hero; and, paradoxically, the question that remains to be solved concerning Pip is precisely whether he is not an old-fashioned hero in a very modern novel.

Or, to use Robert's terminology, is he still at the end the modern Oedipal 'bastard' that we first discovered on his father's grave or has he not regressed into the more archaic type of the Romantic 'foundling', reading backward, in this event, his *Entfremdungsroman* or 'family romance'?

The 'family romance' in the Freudian theory is a story which the child makes up for himself 'as a correction of actual life', a day-dream which serves 'as the fulfilment of wishes' during the early years of his life when he has to free himself from parental authority and which might be compared to a serial story in two main episodes, each corresponding to a new stage in the child's mental and psychic development.

The first episode begins with the child's disappointment with his parents after an early period of idolatry. As he grows up and comes to realize that he is not, or no longer, the sole object of parental care and loving-kindness, has to face the necessity of sharing his father's and mother's dispensation of love, food and security with unwanted siblings, and as he furthermore 'gets to know other parents and compares them with his own, and so acquires the right to doubt the incomparable and unique quality which he had attributed to them', he feels betrayed and humiliated and embarks upon a compensatory dream in which he re-writes his life-story and imagines himself to be a lost child adopted by strangers. He is the noble 'foundling' whose true parentage will of necessity be discovered some day and things will be set to right at last.

The second episode takes place when the child grows aware of a sexual difference between his genitors and realizes that only his father's parental authenticity can be a matter of doubt. He then focuses on his father his genealogical uncertainty and takes on a new part as 'bastard' child of a familiar mother and of some distant, preferably aristocratic, father. This new-born bastardly Oedipus, having thus rid himself of his father, can keep the mother to himself and live in perfect bliss with her.

If, as Freud invites us to do in 'Creative writers and day-dreaming', we consider that fiction, especially popular romance, is primarily based on wish fulfilment, we may assume with Marthe Robert that the two heroic types of the family romance have quite naturally found their way into literary works of fiction: the foundling, a romantic dreamer, had developed into the fairy-tale hero, relying on benefactors, benevolent uncles and fairy godmothers; the bastard, a realist, is the hero of modern fiction, pugnacious, self-reliant and solitary. Among Robert's long list of 'bastards', whether real or fictitious, we may select Empire-builders like Napoleon, colonists like Robinson Crusoe, or lesser figures of ambitious young men like Rastignac or Julien Sorel.

If we now try to sort out Dickens's heroes according to these criteria, we will find few pure types and plenty of overlapping. Oliver Twist, the lost child whose sole *raison d'être* is to find his origins, will appear as the ideal, almost paradigmatic 'foundling', and no 'bastard' in spite of his illegitimate birth; but bastardy is as much a moral quality with Freud as 'true legitimacy' is with Dickens.

At the other end, the legitimate, high-born Charles d'Evrémonde, alias Darnay, who, in hatred of his father, renounces his patronymic, his patrimony and his fatherland and opts for self-reliance in a democratic country with no thought of ever reconsidering his choice, will qualify as the ideal 'bastard'.

David Copperfield, the runaway child who fights his way up into society, makes his own fortune and achieves literary success after the fashion of his creator, is very much on the bastard side, though, in seeking the help of his aunt Betsey, who acts as surrogate and foster parent, the young Oedipus shows that he cannot entirely resist the old attraction of Telemachus for some protective parental figure.

The double temptation is in fact shared by many other Dickens heroes, none so well as John Harmon who early quarrels with his much hated father, leaves home and country with no intention ever to return, yet comes back, years later, at the news of his father's death, attracted by 'the accounts of [his] fine inheritance', though' 'shrinking from [his] father's money' and '[his] father's memory', changes his mind on setting foot in London, passes himself for dead, takes on a pseudonym (thus performing a symbolic parricidal

gesture), proves to himself that he can work for a living and needs no
financial support, lets, meanwhile, other people come into his inheritance
and, after more than 700 pages of masquerading and tribulations, eventually
takes possession again of his 'rightful name and . . . London house',
ambiguously asserting himself both as the son of his father and as the heir of
the latter's servant. With the notable exceptions of Oliver and of Darnay, the
Dickens hero is very self-contradictory and it is significant that Dickens's last
completed novel should offer such a glaring example of ambivalence, for it
shows that to the last Dickens was desperately trying to settle his own oedipal
conflict and was still working on this disturbingly inexhaustible theme, the
father/son relationship, which is at the heart of his fictional matter.

The Dickens novel might in fact be described as an oedipal novel with
Telemachus in the leading role. The hero, in most cases, is a male orphan
whose father died before chapter 1. No father-killer himself (the murder is
always committed in his stead and for his benefit by the impenitently
parricidal novelist), he will have to redeem the deed and feel guilty in spite
of his innocence before, let us hope, coming to terms with the past and with
himself. The movement is always away from the father and back again, back
to his origins.

Structurally, *Great Expectations* follows this pattern. When, after long years of
absence in Cairo, Pip comes back to his native place and visits his friends at
the forge, he finds himself in the presence of another little Pip, his namesake
and *alter ego:*

> and there, fenced into the corner with Joe's leg, and sitting on
> my own little stool looking at the fire, was—I again!
> 'We giv' him the name of Pip for your sake, dear old
> chap,' said Joe, delighted when I took another stool by the
> child's side . . . 'and we hoped he might grow a little bit like
> you, and we think he do.'

The next morning, he takes the child for a walk to, of all places, the old
churchyard where it all began:

> I thought so too, and took him out for a walk next morning, and
> we talked immensely, understanding one another to perfection.
> And I took him down to the churchyard, and set him on a
> certain tombstone there, and he showed me from that elevation
> which stone was sacred to the memory of Philip Pirrip, late of
> this Parish, and Also Georgiana, Wife of the Above.

We have now come full circle and reached the end of the novel. Two or three pages follow on the Estella/Pip relationship, but this love-story is of such limited significance to the novel as a whole that Dickens could rewrite its conclusion at will and reorientate it without damaging the book or improving it overmuch. Altering or suppressing the return of the son to the graves of his parents would, on the contrary, have greatly impaired the meaning of the novel; and when Dickens reworked his ending, he knew better than to rework this scene and reconsidered only what came next.

This act of filial piety is really essential: it confirms to the reader that *Great Expectations* is first and foremost the novel of a son and, more important still, it reminds him that it is the novel of the son of Philip Pirrip. This is all the more necessary as, in between, the relationship between this son and this father is not openly made the subject of the plot: it even seems erased, ruled out of the book. Pip, unlike Oliver, has no reason to seek his father when he knows so well where to find him. He has no reason either to hate or despise him, as John Harmon or Arthur Clennam do their own fathers, and between chapter 1 and the final chapter he never mentions him, never gives him a thought. He has, we remember, never set eyes on him and no one, as far as we know, ever told him anything about his physical appearance or his character. The return of the prodigal son is therefore not a return to someone he ever knew, but to someone he imagined in the days when he was a young epigraphist. His filial pilgrimage is a journey back towards some idea, or some ideal maybe, early derived from a few words inscribed on a tombstone.

We might well also make the journey back to this first chapter, as the conspicuously self-referential narrator invites us to do, if we are to appreciate what exactly he is returning to. He is returning, of course, to his 'first fancies' which, on reflection, prove to have been rather stereotyped images of a fragile mother and of a strong, dark, impressive father, the sort of man that any boy would like to take after or to imitate to strengthen his own image of himself. He is also returning to the poetic appeal of their epitaph and to his misreading of its convoluted phrasing:

> At the time when I stood in the churchyard, reading the family tombstones, I had just enough learning to be able to spell them out. My construction even of their simple meaning was not very correct, for I read 'wife of the Above' as a complimentary reference to my father's exaltation to a better world.

A father in Heaven, a mother magnified by the magic formula which commemorates her—'Also Georgiana. That's my mother'—, two people whom the popular, conventional poetry of an inscription have immortalized into almost mythical figures, such are the parents he is returning to.

These wishful representations do not, unfortunately, provide the whole picture. The child sobbing among the graves is also, as we have seen, a child who has been cruelly slighted by the very people whom he is so willing to idealize; he has been slighted by their death, their inability to provide for him, and even their lack of concern in not taking him with them like the other five little boys. The scene in the churchyard precisely takes place at a crucial moment of awareness when Pip is beginning to estrange himself from his genitors and to 'bastardize' himself, when, in other words, he has just set about adding a new episode to his family romance 'as a correction of actual life' or in retaliation for being mishandled.

But something strange occurs then. For the narrating agencies, who are dreaming on his behalf, help by beginning to write his family romance for him in order to turn him eventually into an adopted son. Instead of remaining a bastard for life, he will thus be given a chance of becoming a foundling and being provided for. But, left in the dark about the identity of his adoptive parent, he will also be given the liberty of projecting his parental ideals on whomsoever he wishes. As blind as Oedipus, he blindly goes on living his oedipal drama through vicarious relationships, imaginary experiences, adapting his dreams to these mysterious new circumstances, misplacing his affections and expectations, faithless to his origins, faithful to his ideals.

The romance begins as early as chapter 1, when Pip is still weeping on his father's grave. What once were David's fearful apprehensions and unavowed dream of seeing Lazarus Copperfield the Elder rise from the dead suddenly comes true at long last: '"Hold your noise!" cried a terrible voice, as a man started up from among the graves at the side of the church porch.' Even before being identified as a convict 'in coarse grey, with a great iron on his leg', the new comer is unmistakably recognized as 'the ghost of a man's' or for that matter of a boy's 'own father' and the recognition is greatly helped by associations with the earlier novel: are we not, after all, reading a new episode of Dickens's huge 'Family Romance'?

Only years later, when the convict returns and proclaims himself to be Pip's 'second father', will the reader grasp the full meaning of this ghostly apparition. But, meanwhile, the mystery attached to the event will not impair his innermost conviction that the man who sprang up as a father-figure might reappear some day as something like a father, a conviction often strengthened in the course of the novel by incidental, premonitory coincidences and narratorial side-lighting. Pip, for his part, will not see beyond the event itself until, some sixteen years later, 'the truth of [his] position' comes 'flashing' on him. And it is certainly the greatest dramatic irony of this first-person narrative that the hints dropped throughout for our benefit and information should come from the very man who, as a character, was primarily concerned, yet remained so long in the dark.

Another, concomitant, irony concerns the child's identity in its long unsuspected relation with the newcomer:

> 'Tell us your name!' said the man. 'Quick!'
> 'Pip, sir.'
> 'Once more,' said the man, staring at me. 'Give it mouth!'
> 'Pip, Pip, sir.'

That an escaped convict should prove so eager to know the name of a child whom he has just met by chance and whom in all likelihood he will never meet again (there is at this stage no reason why he should) seems quite inexplicable, even goes against commonsense. This behaviour cannot be ascribed to vain curiosity or be taken for convict 'manners'. Yet the question is asked twice, as if the man wanted to make sure that he gets the answer right. The obvious explanation that comes to mind is that this verbal exchange meets dramatic requirements: Dickens wants to secure the future of his story and how could the sheep-farmer from the depths of Australia ever find the track of the boy unless he knew him by name?

But there is more than to it than that. For, when Jaggers comes to the forge eleven years later to acquaint him with his good fortune, he does not merely satisfy himself that Joe Gargery's apprentice answers to the name of Pip, but he imparts to him the peremptory and sole condition demanded by his mysterious benefactor, namely that he should always go by that name:

> 'Now, Mr Pip,' pursued the lawyer, 'I address the rest of what I have to say, to you. You are to understand, first, that it is the request of the person from whom I take my instructions, that you always bear the name of Pip. You will have no objection, I dare say, to your great expectations being encumbered with that easy condition. But if you have any objection, this is the time to mention it.'
> My heart was beating so fast, and there was such a singing in my ears, that I could scarcely stammer I had no objection.
> 'I should think not!'

In a novel so meticulously sifted by the critics, little attention has been paid to this strange demand. No explanation, of course, is offered by Jaggers.

None will ever be offered by Magwitch either. But this is no sufficient reason not to give it proper consideration.

Magwitch's likely motivations seem easy enough to detect. The former runaway convict wants to express his gratitude to the boy who once brought him food, a file and a glimpse of humanity, and whose name in his memory stands (rightly or wrongly) for human fellowship. In asking him to stick to his name, he is trying, not unlike Miss Havisham, to stop the clocks and arrest time. His money will go to the little child as he knew him and as he wishes to imagine him always, unchanged, unspoilt by time, child-like, generous, loyal, and weak enough, moreover, still to require his protection.

Other, less noble motives may be hazarded. The social outcast who intends to have his revenge on the oppressive and unfair society that has victimized him ever since he was born may wish to confer respectability on a name that connotes destitution and misery, as he turns this little speck, self-dubbed 'Pip', into a moneyed gentleman. And his vicarious ambition seems gratified: 'I tell it, fur you to know as that there hunted dunghill dog wot you kep life in, got his head so high that he could make a gentleman—and, Pip, you're him!'

But more important still, Magwitch has decided to make Pip his son and heir: 'You're my son', he says, 'more to me nor any son. I've put away money, only for you to spend'. Under normal circumstances (especially in a Dickens novel), the new father would naturally wish to bestow his name as well as his fortune on his adopted child: once in Dover, David begins a 'new life, in a new name' and it is as David 'Trotwood Copperfield' that he eventually inherits what little is left of his aunt Betsey's property; and in the novel we are considering, Estella, the chosen heiress, is named 'Havisham' after the name of her patroness and adoptive mother. But if a convict's money can be bequeathed easily enough (for *pecunia non olet*), how could a man who lives in banishment bestow a tainted name on someone he loves dearly and wishes to protect from such misfortunes and humiliations as he himself has had to endure? Not to mention the fact that he must long remain anonymous to ensure the suspense of his own plotting and that on his return he has to go by a false name. Besides, the name of 'Provis' that this *provi*dential father assumes for a pseudonym, if it corresponds well to the role of donor that he has assigned himself, would ill suit the one placed at the receiving end. If the adoptive father's liberality is unfettered, his power on onomastics is, as we see, very limited and his choice to have Pip stick to the name of 'Pip' may appear as a poor makeshift. It is, none the less, a means of strengthening the father/son relationship between him and his protégé: in compelling his adoptive son to renounce his rightful identity, Magwitch gets the upper hand of an old rival, Philip Pirrip the Elder, the dead and buried father. Should Pip, in growing up, decide to revert to the name of Philip Pirrip (a not unlikely hypothesis), the ghost of the real father would forever be in the way, a constant reminder of the laws of genetics, disturbingly suggestive of usurpation, whereas, thanks to a little clause in a legal document, he is ousted for good. Or should we say that it is 'as if it were all over with him'? And does not the new father run the risk, in time, of being double-crossed by his own stratagem?

The question is well worth asking, given the rather paradoxical character of the benefactor's demand; for it is only, as we must realize, on the understanding that he will keep his bastard's or, more exactly, his semi-bastard's name that Pip is allowed to become a foundling. And, as the narrative proceeds, this request will prove indeed to have harboured one of the major ambiguities of the book, the enduring enigma being whether the foundling will turn out to be 'somebody's child', 'anybody's', or 'nobody's'.

Jaggers, the man who takes 'nothing on its looks . . . everything on evidence', is unduly hasty in his judgement when he calls the demand of Pip's protector an 'easy condition'. On second reading it even sounds rather ironic, though whether the irony be the speaker's or the writer's is a conjectural matter. To be Pip by order is just as absurd as to play to order, and the hero finds himself once again in the impossible situation of one whose wish has become another's command; direly put to the test, he must from now on be at once free and obedient, true to himself and true to his word. Self-naming had made the child father to the man, but now that a man is father to the self-named child, the meaning of Pip's name is as double-edged as its graphic appearance, a mirror-image of itself.

Pip's name is officially made the touchstone of his moral strength and of his loyalty to himself and to the past. Unfortunately, the child has early learnt to distrust and disown himself. Hectored by grown-ups, rebuked and ordered about by his sister, always under the threat of Tickler, and the subject of the most contemptuous conversations, only solaced by Joe's spoonfuls of gravy and inefficient outpourings of love, how could he be expected to be strong and self-reliant? On the occasion of his first visit to Satis House, his weakness and diffidence already induced him to betray himself, even before crossing the threshold of Miss Havisham's dressing-room:

> 'Who is it?' said the lady at the table.
> 'Pip, ma'am.'
> 'Pip?'

His name is returned to him like a slap on the face or a misdirected note: 'Not known at the address', says the question-mark. So deep is the humiliation, so strong the desire to be recognized and acknowledged that, with no hesitation, Pip disowns his name at once and places himself in the most disgraceful bondage: 'Mr Pumblechook's boy, ma'am. Come—to play', he explains. Not Joe's boy, or even Mrs Joe's, but Pumblechook's, of all men. Common-sense readers will argue that this is the best means for Pip of making himself known to the mistress of the place, since Pumblechook is the very man who recommended him to her and who has just brought him there. But was it necessary to put it that way, to create this grammatical dependence as if in testimony of some filial or menial connection with a most hated self-imposed benefactor? And when, a moment later, Pip is asked to play, why should he hit upon the 'desperate idea of starting round the room in the assumed character of Mr Pumblechook's chaise-cart'? The answer rests in one word: 'gigmanity'. For Pip who has seen so little of the world, but heard so often his sister's praises of the man, the local corn-chandler is a paragon of gentility and his chaise-cart, by any conceivable stretch of imagination, the most enviable symbol of prestige. The chaise-cart is part and parcel of Pumblechook: 'Uncle Pumblechook . . . was a well-to-do corn-chandler in the nearest town, and drove his own chaise-cart'. Pumblechook's *own* chaise-cart clinches any argument: 'as Mr Pumblechook was very positive and drove his own chaise-cart—over everybody—it was agreed that it must be so'. Pumblechook's *own* chaise-cart is the proper vehicle to carry young boys with expectations up to town: 'you do not know', Mrs Gargery says to Joe, 'that Uncle Pumblechook, being sensible that for anything we can tell, this boy's fortune may be made by his going to Miss Havisham's, has offered to take him into town to-night in his own chaise-cart'. Pumblechook's own chaise-cart is such an object of veneration that Pip feels 'unequal to the performance' of impersonating it on that memorable occasion, though he will succeed better on his next visit: 'I started at once, . . . and we went away at a pace that might have been an imitation (founded on my first impulse under that roof) of Mr Pumblechook's chaise-cart'. (We note that the 'own' is dropped as soon as the imitation succeeds.)

This instance of self-betrayal is a minor offence compared to the next, which takes place after Pip has pledged himself to Jaggers always to bear the name of Pip. Only too pleased to be removed into the upper spheres of gentility, the young Rastignac has just arrived in London, where he will share house with Herbert Pocket, whom he has identified as 'the pale young gentleman' of Satis House: 'Will you do me the favour to begin at once to call me by my christian name, Herbert?' asks Pip's new friend. Pip assents quite willingly and in his turn introduces himself, though under a name more genteel-sounding than Pip: 'I informed him in exchange that my christian name was Philip'. But, genteel as it may sound and authentic as it may be, Philip will not do: 'I don't take to Philip', Herbert replies, 'I tell you what I should like. We are so harmonious, and you have been a blacksmith—would you mind it?' 'I shouldn't mind anything that you propose', Pip answers, 'but I don't understand you'. Herbert then explains himself: 'Would you mind Handel, for a familiar name? There's a charming piece of music by Handel, called the Harmonious Blacksmith.' 'I should like it very much', acquiesces Pip, who has already forgotten the 'easy' condition to his great expectations.

As on the previous occasion, Pip acts on the initiative of a social better: the 'bastard' will go by any name to rise in society. But, in so doing, he is also the victim of irony, lets himself be 'handled' by others and aligned with the comic or hateful characters to whom, as Sylvère Monod remarks, Dickens mischievously allots preposterous names ending in 'le'. Drummle, Wopsle, Hubble, and even the venerable and respectable Pumble(chook). The musical reference, besides, is as jarring as it is harmonious: in rechristening Pip, Herbert unwittingly performs variations on the theme of social determinism, 'once a blacksmith's boy, always a blacksmith's boy'.

Pip, of course, is deaf to these prophetic undertones. He even takes his new identity as a token of enfranchisement and is soon greatly helped in this delusion by curious circumstances. When he next goes down to the village by stagecoach, convicts are among his fellow-travellers and one of them he recognizes as the man who had once brought him to two greasy one-pound notes on behalf of his old fugitive friend of the marshes. The newly-made gentleman dreads mutual recognition and is happily relieved on realizing that his new name may prevent it:

> 'Good-bye, Handel!' Herbert called out as we started. I thought what a blessed fortune it was, that he had found another name for me than Pip.

The coach journey is nevertheless a journey back into the past, a nightmarish revival of Act 1, scene 1, as the convicts' conversation precisely runs on his own adventures in the marsh country and his connection with the man who since then 'got made a Lifer'. Throughout the journey, Pip is obsessed with the fear of being identified, as if the mask of pseudonymity was thinning down to transparency:

> After overhearing this dialogue, I should assuredly have got down and been left in the solitude and darkness of the highway,

but for feeling certain that the man had no suspicion of my identity . . . Still, the coincidence of our being together on the coach, was sufficiently strange to fill me with a dread that some other coincidence might at any moment connect me, in his hearing, with my name.

Reading this, we think we can hear Miss Havisham's voice still ringing from the distance: 'Good-bye, Pip!—you will always keep the name of Pip, you know', she had said to him when he had come to take his leave before starting for London. In its immediate context, her 'you know' could be understood to mean 'I know' or, more precisely, 'I want you to know that I know'. Miss Havisham in that scene was, as Pip will later tell her reproachfully, leading him on to believe, and leading the Pockets on to believe, that she was his benefactress: 'In humouring my mistake, Miss Havisham, you punished—practised on—perhaps you will supply whatever term expresses your intention, without offence—your self-seeking relations.' And she was described indeed as 'gloating on' the questions and answers that constituted the conversation, 'so keen was her enjoyment of Sarah Pocket's jealous dismay'. But the reach of the sentence goes much beyond the narrow bounds of petty family conflicts and the meanness of immediate psychological implications; in the broader context of the novel, the remark, after a time, acquires some autonomy and may read as a key sentence, possibly *the* key sentence of the novel, an ironic summary of the plot, a cruel epitome of the social fable. Dickens often entrusts his cynics with the task of lending their voices to his sternest messages, and it seems that in this novel Miss Havisham, a disillusioned, clear-sighted, cynical woman, has been assigned the part of prophet and truth-teller, though she performs it most ambiguously, behaving like Rousseau's *faux sincères* 'who wish to deceive in speaking the truth'. What she knows, and what Pip will come to know, is that he is no foundling of hers and has no future except in his past and self-reliant bastardy.

But the crowning irony of Pip's fantastic journey down to the end of the night is that it ultimately takes him to the discovery, on reading the local paper, that he is a most ludicrous father-seeker:

Our readers will learn, not altogether without interest, in reference to the recent romantic rise in fortune of a young artificer in iron of this neighbourhood . . . that the youth's earliest patron, companion, and friend, was a highly-respected individual not entirely unconnected with the corn and seed trade . . . It is not wholly irrespective of our personal feelings that we record HIM as the Mentor of our young Telemachus, for it is good to know that our town produced the founder of the latter's fortunes. Does the thought-contracted brow of the local Sage or the lustrous eye of local Beauty inquire whose fortunes? We believe that Quintin Matsys was the BLACKSMITH of Antwerp. VERB. SAP.

For all its preposterous, convoluted style, the paragraph that Pip lights upon as he rests at the local inn, holds much truth about his character and destiny. It cruelly reminds him that if Miss Havisham is to be his Ulysses, he must needs accept his old Mentor into the bargain and remain to the last 'Mr Pumblechook's boy'. It says in funny terms what the novel reveals in more heart-felt accents: the incompetent Oedipus is also doomed to be a pathetic Telemachus.

When 'our young Telemachus' discovers his 'real' father, he is quite dumbfounded and Oedipus wakes up again. Reluctant at first to recognize him, he is bound, after a time, to identify the man with a 'strange' face as *his* convict: 'for I knew him! . . . I could not have known my convict more distinctly than I knew him now . . . I knew him before he gave me one of those aids, though, a moment before, I had not been conscious of remotely suspecting his identity.' But he immediately estranges him again as '*the* Convict' (my emphasis), 'some terrible beast'; words of hatred and rejection crop up, 'repugnance', 'abhorrence', 'dread': 'I recoiled from his touch as if he had been a snake', he writes. He is on the verge of fainting—'the room began to surge and turn'—, on the verge, that is, of performing a suicide in effigy, behaving as if, short of destroying the unwanted father, he wished to destroy the father's unwilling son. Even his sense of identity is shaken for a while: 'I hardly knew . . . even who I was'.

This aggressive stage is short-lived, however, and, after a few days, Pip, quite reasonably, opts for a compromise: he decides simultaneously to renounce his benefactor's patronage and to stand by the man who, at the peril of his life, has crossed the seas just to see him. But both his decision and the words he chooses to account for it betray fundamentally oedipal motivations. Fearing that, 'under the disappointment', Magwitch might put himself 'in the way of being taken', which, since he is a lifer, would mean death by hanging, he thinks it wise not to impart to him his intentions concerning the inheritance and explains himself as follows:

I was so struck by the horror of this idea, which had weighed upon me from the first, and the working out of which would

make me regard myself, in some sort, as his murderer, that I
could not rest in my chair but began pacing to and fro.

If Dickens had read Freud, he would never have dared to write this sentence!
But what post-Freudian reader can fail to react at the word 'murderer' in
such a context? And, in expressing his fear of being the 'murderer' of the man
who calls him 'my son', how could Pip fail to draw our attention to the
parricidal drive of his nature and to remind us of Pumblechook's oracular
words, 'Take warning, boy, take warning!', which had been uttered, as Pip
had remarked at the time, 'as if it were a well-known fact that I contemplated
murdering a near relation, provided I could only induce one to have the
weakness to become my benefactor'. Pip, like Oedipus, is afraid of the oracle
and his fears are even better justified because, unlike Oedipus, he has from
childhood, and long before hearing the Pumblechookian warning, been
obsessed with fears or visions of murder of a parricidal type.

The avuncular Pumblechook himself had been the victim of his very
first imaginary murder of a near relation and would-be 'patron': at the end of
the Christmas meal, having absorbed a glassful of the Tar which Pip had
poured into the brandy bottle, the uncle had performed such 'an appalling
spasmodic whooping-cough dance' that the miserable child, believing that
his end had come, had immediately looked upon himself as his murderer: 'I
had no doubt I had murdered him somehow.'

Then, there had been the hallucination at the end of his first visit to
Satis House, when he had seen, or fancied that he saw, his new 'patroness'
hanging by the neck from a beam of the brewery. Then, there had been his
fear (prompted by Pumblechook) of his having had a hand in his sister's
murderous aggression. All this, assuredly, was expressed in terms of
apprehensions and nightmarish visions, but the phenomenon on each
occasion could also be read as an inverted wish. And so can this new
manifestation of the Oedipus complex. Pip's fear is even so extreme that,
again like Oedipus, he does his best to make the murder impossible: 'I did
not wish to be a parricide', Oedipus explains to the Corinthian messenger
who wants to know why he left the town where his parents live. Pip cannot
run away (which would be the death of Magwitch) but, by giving up his
financial expectations, he cuts off any filial bond that might link him to his
provider. He will help the man, he will protect him, he will be true to him,
even to the death, he will indulge his illusions, let him be a father, or rather
let him take himself for one, he will act as a son, but knowing all the time that
he is playing a part, with this secret like a barrier between them.

Even towards the end, when his 'repugnance' to Magwitch has all
'melted away', Pip writes: 'in the hunted wounded shackled creature who

held my hand in his, I only saw a man who had meant to be my benefactor'. But 'had meant to be' is a far cry from 'had been'!

It must be conceded that there is ironic bitterness in this 'had meant to be' and that the convict's money would now be less unacceptable than it had been a few weeks earlier. Pip's prejudices have melted away with his repugnance as we gather from a conversation he has with Jaggers about the 'fate' of the convict's wealth on the day that follows Magwitch's recapture:

> I imparted to Mr Jaggers my design of keeping him in ignorance of the fate of his wealth. Mr Jaggers was querulous and angry with me for having 'let it slip through my fingers,' and said we must memorialize by-and-by, and try at all events for some of it. But, he did not conceal from me that although there might be many cases in which the forfeiture would not be exacted, there were no circumstances in this case to make it one of them. I understood that, very well. I was not related to the outlaw, or connected with him by any recognizable tie; he had put his hand to no writing or settlement in my favour before his apprehension, and to do so not would be idle. I had no claim, and I finally resolved, and ever afterwards abided by the resolution, that my heart should never be sickened with the hopeless task of attempting to establish one.

Hopeless the task would certainly be. Dickens has hurried things and plotted against his hero's possible change of mind, allowing just enough time for him to be cured of his prejudices and intolerance, yet not enough for him to get an inheritance to which he has no lawful claim.

For the novelist has no wish to spoil the meaning of his moral and social fable. During the third stage of his adventures, Pip's progress has been towards solitude and renunciation, and, after renouncing the convict's money, he has declined all forms of patronage, even from the person whom he has so long imagined to be his benefactress: 'Miss Havisham', he tells Wemmick, 'was good enough to ask me . . . whether she could do nothing for me, and I told her No'. Pip will get no money from anyone who is not related to him or 'connected with him by any recognizable tie'; and, by so doing, by thus giving up all thoughts of being a 'foundling', he will return to the beginning and accept himself as the son of a poor man.

The real father's poverty is actually sublimated by the death of the adoptive one. With no legacy to hand down to his would-be son, Magwitch in the prison dies like a pauper. In fact, he dies two deaths: his own, which rehabilitates him as a man, even as a gentle man, and the death of the father long buried in the churchyard, whose ghost he had been when he had first 'started up from among the graves' and whom he impersonates to the very last.

Now that the ghost has gone to rest for good, Oedipus is cured of his parricidal leanings and Telemachus can give up his quest. A timely fever will help the hero exorcize old dreams and borrowed identities and become himself again:

> That I had a fever and was avoided, that I suffered greatly, that I often lost my reason, that the time seemed interminable, that I confounded impossible existences with my own identity . . . that I passed through these phases of disease, I know of my own remembrance, and did in some sort know at the time. That I sometimes struggled with real people, in the belief that they were murderers . . . I also knew at the time.

Pip recovers from this cathartic malady to become, after his own terms, if not the Pip of older times, at least one very like him: 'I fancied I was little Pip again', he says. With Joe looking after him 'in the old unassertive protecting way', 'like a child in his hands', Pip is born again to himself.

But it would certainly be a gross misreading of the book to say that in this scene Pip finds a new father or that a son is born to Joe. The relationship between these two characters has never had that kind of ambiguity. Joe is assuredly a 'fatherly', even a 'motherly' man: he feeds, protects, nurses; but he is, and always was, too honest, too 'unassertive' and too much like 'a larger species of child' ever to play father to his 'best of friends'. Significantly, when the stranger at the Three Jolly Bargemen enquired about their relationship, he felt unable to define it:

> 'Son of yours?'
>   'Well,' said Joe, meditatively . . . 'well—no. No, he ain't.'
>   'Nevvy?' said the strange man.
>   'Well,' said Joe . . . 'he is not—no, not to deceive you, he is *not*—my nevvy.'
>   'What the Blue Blazes is he?' asked the stranger.

It is precisely because he is no prevaricator that Joe can be a mediator between the true and the false Pips. The moral touch-stone of the book, he alone can help the hero find his true metal and his true identity. Joe is the father who might have been, not the father who was or ever pretended to be. And this is the reason why, at the end of the novel, he can still father a Pip of his own, a little Pip Gargery whose happy story will never be worth telling.

For repetition implies difference. 'There . . . was—I again!' exclaims Pip who has had a sudden vision of what he used to be like when he was living at the forge; but Joe is more matter-of-fact: 'We giv' him the name of Pip for your sake, dear old chap', he says, 'and we hoped he might grow a little bit like you, and we think he do'. Not Pip's double, but his mirror, Pip Gargery will merely help the son of Philip Pirrip to recognize and accept himself, draw the line between what is, what was and what might have been, and return to his origins.

Thus, Pip's Odyssey brings him back to familiar shores, where Pip is waiting for him. He will now learn 'for certain' that his 'true legitimacy' rests on his semi-bastardy, half Philip, half Pirrip, 'as if in the Family Romance there were some sort of secret pact between aesthetics and logic, stipulating that the Bastard can never betray the Foundling who survives within him without running the risk of a *literary* impoverishment—a loss of depth, ambiguity and poetry—and of losing at least some of the social advantages due to him'. Oedipus will survive and learn self-reliance only in harbouring Telemachus somewhere in his heart of hearts, but their different roles will no longer be confused. For was it not Oedipus who had embarked on a foolish voyage, looking for imaginary fathers and accepting self-imposed ones? Was it not Telemachus who had lost his bearings, blindly murdering parental figures in his dreams and *actes manqués*? But this strange comedy of errors ends with the hero's wanderings when the Tale of Lost Illusions becomes the Novel of Regained Identity.

Chronology

1812   Charles John Huffam Dickens, the second of eight children, born February 7 to John and Elizabeth Dickens.

1814   John Dickens, a clerk in the Navy Pay Office, is transferred from Portsea to London. During these early years, from 1814 to 1821, Dickens is taught his letters by his mother, and he immerses himself in the fiction classics of his father's library.

1817   John Dickens moves family to Chatham where Charles Dickens attends Dame School with his sister Fanny.

1821   Dickens begins at the Rev. William Giles School where he learns the basics of Latin and grammar. Charles remains at this school for a time even after his family is transferred again to London in 1822.

1822   Charles Dickens composes his first tragedy, *Misnar, the Sultan of India*, modeled on *The Tales of the Genii*.

1824   John Dickens is arrested for debt and sent to Marshalsea Prison, accompanied by his wife and younger children who take up residency at the jail. Charles soon finds lodging in a poor neighborhood and begins work at Warren's Blacking Factory, a place where "no words can express the secret agony of my soul." His father is released three months later under the Insolvent Debtor's Act.

1824–26   Dickens attends Wellington House Academy, London where he wins the Latin prize and where he participates in school theatricals until he is again forced to leave because of his father's financial embarrassments.

1827   Works as a law clerk and spends time reading in the British Museum.

1830   Meets Maria Beadnell, the daugher of George Beadnell, a prosperous banker. He eventually falls in love with her, but by 1832 her parents begin to discourage the relationship. Upon her return from a trip to Paris in 1833, Maria loses interest in him, causing Charles to feel socially inferior.

1831   Becomes a reporter for the *Mirror of Parliament.*

1832   Becomes a staff writer for the *True Sun.*

1833   Dickens's first published piece, "A Dinner at Poplar Walk," appears in December issue of the *Monthly Magazine* under the pen name "Boz."

1834   Dickens becomes a staff writer on the *Morning Chronicle.* His "street sketches" begin to appear in the *Evening Chronicle.* Dickens meets his future wife, Catherine Hogarth. John Dickens is arrested again for debt.

1836   *Sketches by Boz,* illustrated by George Cruikshank, published. Dickens marries Catherine Hogarth in April. His first play, *The Strange Gentleman,* runs for two months at the St. James's Theatre. A second play, *The Village Coquettes,* is produced at the same theater. In late 1836, he becomes the editor of a new magazine, *Bentley's Miscellany.* Dickens meets John Forster, who becomes a lifelong friend and his biographer.

1836–37 *Pickwick Papers* published in monthly installments from April through the following November.

1837   *Pickwick Papers* appears in book form. *Oliver Twist* begins to appear in *Bentley's Miscellany* and in its depiction of brutality and crime, it is a marked change from the previous novel. Nevertheless, the success of *Oliver Twist* enables Dickens to rent a terrace house at 48 Doughty Street in Bloomsbury (today this house is one of the most successful literary museums in London). *Is She His Wife?* produced at the St. James's. Dickens's first child, a son, born, and the family moves to Doughty Street. Catherine's sister Mary, deeply loved by Dickens, dies suddenly.

1838   *Nicholas Nickleby* appears in installments and is completed in October of 1839. Dickens's first daughter born.

1839   The Dickenses move to Devonshire Terrace. A second daughter is born. *Nickleby* appears in book form.

1840   Dickens edits *Master Humphrey's Clock*, a weekly periodical, in which *The Old Curiosity Shop* appears.

1841   *Barnaby Rudge* appears in *Master Humphrey's Clock*. Another son born.

1842   Dickens and his wife tour America from January to June. Dickens publishes *American Notes* and begins *Martin Chuzzlewit*.

1843   *Martin Chuzzlewit* appears in monthly installments (January 1843–July 1844). *A Christmas Carol* published.

1844   Dickens tours Italy and Switzerland. Another Christmas book, *The Chimes*, completed. A third son is born.

1845   Dickens produces *Every Man in His Humour* in England. *The Cricket on the Hearth* is written by Christmas, and Dickens begins *Pictures from Italy*. A fourth son is born.

1846   Dickens creates and edits the *Daily News*, but resigns as editor after seventeen days. Begins *Dombey and Son* while in Lausanne; the novel appears in twenty monthly installments (October 1846–April 1848). *The Battle of Life: A Love Story* appears for Christmas.

1847   Dickens begins to manage a theatrical company and arranges a benefit tour of *Every Man in His Humour*. A fifth son is born.

1848   Daughter Fanny dies. Dickens's theatrical company performs for Queen Victoria. It also performs *The Merry Wives of Windsor* to raise money for the preservation of Shakespeare's birthplace. Dickens's last Christmas book, *The Haunted Man*, published.

1849   Dickens begins *David Copperfield* (published May 1849–November 1850). A sixth son is born.

1850   *Household Words*, a weekly periodical, established with Dickens as editor. A third daughter is born and dies within a year.

1851   Dickens and his company participate in theatrical fundraising. Dickens's father dies.

1852   *Bleak House* appears in monthly installments (March 1852–September 1853). The first bound volume of *A Child's History of England* appears. Dickens's last child his seventh son, is born.

1853   Dickens gives first public readings, from the Christmas books. Travels to France and Italy.

1854   *Hard Times* published in *Household Words* (April 1–August 12) and appears in book form.

1855   *Little Dorrit* appears in monthly installments (December 1855–June 1857). Dickens and family travel at year's end to Paris, where the novelist meets other leading literary and theatrical persons.

1856   Dickens purchases Gad's Hill Place from the writer Eliza Lynn Linton. In the fall, Wilkie Collins's *The Frozen Deep*, one of the sources for *A Tale of Two Cities*, is rehearsed.

1857   Dickens is involved primarily with theatrical productions. Hans Christian Andersen is invited to visit Gad's Hill for two weeks, but instead stays for five.

1858   Begins his first public readings for profit. Dickens announces his separation from his wife, about which he writes a personal statement in *Household Words* to dispel rumors of having an affair with Ellen Ternan.

1859   Dickens concludes *Household Words* and establishes a new weekly, *All the Year Round*. *A Tale of Two Cities* appears there from April 20 to November 26, and is published in book form in December.

1860   Begins series of papers, *The Uncommercial Traveller* for *All the Year Round*. *Great Expectations* underway in weekly installments (December 1860–August 1861).

1861   *The Uncommercial Traveller*, a collection of pieces from *All the Year Round*, published. First installment of *Great Expectations* (first two and a half chapters) published in *Harper's Weekly*, New York, in November.

1862   Dickens gives many public readings and travels to Paris.

1863   Dickens continues his readings in Paris and London. His daughter Elizabeth dies and his own health is seriously declining, showing symptoms of thrombosis.

1864   *Our Mutual Friend* appears in monthly installments for publisher Chapman and Hall (May 1864–November 1865).

1865   Dickens suffers a stroke that leaves him lame. He is involved in a train accident with Ellen at Staplehurst, Kent, which causes him to change the ending of *Our Mutual Friend*. *Our Mutual Friend* appears in book form. The second collection of *The Uncommercial Traveller* is published.

1866   Dickens gives thirty public readings in the English provinces.

1867   Dickens continues the provincial readings, then travels to America in November, where he reads in Boston and New York. Dickens is invited to a meal at the White House with President Andrew Jackson. This tour permanently breaks the novelist's health.

1868   In April, Dickens returns to England, where he continues to tour and entertains American friends at Gad's Hill.

1869   The first public reading of the murder of Nancy (from *Oliver Twist*) performed, but his doctors recommend he discontinue the tour. *The Mystery of Edwin Drood* begun.

1870   Dickens gives twelve readings in London. Six parts of *Edwin Drood* appear from April to September. On June 9, Charles Dickens dies, aged 58. He is buried in the Poets' Corner, Westminster Abbey.

Contributors

HAROLD BLOOM is Sterling Professor of the Humanities at Yale University and Henry W. and Albert A. Berg Professor of English at the New York University Graduate School. He is the author of over 20 books, including *The Anxiety of Influence* (1973), which sets forth Professor Bloom's provocative theory of the literary relationships between the great writers and their predecessors. His most recent book, *Shakespeare: The Invention of the Human* (1998), was a finalist for the 1998 National Book Award. Professor Bloom is a 1985 MacArthur Foundation Award recipient, served as the Charles Eliot Norton Professor of Poetry at Harvard University in 1987–88, and has received honorary degrees from the universities of Rome and Bologna. In 1999, Professor Bloom received the prestigious American Academy of Arts and Letters Gold Medal for Criticism.

MURRAY BAUMGARTEN is the author of *City Scriptures: Modern Jewish Writing* (1982); he is the co-author with Barbara Gottfried of *Understanding Philip Roth* (1990) and co-author with H. M. Daleski of *Homes and Homelessness in the Victorian Imagination* (1998).

PETER BROOKS is Tripp Professor of the Humanties at Yale University. He is the author of *Psychoanalysis and Storytelling* (1994) and *Body Work: Objects of Desire in Modern Narrative* (1993).

CAROLYN BROWN is a lecturer in English at Thames Polytechnic. Her articles include "Utopias and Heterotopias: The Culture of Iain M. Banks" (1996) and "Feminist Strategies in the Post-Modern Condition" (1989).

WILLIAM A. COHEN is Professor of English at the University of Maryland. He is the author of *Sex Scandal: The Private Parts of Victorian Fiction* (1996) and "Trollope's Trollop" (1995).

EDWIN M. EIGNER is Professor of English and Creative Writing at the University of California, Riverside. He is the author of *The Dickens Pantomime* (1989) and *The Metaphysical Novel in England and America: Dickens, Bulwer, Melville and Hawthorne* (1985).

DAVID GERVAIS is a Lecturer in English Literature at the University of Reading. He is the author of *Flaubert and Henry James: A Study in Contrasts* (1978) and *Literary Englands: Versions of "Englishness" in Modern Writing* (1993).

ELLIOT L. GILBERT is Professor of English at the University of California, Davis, where he teaches Victorian Literature, Popular Culture, and Creative Writing. He is the author of *The Good Kipling: Studies in the Short Story* (1971) and the editor of *Critical Essays on Charles Dickens's Bleak House* (1989).

GAIL TURLEY HOUSTON is Professor of English at the University of New Mexico. She is the author of *Consuming Fictions: Gender, Class, and Hunger in Dickens's Novels* (1994) and "Broadsides at the Board: Collations of *Pickwick Papers* and *Oliver Twist*" (1991).

JEROME MECKIER is Professor of English at the University of Kentucky. He is the author of *Victorian Perspectives: Six Essays* (1989), *Innocent Abroad: Charles Dickens's American Engagements* (1969), "Aldous Huxley: Dystopian Essayist of the 1930's" (1996) and "Dickens, *Great Expectations*, and the Dartmouth College Notes" (1992).

CHRISTOPHER D. MORRIS is the author of *Models of Misrepresentation: On the Fiction of E. L. Doctorow* and "The Direction of North by Northwest" (1997).

JAMES PHELAN is associate professor of English at Ohio State University. He is the author of *Worlds from Words: A Theory of Language in Fiction* (1981) and *Narrative as Rhetoric: Technique, Audiences, Ethics, Ideology* (1996).

JEREMY TAMBLING is the author of *Dickens, Violence, and the Modern State: Dreams of the Scaffold* (1995) and *Confession: Sexuality, Sin, the Subject* (1990).

WILLIAM A. WILSON is a Professor of English and the Humanities at San Jose State University. In addition to publishing on Dickens, Swinburne, and Tennyson, he has written on contemporary Irish poetry, especially the works of Ciaran Carson and Paul Muldoon. A book titled *Modernity and the Poetry of Paul Muldoon* is forthcoming.

ANNY SADRIN is the author of *Parentage and Inheritance in the Novels of Charles Dickens* (1994) and "Charlotte Dickens: The Female Narrator of Bleak House" (1992).

Bibliography

Ackryod, Peter. *Dickens*. London: Sinclair-Stevenson, 1990.

Barickman, Richard, Susan MacDonald and Myra Stark. *Corrupt Relations: Dickens, Thackeray, Trollope, Collins and the Victorian Sexual System*. New York: Columbia University Press, 1982.

Bolton, Philip H. *Dickens Dramatized*. London: Mansel, 1987.

Carlisle, Janice. *The Sense of an Audience: Dickens, Thackeray and George Eliot at Mid-Century*. Athens: University of Georgia Press, 1981.

Collins, Philip, ed. *Dickens and Crime*. London: Macmillan, 1962.

Dabney, Ross. *Love and Property in the Novels of Charles Dickens*. Berkeley: University of California Press, 1967.

Daldry, Graham. *Charles Dickens and the Form of the Novel*. Totowa, NJ: Barnes & Noble, 1987.

Davies, James A. *The Textual Life of Dicken's Characters*. Houndmills, Basingstoke, Hampshire: Macmillan, 1989.

Dessner, Lawrence Jay. "*Great Expectations*: The Tragic Comedy of John Wemmick," *Ariel* 6, 2 (1975).

———. "*Great Expectations*: The Ghost of a Man's Own Father," *PMLA* 91 (May 1976).

Ford, George. *Dickens and His Readers: Aspects of Novel Criticism Since 1836*. Princeton: Princeton University Press, 1955.

Forker, Charles R. "The Language of Hands in *Great Expectations*," *Texas Studies in Language and Literature* 3 (1961): 280–93.

Garis, Robert. *The Dickens Theatre: A Reassessment of the Novels*. Oxford: Clarendon Press, 1965.

Ginsburg, Michal Peled. "Dickens and the Uncanny: Repression and Displacement in *Great Expectations*," *Dickens Studies Annual* 13 (1984): 115–24.

Hagan, John. "Structural Patters in Dickens's *Great Expectations*," *ELH* 21 (March 1954).

Hardy, Barbara. *The Moral Art of Charles Dickens*. London: Athlone Press, 1970.

Herst, Beth F. *The Dickens Hero: Selfhood and Alienation in the Dickens World.* New York: St. Martin's Press, 1990.

Hornback, Bert G. *Great Expectations: A Novel of Friendship.* Boston: Twayne, 1987.

Kelly, Mary Ann. "The Functions of Wemmick of Little Britain and Wemmick of Walworth," *Dickens Studies Newsletter* 14 (December 1983).

Kincaid, James R. *Dickens and the Rhetoric of Laughter.* Oxford: Clarendon Press, 1971.

Leavis, Frank R. and Queenie D. Leavis. *Dickens: The Novelist.* London: Chatto & Windus, 1970.

Lerner, Laurence. *Angels and Absences: Child Deaths in the Nineteenth Century.* Nashville: Vanderbilt University Press, 1997.

Levine, Richard A. "Dickens, the Two Nations, and Individual Possibility," *Studies in The Novel* 1, no. 2 (Summer 1969).

Lucas, John. *The Melancholy Man: A Study of Dickens's Novels.* London: Methuen, 1970.

Meckier, Jerome. *Hidden Rivalries in Victorian Fiction: Dickens, Realism and Revaluation.* Lexington, KY: University Press of Kentucky, 1987.

Miller, J. Hillis. *Charles Dickens: The World of His Novels.* Cambridge, Mass.: Harvard University Press, 1958.

Mose, Ron. "Autobiographical Narration and Formal Closure in *Great Expectations*," *Hebrew University Studies in Literature*, vol. 5 (Spring 1977).

Rosenberg, Edgar (ed.). *Great Expectations: Authoritative Texts, Backgrounds, Contexts, Criticism.* New York: Norton, 1999.

Sadrin, Anny. *Great Expectations.* London: Unwin Hyman, 1988.

Schlicke, Paul. *Dickens and Popular Entertainment.* London: Allen and Unwin, 1985.

Scott, P. J. M. *Reality and Comic Confidence in Charles Dickens.* London: Macmillan, 1979.

Schad, John. *The Reader in the Dickensian Mirror: Some New Language.* New York: St. Martin's Press, 1992.

Smith, Grahame. *Charles Dickens: A Literary Life.* New York: St. Martin's Press, 1996.

Spenko, James L. "The Return of the Repressed in *Great Expectations*," *Literature and Psychology* 30, (1980): 3–4

Stoehr, Taylor. *Dickens: The Dreamer's Stance.* Ithaca: Cornell University Press, 1965.

Stone, Harry. *Dickens and the Invisible World: Fairy Tales, Fantasy and Novel-Making.* London: Macmillan, 1980.

———. *The Night Side of Dickens: Cannibalism, Passion, Necessity.* Columbus: Ohio State University Press, 1994.

Traill, Nancy H. *Possible Worlds of the Fantastic: The Rise of the Panoramal in Fiction.* Toronto: University of Toronto Press, 1996.

Trudgill, Eric. *Madonnas and Magdalenes: The Origins and Development of Victorian Sexual Attitudes.* New York: Holms & Meier, 1976.

Vogel, Jane. *Allegory in Dickens.* Tuscaloosa: University of Alabama Press, 1977.

Walsh, Susan. "Bodies of Capital: *Great Expectations* and the Climacteric Economy," *Victorian Studies* 37 (1993).

Welsh, Alexander. *The City of Dickens.* Cambridge, Mass.: Harvard University Press, 1986.

Westburg, Barry. *The Confessional Fictions of Charles Dickens.* DeKalb: Northern Illinois University Press, 1977.

Young, Melanie. "Distorted Expectations: Pip and the Problems of Language," *Dickens Studies Annual*, vol. 7 (1978).

Acknowledgments

"Calligraphy and Code: Writing in *Great Expectations*" by Murray Baumgarten from *Dickens Studies Annual* no. 11 (1983). Reprinted with permission.

"Repetition, Repression, and Return: The Plotting of *Great Expectations*" by Peter Brooks in *Reading for the Plot: Design and Intention in Narrative* (1984). Reprinted with permission.

"*Great Expectations*: Masculinity and Modernity" by Carolyn Brown from *Essays and Studies 1987* no. 40 (1987). Reprinted with permission.

"Manual Conduct in *Great Expectations*" by William A. Cohen from *ELH: Journal of English Literary History*, vol. 60, no. 1 (Spring, 1993). Reprinted with permission.

"The Absent Clown in *Great Expectations*" by Edwin M. Eigner from *Dickens Studies Annual* no. 11 (1983). Reprinted with permission.

"The Prose and Poetry of *Great Expectations*" by David Gervais from *Dickens Studies Annual* no. 13 (1984). Reprinted with permission.

"'In Primal Sympathy': *Great Expectations* and the Secret Life" by Elliot L. Gilbert from *Dickens Studies Annual* no. 11 (1983). Reprinted with permission.

"'Pip' and 'Property': the (Re)Production of the Self in *Great Expectations*" by Gail Turley Houston from *Studies in the Novel*, vol. 24, no. 1 (Spring 1992). Reprinted with permission.

"Charles Dickens's *Great Expectations*: A Defense of the Second Ending" by Jerome Meckier from *Studies in the Novel*, vol. 25, no. 1 (Spring 1993). Reprinted with permission.

Christopher D. Morris, *ELH*, "The Bad Faith of Pip's Bad Faith: Deconstructing *Great Expectations*, pp. 941–52. © 1987 The Johns Hopkins University Press. Reprinted with permission.

"Progression and the Synthetic Secondary Charter: The Case of John Wemmick" by James Phelan in *Reading People, Reading Plots: Character, Progression, and the Interpretation of Narrative* (1989). Reprinted with permission.

"Prison-Bound: Dickens and Foucault" by Jeremy Tambling from *Essays in Criticism*, vol. 36, no. 1 (January 1986). Reprinted with permission.

'The Magic Circle of Genius: Dickens' Translations of Shakespearean Drama in *Great Expectations*" by William A. Wilson © 1985 by The Regents of the University of California. Reprinted from *Nineteenth Century Fiction* vol. 40, no. 2 (1985), pp. 154–174, by permission.

"Oedipus and Telemachus" by Anny Sadrin in *Great Expectations* (1988). Reprinted with permission.

Index